'This is a compelling book, well-researched and authoritative, with powerful messages in each of the chapters, and practical suggestions that are both helpful and realistic'
Marion Dowling,
former President of the British Association of Early Childhood Education

'Essential reading for all those who work with children. It has fascinating and sometimes startling revelations about the damaging influences on the young within our society and offers some practical and very readable ideas and recommendations for all those who endeavour to give children the very best we can'   Gervase Phinn, author

'Sue Palmer brings together the information parents need all in one place – research that reinforces what most parents really believe. We're under so much pressure to sign up to a status quo that so often feels wrong; this gives us the courage to seek the best for our children'
Wendy Thomas, mother, Southampton

'As a teacher with 15 years experience I can only agree about the devastating effect our lifestyles are having on children today. Many of the chapters had me in tears! The book should be made compulsory reading for all politicians, health visitors, social workers, teachers and parents!'
Julia Colley, teacher, Essex

'Very well written and well researched'
Mick Brookes, former General Secretary, National Association of Headteachers

'A compact, accessible and research-based "bible" in how to "detox childhood" . . . an ideal, if not essential, read for parents and all those working with children'
Early Years Educator (EYE)

SUE PALMER, M Ed, FRSA, FEA, is a former primary headteacher, now a writer, broadcaster and consultant on child development and education. As a specialist in literacy for over thirty years, she has written over two hundred books, TV programmes and software for three- to twelve-year olds, frequently contributed to the educational and national press, and acted as an independent adviser to many organisations, including the Department for Education and the BBC. Since the first edition of *Toxic Childhood* in 2006, she has been involved in campaigns around wider aspects of children's lives – especially play, commercialisation and early years education – and is a popular speaker on these subjects to audiences of parents and professionals across the UK and around the world. She is regularly consulted by the media, and in 2014 became a Trustee of the charity *Save Childhood*, which works to raise awareness of child development and ensure that children's well-being is at the heart of public policy-making. She lives in Edinburgh, close to her daughter's family, including her first grandchild.

Other books by Sue Palmer on child development in the modern world:

Detoxing Childhood: how to raise bright, balanced children

21st Century Boys: how modern life is driving them off the rails and how to get them back on track

21st Century Girls: how the modern world is damaging our daughters and what we can do about it

TOXIC CHILDHOOD

How the Modern World is
Damaging Our Children and
What We Can Do About it

Sue Palmer

An Orion paperback

First published in Great Britain in 2006
by Orion Books Ltd.
This updated paperback edition published in 2015
by Orion Books Ltd,
Carmelite House, 50 Victoria Embankment,
London EC4Y 0DZ

An Hachette UK company

1 3 5 7 9 10 8 6 4 2

A CIP catalogue record for this book
is available from the British Library.

ISBN 978 1 4091 3752 8

Designed in Quadraat by Geoff Green Book Design, Cambridge

Printed in Great Britain by Clays Ltd, St Ives plc

The Orion Publishing Group's policy is to use papers that
are natural, renewable and recyclable products and made
from wood grown in sustainable forests. The logging and
manufacturing processes are expected to conform to the
environmental regulations of the country of origin.

CONTENTS

ACKNOWLEDGEMENTS

The first edition of *Toxic Childhood* opened with a long list of thanks to the many experts and parents who had advised and guided me in writing and researching the book. Almost a decade later, I've lost count of the number of people who've helped me extend my understanding of child development and the ways it can be influenced by contemporary culture, so I'll just have to thank them all en masse.

Special thanks must, however, go to the expert advisers I interviewed during the updating of each chapter, and who kindly checked the revised manuscript: Dr Alex Richardson, Cath Prisk, Dr Helen Ball, Professor Jan Born, Virginia Bearshaw, Marie Peacock, Wendy Ellyatt, Jill Curtis, Warwick Mansell, Margaret Morrissey, Professor Agnes Nairn, Susan Linn and Dr Aric Sigman.

I should also like to thank Beth Brinton, Dave McLean and their friends for keeping me in touch with the issues confronting modern parents, and Gail Paten my editor at Orion Books.

But the most special thanks of all go to the indomitable childhood campaigner Dr Richard House, who reviewed *Toxic Childhood* in its first incarnation and has since been a friend, support and inspiration. This edition is dedicated to Richard.

PREFACE TO THE SECOND EDITION

It's now almost a decade since the original manuscript for *Toxic Childhood* went off to the publishers, and well over fifteen years since the teachers I met around the UK first set me worrying about the effects of modern lifestyles on children's development. As all my previous publications were on teaching aspects of literacy (particularly grammar and spelling), research for this book took me well out of my comfort zone. I've found myself navigating through uncharted, and somewhat scary, waters ever since.

The first edition of *Toxic Childhood* in May 2006 was well-received among teachers and other professionals working with young children but, to begin with, made little impact on its target audience – parents and politicians. It did, however, introduce me to many other people similarly concerned about child development, including a psychologist called Dr Richard House.

Richard and I organised an open letter on the subject, signed by more than 200 experts (including many of the interviewees for this book), which appeared in the *Daily Telegraph* in late 2006, causing a brief media storm. The then Archbishop of Canterbury seized on this interest to publicise a forthcoming Children's Society enquiry into the subject (*A Good Childhood*); and a couple of months later UNICEF published a survey of childhood well-being, in which, of 21 countries in the developed world, the UK came bottom.

Suddenly, children's lifestyles were on the political map

(although, so far, the responses of most politicians have been far from reassuring), and I found myself transformed into a 'childhood campaigner', combining a literacy day-job with Toxic Childhood talks for parents, trailing around broadcasting studios and commenting in the press on everything from early childcare to the sexual habits of teenagers. It also led to two further research projects, for 21st Century Boys (2009) and 21st Century Girls (2013).

After eight years on this campaign trail, I'm therefore very grateful to my publishers Orion for the opportunity to revise and update Toxic Childhood, drawing on the considerable expertise of many wonderful people from a wide range of disciplines, all as desperate as me to alert the wider world to the challenges of raising children in a hyper-competitive, screen-based culture. My personal experience suggests that responsible parents are now as concerned about this issue as childhood professionals so I hope the book will help any new parent-readers make informed choices about child-rearing in the modern world.

It's written in ten self-contained chapters, each of which covers a key aspect of children's daily lives, so is highly suitable for skimming if a particular topic isn't of interest; and, thanks to my first editor, at the end of each chapter there's a list of 'parenting hints and tips' supplied by the experts I consulted. But while I hope these may help mums and dads detoxify their own children's lives, my main aim was never to produce a 'parenting manual'. Since the child is father of the man (and mother of the woman), the way a culture treats its children will have profound effects on that culture fifteen or twenty years down the line. Toxic Childhood was intended as a social treatise, linking new research on child development to the realities of twenty-first-century children's lives.

For me, the scariest aspect of the last decade has been watching how small changes in children's behaviour noted by teachers in the 1990s (see Introduction) are playing out in the teenagers and young adults of the present day. Researchers in the UK and USA have noted a serious increase in mental health problems and addictions of various kinds (not least to technological devices), widespread difficulties in controlling the focus of attention and an alarming decline in empathy. At present, these problems are contained by professional interventions, but if they continue to increase there are dangerous times ahead for our society, on both the economic and social fronts.

As I write this Preface, the radio informs me that the 'obesity explosion' (to which nutritionists alerted us in the early years of the century – see Chapter 1) has precipitated a 'national health emergency', which threatens the future of the NHS. Obesity is much easier to spot than social and emotional problems, and the economic consequences of a physical health crisis are far more immediately obvious than those associated with emotional well-being. But, in the long run, a society with a mental health crisis among its young people is a society in decline.

So, dear reader, I'll end with a plea that you check out the 'Mind the Gap' sections at the end of each chapter, and lend your weight to movements like the Campaign for a Commercial-Free Childhood (www.commercialfreechildhood.org) and Save Childhood (www. savechildhood.net) which work to improve the lot of all children, including those whose parents would never dream of picking up a book like this one.

Children are the future: the way we care for them – all of them – will determine the future they inherit.

Sue Palmer (childhood campaigner)
Edinburgh, November 2014

INTRODUCTION
TOXIC CHILDHOOD SYNDROME

She was standing on the steps of the Uffizi Gallery in Florence – a short, dark-haired girl, slightly overweight, sulkily licking an ice cream. I guessed from her face she was no more than ten years old, but the angry scowl and scrunched self-consciousness looked more like a teenager, wracked with adolescent angst. Her clothes were too old for her too – a low-slung miniskirt and high-cut top, exposing a plump little midriff. And across her little girl's chest was printed her message to the world: 'I ♥ my attitude problem'.

In the building behind her were some of western civilisation's greatest treasures – paintings by Botticelli, Leonardo, Michelangelo – which presumably her parents had dragged her across Europe (maybe across the world) to see. She clearly wasn't remotely interested. I suspect the only thing that small lost soul wanted to do was curl up in front of a widescreen TV and lose herself in something mindless – a cartoon, maybe, or one of the endless American sitcoms on the Disney Channel. Her feelings about life were written all over her: anger, self-obsession, boredom, lack of engagement – the multiple trademarks of the brat.

Poor child. Poor parents. Poor western civilisation – indeed the whole of the developed world – which now teems with miserable little creatures like that one, male and female, toddlers to pre-teens. In a global culture whose citizens are wealthier, healthier and more privileged than ever before in human history, children grow unhappier every year. From the disgruntled and discontented to the depressed and dysfunctional, we seem to be raising a generation with nothing to love but its attitude problem.

What's happening to children?

In the decade since I spotted that little girl, there's been increasing recognition that all is not well for children in the wealthy west, particularly the UK and USA. By 2014, it was well established that 10 per cent of British children have a diagnosable mental health disorder, while 20 per cent are estimated to suffer from mental health problems of some kind, and the figures for the USA are around the same (13–20 per cent). The problem of children's mental health was brought firmly to public attention in 2007, when a UNICEF survey of childhood well-being in the developed world confirmed that these two countries do indeed have particular issues in this respect: out of 21 countries surveyed, the USA came 20th and the UK 21st.

The knock-on effects of this epidemic are obvious in statistics on drug and substance abuse among teenagers, along with binge drinking, eating disorders, self-harm and suicide (attempted and successful). Add these to the figures for teenage crime and anti-social behaviour, and there's plenty for the parents of a ten-year-old with an attitude problem to worry about. Occasional headline-grabbing incidents – such as high school massacres in the States or England's 2011 summer riots – bring the problems to wider public attention.

So what's going wrong? As one who's worked with children for forty years – the last dozen of which have been spent researching this issue, and talking to experts on aspects of child-rearing around the world – I've come to the conclusion that there isn't one simple answer. There's no point in singling out parents for blame, or teachers, or junk food manufacturers or anyone else – it's a complex cultural problem, linked to the incredible speed of human progress and the worldwide triumph of consumer capitalism.

We've created an amazingly exciting global culture but, over the last thirty years, progress has accelerated so much that our species simply can't keep up. In a nutshell, our culture has evolved faster than our biology.

This clash between technological culture and biological heritage is now damaging children's ability to think, learn and behave. And unless we do something about it, the twenty-first-century global village is going to be in trouble. To put it bluntly, the next generation may not be bright or balanced enough to keep the show on the road...

The 'special needs' explosion

What first started me fretting over this issue was the steady escalation, over my time in education, of what are known as 'developmental disorders'. A number of learning difficulties, which didn't even enter the public consciousness until the late twentieth century, began to affect a growing number of children.

First and foremost among these syndromes is ADHD (attention deficit and hyperactivity disorder), which only appeared on the scene about forty years ago but is now the most common behavioural disorder affecting children in the USA and UK. In 2012, nearly one in ten American children had been diagnosed with ADHD, which affects their ability to concentrate and control behaviour, and rates are soaring around the world, with particular concern about the subject in Australia. Estimates are lower in the UK than across the Atlantic (around one in twenty), but that's probably because diagnosis is less frequent due to revised health service and educational guidelines.

Another type of learning disorder that's been around much longer than ADHD is dyslexia, a specific difficulty with literacy skills. Approximately 20 per cent of young people regularly leave school with inadequate reading skills and the Dyslexia Research Trust estimates that half of these are due to dyslexia – that is, the students are generally bright and able to learn but have specific problems in decoding and comprehending the written word. There's considerable debate about dyslexia among psychologists because they can't agree what causes it (there seem to be many different ways of being dyslexic) and every so often this leads to headlines like 'Dyslexia may not exist', from academics at Yale and Durham in early 2014. Dyslexia's close cousins – dysgraphia (difficulty with handwriting) and dyscalculia (difficulty with maths) – are less well publicised but similarly prone to academic dispute.

In the 1990s, another 'dys-function' – dyspraxia (difficulties with physical coordination, spatial awareness and sensory perception) – raised its head, and by 2014 the NHS estimated that the condition affected at least one in fifty children. It's often linked to other developmental disorders, such as ADHD and Asperger syndrome (see below). As a seasoned special needs watcher, I suspect we'll hear much more about dyspraxia in the years to come.

However, the most alarming increase in developmental conditions has been in autistic spectrum disorders (ASD), which involve children's ability to relate to the world and communicate with others. Autism affects children in many different ways – hence the term 'spectrum'. At one end are 'high functioning' Asperger syndrome children – often academic high achievers but restricted in their interests and socially inept – and at the other are very severely autistic children, completely cut off by their disability and unable to communicate with the rest of the world. The unifying features of autistic spectrum disorders are difficulties in social functioning and communication, and sometimes unusual, often repetitive, behaviours.

According to the American Academy of Paediatrics, in the early 1980s the incidence of autism in the USA was about 1 in 50,000. By 2004 it had rocketed to 1 in 166, and in 2014 was estimated to be affecting one child in every sixty-eight. Estimates elsewhere vary from roughly one in a hundred children in the UK to about 1 in 600 in Japan but the problem appears to be on the increase in all countries of the developed world. It's a frightening escalation of a condition which, even in high-achieving children, can be the cause of much social and emotional suffering.

It's likely that the huge increase in these 'special educational needs' is to a large extent due to increasing knowledge and understanding among doctors and teachers, meaning conditions that went undiagnosed in the past are now routinely recognised. Another possibility is that parents these days prefer to medicalise problems that were once simply labelled 'under-achievement'. This argument is often put forward by critics of the growth in drug-treatment for ADHD – mind-altering drugs such as Ritalin or Dexedrine, prescribed to correct the chemical imbalance in the child's brain.

However, even taking these arguments into account, the increases are phenomenal. Improvements in teachers' professional knowledge, schools' specialist provision and various strategies for teaching and behaviour management have all developed alongside – and in response to – children's special needs. But it seems that, just as schools find ways forward for helping with one type of developmental condition, another arises to take its place. I reckon that educational authorities have been keeping the lid on this problem for several decades ... but it's getting harder every year.

Nature, nurture and behaviour

It's now widely accepted that developmental disorders have a genetic – or, at least, neurological – component. 'Nature' plays a major part. But it's also widely agreed that the way children are brought up inevitably influences their development. The nature-nurture debate about how much an individual's personality is due to one or the other is tediously familiar – indeed it assumed a similar status during the twentieth century to the medieval debate about how many angels can dance on the head of a pin. But most scientists now take the view that, while genes are indeed significant, upbringing and outside influences make a great deal of difference. Nature and nurture are vibrantly interactive.

When a predisposition is strong – as in the case of those unfortunate infants locked into profound autism – nurture may have little effect. But in most cases the environment in which a child grows up will significantly affect the way any genetic traits – good or bad – develop. In one particularly memorable American research project two groups of identical, genetically-vulnerable monkeys were brought up in different circumstances and then given access to alcohol. The monkeys who'd had a tough childhood consoled themselves with drink, while those who'd been carefully cared for and mothered actually drank less than the average monkey.

So could there be something going on in the successful nations of the world that is making it more likely that genetically vulnerable children develop their special needs? Might it be that – despite our economic success – childhood today is actually tougher than it was a few decades ago?

The reason psychologists call ADHD, dyslexia, dyspraxia and ASD 'developmental disorders' is that, in terms of social behaviour and/or achievement at school, the children concerned don't develop along a 'normal' trajectory – something holds them back. There's a sort of developmental continuum we expect children to move along during the first ten or so years of life. At birth, they're all helpless little bundles of egocentricity, but as time goes on we assume they'll move slowly (with occasional understandable regressions) towards more 'grown-up' civilised behaviour. We don't consciously teach this civilised behaviour, except hopefully by example – we just expect it to emerge (or develop) as children mature, in the same way we expect them to walk and talk. Along the way, we also expect them to learn the basic skills covered in primary school: the three Rs of reading, writing and reckoning.

If something is happening to interfere with the normal course of children's development – and thus contributing to the huge increase in developmental and behavioural disorders – you'd expect to see it affecting children in general, not just genetically vulnerable ones. And that's exactly what people have been seeing. Over the last couple of decades, I've heard reports from many thousands of teachers around the UK of a steady deterioration in the behaviour and learning potential of children in their classes, not just those diagnosed with a special educational need. Reports from educators in the USA, Japan and other developed countries bear it out. In *general*, children in the world's most successful nations are not as well behaved or as well-equipped to learn as they were in the past.

Learning to behave

Of course, all children sometimes act up. When over-tired, over-excited or feverish, any child can regress to the level of a two-year-old on a bad day. But in a civilised society we expect a decline in self-obsession and an increase in 'grown-up' behaviour as the years go by – the proportion of good days to bad gradually increasing, until by the time a child's age is in double figures, his or her behaviour is relatively stable. The fact that children then enter that long dark tunnel known as adolescence is, of course, something of a backward step, but if all's gone well in the preceding years, there's hope they'll come out of the tunnel unscathed. (As St Ignatius Loyola, Miss Jean Brodie and Hillary Clinton have all pointed out, the most important learning happens well before the teenage years.) This change from a tantrum-throwing two-year-old to a relatively civilised pre-teen depends on many things, but there are three key principles children must grasp on their journey, principles which have been at the heart of civilisation throughout human history.

The first is the ability to control and maintain attention even when something doesn't particularly interest them. All children – even very young ones – can focus for long periods on chosen activities (as parents forced to play endless games of peek-a-boo or 'I'll-drop-the-rattle-You-pick-it-up' know only too well). However, once children begin to socialise with others, they must learn sometimes to focus on other people's choices; and by six or seven, they're expected to focus on what the teacher is teaching them. If you can't attend – or if you're only prepared to attend to the things that interest you – you're going to have trouble at school.

The second is self-regulation. According to research, this is associated with the developing capacity for physical self-control and is related to children's ability to 'defer gratification'. To get along in the real world, they have to understand that the rewards for actions are not always immediate, and that sometimes people just have to knuckle down to dreary, boring, repetitive tasks because they'll pay off later – perhaps in the fairly remote future. An experiment from the 1960s illustrates how important the appreciation and acceptance of deferred gratification can be. Researchers left children, one by one, alone in a room with a plate containing a single marshmallow. The children were told that, if they wished, they could eat this marshmallow; but if they waited till the researcher's return, they'd be given a whole plateful of marsh-mallows. Some children cracked and wolfed down the single treat; others managed to resist temptation and held out for a plateful. Twenty years later researchers hunted down the subjects of this experiment, and discovered that those whose self-restraint had earned them multiple marshmallows had led more successful and happy lives than those who'd been impulsive.

The third principle is that living happily in a group of any size involves balancing your own needs against the needs of everyone else. This is summed up very succinctly in the name of a character in the children's book *The Water Babies*: Mrs Doasyouwouldbedoneby. Doing as you would be done by, and thus making the wheels of domestic, institutional and social life turn smoothly, requires an awareness of others (the ability to empathise with their point of view) allied with the sort of self-control I've described above. Human beings who do not have these qualities are likely to have a very hard ride through life – and so are the people around them.

Children with profound developmental disorders – conditions which completely impair their quality of life (and, indeed, that of their parents) – don't grasp these principles and their behaviour remains sadly primitive. But 'normal' children progress steadily towards civilised self-control. Then there are the ones in the middle

– those who make some progress but not enough, whose education begins to suffer, and who may have real problems 'fitting in'.

The point at which psychologists diagnose a developmental disorder is, of course, moot – indeed, everyone in education knows diagnosis is partially dependent upon a child's background (the apparent incidence of dyslexia, for instance, is much greater in affluent areas than in disadvantaged ones where reading problems are often widespread). But the point is that, year on year, fewer children seem to be making what used to be called 'normal' progress. Increasingly, children in general have problems in focusing their concentration, exercising self-restraint and taking account of other people's needs and interests. Indeed, in 2010 the definition of Special Educational Needs in England had to be revised. If it hadn't there was a danger that, by 2020, around a quarter of the nation's children would be considered 'special'.

A twenty-first-century report card

Primary teachers are well qualified to assess the behaviour of pre-teen children, since they can compare the way classes behave over time. Over the last few decades, UK primary teachers' concern about children's deteriorating behaviour – especially in dis-advantaged areas – has mushroomed. We had heard such reports coming out of America for years, and I also hear them increasingly now from the teachers I meet in South-East Asia and on mainland Europe. The general opinion is that as the proportion of children with diagnosed special needs increased, so did the proportion who don't have a specific diagnosable disorder but are just distractible, impulsive or badly behaved.

This shift has caused many problems for schools because dis-tractible, impulsive children are difficult to teach. It's particularly difficult teaching them to read and write, since the various sub-skills of literacy take a long time to acquire and – no matter how hard teachers try to jazz it up – involve plenty of dull, repetitive effort. The eventual rewards, however, are well worth having:

beside the obvious advantages psychologists believe the very process of learning to read actually develops children's powers of thought and understanding. It's a classic example of the importance of deferred gratification.

Another major problem is that, as children's behaviour gets worse, teachers must spend more time and energy on crowd control. At the lowest level, they've noticed a decline in manners and respect for adults, with general 'cheekiness' and backchat making day-to-day classroom management more demanding. More significantly, there are many more incidences of rule-breaking, violence and bullying. Discipline problems take up teaching time, and distract from the business of learning.

Readers blessed with well-behaved offspring, or those who do not mix much with children at all, may think teachers are overstating the case. Janet Street-Porter, a British writer and broadcaster, used to feel that way – until she agreed to spend two weeks teaching eight-year-olds in a primary school. Ms Street-Porter is renowned as a forceful woman, capable of withering hardened BBC executives with a glance. In her new role, however – despite an armory of guidelines for dealing with problem children – she found herself leaving school at the end of each day 'weeping with frustration that several of the worst offenders would simply run rings round me. Quite simply, they had no idea of discipline whatsoever.'

These opinions are reflected in teachers' comments around the world. Even in Japan, where a formal educational system has meant that discipline was not a problem in the past, elementary teachers now speak of widespread impulsive behaviour, including bullying (the Japanese word for this, *ijime*, didn't enter the public consciousness till the early 1980s, but is now a household word). They also report an apparent lack of guilt among the children concerned – deeply worrying in a society where respect and honour is of supreme importance. Why then, in all the most advanced and advantaged countries of the world, should children be growing less able to exercise self-control and more difficult to teach?

The blind men and the elephant

Like most teachers I meet, my first instinct was to lay the blame for deteriorating behaviour on electronic media. To a literacy specialist it seemed self-evident that children who spend their days slumped in front of TV or playing computer games miss out on other important activities, such as conversation and reading for pleasure. Commentators have been complaining about reduced attention span ever since television became widespread in the 1950s, and over the last twenty years children's viewing has escalated wildly as TV became a round-the-clock global presence, with endless channels aimed specifically at them: Nickelodeon, Disney, Fox Kids, CBBC, Toonami and so on. I began to take a keen interest in the issue and often wrote about it for the educational press.

Then one day, while looking into reports that Ritalin prescriptions in the UK had increased ten-fold in a single decade, I bumped into another researcher, an expert on children's play. She put the apparent increase in attention deficit down to something quite different: the fact that many parents were too frightened to let their children go outside and run off excess energy. In conversation, we discovered that, while her argument and mine were clearly linked (in both cases, TV was implicated), neither of us had hitherto given much consideration to the other's point of view.

Suddenly I noticed how many other experts seemed to be digging away at this issue. They began to turn up everywhere – the newspapers, the bookshops, the Internet – and each had his or her own speciality. They seemed to be all over the world – from the USA in the west to Japan in the east – worrying away at the same problem, despite differences in cultural traditions. Some put the change in children's behaviour down to diet or lack of exercise; others chose working mothers, marriage breakdown, defects in the educational system, excessive consumerism or other effects of technological or social change ... The world was teeming with experts on children's behaviour, and most of them seemed completely oblivious of all the others.

The trouble is, expertise nowadays is increasingly specialised: researchers are trapped in their own disciplines, knowing more and more about less and less; social commentators are trapped in their own countries, addressing the minutiae of national concerns. So, although there's worldwide concern about changes in children's behaviour patterns, investigation into the issue is proceeding like the blind men of Indostan's investigation of the elephant. In the poem, each blind man caught hold of one bit of the animal – the trunk or the leg or the tail – and on the basis of this worked out his theory of what an elephant looked like. At present, each expert latches on to one element of the decline in children's behaviour and ability to learn – and in so doing we fail to grasp it in its entirety. We haven't observed the whole elephant.

The more I read, the more I became convinced that there was not just one cause behind the changes in children's behaviour, but a vast array of causes, all interrelated and deeply ingrained in contemporary culture – a complex and alarming mix. And, while it seemed to be affecting children across the developed world, it was particularly noticeable in the USA and UK. This is why, a dozen years ago, I stepped off my personal professional tramlines and began research into childhood in general.

The past is another planet

My first reaction was deep sympathy for contemporary parents. How in the world could they be expected to cope with the astonishing amount of information generated by these legions of experts? And if those same experts haven't worked out what 'the elephant' in the middle of all their research looks like, how are parents supposed to guess what's significant in their findings?

Bringing up children has never been easy, but nowadays it's a minefield. Twenty-first-century parents pick their way gingerly through the sound bites – *junk food, sugar highs, cotton-wool kids, battery children, pester power, electronic babysitters, technobrats,* and so on – but with a distinct shortage of reference points. When my husband and I were bringing up our daughter a quarter of a century ago, the world we lived in was not vastly different from the one in which we'd grown up ourselves. But since then, the pace of change has been phenomenal. In less than a couple of decades, technology has transformed our homes: PCs, laptops, email, the worldwide web; cable, satellite and digital TV, tele-recording and DVD players; computer games, PlayStations, social networking sites; iPods, tablet computers and apps; mobiles, text messaging, smartphones ... And everything happens much, much faster than it did in the past.

Social changes have been no less startling. Across all wealthy countries, there are now far fewer extended family groups than there were; mothers are much more likely to work and, in a fast-moving, fast-changing workplace, the pressures of work for all parents have hugely increased; marriages are less stable and cohabitation and divorce widespread – even in countries, such as Japan and Spain, where such behaviour was unthinkable twenty years ago. The old certainties have gone, and 'moral relativism' doesn't make for easy parenting.

Technology has meant families across the developed world have more and more in common – an exciting development – but it also means that they have less and less contact with their own cultural past. Back in 1950, L.P. Hartley began his novel *The Go Between* with the famous words: 'The past is a foreign country. They do things differently there.' These days the past isn't just a foreign country, it's another planet.

The Canadian media visionary Marshal McLuhan called this phenomenon 'electric speed'. It began with the growth of global mass media in the middle of the twentieth century, but has accelerated wildly – as evidenced above – since the 1980s. McLuhan predicted that the contraction of time and space within the global village would be a great leap forward for mankind, and in many ways, he was right: for adults, it's an amazing period to be alive, and most of the time we manage to keep up with the electric speed of modern life.

But children are not fully-developed adults – they still have to move along that biological developmental continuum, acquiring the habits of civilised behaviour. Focused attention, self-regulation, deferred gratification, empathy and other important lessons can't be learned at electric speed. Human development happens in 'slow time', and contemporary children still need the same time-consuming, old-fashioned nurturing that small, highly intelligent primates have needed through the ages.

The elephant in the house

In the tumult of change, it's not surprising if some parents have lost sight of age-old truths about child-rearing, especially as many of the old reference points – lore from the extended family, cultural and religious traditions – have been swept away. But the problem is compounded because the cultural changes of the last quarter of a century have brought with them a toxic mix of side-effects that have made the task of rearing children more difficult than ever before. Parents haven't had the time (or the clarity of information) to make adjustments for these side effects. As a result, every year children become more distractible, impulsive and self-obsessed – less able to learn, to enjoy life, to thrive socially. So even though it's more difficult than in any previous generation, good parenting is essential. In a complex contemporary culture, children are in greater need of parental wisdom, guidance and support than ever before.

The needs of a small human being are much the same as they ever were. They need physical nurture: nourishing food; plenty of exercise and play; adequate sleep. But they also need emotional and social nurture, which means time, attention, communication and love from the people closest to them. As they grow older, they must widen their social circle and start to learn essential academic skills, including the three Rs. And throughout childhood they need moral guidance, to help them navigate through the increasingly complex web of contemporary ethics.

My researches suggest that children's development in every

one of these areas is threatened by the side effects of technological and cultural changes. A great many – probably a majority – of our children have developed a taste for unhealthy food and a couch-potato lifestyle, and have related problems with sleeping. An unacceptable number also suffer from inadequate early emotional bonding, lack of interaction with their parents and a high level of emotional instability. Instead of stimulating, real-life experiences, contemporary children have electronic entertainment and communication at home, and – all too often – a narrow test-and-target driven curriculum at school. Moral guidance has suffered as societies become increasingly confused, while children are constantly exposed to manipulative advertising and the excesses of celebrity culture.

Any one of the vast array of cultural side effects I discovered would be enough to trigger developmental delay in a genetically-vulnerable child; the whole toxic brew could trigger it even in the most genetically robust of individuals. This is the 'elephant' standing full square in the living room of every family home in the developed world.

Toxic childhood syndrome

There's no point standing around wringing our hands about this problem, or indeed looking for someone to blame. No one intended it, and the culture changes so rapidly nowadays that hand-wringing and blaming are just a waste of precious time. And I'm not suggesting we turn the clock back on our cultural revolution. Personally I *love* new technology and would hate to go back to an earlier age – indeed, without email and the worldwide web, this book couldn't have been written. I love the buzz of twenty-four-hour living, the improvements in women's status, the comfort and convenience of a contemporary lifestyle, the excitement of change. But, in order to maintain the new global culture, we must acknowledge what it's doing to our children and work out how to detoxify their lives.

Toxic Childhood assembles evidence from a wide range of disciplines – from psychology and neuroscience to economics and marketing. The initial research took several years' work (by myself and two hard-working research assistants), hundreds of discussions with children, parents and teachers around the world, and – most importantly – interviews with scores of scientists and other experts, who gave generously of their time and expertise to explain the effects of 'toxic childhood syndrome' in their particular disciplines. In the eight years since first publication, I've moved in a wide range of academic, political and social circles formerly beyond my wildest dreams, which have provided me with many new sources of information and extra insights.

The more I've found out, the clearer it's become that trying to tackle any one of these elements independently of the others is a waste of time – they all swirl together in a toxic mix. So just trying to improve a child's diet, for instance, isn't enough – all sorts of other things impinge on it: TV and marketing messages, exercise and sleeping habits, childcare arrangements, parenting style. Anyway, just as we can't know a child's genetic blueprint, we can't guess which elements of contemporary culture might be particularly poisonous for each individual. Toxic childhood is a syndrome, and we have to tackle the whole thing, not just odd symptoms. The good news is that doing so isn't particularly difficult, shouldn't cost much (except in time and attention) and parents who are already detoxing their children's lives find it extremely rewarding and enjoyable.

Detoxing childhood

After each chapter, there are a few guidelines for 'detoxing childhood', based on advice offered by experts and ideas from parents I have met on my travels – the sort of hints and tips I'd find helpful if I were raising children myself. On the same basis, I've also recommended books and websites offering further insights and advice. However, I'm not a parenting expert and Toxic Childhood was never intended to be a child-rearing manual. Indeed, one of the problems I recognised in my research was that the burgeoning 'parenting industry' can contribute to the syndrome, as many parents feel de-skilled, overwhelmed with advice (often conflicting) and unable to trust to their instincts. My aim has simply been to pull together in one place (and hopefully, to demystify) up-to-date scientific information about child development and the ways that children's biological blueprint can be compromised in a fast-moving consumer culture.

Anyway, tackling toxic childhood syndrome isn't merely a question of what individual parents can do. It's also an important social project, one that affects everyone in the developed world. Children are our most significant investment for the future and the toxic cocktail described in these pages is already undermining the social, emotional and intellectual development of an unacceptable number. Even if your own offspring have escaped unscathed, the world they're growing up in is full of others who've been less fortunate. When children in general become more distractible, impulsive and lacking in empathy, there's inevitably a corresponding increase in mental health problems and anti-social behaviour.

We could, of course, try to solve the problems by doling out drugs, as already happens in the case of many children diagnosed with ADHD. I would be the last to deny that some families desperately need the relief that comes from a timely dose of Ritalin – living with a severely ADHD child can be utter hell. But as prescriptions soar (in the decade between 1999 and 2010, they increased fourfold in the UK), we must ask ourselves whether pathologising childhood in this way is an acceptable option.

Apart from anything else, drugging a growing proportion of the nation's youth is an expensive option, and may have many unintended consequences. I once visited a school where an eight-year-old boy had saved up his Ritalin in an attempt to kill himself with an overdose: 'Because I'm too naughty,' he explained. 'I'm just a nuisance to everyone.' Another possibility is that, like the rock stars Kurt Cobain and Courtney Love, both on Ritalin as children, it may contribute to drug dependency. After Cobain's suicide, Love ruminated: 'When you're a kid and you get this drug that makes you feel that feeling, where else are you going to turn when you're an adult? It was euphoric when you were a child – isn't that memory going to stick with you?'

A much more sensible solution is for medical, educational and political establishments to address the underlying causes of these changes in children's behaviour, and support parents in doing the best for their children. Governments across the world already recognise that investment in the next generation's physical, mental and emotional health is a worthwhile cause, but often base their responses on experience that ignores the effects of cultural change – experience from that other planet known as the past. Awareness of, and attention to, toxic childhood syndrome is essential if their investment is to succeed. Above all they must be prepared to challenge adverse commercial influences on children's health and well-being.

So big business needs to listen too. Large corporations have been slow to recognise that, when short-term profit undermines society's long-term prospects, it's not just the punters they're screwing, it's themselves. Fortunately, there are some signs that, with sufficient public outrage and threats of litigation, they can be persuaded to change direction. It's even possible they'll recognise that there's money to be made in creating and marketing products that develop a healthy rather than unhealthy lifestyle for children. In helping big business along this road, parental pressure is an extremely powerful force.

$$\star\star\star$$

All adults – not just parents, teachers and politicians – have a social responsibility for the well-being of the next generation. We all have to wise up, shrug off the social paralysis fuelled by a combination of rapid change, information overload and selfish materialism, and help to create a secure, healthy environment in which children can grow. The suggestions in this book are not rocket science – but if we care about the future of our global village, they're more important than rocket science. And, in a world moving at such breakneck speed, successful child-rearing depends not just on the advice of scientists playing catch-up, but on age-old, tried-and-tested human wisdom.

Mind the gap

One advantage of being a travelling literacy specialist is the opportunity to visit schools in every part of the UK, from prestigious prep schools set amid verdant play areas and well-manicured sports fields, to run-down inner-city institutions with cramped tarmacked playgrounds and high spiked railings to keep out the vandals. I know from twenty-five years of personal experience about the gap between rich and poor in this country, and its impact on the next generation.

Since all parents want the best for their children, it's no surprise that those who value education seek out the best possible schools, or that wealthy parents are prepared to pay for excellent facilities. Well-educated families thus tend to raise well-educated children. As concern about childhood well-being grows, these parents are also likely to find out more about the subject, and to take steps to detoxify their own children's lives.

But parents in Britain's meanest streets have no such choices. Poverty tends to go hand in hand with lack of educational qualifications, low income, poor diet, physical and mental ill-health, housing problems and – increasingly – debt. These mums and dads have no alternative but to send their offspring to the nearest school where, no matter how hard the teachers work, children's home circumstances constantly impact on their educational achievement. What's more, anyone struggling to raise a family in an area where crime, violence, drug and alcohol abuse are facts of daily life is unlikely to be well-read on the subject of child development. So the effects of toxic childhood syndrome are much worse for the children of the poor than they are for those from more fortunate backgrounds.

As one whose own family was 'lifted out of poverty' by improved educational opportunities over the course of the twentieth century, I began my teaching career believing that, in terms of social mobility, things could only get better. However, by the early 2000s it was pretty obvious to anyone travelling around Britain's schools that the beneficial effects of education had ceased to work their spell – the rich were getting richer, and the poor poorer. In fact, the Labour government's attempts to close the gap by 'raising educational standards' seemed to me to be making things worse. That's why I began my research into child development, and why, at the end of each chapter of *Toxic Childhood*, I added a PS called 'Mind the Gap'.

In 2006, these postscripts were not well received. Some commentators accused me of 'demonising poor children', which was the last thing I intended. Perhaps the problem was that, before UNICEF's 2007 survey brought the subject to public attention, childhood well-being and its intimate connection with inequality was little understood. Perhaps also, as social scientists Richard Wilkinson and Kate Pickett suggest, until the global financial crisis 'there was an assumption that inequality mattered only if it increased poverty, and that for most people "real" poverty was a thing of the past.' However, after several years of recession, anyone who has any contact with the real world can be in no doubt that real poverty is alive and well in the UK.

Wilkinson and Pickett's own book, *The Spirit Level*, appeared in 2009. In it, they argued that inequality is bad for everyone, rich and poor. It feeds fear and the breakdown of trust, so unequal societies as a whole suffer from more violence, mental illness, drug addiction, loss of community life and poor well-being for *all* children.

My argument is that poor childhood well-being is not merely the *result* of social inequality but, in a screen-based, hyper-competitive culture, it's also one of the most significant *causes*. Those of us lucky enough to be born in the mid-twentieth century benefited not only from educational opportunities but from other aspects of 'a good childhood' that were taken for granted in the past, but swept away by the socio-cultural changes described in this book. If, as a society, we truly want to close the poverty gap we must find ways to reinstate these factors for all our children.

It may not be possible to provide every primary school in Britain with verdant play spaces and well-manicured sports fields (although I ardently hope that, one day, it will be), but – by attending to the messages from developmental psychologists and other experts quoted in this book – we *can* ensure that every primary school pupil is physically, socially and emotionally equipped to learn. In the words of Nelson Mandela, 'there can be no keener revelation of a society's soul than the way in which it treats its children.'

CHAPTER ONE

FOOD FOR THOUGHT

In the early years of the twenty-first century, the people of the developed world suddenly noticed we had been poisoning our children. The food we'd let them eat over recent decades – ever-richer in sugar, salt, additives and the wrong sort of fat – now contained very little actual nourishment. Instead of building healthy bodies, it was simply making children fatter and more unhealthy by the year.

Although nutritionists had been warning about these developments for years, it wasn't until the physical effects of the 'obesity explosion' were clearly visible in a growing number of children that the media recognised a 'story'. Parents were suddenly bombarded with terrifying information about long-term implications for physical health, including the possibility that today's children might be the first generation in history to have a shorter lifespan than their elders. There was less media attention to the fact that junk food can also damage children's mental health, but at an international symposium on brain research and learning in Germany in 2003, delegates were told: 'If we do not pay attention to the diets of our children, we may be faced with a future of brain degenerating problems which are closely linked to learning problems.' Ten years on, this concern among scientists continues: it was voiced again at two international seminars in London as I revised this chapter in 2013 and updates on recent research are regularly collated by the Institute for Food, Brain and Behaviour.

Urged on by medical authorities and nutritionists, governments around the world have produced guidelines about healthy eating for decades, often with flashy illustrations: Canada developed a food rainbow; Germany a dietary circle (with a healthy glass of water in the middle) and China a food pagoda. In 2005, the US Department of Agriculture upgraded its food pyramid into a multicoloured, individualised animation – MyPyramid. This revamp was hailed by nutritionist Michael Jacobson as 'the strongest dietary guidelines yet produced', yet by 2010 it had been supplanted by MyPlate, giving specific advice for different age and ethnic groups. The UK now has a MyPlate website too, on which Alisha and Ronnie invite schoolchildren to choose a sensible day's food.

So, now that the twenty-first century is well into its second decade, most adults and older children are well-informed about what the younger generation *ought* to be eating, but in a multi-media world running at electric speed, it's not just parents who feed children – it's a global competitive consumer culture. And even though today's parents are increasingly aware of the dangers, they also know to their cost how difficult it is to turn the effects of that culture round.

Junk-food junkies

Despite all we know about it, highly processed junk food is still extremely popular throughout westernised society, and among children in particular. In a quick-fix world, it's the fastest, easiest way to satisfy hunger – pre-prepared, readily accessible and requiring no effort. It doesn't even need eating implements: burgers, hotdogs, pizzas, pies and pastries are all finger-foods, and fizzy drinks can be consumed straight from the can. What's more, mass-produced finger-foods are 'tasty', because the high quantities of fat, sugar, salt and food additives disguise poor quality ingredients. Fizzy drinks feed our human craving for sweetness (there's the equivalent of three tablespoons of sugar in each can), as do sugary snacks like cupcakes, biscuits and chocolate bars.

The addiction has been building up for some time, especially since fast food outlets proliferated over the second half of the twentieth century and restaurants like McDonald's became associated with days out, treats and parties. As children grew increasingly keen on the taste of quick-fix meals, manufacturers responded by creating many more products for the home: foods which are quick and easy to prepare in the microwave; ever-sweeter cereals; salty snacks to be popped into school lunch boxes or scoffed while watching TV; fatty foods suitable for 'grazing' throughout the day. The more of this stuff children eat, and the more cans of sugary fizz they drink, the more they want.

It's not an exaggeration to talk about contemporary children being addicted to junk. Psychologist Deanne Jade, founder of the Centre for Eating Disorders explains that highly flavoured food works in the same way as drugs. 'It changes our mood and it impacts on the chemicals and neurotransmitters in the brain in a similar way to alcohol, nicotine and cocaine.' The extent of physical addiction is considerably less, of course, but as the British nutritionist Dr Susan Jebb puts it: 'Children develop very strong learned preferences – junk food can become a psychological addiction.'

Sadly, it's often loving adults who inadvertently initiate children into the junk-food habit. Most of us have been conditioned by our own upbringing to see certain products as 'treats', which we enjoy and use as a quick comfort fix. Since we love our children, we want to give them treats too, and certain foods swiftly become associated with love, comfort and reward. This can start very early in life, when parents add sugary flavourings to toddlers' drinks or provide fruit juice instead of water. As Susan Jebb points out, this is quite unnecessary – children are perfectly happy with milk or water if we don't give them anything else, just as they are happy with fresh, wholesome food if no one introduces them to the unhealthy stuff.

But it's not that easy. Even if mum and dad try to keep sugar, salt and fat intake down, other adults (grandparents, neighbours, playmates' parents) like to indulge children with 'treats', and the thrill of forbidden food makes it taste all the sweeter. As they grow older, children compare notes with friends at pre-school or day centre, so they're soon aware of the range of goodies on offer. Add to this the impact of marketing – not just the obvious TV and Internet ads, posters and packaging, but the subliminal marketing wherever we go, such as vending machine displays and product placement in films and TV programmes – and it seems practically impossible to keep children away from unhealthy food for long.

Marketing messages

In the last few decades, the marketing industry has made increasingly insidious inroads into consumers' minds, affecting the way we all think and act. Most people in the developed world now believe that choice – in food as in all other consumer products – is a fundamental right. (In fact, for most of human history, choice hardly existed – most people ate, drank and wore what they could get, if they were lucky enough to get it.)

As a result, many parents feel guilty when they deny their children the choice of their favourite food. But, as celebrity chef Jamie Oliver put it when asked why he thought children shouldn't have any choice over their school meal: 'You wouldn't ask them what they wanted to read in an English class. If they'd asked me, I'd have chosen ... comics or porn.' In a consumer society, children do need opportunities to learn to make choices, but it's up to parents to decide which choices to offer.

Marketing has also conditioned us to care about brands. Neuro-imaging technology has shown that for many Americans the mere sight of a can of Coca-Cola excites activity in sections of the brain associated with feelings of self-image, memory and cultural identity. Since the early 1990s, when it became clear that even two-year-olds recognise and ask for specific branded products, there has been a particularly concerted effort to win the hearts and minds of juvenile consumers. A UK government report on children's food and advertising in 2004 found that children associate highly advertised, branded food with 'fun', influenced not just by the taste but by the colourful packaging and use of pictures, cartoons and characters from TV or films. It added that 'effectively marketed brands generate recognition, familiarity and even affection amongst children. Well-known brands can impart status/'cool' to the user'.

Marketing aimed at children – such as links to popular films and TV programmes, toys in cereal packets and 'Happy Meals', etc. – creates a very powerful form of 'pester power'. So when parents are conditioned by marketeers to feel that allowing choice shows love for their children, and children are persuaded by those same marketeers to choose certain products, it can be extraordinarily difficult to resist the pressure. And that pressure now is immense: marketing techniques have become enormously sophisticated in recent years, and parents are often unaware of the ways their children are being targeted.

A confidential report about one advertising agency's successful child-focused promotion – for a fruit-based sugary snack – caused a furore when it fell into the hands of a British journalist. The report described how the agency had used a 'viral' approach – designed to create interest in the brand by word of mouth before the launch. Their task was to ensure children recognised images associated with the snack ('mutant fruit characters'), and saw them as 'cool'. The first target, therefore, was not the children themselves, but older youngsters whose tastes would influence children. So they 'seeded' the characters, along with a secret language, at concerts, in magazines and in cinemas, to put the word on the street. Using gifts of clothing, they also adorned children's celebrities with pictures of the characters, thus gaining exposure on television shows and music channels that children watch. They featured their characters on Internet pop-ups and created micro-sites on popular children's websites. Only when demand had been created among the infant audience was the product also marketed to their parents, this time as a 'healthy snack'.

It's just a bit of fun …

Since the media noticed the obesity explosion, there have been many campaigns to prevent the marketing of unhealthy food to children. Unfortunately, small groups of earnest campaigners, working within the constraints of their home nation's political system, tend to make little impact in the face of global corporations with immense political influence and multi-million dollar marketing budgets. As a result, most regulations end up being cosmetic rather than effective.

For instance, in 2007 the UK government banned junk-food advertising during children's TV programmes, a move which was trumpeted to anxious parents as a great step forward in market regulation. However – as the market researchers had always known – the vast majority of the TV shows watched by children under 12 aren't specifically aimed at children. They're traditional family viewing such as soap operas and talent contests, in which commercial breaks still teem with ads for burgers, confectionary, fizzy drinks and so on.

And, anyway, the ability of national governments to regulate screen-based marketing has more-or-less evaporated as, over the last ten years, advertising budgets have been directed steadily webward. Today's children, equipped with laptops, smartphones and tablets, habitually see the food and drink ads 'officially' aimed at adults. They can also enjoy free branded 'advergames', apps and other special offers that pop up on their favourite social networking and gaming sites.

The commercial websites to which these ads direct children often feature the cool, cuddly characters who inspire their affection and brand loyalty, such as Sugar Puffs' Honey Monster and the Nesquik Bunny. Although the 2004 report cited above led to UK regulations about the use of celebrities or 'licensed characters' like Winnie the Pooh to promote unhealthy foodstuffs, there's no ban on branded characters devised by the companies themselves, so marketing departments invest heavily in devising them. As young children's screen use moves inexorably towards the Internet, we can expect a host of cute cartoon heroes inviting them to share this web-based fun.

Trapped in the junk-food jungle

Wise parents try to keep ahead of marketing tricks and educate their children to do so too (see Chapter 8 and suggestions in 'Turning children into healthy eaters', page 44). But even where parents are able to withstand the marketing assault and convince their offspring that love is not the same thing as indulgence ('We *love* you; the marketing men just want our money!'), children also have to live in a world beyond the family. Peer pressure exerts a strong influence – children don't want to seem 'different', parents don't want their offspring to be an oddball in the playground – and the wrong sort of packaging in your lunch box can be social suicide.

Schools themselves have even been drawn into promoting unhealthy food, through marketing promotions where resources are exchanged for children's snack food wrappers, or by topping up school funds through the sale of junk foodstuffs and fizzy drinks in vending machines or tuck shops. Recent 'Healthy Eating' initiatives have put paid to most of these practices, but there are other ways that the food industry can make inroads into the classroom. The Nesquik bunny may not appear in Nestle's 2012 *Healthy Kids Programme*, but when cash-strapped schools use its free literature they ensure that the brand is well-promoted ... and associated with 'a healthy lifestyle'.

Despite the sterling work of restaurateur Jamie Oliver, even school lunches can still help to feed the junk-food habit. In 2005, Oliver caused a national outcry with a TV series about the nutritional content of the food being fed to large numbers of the nation's children. It was summed up by the notorious 'turkey twizzler', then a popular item on many school menus, consisting of reconstituted bits of poultry (the bits you'd rather not think about) mixed with fats and additives. Oliver's efforts to change the eating habits of primary school children made fascinating viewing – and caused the British government to establish stricter controls on school food standards.

But he also showed how difficult it can be to wean children off junk. As his dinner ladies pointed out, the reason they served up turkey twizzlers and other nutritionally appalling dishes wasn't just a question of cost and convenience. It was because the children refused to eat anything else. Despite legislation, this is still the case in many schools where, as one teacher told me in 2013: 'the children's plates are filled with pizza, pasta, bread and a sweet dessert ... [They] may have been given vegetables or salad with their meal but these are left to go cold or 'accidentally' end up on the floor. So on paper the meal may appear balanced but what the children actually ingest is not.'

The problem is that once kids are hooked on rubbishy food, their sense of taste is suppressed by excessive amounts of salt, sugar and additives, and other foods begin to taste bland and unappetising. This is when they turn into 'fussy eaters', holding adults to ransom to provide the type of highly flavoured food they crave. So no matter how hard parents try to provide healthy options, many – like the dinner ladies – still allow their offspring to feast on junk, simply because it's the only food they'll eat.

It's easy for parents to find themselves loving their offspring 'not wisely, but too well'. When a child refuses to eat, panic can set in. To the heady mix of pester power, 'the right to choose', peer pressure and a quick-fix culture, is added parental panic that their children might waste away (or acquire one of those much-hyped eating disorders). So children across the world continue to be hooked on a diet that threatens the healthy development of their growing bodies – and brains.

Sugar rush

The brain is a greedy organ, needing almost one third of the blood pumped from the heart to supply it with the oxygen and nutrients it needs to work efficiently. Deprived of these nutrients, it won't work as well as it should, so a balanced diet is essential for growing, learning children. Filling up on the wrong foods doesn't just threaten their physical health, it threatens their brain chemistry and thus their capacity to learn.

One of the main dietary culprits is sugar, which children – left to their own devices – often use as a major source of dietary fuel. They start the day with a sugary cereal, and continue at regular intervals with cans of fizzy drinks, cakes and biscuits, chocolate bars and sweets. As a body fuel, sugar is worse than useless. It provides an immediate 'sugar high', which in many children can lead to hyperactivity and impulsiveness, so they're unable to settle to learn in school. But this high soon wears off, leaving the body craving more sugar. The child then has the option of feeling cranky and miserable, or fuelling up on sugar again for another high. Hence the regular sugary snacks.

However, cereals, sweets and fizzy drinks are merely the visible face of sugar addiction. Over the last thirty years, the amount of sugar in western diets has soared because of its steadily increasing presence (often in the form of 'fructose' or 'corn syrup') in processed foodstuffs of every kind. The food industry relies heavily on sugar to mask the poor quality of other ingredients because, in the words of endocrinologist Professor Robert H. Lustig, 'You can make dog poop taste good with enough sugar. In essence, this is what the food industry has done.' The result is a double-whammy for the manufacturers, because the more sugary foods and drinks we consume, the more we want. 'It's addictive,' says Lustig. 'The food industry knows that when they add fructose we buy more...'.

There's no doubt that excessive sugar consumption has contributed to the obesity explosion. But just as significantly, the calories in refined sugar are 'empty calories'. Sugary drinks and snacks don't provide any of the nutrients and dietary fibre children gain from eating healthy snacks like fruit, vegetables, nuts, dairy produce and grain. This means children with a sugar habit are likely to end up deficient in the minerals and vitamins found in a balanced diet. For instance, in a review of studies in 2005 the British Nutrition Foundation found that 50 per cent of children had a marginal intake of Vitamin A and 75 per cent had a marginal intake of zinc, both essential nutrients.

A long-term study at the University of Southern California claimed that if children's diets lacked a variety of minerals in the first three years, they were more likely to be irritable and aggressive at eight years old, more likely to swear and cheat at eleven, and more likely to steal and bully at seventeen. Over the years, studies of children with ADHD and dyslexia have frequently pointed towards various mineral and vitamin deficiencies, usually resulting in a surge in the sales of food supplements. But when human beings eat a balanced diet, supplements aren't generally necessary. Too much sugar is a sure way of putting the diet out of balance. In the words of Oxford scientist Bernard Gesch, 'There is evidence that nutrition can improve [developmental conditions]. More importantly, if careful diet can be used to treat these, it's possible we can also prevent them in the first place.'

The additive cocktail

While children may be missing out on essential nutrients, they are usually getting high dosages of inessential additives. Controversy has raged for years about the safety of additives, such as tartrazine, caffeine and monosodium glutamate, which are used to colour, flavour or preserve food, and certain additives are banned in some countries but not others. Since additives often have long, complex chemical names (not made any easier in the European Union by the convention of also giving them E-numbers), the whole subject can be bewildering to consumers, adding to parental confusion and concern about diet.

Recent studies suggest that the 'cocktail' of additives consumed in a diet of processed food and soft drinks could be a contributory factor in behavioural problems. British toxicologist Vyvyan Howard points out that additives are tested by food companies one at a time, and little is known about how they react in mixtures: 'A number of these substances are related very closely to transmitter substances in the brain, which is the way nerve cells talk to each other. If you interfere with that, you interfere with brain function.' But establishing whether this is the case, and then the exact nature of each additive's contribution, will be difficult and could take decades.

Research studies into the effects of dietary factors on brain function are few and far between (in a world financed mainly by commerce, it can be difficult for scientists to access funding), and the food industry is quick to find fault with them. There's also the problem of identifying which ingredients specifically affect particular children – indeed, it seems possible that different cocktails of sugar, additives and other ingredients have adverse effects on different children, and maybe even the same children at different times. Reporting on a 2011 study of food colourings for the US Food Advisory Committee, psychology professor Andrea Chronis-Tuscano announced herself unconvinced that the substances are dangerous, but similarly unconvinced that they aren't. Like all independent researchers before her, she concluded that more research is needed: 'appropriate toxicology studies have not been conducted to determine the effects of these additives on developing brains at different ages.'

But even if scientists aren't yet able to reach definite conclusions about individual food additives, these are clearly among the 'usual suspects' within an impoverished western diet. And now that science has proved without doubt that such a diet damages the human body, we must also take seriously its potential effects on the brain. In 2013, Dr Alex Richardson, currently researching the effects of diet on children's brain development at Oxford University told me: 'We're seeing nutritional deficiencies and imbalances in children that are almost certainly negatively affecting their mood, behaviour and learning. We are pretty sure why this is happening. But there's a dearth of funding for independent research to prove it conclusively, because the food industry doesn't want us to prove it.'

Fats and fish oil

An important ingredient in any balanced diet is fat – or, at least, the right sort of fat. As well as being greedy, the brain is a fatty organ – in fact, it's almost two thirds fat. Some of the key nutrients required to keep it going are essential fatty acids, which the human body cannot make, and which we therefore have to ingest in the form of food. The demonisation of fats in general – due to the twin terrors of heart disease and obesity – have blinded many people to the fact that some fats are essential to health, especially for children, whose brains are still developing. Breast milk is 50 per cent fat, and paediatricians advise parents not to restrict fat intake in children under two, when brain development is at its most rapid.

As children grow older, the advice is that – like adults – they should avoid saturated fats (solid, hard animal fats like butter and lard) in favour of healthier vegetable oils, keeping fried food to a minimum. However, as long ago as the 1970s, Professor Michael Crawford (now at Imperial College, London) showed that the 'long-chain' Omega 3 and 6 hard fats are indispensable for brain structure and function. Since then, scientists around the world have backed up Crawford's findings, but the information has failed to filter through to either policy or practice in child nutrition.

In the distant past, a typical human diet included two essential fatty acids: Omega 3 (found in oily fish and seafood), and Omega 6 (found in meat and dairy products). Our hunter-gatherer ancestors consumed these in about equal measures. Over time, as people ate less fish, the ratio has changed – nowadays, we consume up to twenty times more Omega 6. Indeed, Omega 3 has virtually disappeared from the diets of many people in the developed world – especially vegetarians.

There's mounting evidence that (among other contemporary ills) Omega 3 deficiency in children is related to distractibility and learning difficulties, and – as studies on the subject appeared – many parents have started giving their children fish oil supplements. However, recent research suggests the beneficial effects for many aspects of mental and physical health come only from long-chain Omega 3 fatty acids. Short-chain Omega 3s, which are often used in 'enriched' foodstuffs and health store supplements, don't convert reliably into the long-chain fatty acids that the body and brain need so, as usual, it's important to check the label carefully (long-chain Omega 3s are known as EPA and DHA).

The wrong sort of fat

There's a further worrying factor in the fat story. Many processed foods contain 'trans-fats' (sometimes listed on labels as 'hydrogenated vegetable oils' or HVO). Like sugar, trans-fats are popular with manufacturers – they're cheap to produce and prolong shelf life – but they also pose a greater health threat than saturated fats such as butter and lard. In 2009, the World Health Organisation declared them 'toxic', adding that there is no safe level of consumption, and in 2010 the National Institute for Clinical Excellence (NICE) urged the UK government to ban them completely from the national diet, as has already happened in Denmark, Switzerland, Iceland, Sweden, Austria, New York City, Seattle and the state of California. Unfortunately, the influence of the food industry in modern Britain is so great that, in 2011, it was merely suggested that the market should 'self-regulate', on a voluntary basis.

Self-regulation may be successful if consumers care about what they're eating – and, in fact, more upmarket stores such as Marks & Spencer and Waitrose (as well as the ethically-inclined Co-op) removed trans-fats from their products many years ago, on the assumption that well-educated customers would soon be up to speed on the trans-fat question. Other companies, including Tesco, Asda and Burger King, have since responded to the government request, but there's still a long way to go before these toxic substances disappear from the national diet.

Trans-fats still appear in cheaper brands and are regularly used by many fast-food outlets, which aren't required by law to list the ingredients in their meals. These, of course, are the products and places which often furnish the entire diet of families in poorer areas of the country. They're also popular with children and young people across the social spectrum, because kids get more for their pocket money and teenage culture tends to have a rebellious downmarket edge.*

In terms of mental health, manufactured trans-fats don't lubricate the brain in the way natural long-chain fatty acids do – in fact, they're more likely to inhibit brain function. Animal studies have shown trans-fatty acids alter the efficiency with which brain cells communicate with each other. As Alex Richardson explains, 'Every time children eat cheap processed food (especially baked goods) or fast food they are filling themselves with what are, essentially, toxic fats ... They are replacing the essential fats that would make their brains and bodies work properly with ones that are clogging up the machinery.'

The decline of the family meal

The message is clear. If parents want to ensure a healthy diet for their children, the fewer highly processed foodstuffs they provide, the better. But there's another huge influence on contemporary children's eating habits that I've so far failed to mention: the changes over recent decades in family structures and working habits. This subject is covered in Chapters 5 and 6, but its effects are felt in every single chapter in the book. In terms of diet, the greatest impact has been the decline of the family meal.

Throughout human history, eating has been an important social event and in countries where food traditions are still highly valued, enjoyment of food is closely related to the circumstances of eating: preparation and presentation, family gatherings and

---

* Incidentally, there's also the chance that adults across the social spectrum might unknowingly be ingesting trans-fats when they eat out. One of the 'expert witnesses' I interviewed about diet was sitting with a colleague outside an expensive London restaurant when they saw a consignment of cooking oil arrive. After reading the chemical formula on the container, they decided to eat elsewhere.

mealtime conversation. But in developed nations, meals have become increasingly solitary experiences, with preparation often involving little more than piercing a film lid and switching on the microwave. The habit of 'grazing' on snacks throughout the day means that in many homes set mealtimes have all but disappeared; in others, there is not even a dining table.

Many families around the world would identify with American journalist Sheila Pell's description of a typical mealtime – husband and children eating in different rooms in front of different screens, while she perches alone in the middle, tucking into a microwavable snack-meal: 'Like much of the nation, everyone in the family is so busy that we long ago became used to eating in shifts. Dining has become dinner, interrupted. It is often a staggered affair, where people wander in on their own schedules, gaze into the refrigerator as if it were a 1950s automat, and make a selection. Our seating arrangements evolved out of this moveable feast.'

The highly significant social shift from communal to solitary eating happened almost without comment, a knock-on effect of many other cultural changes happening at electric speed. These include: the rise of dual-income households; the availability of pre-prepared 'ready-meals'; the increase in television channels and screen-based socialising ... and, of course, children's addiction to junk food, which means they're not really interested in sharing something 'gross' with the rest of the family – they'd rather 'grab a burger and chill out' on their own.

When one day we woke up to find ourselves eating like Sheila Pell's family, people began to worry, and there's evidence that families have been making much more of an effort to eat together over recent years: in 2006, researchers at Rutgers University in New Jersey reported that 'there is definitely an awareness about family meals that was not there a few years ago' and I've noticed growing concern about the issue among the thousands of parents I meet every year in the UK.

Unfortunately, with the steady proliferation of handheld devices, today's family meal may not be the close communal occasion of old. In a 2013 survey about toddlers' eating habits, six out of ten parents admitted to using a smartphone at mealtimes to answer emails or check Facebook. Not surprisingly, two-thirds of their toddlers also preferred to engage with screens as they ate (TV, DVD, iPads, smartphones, hand-held games devices). Their parents claimed these distractions improved their offsprings' behaviour at the table, but it also meant the children were more familiar with cartoon characters than the food on their plate: three in five toddlers could identify Peppa Pig, while just over a third were able to name broccoli.

Meals, manners and marijuana

And yet, as child psychologist Robert Wolfson explains, 'The family meal can be such a wonderful time for parents and children alike. It allows them to share their feelings, thoughts and ideas through face-to-face communication, while giving parents the opportunity to encourage positive eating habits and provide good nutrition to support this amazing period of toddler development.'

It's also where young children can – slowly but surely – learn table manners, by watching the adults and copying their behaviour. Imitation is one of the most important learning mechanisms, and toddlers are very keen to appear 'grown-up' so this is a critical period in their social education. But teachers in western countries frequently complain nowadays that children can no longer handle a knife and fork (a 2005 survey of one thousand pre-teens eating in a restaurant chain in the UK found 20 per cent eating with fingers more than cutlery, 49 per cent only using a fork and three-quarters failing to put their knife and fork together at end of meal).

It seems to be not much better in Japan – a country famed for its addiction to manners – where nutritionist Dr Yukio Hattori complains that nearly 40 per cent of children can't use chopsticks properly. As social psychologist Pat Spurgin puts it, table manners have an important social function: 'It's an important social skill to be able to sit at a table and not embarrass yourself and other people with your manners – to not lean over people and grab things, not take the last potato and to recognise that other people are with you.'

But there's more to social development than table manners. In a world where opportunities for adults and children to talk together grow fewer and fewer (see Chapter 4), a regular shared meal is the ideal opportunity for chatting over the events of the day, swapping gossip and planning future activities. This sort of family interaction might seem trivial at first sight, but its long-term implications are profound. Richard Harman, headteacher of Uppingham School, explained at an educational conference in 2012: 'the decline in family meals has led to an erosion of social skills amongst youngsters, despite the fact that it's becoming increasingly clear for the future that an ability to get on with people and share ideas will be just as vital for the workplace as the ability to master maths and English.'

As the years go by, the social significance of regular family meals becomes ever more apparent. Researchers at the University of Minnesota found that the more frequently teenagers ate with their parents, the less likely they were to smoke, drink, use marijuana, or show signs of depression. There's even a US research study showing that the only common denominator among National Merit Scholars of all races and social classes is that they eat dinner with their families. It doesn't take a rocket scientist to recognise that regular family get-togethers have a civilising effect on children at all ages.

Feeding a family

Family meals also tend to be healthier. Japanese nutritionist Asako Aranaki points out that people who eat with chopsticks tend to eat a more balanced diet than members of the 'hashi-nashi zoku' (chopstick-less tribe), who are 'particularly careless about eating a good breakfast ... take dinner at irregular hours and nibble constantly at snacks during the day.' Shared mealtimes, of course, allow parents greater supervision of the food children eat (and when they eat it) and opportunities to counter the fussy-eater syndrome, thus weaning them off junk food.

If possible, the best way to avoid fussy eating habits is to stop them before they begin, by ensuring children eat a wide variety of food from the earliest age. In Italy, there's a long-established detailed feeding routine for babies, weaning them off milk and on to a range of tastes. This seems eminently sensible. As pointed out earlier, parents have control over children's diet in the first few years and it's not till the age of two that children really begin to be fussy about food. Evolutionary biologists explain that this is when they become aware that unfamiliar foods might be poisonous – and marketeers tell us it's the age at which they become aware of brands. The collision of old and new 'instincts' is a powerful one.

Once children have become addicted (or even quite partial) to junk foods, changing their eating habits is much more difficult, and without careful forethought parents' efforts could be counter-productive. The combination of work-frazzled adults and junk-demanding children could easily mean that mealtimes turn into a battleground – and unless family meals are a pleasant social occasion, no one's going to benefit. Indeed, it's possible that continual struggles with parents over food can, in the long term, drive children into eating disorders (although other elements are undoubtedly involved – see Chapter 8).

A brief battle-plan for detoxing junk food addicts, culled from discussion with a range of experts, is provided on page 45, but its success depends on parents sticking to three key principles:

- mealtimes should be enjoyable
- everyone eats the same meal – no special dishes
- parents decide which choices to offer to children.

To convince children to be more experimental, experts suggest the repeated offering of 'a little taste' during the family meal. If the child enjoys it, you offer more. If not, the key is not to push it – but not to offer an alternative dish. If you provide plenty of bread, rice, vegetables or other staples to choose from the child won't go hungry. The next time you eat that dish, offer 'a little taste' again . . . and so on. The American nutritionist Ellyn Satter has a useful rule of thumb for establishing mealtime harmony: adults decide *what*, *when* and *where* children eat; children decide *how much*, and even *whether*.

For working parents, preparing and sharing a pleasant meal each evening is clearly not easy to arrange – but it's worth putting in some thought on the subject. The ideal would be to arrive home at a regular time themselves, and build up a repertoire of simple meals using fresh ingredients that can be prepared relatively quickly. There are plenty of recipe books with suggestions for quick, healthy suppers. But if they can't always be there themselves, parents could at least ensure that whoever minds the children in their absence – hopefully other committed adults – reads clearly from the same nutritional and behavioural hymn-sheet (see Chapter 6).

The key elements are consistency and regularity – agreed attitudes to food and behaviour at the table, and an agreed regular mealtime – so children know what to expect and when and where to expect it. This might seem an effort to organise, but it's a question of priorities. When their children are ill, working parents move heaven and earth to ensure correct medication is administered at the right time. Regular healthy meals on a daily basis are as significant for children's long-term health as medication is for acute conditions – and in this respect, as in every area of child-rearing, consistency is essential. The nutritionist Susan Jebb believes that establishing eating habits to keep children in good shape for the rest of their lives is 'a key way to invest in their futures.' As she explains, 'They are not called 'eating habits' for nothing – habits are ways of behaving which have become very deep-seated, and are therefore difficult to change. Habits acquired in childhood tend to stay with you life-long.'

Cutting back on snack attack

Regular family meals are the best way to provide children with a balanced diet – and with ring-fenced 'family time' in which to consume it – whilst also making them less likely to gorge on unhealthy snack foods. Indeed, if you're going to the trouble of cooking, it's essential they don't eat snacks in the couple of hours leading up to the main meal. If children come to the table full, they'll have a far higher fussiness quotient. This is another reason for insisting on a regular mealtime – so that everyone knows when food is going to arrive on the table and, out of courtesy to the cook, snacks are banned during the preceding couple of hours.

Children do, however, sometimes need snacks to stave off hunger – for instance on arrival home from school. Susan Jebb recommends the best way to ensure these are healthy snacks is to make your home a junk-free zone. This removes the temptation for anyone – including adult role models – to snack on unhealthy food. (While researching this chapter, I found the following list of suggestions on an Australian government website, and stuck it inside my kitchen cupboard door: *fresh and dried fruit; crackers with cheese or peanut butter; yogurt; raisin bread, fruit loaf, toasted muffins; dips and biscuits or vegetable sticks; plain biscuits, scones or buns.* My family added to it as we thought of others, such as *popcorn, sardines on toast* and *boiled egg.*) Similarly, to save children from the soft drinks trap, have only water, milk, diluted fruit juice or hot chocolate available.

If food at home is kept relatively junk free, parents can afford to be more relaxed outside the home. A total ban on junk food isn't a good idea, as it leads to interest in the forbidden foods. Allowing the over-fives *occasional* burgers and snacks when out shopping or when eating out as a family is unlikely to do much harm, and ensures they're worldly-wise about such things among their peers.

While interviewing a nutritionist about this, I was reassured to find she took an '80-20 approach' with her own family – 80 per cent healthy food, 20 per cent not so healthy. 'If they don't have the occasional sweets or McDonalds they aren't part of the peer group, and that causes other problems. As long as the overall diet's healthy, a bit of junk shouldn't do that much harm. The trouble is that many parents now get it the wrong way round – 80% rubbish food and 20% nourishment.'

* * *

The essence of this chapter is that the caring adults in children's lives must reassume responsibility for what they eat. We have to reassert the grown-ups' right to decide what, in terms of nutrition, is good for growing bodies and brains. 'Choice', the siren call of the marketing men, depends upon informed decision-making, and children don't know enough about nutrition to make informed decisions. Adults must therefore make choices on their behalf, to counteract damaging marketing messages.

This doesn't mean coercing children to eat particular foods – which could be just as damaging in other ways. It means ensuring attractive healthy options, associating these with pleasant family rituals, and thus gradually weaning children away from an unhealthy diet. If the significant adults in every child's life genuinely believe healthy food is better choice than junk, then we'll make the effort to provide food that nourishes our children rather than poisoning them.

DETOXING MEALTIMES

- Serve the main meal of the day at a regular time, and eat together as family as often possible, even if only one parent (or a parent substitute) can be there.
- Make a list of healthy meals your family enjoys, and add to it as you find new ones. Then you don't have to think so hard when deciding what to make.
- Don't make different dishes for different members of the family – all eat the same food.
- You decide what, when, where your child eats; let the child decide how much (or even whether) – if there's plenty of bread, potatoes, rice or other staples available, children need never go hungry.
- Teach table manners by:

    – deciding with other adults and older children what to emphasise and why
    – modelling good manners yourself
    – building up younger children's eating skills and manners
    – gradually (focus on one aspect at a time and give plenty of praise when they get it right).

- Eat in a screen- and mobile-free zone. Concentrate on the food and the chance to chat (see Chapter 4 for ideas on what to chat about).
- Don't allow any snacking for an agreed period (say 1½-2 hours) before a mealtime.
- Don't let mealtimes turn into battlegrounds: aim for enjoyable social occasions.
- Try not to panic if your child goes through a 'fussy' stage. Not eating a balanced diet for a while is unlikely to be too harmful (see the doctor and look into food supplements if you're really worried). Getting into food battles is more likely to do long-term harm.
- As often as possible, let your child help with planning (e.g. choosing new dishes from recipe books), shopping and preparing meals.

- Be laid back. Meals are a time for enjoying your family's company, so try to make them occasions to remember with pleasure.
- If you're not going to be at home, make sure everyone responsible for your child's meals keeps to your ground rules (show them these detox lists).

TURNING CHILDREN INTO HEALTHY EATERS

- Start as you mean to go on – for instance, from the beginning provide water or milk rather than sugary drinks. If you later include fruit juice, dilute it.
- Keep an eye on your children's behaviour in relation to food, and try cutting out any foodstuffs that seem to create a bad reaction – check the labels to work out what ingredient (especially additives) might be the cause.
- Follow healthy eating guidelines, such as MyPlate and use low-fat milk products where possible (but remember that the under-twos need full-fat milk).
- Ensure children have both long-chain Omega 3 (oily fish, seafood) and Omega 6 (animal fats, dairy products) – if necessary, look into fish oil supplement (see the independent Food and Behaviour Research website).
- Avoid trans-fats (e.g. hydrogenated vegetable oil) at all costs.
- Help children recognise the difference between *your* interest in their health and fitness, and the marketeers' interest in your money.
- Don't use food – especially unhealthy snack food – as a reward or treat. Try to persuade grandparents and others to follow this rule too!
- Parental example is very important. If you have a sensible, balanced attitude to food and eating, your child will pick it up – but if you gorge on unhealthy snacks, they'll want to too. Raising a healthy child is great motivation to sort out your own eating habits.
- Don't keep any junk food or unhealthy snacks in the house. Have a

selection of healthy snacks available (but no snacking before meals!). If an adult member of the family is unable to curb his or her need for some type of junk, explain that adults are old enough to make their own choices – children's bodies and brains are still developing, so junk is far more damaging for them.

- When shopping or watching ads, alert your children to unhealthy food. For instance:

    – the more 'pre-prepared' the product, the more likely it is to contain damaging ingredients (e.g. frozen peas are probably OK; frozen pizza probably isn't)

    – the longer the list of ingredients, the more suspicious you should be

    – be wary about long shelf-life, very unnatural colours, 'cool' packaging

    – just because something claims it's good for you doesn't necessarily mean it is: vague claims like 'full of goodness', 'wholesome', 'nutritious' are probably disguising something (for instance, for 'energy' read 'corn syrup' or 'sugar').

- Don't ban junk food altogether – allow occasional snacks, drinks, fast food (for instance, when away from home) – but don't view them as 'treats', and make your disdain apparent.

HOW TO DETOX A JUNK-FOOD ADDICT

This takes time, so don't expect too much too soon. Use the techniques listed above, and at mealtimes try the following:

- Offer a mixture of new foods and the healthiest of children's old favourites (gradually transferring to home-made burgers, fish cakes, pasta sauces, etc).
- Offer 'tastes' of new foods to start with, not whole portions. If the child

doesn't like it, don't insist. Wait a month or so and offer the same dish another time … and again, and again…

- Present food as attractively as possible. Borrow the marketeers' ideas, e.g.:

    – cut food into interesting shapes, make 'faces' or other pictures on the plate

    – invent names to make dishes sound special ('Cheesy Delight', 'Sardine Special').

- So your child doesn't go hungry, make sure there are plenty of 'staples' on the table.
- Soups, stews, casseroles and smoothies are great for disguising unfavourite vegetables (switch to mince or grate on the food processor). This can help familiarise a fussy eater with a new taste.
- Some children prefer vegetables raw (for instance, with a dip).
- Always have water at the table for drinking (this is good for adults too! – if you're drinking wine, intersperse with glasses of water). Make it more enticing by adding ice or serving in fancy glasses or with a special straw.
- Don't force or bribe your child to eat – for instance, don't offer dessert as a reward for finishing a main course. (Ellyn Satter recommends that if you're having dessert you put out a single portion for each person *before* the meal, and children can eat their dessert first if they prefer. But only a single portion – no seconds!)
- Fresh fruit is a healthy dessert. You can make it special by peeling, cutting into shapes, cooking (baked or stewed fruit) or creating a fruit salad.
- See Satter's book (below) for many more ideas.

PARENT POWER: CHANGING THE WAY WE EAT

Public opinion is a potent force. International reaction to the film *Supersize Me* stung McDonalds into changing its menus; support for celebrity chef Jamie Oliver's campaign forced the UK government to improve school meal provision. When people get together they can change the world.

Parents may come in all shapes, sizes, colours and creeds, but they're united by one overriding ideal – they want their children to grow up happy and healthy. Working together, parents could become the world's most powerful and positive pressure group. So, as well as detoxing your own child's diet, look for ways of helping detox the culture they live in:

- Talk to other parents about children and food. Tell them what you know; find out more. Support local, national and international campaigns to improve food quality.
- What is your child's school doing to promote healthy eating? If they haven't already done so, suggest they:

    – provide water coolers and/or milk to drink and discourage (or preferably ban) the consumption of sugary drinks on school premises

    – provide healthy snacks (e.g. toast, fruit, homemade scones and biscuits) at break times and stop children from bringing unhealthy snacks as tuck or packed lunches

    – provide appetising, healthy school lunches and encourage all children to eat school lunch (one of the best ways to do this is to make the bringing of packed lunches an unattractive option, e.g. by providing less pleasant facilities for eating them)

    – provide a pleasant, calm environment for school lunches, and use them as an opportunity to develop good manners and civilised behaviour

    – interest children in food production and preparation by growing food in school gardens, keeping hens, etc. and with clubs to involve the children in gardening and/or caring for livestock

– involve children in devising menus, preparing food, simple
cookery lessons and cookery clubs.

- If you have particular expertise in any of these areas and time to spare,
  offer help with school and childcare activities (see Chapter 7).
- Support campaigns to tackle the effects of marketing – for instance,
  the banning of all advertising to children under twelve (as has already
  happened in Sweden) – see Chapter 8.

Further reading

Alex Richardson, *They Are What You Feed Them* (Harper Thorsons, 2005)
Ellyn Satter, *Secrets of Feeding a Healthy Family: How To Eat, How To Raise
     Good Eaters, How to Cook* (Kelcy Press, 2008)
Joanna Blythman *The Food Our Children Eat: How To Get Children To Like
     Good Food* (Fourth Estate, 2011)

Useful websites

Independent research findings on food and behaviour – FAB Research:
     www.FABresearch.org and The Institute for Food, Brain and
     Behaviour: www.ifbb.org.uk
Sustain (the alliance for better food and farming) campaigns about
     children's food and advertising: www.sustainweb.org
Lots of useful family diet tips: www.parentsforhealth.org
US MyPlate site: www.choosemyplate.gov
Children's recipes: www.bbcgoodfood.com/recipes/collection/kids-
     cooking

Mind the gap

Thirty years ago, when I first began visiting schools around the UK, I was struck by the size of children in poorer areas of the country. I'd expected them to be small and undernourished, but many were huge, heavily-built and lumbering. They were indeed malnourished, the products of a high-fat junk-food diet.

There are many reasons why poorer families feed their children less well than others: transport problems that prevent them shopping around or buying in bulk for economies of scale; costs of buying fresh and organic products; the proliferation of cheap fast food outlets in inner-city areas; less knowledge about healthy eating and more susceptibility to marketing messages. So while recent health campaigns, films and television programmes have made an impact on diet in wealthier homes, many children in poor homes remain trapped in poor eating habits.

A nursery nurse working in a school in a deprived area of the country sent me this note:

> As I live near the school where I work, I shop at the same store as most of the parents. I've noticed that many buy poor quality or cheap basics like white bread, small and limited variety of fruit and vegetables, but seem quite happy to spend more money on branded expensive cakes, chocolates, snacks, etc... In school we give free fruit and milk at break time. Some parents insist their children will not eat fruit and send them with a chocolate biscuit or crisps every day. An even larger number of children don't have the free milk provided and bring high-sugar, coloured drinks.

In an international comparison of social mobility – the extent to which children from poor homes are able to overcome the circumstances of their birth and prosper in the educational system – two of the most successful countries were Spain and Finland. During my research for *Toxic Childhood,* I visited both these countries and ate school meals in each. The food was fresh, locally-sourced, highly nutritious and appetising; all the children ate it (no packed lunches); and teachers sat down to eat with them, insisting on the sort of civilised behaviour you'd expect at a pleasant family dinner. The contrast between this and the noisy eating areas, highly variable school food and junk-filled packed lunchboxes in the UK and USA (two countries with very poor social mobility) was stark.

Schools in the UK try valiantly to pass on the message about healthy diets, but in deprived areas it's an uphill battle. One headteacher told me that, as part of a healthy food campaign, his school began to provide milk, fruit and toast for the children at break time, but the campaign was undermined because some children continued to bring in crisps, chocolate bars and sugary drinks. After much debate, it was agreed the only way to stop the drift back to unhealthy food was to ban it. Within hours, one father was in school threatening the headteacher with (a) violence and (b) a trip to the European Court of Human Rights if he didn't reinstate his daughter's right to eat junk.

But schools in poorer areas of the USA and UK where healthy eating campaigns *have* been successful report considerable improvements in children's behaviour. It seems the best way to make a real change in the eating habits of under-privileged children would be for government or individual schools to be heavy-handed about school meals. If there were a national policy of compulsory, nutritionally-balanced school lunches for all (as is often the case in private schools), campaigning parents in the leafy suburbs would soon ensure high quality appetising food, all children would have access to at least one healthy meal a day, and parents would be let off making packed lunches. It sounds a good deal to me.

CHAPTER TWO

OUT TO PLAY

Centre-screen, a lion is basking in the sun. Three young cubs tumble, prowl and pounce around him – play-hunting, play-fighting, and occasionally launching themselves at their father, until he loses patience and brushes them away with a mighty paw. Into this picture edges the natural historian, David Attenborough, speaking softly into the mike so as not to disturb the family group. 'Play,' he breathes sonorously, 'is a very serious business.'

It certainly is. Those lion cubs are learning some of the most important lessons of their lives. They're developing the physical control and coordination they'll need for the hunt; they're establishing the social pecking order within their family pack; and they're discovering – in a safe, controlled environment – what it's like to take risks ... and what happens when you step over the line. What's more, they're enjoying it. The glorious thing about play is that it is fun: the young of every species is designed by nature to learn fundamental physical, social and emotional lessons through sheer enjoyment. As the Scottish poet Robert Louis Stevenson put it over a century ago:

> Happy hearts and happy faces
> Happy play in grassy places –
> That was how, in ancient ages,
> Children grew to kings and sages.

Unless, of course, they are denied the opportunity to play outside, or are lured away from Stevenson's 'grassy places' to some sort of virtual unreality.

One major side effect of the technological revolution has been, for many children, the replacement of age-old play activities (running, climbing, pretending, making, sharing) with a solitary, sedentary screen-based lifestyle. This is an alarming development. TV, computer games and the Internet have many merits, and our lives would be much the poorer without them, but they aren't a substitute for real life – and if children are to develop healthily in mind and body, neither are they a substitute for real play.

This change in children's play habits happened over a single generation, and two side effects of contemporary culture helped it along. First, the development of technological (and overwhelmingly indoor) options mentioned above, the pros and cons of which are discussed in Chapters 8 and 9, provided a seductive alternative to outdoor play. Second, a huge increase in parental anxiety led to restrictions on children's physical activity, their play and their freedom to roam beyond the confines of home, school and other supervised environments. Part of this anxiety is rational – for instance, a huge increase in traffic on the roads means the outdoor environment has become less safe every year, and now that most mothers are out at work there are fewer 'eyes on the street' to watch out for children's welfare – but part of it is highly irrational, and itself a consequence of our multimedia culture.

The fear of fear itself

One summer afternoon in 2002, two little girls went out for a walk in an English country village ... and disappeared. For weeks, the world's media camped in Soham, Cambridgeshire, and the last photograph of ten-year-old Holly and Jessica shone out from TV screens across the developed world – until the discovery of their bodies in a ditch wiped out all hope. A couple of months later, the TV cameras moved to Washington, USA, where deranged snipers were picking off parents and children from their car, leaving unnerving messages that no child was safe. The faces and voices of terrified parents spoke directly to mothers and fathers all over the world. Fast-forward to 2007 and the disturbingly ubiquitous image of three-year-old Madeleine McCann, who mysteriously disappeared from her family's holiday apartment; then to 2014, when the reopening of the McCann case revived the terrifying spectre of abduction for another wave of anxiety-stricken mums and dads.

Horrific news stories like these don't just shock us. They affect the way our brains work. We can now view (and repeatedly re-view) extraordinarily distressing images as if they are actually happening in front of us. This has a much greater effect on our mental stability than hearing or reading about them. Neuroscientists have found that horrific pictures affect the emotional centres in the brain and the more frequently they're viewed, the more they induce feelings of anxiety. When you read news, or listen to the measured tones of a newsreader, your responses are less immediate, more open to reason. What's more, in reading a newspaper, you can choose which stories to look at, while television news involves sitting through the whole thing – and studies show that that the large majority of television news stories are negative, depicting issues such as conflict and abuse.

Psychologists researching the effects of the 9/11 attack on the people of America found that the more TV people watched, the more likely they were to suffer psychological effects, even though they had no personal connection with the atrocity. Terrorists have been swift to capitalise on this finding, and to use video images as a primary instrument of terror. In the same way, news coverage of horrific news about children and families forces parents to confront their worst fears over and over again. The fact that this coverage continues remorselessly, night and day – in the corner of our living rooms, on the smartphones or tablets that now accompany us everywhere, even in the bedroom just before sleep – makes it even more powerful. So, even though we know the chances of our child being murdered by a maniac, hit by a sniper's bullet or spirited away by some unknown hand are infinitesimally small, we are still afraid. We have fallen victim to the worst fear of all – fear of fear itself.

When a National Lottery was introduced in Britain in the 1990s, its TV slogan, accompanied by a pointing cosmic finger was: 'It could be you!' although the chances of any family winning a life-changing amount are statistically negligible. Whenever any terrible event happens to children – however far away – we now know about it immediately, share vicariously in the parents' anguish, and think: 'It could be us.' As one newspaper columnist put it in the week of the terrible siege in Beslan's School Number One in Bello-Russia, 'that was the overpowering feeling as we watched the images of women, their faces contracted with stress and grief ... the men outside the siege school swearing at their impotence. It could have been us.' Through the power of the electronic media, human empathy is now transformed into debilitating fear.

Cotton wool kids

Children too are becoming more fearful. Despite restrictions on many types of television programming during the daytime and early evening, there's little restriction on the content of the news. Young children cannot distinguish between real events in real time and drama or video footage: to them, what's happening on TV is happening now. Neither do they understand geographical distance: as far as they're concerned, these scary events could be going on just down the road. As, over the twenty-first century, TV coverage of catastrophic events has grown ever more graphic and all-pervasive, psychiatrists have become concerned about the levels of stress and anxiety it can raise in children. In the words of the Professor of Clinical Child Psychology at the University of Kansas, 'The news media may inadvertently amplify and increase traumatic exposure ... by showing graphic and emotionally laden images of terrorist acts and the aftermath; in previous eras, the public could only imagine such a scene of violence, whereas today we can experience it over and over again in Technicolor.'

Now that the twenty-first century has moved into its second decade, access to destabilising images is even more widespread, as the viewing habits of both adults and children steadily transfer to the Internet, where there are no 'watershed' time restrictions and far more graphic material on view. So parental anxiety and children's fears go hand in hand, and the outside world has begun to seem an infinitely frightening place. This is in spite of the fact that, for most of us in the developed world, life is generally safer than it's ever been.

In his book *The Invention of Childhood*, Professor Hugh Cunningham catalogues the many risks, hardships and horrors that confronted children in western societies over the last millennium, and the remarkable resilience they showed as they grew to adulthood. He has high hopes that the younger generation of today will overcome the challenges of modern childhood – with one significant reservation, summed up in this passage from his book: 'A concern for safety, for assessing and managing risk, has become a dominant concern for many adults in their dealings with children. And children take on this concern. When some 700 children, mostly aged ten, were asked recently what they thought was of most importance in their upbringing, they placed highest of all, "stay safe". It is difficult to imagine this would have been the highest priority for any previous generation of children.'

Anxiety is insidious. It amplifies rational fears and stimulates irrational ones. There seem so many things now to worry about – health issues, all sorts of possible accidents, crime and violence, paedophiles and other people with evil intent, natural disasters – and all of these receive copious coverage in the media. But when the gathering paranoia begins to threaten children's emotional, social and intellectual development, we have to confront the problem.

One obvious way to avoid unnecessary anxiety is to limit

exposure to distressing news. I'm not advocating ostrich-like head-in-sand behaviour – in a global village, we all need to know what's going on in the world, and to wise up to real risks. But we don't need to invite constant messages of doom and destruction into our daily lives, and we certainly don't need to wallow in the misery of other people. The best advice for adults seems to be to read the news rather than watch it, monitor and mediate screen-based activity when young children are up and about, avoid acting like a rubbernecker when tragedy strikes other unfortunate parents – and definitely don't keep tuning in to distressing re-runs of news stories. Advice regarding children's viewing habits is given in Chapter 9.

We also have to be aware that there's a huge market in safety, so it's in the interests of marketing men to keep anxiety on the boil. All parents need to take sensible precautions, of course, but there's a limit. There's currently debate among experts about the efficacy of both safety surfacing in playgrounds and cycling helmets in reducing serious accidents to children, but the commercial flood of 'safety equipment' continues. Tim Gill, who researches the significance of risk in play, commented in 2013 that the latest outbreak of safety equipment appeared to be helmets for children to wear outdoors: 'not cycling helmets, but just "life helmets", that will protect children from flying objects coming from different directions.'

In fact, attempts to make life super-safe frequently backfire. It's now believed by many experts that the asthma boom of the last two decades (and perhaps increases in allergies and other diseases of the auto-immune system) is related to excessive levels of cleanliness in contemporary homes. When all the everyday bacteria are wiped out, children's bodies don't get the chance to build up resistance. Too great a preoccupation with safety can be as harmful as too little, and wrapping children in cotton wool carries a very strong risk of suffocation.

How fear turns children into couch potatoes

Healthy development of both body and mind depends on activity and experience. From the very beginning, babies learn about the world around them through touch and movement. To refine their physical control and coordination, they need plenty of opportunity to flex developing muscles. If parental anxiety gets in the way, development is inhibited.

For instance, the 'Back to Sleep' campaign (aimed at preventing Sudden Infant Death Syndrome or 'cot death') advised that babies should be put to sleep on their backs, but parents who over-reacted to the advice became frightened of placing their children on their stomachs. Dr Amanda Kirby, director of the Dyscovery Centre for Specific Learning Difficulties, believes this may help account for a sudden rise during the 1990s in cases of dyspraxia, since babies don't get adequate exercise unless they also spend time lying on their fronts and sitting up in baby seats. 'Children need to exercise all their bodies,' she says, 'If an adult did exercises just for the biceps, and none for the triceps, he'd have flabby triceps.'

If babies are seldom put down on their fronts they'll be slow to lift themselves on their arms, and then to crawl, and some never crawl at all. The act of crawling – alternately leading with opposite arms and legs – helps open up connections between the two sides of the brain, vital for later learning. Opportunities to move about – touching, grasping, and exploring objects in a carefully monitored environment – are also essential for every aspect of infant brain development. Dr Christine Mcintyre, an expert in children's physical development at the University of Edinburgh, told me that 'poor movement is part of all the specific learning difficulties and syndromes such as Asperger's.' Yet in many contemporary homes, parents obsessed with cleanliness or accident-prevention often decide it's safer to keep their offspring stationary. Children now spend much more time strapped 'safely' into baby seats, high chairs, car-seats and strollers than ever in the past.

Once old enough to be up and moving, small children by nature want to walk, run and climb – and some are genetically programmed to need more of this type of physical activity than others. Without sufficient opportunities to work off excess energy, any child (genetically vulnerable or not) will be frustrated and fractious. But in a home full of electronic equipment – TVs, DVDs, computers, music centres, smartphones and tablets – lively physical play can prove both dangerous and expensive. And with the amount of traffic now zooming around even in rural areas, play outside in the street or lane is definitely off limits for toddlers.

This sort of activity is therefore increasingly confined to 'specialist environments' – playgrounds, 'soft play' areas, activity clubs or, if you're lucky, the family garden – where toddlers require supervision. As parental time is at a premium nowadays (quite apart from work demands, all that electronic equipment around the house keeps adults pretty busy), many young children spend precious little time in the sort of places where they can indulge their need for active play. It's much easier to let them watch other people moving about on TV. Even getting to and from from play-places seldom involves much physical activity. Time pressures and fears of traffic mean small children are usually transported by car – or strapped, for safety reasons, into a stroller, even when they are perfectly capable of walking.

If the weather's good, some parents have another reason for keeping children indoors: fear of the sun. Several decades' worth of warnings about ultraviolet rays mean they've become paranoid about skin cancer. But like the Back to Sleep campaign and sensible hygiene rules, this issue calls for a bit of common sense. Apart from the importance of outdoor exercise, children of all ages need exposure to sunlight to meet their body's requirement for Vitamin D. Although in hot sunshine children should take precautions (the fair-skinned particularly need good dollops of suncream, broad-brimmed hats and advice to keep in the shade), there are too many benefits to outdoor play to let fear keep our children indoors.

Longitudinal studies have found that children who are outdoors and active from their earliest years have a greater chance of developing a healthy active lifestyle as they grow older. It's in toddlerhood – as lack of exercise and interest in all that unhealthy junk food collide – when the fuse on many children's personal 'obesity time bombs' is ignited. From now on, the more sedentary they are, the more time is available for screen-based snacking and grazing. And the more over-weight and sluggish they become, the less interested they are in taking exercise. These two side effects of our technological culture begin to swirl together in the toxic mix, and we can't tackle one without bearing in mind the effects of the other. What's more, as future chapters will show, the toxic brew is enriched by many other contributory factors.

Getting children off the couch

There's an easy way to get children off the couch (and out of the stroller and car seat) while simultaneously defusing parental anxiety. It is simply to spend more time with them, introducing them to non-sedentary activities. This doesn't have to be taxing or tiring and doesn't need any special equipment. For instance, walking with children through the streets rather than driving provides physical exercise, a chance to chat and an opportunity to develop deep-seated awareness of road safety skills through example and experience. Young children need many opportunities to watch adults modelling road safety procedures – in real space and time with traffic moving at real speed – if they're eventually to cope for themselves on today's busy roads.

Parents' fears of traffic accidents mean they often prefer to take children in the car, even on the shortest journeys. But the problem of heavy road traffic isn't going to go away, so modern children need to be extremely streetwise in terms of road safety and risk-awareness. This means that training them in how to negotiate traffic hazards can't start too early, and they need innumerable opportunities to learn and practise under expert adult guidance. Road safety campaigners point out that the highest number of deaths and injuries nowadays occur when children are in their early teens, because that's when so many of them begin travelling independently without having acquired deep-seated pedestrian road-skills.

Sadly most of us are now so used to using the car for all journeys that the thought of walking is off-putting. It can, however, provide opportunities for interaction that simply aren't available when you're driving. When my daughter was at nursery school we didn't have a car, so had to walk a mile or so there and back each day. I still remember impromptu games of hide-and-seek in the churchyard we used as a short cut; squirrel-spotting and hiding peanuts for them to find as we passed through the park; inventing stories about the people we saw regularly in the streets. All these and many other silly games arose naturally and delighted us both, although often we just ambled along in companionable silence. (Mind you, sometimes it wasn't very companionable – not every moment spent with one's child is one of unalloyed joy ... but the two generations also have to learn how to cope with not getting along with each other.) Anyway, after a couple of years we got a car, and I have no more memories of our trips to school – except, of course, the misery of the traffic.

Family time ... and having fun

Spending time with young children in safe outdoor environments (parks, playgrounds, countryside or local wild spaces, your own back garden) gives them a chance to run about and let off steam – and it doesn't have to be a special outing. Indeed, activity doesn't necessarily mean outdoor exertions. As soon as children are old enough, letting them help with everyday chores – such as making beds, emptying rubbish and preparing food – provides shared time for chat and develops physical dexterity and competence. Parents often spend a fortune on expensive 'educational games', forgetting there are many significant life skills to be learned using resources to hand in every home. One mother I met said her toddler's favourite occupation was helping fill the dishwasher; another remembered a happy day defrosting the fridge: 'We started off making snowballs, and ended up paddling'. The lists of 'life skills' for six-and twelve-year-olds in Chapter 5 are starting points for activities you can first model, then share, and finally hand over to your offspring.

The point is that spending time with children doesn't usually require parents to do anything special – just to be with them, getting on with whatever needs doing. What's more, shared time can reduce parental anxiety: it's reassuring to know you've repeatedly modelled safety procedures, and over time you can actually watch a child grow in confidence and ability. As for the children, they get to wallow in what they most crave – parental time and attention – whilst learning skills to carry into their own time and play.

Outdoor family leisure activities – such as ball games, cycling, riding, climbing or just walking the dog – also help keep everyone fit and healthy. In the Netherlands, where practically everyone cycles everywhere and you frequently see family groups speeding down the cycle lanes, there's one of the lowest levels of obesity in the developed world. There's also, according to UNICEF, the highest level of childhood well being. What's more, these active family pursuits don't need to be expensive – indeed, psychologists and paediatricians all agree that parents' major expenditure on their offspring should be in the form of time rather than money. Amanda Kirby finds it sad that people who visit her centre often feel they're not 'good parents' if they're not spending money: 'They've been made to believe by marketing that they have to pay for a package called 'creativity' or some sort of programme to make their children healthy. I find they're often relieved to be given permission just to go swimming or throw a ball about. We seem to have forgotten the secret of just playing with children, just having fun...'.

A research study in 2011 backs up Kirby's insight. Professor Agnes Nairn was asked to investigate why the UK came at the very bottom of the UNICEF league for childhood well-being in which the Netherlands came first. When she asked children what made them happy, they mentioned three things: spending time with family, friends and pets; creative and sporting activities; and just being outdoors, having fun.

PE, playtime and paranoia

There's now concern across the developed world about children's dwindling interest in physical exercise. This has been clearly recorded in Japan, where the Central Council for Education has monitored children's development annually since the 1960s and noted a steady deterioration in physical abilities, beginning in the mid-80s. Children can no longer run as fast, jump as high or throw and catch a ball as well as they did in the past. The Central Council puts this decreasing physical strength down to changes in lifestyle, including more playing of video games, less space for physical activity, and an inadequate diet and concludes 'We are now playing a high price for what we have unconsciously lost.' In 2014 Australian researchers found that in a survey of 25 million children in 28 countries nine- to seventeen-year-olds took on average one and a half minutes longer to run a mile than their parents' generation.

Internationally, the situation has also been fed by changes in attitudes to physical education (PE) in schools during the latter part of the twentieth century. Firstly, a generally liberal educational establishment, influenced by increasingly vocal and anxious parents, has become less keen to enforce participation in school sports and outdoor activities – even in Japan, where the tradition of *rajio taiso*, communal callisthenic exercises, which used to be compulsory each morning of the school vacations, is dying out in some areas.

Secondly, as school curricula throughout the developed world have become ever more exam-orientated (see Chapter 7), there have been changes in both the time available for PE and the way the subject is taught. With the emphasis on literacy, numeracy and other academic subjects required by law, there are now fewer opportunities for physical education in the school day than there were in the past. PE itself has often been 'academicised', even in the pre-teenage years, with teachers required to concentrate on the development of technique rather than general exercise and enjoyment. When lessons are about curricular targets, rather than opportunities for children to run, jump, be active and let off some steam, those who aren't keen on PE – including the overweight or out of condition – are difficult to motivate. 'Fear of injury' then provides a good excuse for reluctance to join in.

Thirdly, another source of fear – fear of litigation – has affected PE in the same way it's affected the rest of the curriculum. As well as influencing what happens on the sports fields, fear of injury also leads to constraints on what children can do at playtime and a reduction in outdoor excursions and classroom activities which could, if anything went amiss, lead to lawsuits. For a couple of decades, the 'health and safety' bogeyman has stalked corridor, playground and sports' field, so that schools have often become bland and unexciting places. When teachers have to fill in a dozen pages of risk assessment forms before taking their class out on so much as a nature walk, many just decide not to bother. Pet gerbils, games of conkers, snowball fights, even using eggboxes for making craft models have all been banned in one British primary school or another on safety grounds.

The irony is that there's actually been very little litigation about this sort of thing. But some insurance companies have exploited the possibility that there might, so spurious health and safety messages grow ever stronger ... and our children grow ever weaker.

And it's not just physical development that's threatened by the changes in society's attitude to PE. As well as promoting physical control and coordination, sporting activities – particularly team games – have always been valued for their contribution to children's social and emotional growth. For many children, especially boys, learning to work as a team on the playing field teaches important lessons about co-operation, rule-following and self-control (see also Chapter 10). For some, success in competitive sport can offset the damage of failure in the classroom – indeed, the boost to self-esteem can sometimes help restore failing academic fortunes.

If schools' attitude to sport is ambivalent, PE lessons fail to motivate, and fear of injury interferes with playground games and after-school clubs, these benefits are lost for many children. Sadly, for those who do catch the sporting bug, an over-emphasis on competitiveness can be just as damaging – when children model their behaviour on that of many sports personalities seen on TV, the values of co-operation, rule-following and self-control are unlikely to figure highly (see Chapter 8).

This complex web of social conditions and conditioning will take some time to unravel, but in recent years UK campaigning groups such as the Play Safety Forum have made a good start. 2013 saw the publication of the PSF document 'Managing Risk in Play Provision' and Scotland's 'Good School Playground Guide', both of which stress that adults should balance awareness of risk in activities for children with awareness of its manifold benefits.

Even more cheering has been the active involvement of the Health and Safety Executive, a government body which in 2012 launched a Myth-Busters Challenge Panel to stop the use of 'health and safety regulations' as an excuse for letting sensible activities go ahead. Judith Hackitt, Chair of the HSE, is particularly keen that children should learn the skills of risk-management through taking part in age-old playtime activities. To coincide with the Myth-Busters launch, she wrote an article for the Sun newspaper with the encouraging headline: 'Why we must let children climb trees and play conkers (a bit of common sense from HSE chief)'.

The decline of the free-range child

Unfortunately, even as schools become slightly less paranoid, there remains a massive constraint on the younger generation's access to exciting challenges that's much closer to home. Until the closing decade of the last century, children didn't have to rely on adult-organised games and activities for their physical, emotional and social development. As they reached school age there was another way they grew in physical strength and learned about themselves and how to relate to others. It was called 'going out to play'.

Nowadays, our generalised anxiety has created a culture in which children's freedom to roam, whether to the park for an informal kick-about or just for a general mooch around with friends, has been greatly curtailed. The National Trust's 'Natural Childhood Report' in 2012 pointed out that over the last thirty years children's 'radius of activity' (the area around their homes where they're allowed to roam without constraint) has declined by almost 90 per cent, while a survey by the Good Childhood Inquiry in 2009 found that almost half of adults thought the earliest age a child should be allowed out unsupervised is 14. Similar restrictions on children's freedom to roam have been reported across the developed world.

This means children no longer experience what writer and play expert Tim Gill calls 'everyday adventures', those small but significant experiences through which the next generation learns about the world, develops physical co-ordination and control, and grows in independence. Everyday adventures are an unpredictable but essential part of growing up – they are opportunities to make judgements, take risks, learn how to make friends and elude enemies. But they depend upon the freedom to be out and about, not closeted in the home.

In stark contrast to these everyday first-hand escapades, today's children have ersatz adventures courtesy of TV or computer games. These adventures are not real – the children aren't moving in real time and space or taking real risks: if it all gets too dull or too scary, they can just switch off. Screen-based activities don't prepare children for the everyday risk assessments adults must make on a moment-by-moment basis – judging speed and distance when crossing the road or driving a car, for instance, or assessing one's own competence to deal with unexpected emergencies. Without the preparation of play and other independent activities involving relatively 'safe' risks, some children become excessively reckless and others excessively timid.

A great deal of children's out-of-school social life has also transferred to the Internet. Despite the fact that its lower age limit is 13, Facebook is one of the most popular websites for children under 10, suggesting that many parents are unconcerned about age restrictions. There are also many other websites that require parental consent – such as Club Penguin and Moshi Monsters – where young children can enjoy virtual friendships through the medium of cuddly cartoon characters. Since they can also keep in contact with school friends through texts and instant messaging, in virtual terms the younger generation is considerably more 'socially-connected' than ever before. But screen-based socialising is very different from interactions with real-life playmates, sharing everyday adventures in their local area. This is where they learn the face-to-face skills of making friends, dealing with fall-outs, negotiating and collaborating over shared tasks. It's where they learn to read facial expressions, body language and tone of voice – essential aspects of human communication which can't be learned from a screen, and which underpin decisions on whom to trust or distrust.

Practically all real-life juvenile socialising now goes on under the eagle eye of adults – who are naturally swift to intervene if things look dicey. Some children are thus being labelled 'naughty' very early in their social careers (and then going on to fulfil the prophecy), while others are learning to call for help at the first sign of danger. The epidemic of bullying recorded in many countries over the last decade may be partly due to over-supervision, which helps create both bullies and victims.

The loss of outdoor play and everyday adventures is particularly significant for children with a tendency to be distractible or impulsive. They often need to run off excess energy and develop self-confidence through confronting physical challenges. In school, these children may be trapped in a vicious cycle of poor school performance, leading to poor self-image, leading to poor behaviour. They need access to other environments and experiences, away from constant adult censure.

Unfortunately, as the general public came to see constant

supervision of children as the norm, older members of the community became increasingly censorious about children and young people 'hanging out' in the local area. In more and more communities, fears about safety have led to a growing perception that parents who let their children play in the street are uncaring and irresponsible, and that any youngster out unsupervised must be an ill-disciplined 'feral child', probably up to its neck in truancy, drug-running and crime. Since it's now become widely accepted that 'good parents' keep their children under constant surveillance, naturalist Stephen Moss doesn't overstate the case when he claims that 'Britain's children in some ways have less freedom than free-range chickens.'

Back to nature

There is, however, some good news in terms of getting children outdoors and active. Over the last few years, there's been growing awareness of children's dwindling connection with nature, much of it arising from Richard Louv's book *Last Child In the Woods* (2005), in which he coins the term 'nature deficit disorder'. Concern about this issue has brought together a powerful coalition of play enthusiasts, educational authorities, environmentalists and natural historians (as David Attenborough put it in 2010: 'No one will protect what they don't care about; and no one will care about what they have never experienced'), which has resulted in a number of welcome efforts to reverse the trend.

In the UK, the Forest Schools movement, which has been taking schoolchildren out into the woods since the early 1990s when a group of teachers brought the idea over from Denmark, found itself moving steadily into the educational mainstream: between 2000 and 2013, the number of trained Forest School practitioners rose from about 200 to around 11,000. It also spawned an off-shoot Beach Schools movement, which seems very appropriate for a country with around 11,000 miles of coastline. A number of outdoor nurseries have also sprung up around the country, and early years specialists who've long advocated more outdoor learning for young children have begun to find schools and local authorities far more amenable to their message. With the help of organisations such as Learning through Landscapes and Grounds for Learning (Scotland) (see page 84), natural playground areas and play materials have transformed many state school grounds.

But institutionalised outdoor play isn't enough: freedom to explore nature starts at home. As the Back to Nature movement gathered force, the UK play organisations redoubled their efforts to entice families into the great outdoors with events like their annual Play Days. A rash of books by nature enthusiasts hit the shops, a group of 'guerrilla geographers' launched Mission Explore to lure children out into their local environment, and TV programmes such Channel 4's *Cotton Wool Kids* began to redirect parental anxiety in what is hoped will be a more productive direction. When, in 2012, the National Trust launched its *Natural Childhood* campaign, the hard-hitting report was eagerly seized on by the media, and the Trust's '50 things to do before you're 11¾' (see page 81) has since helped transform the lives of many middle-class children. The Trust was also one of several prestigious sponsors for a film, *Project Wild Thing*, released in 2013, in which film-maker David Bond appointed himself Marketing Director for Nature and enlisted the help of advertising gurus to sell nature to disengaged youth (the many ideas these creatives helped generate are catalogued on the *Project Wild Thing* website).

Bond's film and Stephen Moss's *Natural Childhood Report* provide a raft of contemporary arguments for Stevenson's 'happy play in grassy places'. As Moss puts it: 'Compared with man-made playgrounds, the natural world is highly complex, with lots of places to hide and explore. It's untidy, which may be off-putting for adults, but adds to its attraction for children; and above all, it is dynamic, changing from day to day, season to season, year to year.' Bond and Moss both stress the importance of introducing the next generation to the great outdoors as soon as possible (young children who don't connect with nature are likely to fear venturing beyond the tarmac as adults) and thus helping them grow up valuing the natural world. They also stress the many health benefits, both physical and mental: people with ready access to green spaces are more likely to be physically active than those without; children are more likely to run, jump, dig or climb in a natural environment than a man-made one; all human beings are less likely to suffer from depression if they have a strong connection with nature; children are less likely to display the symptoms of ADHD; indeed, according to researchers at Essex University, if you get out regularly among the foliage, you even live longer.

So much publicity and so many high-profile initiatives have been very cheering for psychologists concerned about the loss of outdoor play, which many now consider as vital to children's development as food and sleep. And, in the light of a recent UK research finding that only a third of children can identify a magpie while 90 per cent can identify a Dalek, it's certainly time for a national drive to reconnect children with nature. But, sadly, all this activity has merely scraped the surface of the 'out to play' problem. In a world where the global balance of population tipped from rural to urban living (around 2009), opportunities for the majority of children to spend most of their leisure time in wild places are few and far between – trips to the woods, fields and seashore are likely to be occasional treats, like a visit to a theme park (albeit much, much cheaper). Perhaps the greatest question confronting play specialists and parents today is how to ensure that children in built-up, traffic-ridden, child-averse neighbourhoods can play out near their homes – freely, safely and frequently.

It takes a village ...

One of the saddest stories I've heard over the last few years was from a teacher in a North London suburb. While working in her kitchen during the Easter school holidays she enjoyed listening to a small group of boys who were playing behind the house, making go-karts from bits of junk. She was therefore stunned when a letter was posted through her door by a neighbour, urging her to help move the children on. 'They may be making go-karts today,' the letter explained, 'but they could be vandalising our cars tomorrow.' My informant didn't join the witch-hunt, but enough neighbours did, the boys' families were contacted and the lads moved on – presumably back into their homes to be propped in front of the TV or communing with a Gameboy for the rest of the holiday.

It's no coincidence that the decline in outdoor play has coincided with the decline of local communities. Our increasingly atomised lifestyles have made individuals and families less tolerant and more suspicious of anyone beyond our own front doors. For the last couple of years, there's been a TV advertisement for gas that sums up modern lifestyles perfectly: the screen fills with lots of different families, each inhabiting its own little (gas-fuelled) planet, and all ignorant of all the others. Nowadays older people, despite adoring their own grandchildren, are often intolerant of their younger neighbours' offspring; and young families can be scathing about the fussy old lady up the street, even though they worry about their own, geographically-distant, aging mums.

The good news is that getting children out to play is a wonderful way of reviving local community spirit. Two mothers in Bristol discovered this in 2009 when they persuaded the local council to close off their street for a couple of hours after school so their young children could play out near to home. They consulted with the neighbours and, at the appointed time, children came tumbling out from houses all along the street, as if summoned by the Pied Piper. Grown-ups drifted out to watch, and began chatting with other grown-ups. The mums now run a website called Playing Out, to advise other families who'd like to try it.

I've heard many similar stories from parents I've met around the country, who've made lots of new chums when they campaigned to turn their road into a Play Street, organised a street party or rallied the neighbourhood to oppose a planning application that threatened a popular children's play space. The campaigning group Streets Alive has dozens of good ideas for revitalising local communities, many of them centred on children and play. And it's not surprising that these ideas work: there's great truth in the old saying that 'it takes a village to raise a child'. When concerned parents take the trouble to connect with other 'villagers' in their immediate locality, they're supported by both human nature and human history in turning neighbours into valued friends.

Safer streets

However, as well as human resources, parents also need a little help from the Planning Department. When I was first drafting this chapter, a German father emailed me details of his neighbourhood, predominantly made up of young families. With all adults keeping an eye out for all children, houses in cul-de-sacs and the frontage street a go-slow zone for cars, it feels safe to let the children roam: 'It's not uncommon for me to be sitting on the patio reading on a spring or summer afternoon, only to have my kids invade with eight or ten other kids to play on the swing set in the backyard. Half an hour later they're all at the neighbours' next door jumping through the sprinklers; perhaps later the boys split off to ride their bikes while the girls play with their Barbies on the lawn. The whole situation certainly gave me a new appreciation of urban and suburban design once it sank in.'

His email inspired me to investigate urban planning in the UK and my findings so far have been pretty depressing: the new developments I've visited have been distinctly un-child-friendly, with dreary enclosed play spaces, highly manicured greenery on which only the bravest of children would dare to tread, and a great many car-parking spaces protected by 'No Ball Games' notices. In the words of David Sim, a partner in the Danish firm Gehl Architects, famous for its inspired urban design: 'Just like adults, children usually want to be where the action is. There is no substitute for real life. Everyday activity is a great source of

learning – simply watching other children or watching adults
doing stuff. Unfortunately there is not much street life in mono-
functional, residential neighbourhoods – even the modest things
like fish vans, milk floats, pavement games and street football
have disappeared. Any interesting activity is centred around the
car – arriving and departing, packing and unpacking, washing the
car and perhaps mending/servicing the car. I think we need to have
spaces where people (including children) can comfortably share
spaces with cars – and this I think is only possible if the pedestrian
is always given priority.'

While it's fair to expect pedestrians to keep off major roads, it's
also reasonable to expect cars to give way to pedestrians (especially
small ones) in built-up areas. Initiatives to keep heavy traffic out
of residential areas, traffic calming measures and very low speed
limits are a start, but traffic accident figures make it clear that
much more could be done. Urban designer Ben Hamilton-Baillie
points to evidence that where traffic speed is kept to around 20 mph
(30 kph), pedestrian safety is vastly improved. For one thing, an
impact at that speed is unlikely to be fatal; for another, drivers and
pedestrians can still make eye contact at 20 mph, and that sort of
human contact tends to make drivers more considerate.

Some European countries, notably Germany and the
Netherlands, have set up 'home zones' (residential areas where
the needs of pedestrians are considered more important than
those of motorists). With millions of new homes scheduled to be
built in the UK in the next decade or so, there's a real opportunity
for planners to learn from their experience. Another successful
innovation in Scandinavian and Dutch cities is 'shared space',
where cars and pedestrians are given equal rights to the road,
traffic signs are removed, and the design of the street works
alongside interaction with pedestrians to make drivers drive
safely. These measures have achieved significant reductions in
accident figures, while the UK, which is swamped in road signs
and traffic furniture, has the second worst road casualty figures in
Europe for child pedestrians.

Schools could also do their bit to help improve road safety by organising systems to replace 'the school run' that bedevils so many European cities. It's a foolish irony that, by driving their children to school 'for safety reasons', parents add massively to the traffic problem. The long-established yellow school bus system means this is far less of a problem in the USA, and similar systems have been trialled successfully in rural areas in the UK. In built-up areas, the system of 'walking buses' widely used in Japan is worth considering: parents drop their children off at a walking bus stop at an agreed time and older children supervise the walk to school. Rather sadly, the walking buses I've seen in the UK are supervised by several adults, and the children are sometimes hanging on to a rope or a safety contraption called a 'walkodile' – we're obviously less inclined to trust our offspring to develop a sense of responsibility than the Japanese.

Still, the UK effort to reintroduce children to the outdoors has only just begun. In my home country of Scotland, the government published a national Play Strategy in 2013: it requires all local authorities to have regard to children's right to play, as required by Article 31 of the United Nations Convention on the Rights of the Child. When planning departments across the land are as committed to this Strategy as people who work directly with children, I'll know that the enterprise is finally under way.

Places to play ...

Given the findings of report after report, it's clear that town and city planners should take account of the need for children to play outdoors near their homes, the significance of green spaces for everyone's mental health, and the importance of balancing the requirements of car-owners and pedestrians, especially those under the age of ten. It has horrified me, as I've learned more about the problems of getting youngsters outdoors and active, that we seem in the UK to care more about our cars than our children. We also seem to have lost track of our human need for nature, steadily covering all available urban and suburban space with buildings or carefully-tended 'civic' vegetation.

There are, however, still a few areas in every neighbourhood that could be made available and attractive for children's play: 'wild' sections of public parks, green space attached to sports clubs or leisure centres, and – above all – primary and secondary school grounds. As Don Early, CEO of the UK charity Fields in Trust, points out: 'at present they're mostly used for organised activities, but these cost money. School fields and playgrounds could be a much better-used, free resource – a space in the middle of the community for children just to enjoy themselves with friends.' As familiar 'safe' areas, school grounds are also likely to appeal to parents as informal play-spaces for primary-age children.

Sadly, many playing fields were sold off to developers at the end of the last century, but legislation now makes it more difficult for local authorities to dispose of them in this way. Indeed, Don Early contends that we should be making serious efforts to hang on to all remaining urban green space: 'There's a strong lobby for protection of the countryside, but it's time for a planning policy change – land is at a premium in urban areas so whenever possible we should push new development out to the edges of towns, even the green belt, and try to protect the land that's left within the built-up areas.'

In many countries there are now movements committed to greening urban and suburban environments. For instance, in Canada the Evergreen movement is a national charity working for community naturalisation – with government assistance – by transforming school grounds, publicly-accessible land and home landscapes. Northern Europe is similarly enlightened: planners in Freiburg in Germany, for instance, have stopped installing artificial play equipment, and begun creating 'nature playgrounds', full of logs, mounds, ditches and other natural features. If UK parents were really convinced of the importance of outdoor play, the pressure they could exert would be a powerful force in the greening of post-industrial landscapes across the developed world

... and a few more 'grassy places' would be a boon for everyone, children and adults alike.

... People to play with

However, in order to change the current corrosive culture, parents also have a personal part to play. The first steps are the anti-anxiety measures described earlier in this chapter, and one of the best ways to banish irrational anxiety is to spend time in one's children's company, providing them with the life skills necessary to assume greater independence, including full training in road safety and how to avoid 'stranger danger'. The more time parents and children spend together, the more they'll both be able to trust children's judgement and their ability to cope alone. As children grow in self-control and self-confidence, it becomes easier for parents to let them flex their wings beyond the family circle.

Opportunities from as early as possible for loosely-supervised play with friends is another way of building self-reliance and resilience. Former playworker Issy Coles-Hamilton believes this sort of experience is essential if children are later to feel confident enough to make their own decisions, and not be forced by peers into doing something that doesn't feel comfortable. 'If you ban friends or keep your child in, they'll never learn to evaluate risk. And just telling them "Don't do this" isn't an answer. What you should be saying is "This is what to expect if you do this".'

Once you feel it's time (and the time will vary depending on the individual), the first step to giving children a free-range childhood is simply a question of letting them out of your sight for a limited time – to go alone to the local shop, or to the play-park with a friend. Some parents – and I have to admit, I'd probably be one – may feel better if their offspring carries a very basic mobile phone. It seems only sensible to make use of technology to facilitate outdoor play (although, except in dire emergencies, phones should be used for texting only, as there's a possibility their use can damage the developing brain). Once you've done this a few times and your child has demonstrated confidence and competence in being away from you, you can gradually extend the level of freedom to roam on foot, bike or public transport around the local neighbourhood.

Since all parents need to know there are people who will keep an eye out for children, and to whom they can turn in emergencies, there's a real incentive to 'build your own village' by making connections with other parents to share supervision and, as children begin to wander a little further afield, agree curfews and geographical boundaries. Informal contacts like this could widen to take in grandparents, owners of local businesses and any retired neighbours with the time to keep an eye on the streets. Perhaps residents' associations could be drawn into the quest, so that 'keeping an eye out for the children' became a means of strengthening community relations, and dampening down intolerance from older residents.

All this also has implications for the provision of supervised play facilities in school buildings after school hours – a service which is burgeoning internationally in response to the rise in working mothers over the last decade or so (see Chapter 6). National and local providers need to look hard at the environments provided for this extended care, and the quality of the staff they employ to supervise them. Corralling children in paved school yards surrounded by grey city streets is simply not good enough.

One way forward is to extend the influence of playworkers and play rangers, professionals devoted to encouraging and facilitating children's independent play. The playwork movement is already widespread in Scandinavian countries such as Norway and Denmark, and growing internationally. As well as working in day centres and after-school clubs, where they aim to provide less intrusive supervision than that of teachers or untrained helpers, playworkers can also be assigned to particular open spaces for community use.

Here then are the twenty-first-century professionals who can begin the re-establishment of eyes on the street. Not only can playworkers keep a general eye on the children who play in their areas, but they can also run activities and help to build up community usage of open spaces, familiarity with, and ownership of, the area by all who live there. They can be a focal point for the type of community engagement, around the needs of children, that will be necessary if we are to reclaim the outdoors.

* * *

If the key message about food is that adults, especially parents, must reassert control over what children eat, the key message about play and exercise is that once children are of school age we must begin to relinquish excessive anxiety-driven control over this aspect of their development, so that by the end of the primary years they are fit, self-confident, socially competent and growing in independence. Improved attitudes to PE at school would help, but much more important are opportunities for youngsters to run, play, move and grow independently in their own space, learning to make their own choices with steadily diminishing adult attention.

A couple of years ago, while speaking at a child protection conference, a policeman took me aside and asked me to pass on a message to parents: 'They're all so worried about letting their kids play in the park because of the "bad men" in the bushes,' he said. 'Please tell them from me that the bad men aren't in the bushes any more – they're all on-line!' So, rather than keeping our children safe from a supposedly threatening outdoors, the job is to make the outdoors as safe as possible – and exciting and inviting – so our children can once again go out to play.

DETOXING THE GREAT OUTDOORS

- Reduce anxiety by accessing less twenty-four-hour news, and don't have the TV news on during the day when young children might watch it. Read the news rather than watch it.
- Resist irrational fears, and balance worries about letting your child play out with the knowledge of how important outdoor play is.
- Help children become streetwise and safe by walking with them to daycare, shops, and so on, modelling road safety. (By not taking the car you will also incidentally help cut traffic congestion.)
- Make sure you go out with your child in bad weather too, dressing appropriately. Children need to experience all kinds of weather, and if you model wimpishness they'll learn it.
- Explicitly teach about road safety rules and 'stranger danger'. Make sure your child knows what to do in emergencies, and remind them regularly – but try not to give the impression that *all* unknown adults are a likely source of danger.
- Look for safe places where your child and friends can play outside: in your or neighbours' gardens, in parks, recreation grounds, local 'wild places', or on the pavement outside home, if the street's generally free of traffic.
- Help children get to know your local environment by getting out and about in it with them, pointing out potential dangers, and helping them choose safe routes.
- Make sure children also know how to travel by bus, train or tram by doing it with them lots of times.
- When children start going out alone, ask them always to let you know where they're off to and who with. Ask them to check in regularly with you or other trusted adults, particularly if there's any change of plan. Make this such a routine that they wouldn't dream of forgetting.
- Make contact with other local parents and arrange to 'keep an eye out' for all the children in your neighbourhood. If possible, try to involve more of the local community. Agree ground-rules about play, curfews, out-of-bounds areas and so on.

- Accept that occasionally accidents happen – and keep your fingers crossed that the only accidents affecting your child will be minor ones, and useful learning experiences. (Actually, no matter how hard you try to remove risk, accidents *will* happen – so there's no point in losing sleep about them.)
- Remember the robust rallying cry of Lady Allen of Hurtwood, an early twentieth-century play enthusiast: 'Better a broken bone than a broken spirit!'

HOW TO AVOID COUCH POTATO SYNDROME

- Ensure your child has plenty of opportunity for free movement and exercise at all stages in development.
- Babies and toddlers:

    – Give babies opportunities to lie on their tummies and backs (but put them to sleep on their backs).
    – Create safe spaces for toddlers to run, play and tumble – both indoors and out.
    – Don't panic about the dangers of dirt and mud – remember that children reared in 'super-clean' environments may fail to develop resistance to everyday infections.
    – Don't always strap your child into the buggy – as soon as possible, let him or her walk, scoot, or cycle (pedal-less bikes are a great way of helping young children develop the balance skills they'll eventually need to ride a bike for real).

- Spend time with children doing 'ordinary things' like household chores, shopping or cooking – don't try to fill every moment with so-called 'quality time' (see list of life skills in Chapter 5).
- Establish clear rules and routines for safety in the home, garden, street and so on as early as possible (see Chapter 10) so your child knows and accepts the boundaries, and can move around freely within them.

- From as early as possible, share family activities such as walking, swimming, cycling or exercising a dog.
- Introduce your child to exercise by playing with them and demonstrating skills, e.g.:

  – three- to six-year-olds: dancing, catching a ball, bat and ball, playground and party games
  – six upwards: skipping, hula hooping, team games, jogging, aerobics to music, etc.

- Provide opportunities for children of all ages to play with peers – both indoors and out – in a loosely-supervised environment (with adults on hand, but not monitoring every move). As children grow older, encourage 'everyday adventures' and the taking of 'safe risks'.
- Encourage children to sort out problems during play for themselves – don't rush to intervene before they've had the chance. (Teaching 'conflict resolution' helps – see Chapter 4).
- If at all possible, walk your child to school. If it's too far, drive part way and walk the rest. When your child is old enough to walk with friends (or in a 'walking bus'), encourage him or her to do so.
- Encourage children to take part in sports and join activity clubs, dance classes, etc. Always turn up to support them if they're in a match or display. Give plenty of praise not just for winning, but for joining in, trying and taking part.

50 THINGS TO DO BEFORE YOU'RE 11¾

Reprinted by kind permission of the National Trust

Adventurer

1 Climb a tree
2 Roll down a really big hill
3 Camp out in the wild
4 Build a den
5 Skim a stone
6 Run around in the rain
7 Fly a kite
8 Catch a fish with a net
9 Eat an apple straight from a tree
10 Play conkers

Discoverer

11 Go on a really long bike ride
12 Make a trail with sticks
13 Make a mud pie
14 Dam a stream
15 Play in the snow
16 Make a daisy chain
17 Set up a snail race
18 Create some wild art
19 Play pooh sticks
20 Jump over waves

Ranger

21 Pick blackberries growing in the wild
22 Explore inside a tree
23 Visit a farm
24 Go on a walk barefoot

25 Make a grass trumpet
26 Hunt for fossils and bones
27 Go star gazing
28 Climb a huge hill
29 Explore a cave
30 Hold a scary beast

Tracker

31 Hunt for bugs
32 Find some frogspawn
33 Catch a falling leaf
34 Track wild animals
35 Discover what's in a pond
36 Make a home for a wild animal
37 Check out the crazy creatures in a rock pool
38 Bring up a butterfly
39 Catch a crab
40 Go on a nature walk at night

Explorer

41 Plant it, grow it, eat it
42 Go swimming in the sea
43 Build a raft
44 Go bird watching
45 Find your way with a map and a compass
46 Try rock climbing
47 Cook on a campfire
48 Learn to ride a horse
49 Find a geocache
50 Canoe down a river

To find out more, track your progress and discover extra challenges, visit
www.nationaltrust.org.uk/50things

PARENT POWER: GREEN AND PLEASANT PLACES TO PLAY

For children to be able to play out safely in a post-industrial society, policy-makers must be alerted to their needs. At present, in many countries children's needs are very low on the political agenda. This could be changed very rapidly if parents decided to vote for people who promise – and deliver – the following:

- traffic calming measures/car-free streets/very low speed limits/'shared space' design in residential areas (especially in new housing) – children are more important than cars.
- greening of the environment – planting trees, conserving any open spaces (derelict ground, made safe, is great for 'everyday adventures')
- better parks and parklands, and playworkers to supervise open spaces of all kinds and build a sense of community
- daycare and after-school care facilities that involve outdoor activities in exciting environments – and also plenty of opportunities for loosely-supervised, self-directed play
- schools that aren't frightened (or too burdened with red tape) to provide physical exercise and fun outdoor activities as part of children's education
- international laws and policing to ensure that those who threaten children's safety are apprehended and their activities stopped (see also Chapter 9).

If you have the time and energy, campaign for these improvements yourself. Consult the web and local information sources (library, school, advice bureau) to find local pressure groups or get together with other interested parents, grandparents, etc. and start your own.

Further reading

Richard Louv, *Last Child in the Woods: Saving Our Kids from Nature-deficit Disorder* (Algonquin Books, 2005)

Sally Goddard Blythe, *The Genius of Natural Childhood* (Hawthorn Press, 2004)

Peter Gray, *Free To Learn: How Unleashing the Instinct to Play Will Make Our Children Happier, More Self-Reliant and Better Students for Life* (Basic Books, 2013)

Fiona Danks and Jo Schofield, *The Wild City Book: Fun Things to Do Outdoors in Towns and Cities* (Frances Lincoln, 2014) and many other titles by these authors.

Useful websites

Learning through Landscapes UK: www.ltl.org.uk or Grounds for Learning in Scotland: www.ltl.org.uk/scotland

Streets Alive: www.streetsalive.org.uk

Playing Out: www.playingout.net

The National Play Councils: www.playengland.org.uk , www.playscotland.org, www.playwales.org.uk, www.playboard.org (Northern Ireland)

National Trust 'Natural Childhood Campaign': www.nationaltrust.org.uk/what-we-do/big-issues/nature-and-outdoors/natural-childhood/

National Trust 50 things: www.nationaltrust.org.uk/50things

Project Wild Thing: www.projectwildthing.com

Love Parks: community campaigns for local parks: www.love-parksweek.org.uk

UNICEF Child-Friendly Cities initiative (Bath is the UK's first child-friendly city): www.childfriendlycities.org

Canadian Evergreen Project: www.evergreen.ca

Home Zones – safer streets: www.homezonenews.co.uk

Mind the Gap

One of my earliest memories is playing in the street outside my grandmother's back-to-back cottage in Salford, one of the poorest areas of Manchester. I can't have been above four, and some big girls (maybe six- or eight-year-olds) were teaching me hopscotch. In those far-off days there was little danger from traffic and older children were often left to look after the little ones.

A few years ago I revisited the same street, to run a training course for teachers at the school where my gran was once the cleaner. It's still a very poor area, but you don't see small children playing out any more. Their parents are too worried by the high levels of drug-related violence and antisocial behaviour by young teenage and pre-teenage gangs. And in places like this, such fears are perfectly reasonable.

The area where my gran used to live looked like a war zone. Amid the litter in the alleyways behind the houses were broken bottles and discarded hypodermics, and on the day I visited there was a burnt-out car a couple of streets away, the remnant of nocturnal joy-riding by a gang of lads. The teachers at the school warned me to empty my own car completely while I was away from it, so I wouldn't get the windows broken. When I protested that no one would want to steal a load of grammar books and other teaching stuff they shook their heads. 'You'd be surprised,' they said. 'Anything they might be able to flog for drug money.'

I've visited similar areas in many parts of Britain, communities in which civilised behaviour has broken down to the extent that young children can't possibly venture out of doors unaccompanied, while older children (from about the age of eight) wander in gangs, creating mayhem for local residents. You don't leave big girls looking after the little ones any more – you really don't know what they might do to them. Small children here are usually kept safe indoors at all times – tragically, health problems as a result of excessive hygiene are more common in these poorer homes than wealthy ones. But presumably, by the time most children are eight or so, many parents have given up or lost interest in trying to protect them – or the children have become so ungovernable that they break out of captivity and begin to run wild.

Sadly the parents seldom do much to widen their young children's horizons. As the director of a WHO research study on the health of people living in poor areas commented, 'You are less likely to take the baby out in the stroller or walk to the next bus stop or go for a run if you are living in an area that the council doesn't clean up.' Many make little effort to escape from the area even for a day: in rundown estates only a few miles from the seaside you often find large numbers of children who have never been to the beach; in the inner cities, many children never visit the great city parks a bus ride away from home. Uneducated parents often don't see the point of family outings – they're too trapped in the misery of the here and now.

As usual, schools do their best to compensate, organising trips to the countryside, weeks at camp schools and so on. Increasingly often, though, I hear tales of parents refusing to let their children go on such excursions – not because of costs (schools will quietly waive fees in the case of real need) but because of safety fears. To their rational fear of the great outdoors near home, add irrational fear generated by media coverage.

Schools and other agencies also try to provide opportunities for children to play out and experience nature nearer home, by building adventure playgrounds, creating school gardens, vegetable patches or wild areas. All too often, their efforts are destroyed by vandals – those roaming gangs of disaffected teens and pre-teens. Sometimes children help their teachers build gardens or play areas during the day, then go to great lengths overcoming security measures to help their older mates wreck them at night. I once stood in the shell of a school burned down by its own needy pupils, and listened to the headteacher (a nun) explain gently: 'It's not personal. They just have this deep need to destroy.'

So where does it spring from, this cycle of ignorance, poverty and violent destruction, that transforms an environment into somewhere no child can go out to play? In my experience, it takes about ten years to turn human children into impulsive, unempathetic animals, so desperately antisocial that they destroy their own habitat. And the best way to do it is rear them in captivity, malnourish them on junk and expose them to all the other aspects of toxic childhood outlined in this book.

So the best way to break the cycle is to detox childhood. Read on!

CHAPTER THREE

TiME FOR BED

Sleep …
Sleep that knits up the ravell'd sleeve of care;
The death of each day's life; sweet labour's bath;
Balm of hurt minds; great nature's second course;
Chief nourisher in life's feast …

Do you get the impression that Shakespeare enjoyed a bit of shut-eye? If current research is on the right tracks, it's not surprising. In the late 1990s, sleep – which had been practically ignored by scientists for centuries – began to hit the headlines in neuroscience. And since it appears to be the key to both memory and creativity, it's of great significance for children's thinking and learning.

Yet sleep is still not high on the twenty-first-century agenda. When I asked teachers around the UK which aspects of contemporary childhood they think damage children's progress at school, 'lack of sleep' was very near the top of their list. Personally, I think it's not just children's lack of sleep that causes the problems. It's lack of sleep – or, at least, lack of good quality rest – for adults too (and that includes teachers). In a 24/7 world where sleep has been sidelined, tiredness is heavily implicated in the toxic mix affecting contemporary children.

Sleeping problems have been on the rise ever since electric light became widespread and darkness was banished from our lives. Human beings had already learned to extend their waking hours by the regular absorption of caffeine (in coffee, tea, and, most recently, fizzy drinks), to which most of the developed world is now addicted. Gradually, through the twentieth century, people have slept less and less, and rushed about more and more. Indeed, we now seem positively to resent time spent sleeping, or even resting.

As science writer Paul Martin points out in his book *Counting Sheep*, 'Having nothing to do is seen as a sign of worthlessness, while ceaseless activity signifies status and success. Supposedly unproductive activities are deprioritized or delegated. And according to prevailing cultural attitudes, sleeping is one of the least productive of all human activities.' It seems that when electric speed was added to electric light, the developed world moved from mere sleep avoidance to chronic sleep deprivation.

A 2012 review by the UK Sleep Council revealed that 70 per cent of British adults now get by on an average of seven or fewer hours a night, a third manage only five to six hours, and more than a quarter experience poor quality sleep on a regular basis. Even more worryingly, the amount and quality of reported sleep had decreased since the Council's previous survey in 2010.

Tired families

Consider how tiredness impacts on the average family. Tired parents, home late from work, don't have the energy to cook a meal and entice a recalcitrant child into eating something nourishing. Tired children are cranky and unpleasant, more likely to kick up a fuss if they don't get their own way. In these circumstances, only the saintliest of parents sticks to the advice about diet in Chapter 1: most will soon be back to throwing a ready meal into the microwave for the adults, heating up nuggets and chips for the children, then slumping exhausted in front of a screen – or preferably several screens, so everyone can lapse into their personalised electronic world.

Tiredness thus draws whole families into the vicious circle

of poor nutrition and lack of exercise. The sluggishness that comes from poor diet feeds further exhaustion, which leads to more quick-fix junk food and screen-slumping ... and so on, ad infinitum. And all this overlaps with another vicious circle. This is the one where exhausted parents attempt wanly to convince their children it's bedtime. And the children – over-tired and brattish – play up more and more, till their parents give up the unequal struggle and let them 'watch one more programme' or 'play one more computer game'. The next morning everyone wakes up tired again ... and on it goes, the two vicious circles overlapping into a vicious Venn diagram, with a worn-out family trapped in the middle.

A poll by the US National Sleep Foundation (see page 110) found that, on average, children of all ages seemed to be sleeping for one and a half hours less per night than the recommended level:

Age-group	Recommended hours of sleep	Average hours of sleep recorded in NSF poll
Infants (3-11 months)	14–15 (over 24 hours)	12.7
Toddlers (12-35 months)	12–14	11.7
Pre-schoolers (3-6 years)	11–13	10.4
Elementary school age (7-11 years)	10–11	9.5

This sleep deficit seems to apply to British children too, with over 70 per cent having less than the recommended amount of sleep in a 2012 survey, and average six-year-olds failing to put their heads down until after 9.30 p.m. In the same year, scientists surveying international research pointed out that concern about children's lack of sleep is nothing new but, due to societal and family changes over the last thirty years, today's children are sleeping for less time per night than ever before.

A good night's sleep

Scientific interest in sleep was reawakened a decade or so ago by the development of functional magnetic resonance imaging (fMRI) techniques, which allow researchers to watch what is actually happening in the brain. Nowadays neuroscientists are discovering more about the significance of sleep with every passing day (and night), so it really is time the rest of us started taking it more seriously – especially the parents of young children.

It's long been known that there are several distinct kinds of sleep, happening in cycles throughout the night, but it's now becoming clearer what the brain is doing in each of these stages. When we first fall asleep, our brain wave patterns slow down and we drop into something called Stage 1 and Stage 2 sleep. This is quite shallow, so sleepers are easily awakened by activity around them. These stages tend to last longer in adults than children, who only take about five minutes to move into the next stage – slow-wave sleep (Stages 3 and 4 sleep).

Once someone is in Stage 3 or 4 sleep, they're very deeply asleep and difficult to rouse. (This is when you can carry children out of the car and put them to bed without their waking up.) Although much of the brain seems to close down during slow-wave sleep, parts are still active, processing new information. In children, slow-wave sleep is also important for physical development, being the time at which growth hormone secretion reaches its peak.

A phase of slow-wave sleep lasts around 80 minutes; after that, sleepers rise back up through the four levels to a state much closer to consciousness. This is called REM sleep (Rapid Eye Movement – because the eyes dart about beneath the eyelids), and it's here that most dreams seem to occur. Brain activity is much higher in REM sleep than slow-wave sleep, especially the areas of the brain associated with emotion.

During the course of the night, sleepers move through four or five sleep cycles – dropping down into deep slow-wave sleep and drifting up into REM sleep. They spend longer in slow-wave sleep during the first half of the night, but in the second half of the night they get more REM sleep. Not unnaturally, people are much more likely to wake during a period of shallower REM sleep – and, if so, may well remember a fragment of dream.

Learn while you sleep

So why is sleep so important in terms of children's learning? The obvious reason to non-scientists is its effects on mood and behaviour. Every parent knows from bitter experience that over-tired children are cranky and unpleasant. Unlike adults, who grow drowsier when they're tired, sleepy children often just grow more 'wired' and uncontrollable. This, of course, means that sleep-deprived children at school tend to be badly behaved and difficult to teach, while children who've had enough sleep are more likely to be pleasant and alert, finding it easier to concentrate and thus to learn.

However, research over the last couple of decades has shown that sleep is essential to learning in many other ways. It's now become well-established that skills, facts and ideas acquired during the day are transferred into long-term memory by the brain during sleep. Scientists can see this on their fMRI pictures – when someone returns to a new skill or learning task after a night's sleep, different places light up in brain from the ones that lit up when the learning first happened. The memory of what they learned has been transferred to another part of the brain.

It turns out that sleeping time, when everything's relatively quiet because no new input is being received, is when the brain reorganises and tidies information – transferring new stuff into long-term memory and pruning out what's no longer required. US neuroscientist Terry Sejnowski compares falling asleep to leaving your house when workmen come in to renovate it: 'You don't want to live in the house while the construction's going on because it's a mess.' Every night, when children go to sleep, the workmen come in and sort out all the stuff that's been dumped in their brains during the day.

If you think about it, this is a great deal of stuff. Young children have to learn a vast array of physical and practical skills – from walking and talking to riding a bike. This sort of practical 'learning by doing', without much conscious awareness of what's being learned, is known by scientists as 'procedural' learning. As children grow towards school age they also have to learn facts and information. And if they're lucky, they'll also learn how to make connections between the ideas they absorb, developing the skills of imaginative, creative thinking.

Why it's important to 'sleep on it'

Researchers have found that REM sleep is involved in procedural learning of practical tasks. It seems that during REM sleep the brain re-runs experiences from earlier in the day – experiments have shown that patterns of activity in the brain during REM sleep precisely match those shown when people were actually practising the task. Procedural learning happens in 'chunks' (each chunk consisting of physical perceptions and related actions) and REM sleep appears to strengthen the processes involved, leading to better chunking.

To be effective, the REM sleep must occur within at least 24 hours of the learning – otherwise it doesn't improve performance at all. Young children do a great deal of this sort of practical learning, so it's not surprising that the younger the child the longer it spends in REM sleep – as we grow older our REM sleeping time reduces. Not surprising, either, that babies and toddlers need lots of little naps, to consolidate all their learning.

Slow-wave sleep, on the other hand, is important for declarative learning of factual information, which involves concentration and conscious awareness of what's being learned – the sort of academic learning older children do at school. Again, the brain appears to replay the information they've studied, this time during slow-wave sleep, and in the process transfers it into long-term memory, reorganizing and restructuring their understanding. It's therefore very important to 'sleep on it' when you've studied something, as even small reductions in slow-wave sleep have been linked to a decrease in memory function.

It appears that 'sleeping on it' is also involved in creative thinking and problem-solving. Several years ago, the German sleep researcher Jan Born gave some of his students a repetitive number task containing a hidden short cut. None of the students noticed this short cut whilst first practising the task, nor on returning to it after eight hours awake. But those who repeated the task after eight hours' sleep often spotted the short cut very quickly. Born suspects that, when we return to a problem after sleeping on it, the fact that information has started transferring from one part of the brain to another renders us more able to have a creative 'insight': 'What may be happening is that, due to this reorganisation, after sleep you get a slightly different perspective. So you now view the information from two perspectives, which means you could make a problem-solving leap.'

Since then, Born and his team have been investigating the significance of sleep for declarative learning (and creativity) in children, and have found that slow wave sleep is even more important for them: 'It matters at all ages but ten to twelve years is when children really profit from plenty of slow wave sleep.'

Hush, little baby …
stopping sleep problems before they begin

Good bedtime habits and sleeping routines from an early age are therefore clearly important. In the words of Professor Yvonne Kelly, researcher into sleep at University College, London, 'Not having fixed bedtimes [in early childhood], accompanied by a constant sense of flux, induces a state of body and mind akin to jetlag, and this matters for healthy development and daily functioning.'

So, given sleep's significance in learning, we should all be taking much more interest in seeing that children get plenty of it. Unfortunately, as the survey results outlined earlier in the chapter suggest, this isn't happening. Another US survey estimated that around one-third of pre-school-age children have problems of one sort or another with sleeping. The advice of most parenting experts is that the sooner children get into a good sleeping routine, the better for all concerned. But there's considerable debate about the best way to do this.

As most new parents learn to their cost, newborn babies' sleep habits are chaotic – they may sleep a lot, but not usually when you want them to. However, according to the National Sleep Foundation, by six to nine months the vast majority of babies sleep through the night, as well as having a number of short naps during the day. Understandably, most parents would like to achieve this blessed state as soon as possible, especially if they have to return to work, or have older children who are constantly awoken by a crying baby. They're also usually concerned to establish good sleeping habits for their new offspring, which involves helping him or her eventually become a 'self-soother', able to fall asleep independently without needing a parent to be there.

Not surprisingly, therefore, there's a brisk market for baby sleep-training manuals. Professor Helen Ball, of the Parent-Sleep Laboratory at Durham University, is concerned about this development. She suggests that recent trends in Western infant care have led to misperceptions of normal infant sleep development: 'When we ask whether a young baby "sleeps through the night" this reinforces the idea that prolonged infant sleep is important and should be achieved early. It also does not recognise the role of nightfeeding in successful breast-feeding because breast-fed babies wake more often during the night than those who are not breast-fed.' In 2012 she launched a website called the Infant Sleep Information Service (ISIS). It explains the ways our evolutionary heritage influence babies' behaviour and brain development: for instance: 'Throughout our evolutionary history, human babies would not have survived without the constant presence of a caregiver – in most cases the mother. Together with the need to feed frequently, this means human babies are designed to be close to their mother, both day and night.'

ISIS provides wise, research-based information and advice on such knotty questions as co-sleeping (the traditional system of mother and baby sleeping together, now widely frowned upon in many western cultures), the possible causes of Sudden Infant Death Syndrome (SIDS, formerly known as 'cot death') and the much-debated technique of 'controlled crying'. Since 2013, the National Health Service in England has directed all new parents to ISIS, which I reckon is a very good start in preventing sleeping problems before they begin.

The babies who haven't read the book

When parents understand the reasons behind their babies' behaviour, it's easier to cope with disruption to their established lifestyle. If, on the other hand, they expect their little ones to conform to an idealised version of babyhood as soon as they arrive home from the hospital – such as settling down to a good night's sleep in a beautifully-appointed nursery far from the security of mum's embrace – the baby's recalcitrance is likely to make them increasingly anxious. This is when many parents reach for a sleep-training manual which, if their offspring still fails to react as prescribed, may simply become a source of further anxiety. Almost inevitably, the more inadequate the parent feels, the more distressed the baby becomes and the more problems they set up for the future.

Like every aspect of child-rearing, looking for a one-size-fits-all solution is a waste of time. All children are different and so are all parents. In the past, when people were reared in extended families within close communities, they witnessed the raising of many different children and had a reasonable idea of what could be expected at particular ages and what couldn't. This gave them the confidence to adjust and adapt child-rearing procedures to suit their own circumstances. Most contemporary parents have little, if any, experience of children before bringing home their own from the hospital.

Working on the assumption that science is now the only available substitute for experience, it's useful to have up-to-date information on children's brain development and successful parenting strategies. As a mother who went through several years of sleep deprivation and anxiety, I would have found it very helpful to know that babies vary greatly in temperament, some being much more anxious and 'fussy' (especially low-birthweight babies or those born to mothers under stress in the later months of pregnancy) and therefore may take longer than average to settle into a sleeping routine.

According to psychologists, the best parenting style for our contemporary global culture is 'authoritative'. That's authoritative – not authoritarian – and it means being caring, confident, consistent and firm (see also Chapter 10). Research suggests that authoritative parenting works well for all children, but particularly for the anxious, fussy ones. If the adults in charge seem to know what they're doing, children feel more secure and the chances of a good night's sleep for everyone are considerably greater.

The trouble is, parents in thrall to a parenting manual are unlikely to feel personally confident – they've handed over responsibility to some author who knows neither them nor their baby. Confident parenting does not come from slavish adherence to someone else's rules but from being well-informed about child development, watching the patterns of a beloved infant's behaviour, then making one's own judgements about the best ways to help him or her become a self-soother. Helen Ball's reading of the available research suggests that, after the first six months or so, it doesn't make much difference which system they choose: the keys to success are care, confidence and consistency.

Time for a nap

The importance of sleep schedules and self-soothing relates to day-time as well as night-time sleep. Babies and toddlers also need to take naps, thirty minutes to a couple of hours long, between one and four times a day. Again, children vary, and parents have to be sensitive to their own offsprings' needs, working out when and how long seems to be optimal. The number of daytime naps required changes over time, so this also involves awareness of changing needs – usually, by eighteen months, toddlers are down to one nap a day, lasting between one and three hours.

Naps are important. To quote a recent headline in the US Proceedings of the National Academy of Sciences, 'Napping helps preschoolers learn.' On the other hand, paediatric sleep specialist Marc Weissbluth points out that 'when children do not nap well, they pay a price'. He cites research showing that four- to eight-month-old infants who don't nap well have shorter attention spans or appear less persistent when engaged in activities. By three years of age, children who didn't nap or who napped very little are more likely to be 'non-adaptable' or hyperactive. Napping also seems to consist mainly of REM sleep which, as described above, is necessary to consolidate the hands-on physical learning of early infancy. So babies and toddlers need naps, both to restore energy and good temper and to consolidate the huge amount of learning they do every day.

However, our present-day resentment at wasting time asleep means these days we don't attach much benefit to naps. All too often, children's napping habits conflict with childcare arrangements or other facets of modern life, and the naps have to be curtailed or abandoned altogether. Children themselves may become resistant to napping, perhaps because an increasingly sedentary lifestyle means they don't have sufficient exercise to make them physically tired, or enough real-life stimulation to tire them mentally. If they spend too much time in front of the TV, the artificial stimulation of constantly changing images may make it more difficult for them to switch off.

The psychologist Marie Winn suggests screen-based media may affect children's napping habits in another way. She reckons that before the advent of the electronic babysitter, parents had a powerful motivation to encourage their offspring's napping habits – to provide a little uninterrupted time to complete other chores, or just have half an hour to themselves. If the baby can be kept busy staring at the TV or an iPad, there's less incentive to insist on naps.

One way and another, establishing good sleeping habits from the start is probably harder today than it's ever been – but in a high-octane, super-stimulating world it's also probably more important than ever before.

Sleepy schoolchildren

As children grow older, they naturally become more interested in staying up late to find out what's going on in the infinitely interesting adult world. If they haven't already developed good sleeping habits, this is when 'bedtime resistance' – difficulty falling asleep or night-time awakening – can get out of hand.

Many factors can contribute to the problem. Diet may play a part – for instance, children who are sensitive to certain additives may find settling to sleep more difficult. One particular additive, found in most fizzy drinks, is proven to keep people awake: caffeine. Indeed, three cans of Diet Coke deliver as big a caffeine hit as a regular espresso. As the French essayist Jean-Anthelme Brillat-Savarin said in 1825: 'It is the duty of all mamas and papas to forbid their children to drink coffee, unless they wish to have little dried-up machines, stunted and old, at the age of twenty', but many parents, diligent about banning coffee, are unaware of the caffeine cocktail available in fast food and soft drinks.

Many studies have also connected lack of sleep with obesity, possibly because poor sleepers secrete less leptin, an appetite-reducing hormone released during sleep, or because they have more time awake during which to consume unnecessary calories.

Common sense also suggests that lack of outdoor play and exercise may contribute to sleeping problems, since the muscular fatigue induced by exercise should lead to better quality sleep.

Snoring and other worries

Another common condition associated with disturbed sleep is snoring, and research has found that children who snore are more likely to have learning problems at school. Constant loud snoring may be a symptom of sleep apnea, a condition in which sleep is disturbed because the sleeper actually stops breathing periodically throughout the night. But it may also be the result of enlarged tonsils or adenoids – leading to frequent infections and bunged-up noses – or to an allergy, perhaps relating to processed foods or environmental pollution (and possibly enhanced by our over-clean homes – see page 57).

When I worked with special needs children, I noticed that many (especially dyslexics and ADHD-sufferers) suffered from snuffles and runny noses – but I'd always assumed these were connected with hearing problems, which would obviously cause them difficulties with listening skills and probably phonics, rather than disturbed sleep. I've since found plenty of research linking ADHD to poor sleeping patterns. Perhaps, as is so often the case in questions of child development, it's a mixture of lots of things, including both poor hearing and lack of sleep.

As sleep specialist Marcus Weissbluth points out, in the past snoring was often 'cured' by an operation – doctors tended to recommend the removal of tonsils and adenoids for recurrent throat infections. These days the medical profession is less enthusiastic about invasive surgical procedure. However, Professor Jim Horne of Loughborough University has cited research findings that 20 per cent of children with mild to moderate ADHD appear to have sleep disturbances due to chronic colds, enlarged tonsils or breathing problems, and in his opinion the removal of tonsils or adenoids may often solve the behavioural problem. This is an area where medical and educational professionals could usefully work together.

Indeed, there's another developmental condition in which poor sleeping patterns seem to be implicated: autistic spectrum disorder (ΛSD). Sleep problems are common among children with autism and a 2013 study at the University of Missouri linked their prevalence among boys with bedroom access to screen-based media. However, working on my 'toxic cocktail' theory, I wonder if this is a chicken and egg question: autistic boys can't get to sleep so they want to play computer games and/or autistic boys want to play computer games so they don't get to sleep. The researcher, Dr Christopher Engelhardt, explained that boys' sleeping problems may be due to a variety of underlying factors but 'media use may worsen some of these ... and it appears to be an area for future research'. There's certainly room for much more exploration of physical and cultural reasons behind children's learning difficulties, and if it were up to me I'd start by looking at the complex interface between diet, outdoor activity, sleep and screen-gazing.

Other reasons for sleep disturbance among school-age children include emotional difficulties and anxiety, which can cause nightmares, insomnia or bedwetting. As we'll see in succeeding chapters, many contemporary children have powerful reasons to be emotionally disturbed, and emotional problems are among the most difficult to solve. But one of the main ways parents can develop emotional resilience in their children is to provide stability and security. And one of the best ways of doing that is to buttress family life with calm regularity and reliable routine.

A regular bedtime

All child development experts point to the significance of regularity and routine in children's lives, and the more difficult the children, the more they need familiar, comfortable routines. I suspect many of the problems today's children have in going to sleep and staying asleep are simply the result of our contemporary lifestyle. Parents who are frantically trying to juggle work and domestic duties have often lost sight of the importance of ensuring a regular sleep schedule and bedtime routine. Yet both they and their children would benefit from the predictability of established routines, not only for going to bed but for mealtimes, weekday mornings and any other regular parts of family life. The more the mechanics of such occasions are carried along by habit, the more one's brain is free for conversation and just enjoying family time. On the other hand, when life is chaotic and no one's sure what to expect, discord and disharmony ensue.

Sleep specialists specifically point to the significance of routine in preparing for sleep. The connection between properly organised bedtimes and behaviour at school is clear, with researchers reporting 'spectacular improvements in manageability' of ADHD children when bedtime was improved, adding that, 'our clinical impression in these cases was that the changes were too rapid to be accounted for by other changes, such as parental discipline tactics'.

A good bedtime routine involves a comfortingly familiar winding down towards sleep, providing a sense of security while encouraging the child to relax (see page 107). Sadly this sort of restful ritual is a long way from the reality of many families' evenings, with children staying up waiting for parents to return from work, then becoming excited by their arrival and under-standably reluctant to break up the reunion. So either parents vainly try to put them to bed, and bedtime becomes a battleground, or the children stay up far too late ... and eventually drop off from exhaustion.

However, just as working parents have a responsibility to put themselves out to provide regular meals for children, they can't afford to ignore the importance of a regular bedtime. Parents who work late really have only two options: to adjust working hours so that at least one parent is home in plenty of time to supervise bedtime routines; or to sacrifice seeing their children in the evening and ensure someone else settles them appropriately for sleep. If supervision has to be spread among a number of adults over the course of the week (and, in the case of very young children, it should be as few as possible) everyone involved should share a behavioural hymn sheet – every child should be able to look forward to a familiar bedtime ritual every night.

The more 'difficult' and temperamental children are, the more they need the security that comes from regular routines – and the more disruptive any departure from the routine will be. This has implications for parents' social life. If children don't find bedtime and sleeping easy, the disruption caused by holidays or special late-night excursions can play havoc with carefully established procedures. Parents who've struggled to put a regular bedtime into place may find it pays not to disrupt the routine too often. Otherwise, they may have to retrain their child from scratch each time, which is wearing for everyone.

The *real* monsters in the bedroom

Many children go through a phase of worrying that lions, dragons or other monsters are lurking under the bed. I love the idea suggested by a friend of using Monster Repellent Spray (see page 107) to see off these chimera every evening. Children's fears may seem silly to adults, but they're very real to them, and brushing them off as nonsense doesn't help. Parents are only too happy to indulge childish fantasies about the Tooth Fairy and Santa Claus – there's no inconsistency in collaborating in the brisk disposal of monsters if it helps soothe a child for sleep.

There is, however, another sort of monster that's established itself in children's bedrooms around the developed world, which parents have unfortunately collaborated in putting there. Electronic equipment – TVs, computers, games consoles and so on – can be wonderful additions to family entertainment, but they have no place in the 'restful darkened room' prescribed by the sleep specialists. Instead of a calm winding down to sleep, many children settle down in bed to the accompaniment of the flashing bright lights and frantic soundtrack of screen-based entertainment. In 2012 the American Medical Association issued a warning that 'excessive exposure to light at night, including extended use of electronic media, can disrupt sleep or exacerbate sleep disorders, especially in children or adolescents.'

Indeed, the ill-effects of bedroom TV have been catalogued since the 1990s, when researchers found that sleeping problems in children aged between five and nine were more likely among those who watched a lot of television, especially just before sleep. They pointed out that having a television set in the bedroom 'may be an important contributor to sleep problems in school age children', with a worrying knock-on effect on learning. Yet TVs continued to find their way into children's bedrooms – survey results in US and UK in the early 2000s ranged from 30 per cent of four-year-olds and under up to 80 per cent of over-fives, with computers and other equipment not far behind.

Monsters on the move

There has however in recent years been a steady decline in the prevalence of the TV monster: Ofcom's 2013 report on family media use recorded 'a significant downward trend' as regards bedroom TV, beginning in 2007 (although the figures were still high: 22 per cent when children were three- to four-years old, 37 per cent of five- to six-year-olds, 53 per cent in the eight to eleven age range, and 62 per cent of twelve- thirteen-year-olds). This downward trend is almost certainly connected with a recorded reduction in 2009 of TVs in middle-class children's bedrooms, probably due to their parents' awareness of mounting research that linked TV-watching to learning, behavioural and sleep problems.

Unfortunately, as Ofcom points out, it's also almost certainly connected with the rise in ownership of handheld devices – smartphones and tablets, on which children can access TV whenever and wherever they want it. As one sleep-destroying monster is dispatched, another arises to take its place. And there may be even more reason for concern as regards handheld devices. The type of light produced by portable electronic devices – short wave-length blue light – is particularly disruptive of sleep patterns, while the fact that tablets, smart phones and e-readers are held close to the face increases the problem: 'The closer you have a light source to your face, the more intense it is,' says Harvard researcher, Dr Steven Lockley. 'And the further you go away it falls off quite quickly. So having things close to the face is much worse than having a TV which is ten feet away.'

Screen-based entertainment and socialising may not interfere with the sleep patterns of an adult, who's already learned – in an earlier, less frenetic age – how to drop off and, hopefully, stay asleep. But lights from electronic media can be a powerful force in preventing the development of good sleeping habits in children. Scientists at the University of Columbia in USA point out that too much screen-gazing has a knock-on effect on sleep problems later in life. They found late-night TV leaves children in a state of 'heightened alertness' at a time when their minds should be winding down, preventing them from developing natural sleep patterns which would otherwise become ingrained, so they're more likely to have sleep problems throughout their lives.

And electronic media present other potential sources of sleep disruption. A Belgian researcher found the sleep of young teenagers was disturbed by incoming text messages on their mobile phones, and also that they slept at a different level because they were constantly aware of the phone, waiting for communications. His conclusion that this leads to a different – presumably shallower – level of sleep is very worrying, as it's during deep slow-wave sleep that academic learning is transferred to long-term memory. Ofcom's 2013 survey found that 43 per cent of children aged five to fifteen own a mobile phone of some kind, with ownership of smart phones increasing in all age-groups (culminating in 62 per cent of twelve- to fifteen-year-olds), so there's a good chance that these problems are already affecting the school careers of a growing number of UK children.

The message from all the research is clear: if children are to get a good night's sleep and develop healthy sleep habits, the electronic paraphernalia of modern life must be removed from their bedrooms. The sleep experts are all in accord that children need a quiet, darkened, calm environment in which to become effective sleepers. What's more, there are many other pressing reasons why electronic gadgetry in the bedroom is not a good idea, to be explored in Chapters 4, 8 and 9. How about putting a container at the bottom of the stairs, in which *everyone* deposits their mobile devices as they make their way up to bed?

★ ★ ★

Many aspects of contemporary culture seem to contribute to problems with sleep, and research shows clearly that these problems impact on children's learning and well-being. But this particular example of our cultural evolution outstripping our biological needs is not just affecting children. There's mounting evidence that post-industrial society in general has gone too far in the direction of enforced wakefulness – we could all benefit from calming down, dragging ourselves away from the flickering screens and getting an hour or so more shut-eye per night.

Benjamin Franklin's famous aphorism still makes sense: Early to bed and early to rise makes a man healthy, wealthy and wise. Maybe it would also make everyone – adults as well as children – more attentive, self-controlled and civilised.

DETOXING SLEEP HABITS

- If you're a new parent, start as you mean to go on, and establish good sleep habits early.

  – Familiarise yourself with the scientific background to infant sleep patterns and ways of dealing with them that are as well-suited as possible to your family's circumstances (see ISIS website below).
  – If your baby is particularly difficult to soothe, try to find out why (e.g. see *A Good Start* below) and investigate a range of ways of helping to calm him (e.g. see *Sound Sleep* below).
  – Ensure a calm and quiet end to the day, dimming the light, so your baby begins to associate this time with sleep.
  – Put babies down to sleep while they're drowsy and leave them to fall asleep by themselves. Don't feel you have to stay and sing lullabies, or even 'just be there', till they've dropped off – you want them to become 'self-soothers'. See bedtime routines, opposite.
  – Once babies can sleep through the night (i.e. for between five and eight hours), if they wake and cry, don't pick them up immediately. Give them a chance to settle down without your intervention.
  – Create regular daytime and bedtime sleep schedules. The need for daytime naps changes over time, so be sensitive to your child's sleep patterns. By eighteen months, most toddlers are down to one nap a day, lasting between one and three hours.
  – Remember that you are the one who knows the outcomes for which you're eventually aiming – don't let your baby train you into habits that you'll one day regret.
  – Hold on to the watchwords 'confidence and consistency' and aim for both.
  – If you've tried all the recommended techniques and your child still has problems, check with your doctor or paediatrician.

- Ensure your child is getting adequate sleep (see the chart on page 89).
- Don't let children have any electronic equipment in their bedrooms. The one possible exception for older children is a tape recorder or CD player for talking books (see Chapter 4).
- If your child is a frequent snorer or has disrupted breathing patterns consult your doctor (especially if there are problems at school).
- Don't let your child have caffeinated drinks after about 4 p.m. Keep an eye on other foods to see if any cause 'hyper' behaviour, and avoid these foods at all times, but especially in the evening.
- Be authoritative and consistent about the rules for bedtime. Occasionally you will have to adjust timings, routines, etc. as your child grows older – do this in negotiation with your child, but ensure you make the final decision. This is an area, like diet, where adults have to take responsibility to act in the child's best interest – and the child often has other ideas.

HOW TO DETOX A PROBLEM SLEEPER

The key is to establish a bedtime routine that suits you and your child(ren) and stick to it as far as humanly possible.

- Begin the 'wind down' by removing your child from TV or other technological distractions at least an hour before bedtime.
- A bedtime routine should be gentle and calming and might involve:

  – a drink of warm milk
  – bathtime, teeth cleaning, etc
  – a bedtime story and/or songs (see also Chapter 4)
  – a security object, such as a blanket or soft toy
  – a darkened room, if necessary with a nightlight or the door ajar to allow just a little light from the hall
  – soft music (the same gentle lullaby or soft music on CD every night can be a way of conditioning a child to feel sleepy)
  – a particular form of words for goodnight, with your goodnight kiss.

- If your child is fearful of 'monsters', let them watch you give the room a quick spray with 'Monster Repellent' – a water-filled plant spray bottle appropriately labelled.
- If your child's afraid of the dark, turn off the light while you're still in the room, and sing or tell a story in the twilight.
- Don't wait for your child to go to sleep – and don't be cajoled into 'one more story'.
- Use a signal (such as a timer or your phone alarm) to limit time at the bedside to a previously agreed amount – that way there's no question about when to give the goodnight kiss and leave. You can just say 'Oh dear, time's up,' and it's the timer's fault you have to go, not yours.
- Try to ensure your child's bedroom is not only quiet and dark, but cool. A warm bed is more attractive and restful if it's much cooler outside it.
- During the summer time, ensure your child's room stays dark in the morning until the time the family wants to get up.
- As soon as your child moves from a cot to a bed, establish that he/she mustn't get up until it's daytime (you can now buy electronic timers that switch on 'the sun' at your family's getting-up time). Explain that if they wake early, they still need to rest in bed until the appointed hour, so the sensible thing is just to snuggle down and try to go back to sleep. As they get older, they could perhaps be allowed to look at favourite story books or play quietly with toys, but no TV or electronic entertainment.
- If children start getting out of bed at any time between bedtime and getting-up time, establish whether there's a good reason (maybe they need a glass of water beside the bed). If there isn't, don't reward them with adult attention. You have to find a system that keeps them in bed until they fall asleep with as little attention as possible (see *Little Angels*, below, for a variety of approaches) and accept that there's no point in trying to get up before 'lights on'.
- Training children out of bad habits takes time and absolute con-sistency. Once you've chosen and started your routine, don't waver!
- If at all possible, make sure the bedtime routine is very well-

established before interrupting it with holidays, trips or late-night
excursions. If not, you might end up having to start the whole training
programme again from scratch.

- If you go away on holiday, try to keep to the routine as much as
possible.
- Ensure everyone who puts your child to bed knows and sticks to your
chosen routine and schedule. Write them out and post them up where
babysitters, etc. can easily refer to them.

PARENT POWER: SLEEP GUIDELINES

In a culture that has lost sight of the importance of sleep, it would help
enormously if governments issued and publicised guidelines about
children's needs. Many parents simply don't know how much sleep their
children need and others would welcome support in creating and applying
routines. Now that children have assertiveness off to a tee, it would help
many parents to be able to counter 'Why have I got to go to bed?' with
'Because the government says so'.

- If you're a new parent, ask your midwife or health visitors for guidelines
on sleep requirements at various ages. If these aren't available in
published form or on a website, ask why not.
- If your child is school age, ask if the school prospectuses could include
information on the sleep requirements of children at different ages, the
significance of regular bedtimes and routines and the importance of
keeping electronic equipment out of children's bedrooms.
- If the school uses 'home-school contracts', suggest it includes a
requirement to follow sleep guidelines, giving more power to parents'
elbows about bedtime.

Further reading

Sarah Woodhouse, *Sound Sleep: Calming and Helping Your Baby or Child to Sleep* (second edition published by PAM Communications, 2010)
Norbert and Elinore Herschowitz, *A Good Start in Life: Understanding Your Child's Brain and Behaviour from Birth to Age Six* (Dana Books, 2004)
Tanya Byron, *Little Angels* (BBC Active Books, 2005)

Useful websites

Infant Sleep Information Service, information about babies and sleep from a team at Durham University: www.isisonline.org.uk
Useful information from a non-profit body (but worth knowing that it's funded by bed manufacturers): www.sleepcouncil.org.uk
US National Sleep Foundation facts about sleep: www.sleepfoundation.org
Information for children from NSF: www.sleepforkids.org

Mind the gap

Attitudes to bedtime schedules and routines are a good measure of parents' general approach to child-rearing. Many wealthier, better-educated parents, although laxer about bedtime than science would suggest is sensible, nevertheless attempt to rule the roost in this respect. Judging by what they tell their teachers, the experience of children from poorer homes is much less organised.

A few years ago the Chief Inspector of Schools in England caused a furore by claiming that many young children led 'disrupted and dishevelled' lives. Asked for statistical evidence, he was unable to provide it – parents don't tend to invite researchers into their homes to record how they're neglecting their children or, alternatively, letting those children run rings round them. The Chief Inspector's anecdotal evidence came from the same place as mine – thousands upon thousands of teachers worried to death about the chaotic lives led by the children in their classes. Whether statisticians have precise figures or not, the main reason for lack of regularity and system in the homes of disadvantaged families is not difficult to work out: parents whose own lives are chaotic and stressed are unlikely to be able to organise and apply schedules and routines for their children. I frequently hear stories of children from such homes falling asleep in class or arriving late for school (or not arriving at all) because they overslept.

Anecdotal evidence also points strongly to the contribution of electronic entertainment to these chaotic sleeping habits. In the poorest families, children almost inevitably sleep in rooms lit up by screens, either because they share a room with their parents or – if they're lucky enough to have a room to themselves – the first items of furniture tend to be the must-have electronic paraphernalia they hear about at school (see Chapters 8 and 9).

The poorer the home, the greater seems the dependency on electronic entertainment. The agony aunt for the downmarket British newspaper, *The Sun,* says her correspondents rely on TV for company, information, relaxation – and respite from their children. In many such homes it's so important it's never switched off. A correspondent in an industrial area of the north of England, whose job in the fire service takes him out in the depths of the night, records that the light of TV flickers constantly in the windows of most homes even when all else is darkness.

The children in such homes need the security and well-being that comes from a regular bedtime and a calm, restful night's sleep more than any others. Their parents also desperately need quiet time while their children are in bed to recoup from the day. Recommendations from government, health professionals and schools on children's sleep requirements at different ages – and advice on how to establish healthy sleeping habits from their earliest days – could be really helpful to Mind the gap parents.

CHAPTER FOUR

IT'S GOOD TO TALK

It's never been easier to communicate. Technological advances over the last quarter-century mean we can now seek out like-minded people around the world through websites and blogs, register our opinions and order goods via interactive TV, commune across vast distances by email, social networks or videophone sites, chat with family or friends wherever we happen to be by means of a smartphone ... We have even discovered, in text messaging, a unique human ability to communicate by thumb.

Ironically, the more technology has allowed us to communicate with people at a distance, the less we seem to converse with our nearest and dearest at home. As well as worrying about children's lack of sleep, the teachers I meet are particularly concerned about two other factors: lack of talk at home, and too much technology. They see these two elements as highly correlated.

Language development is not an issue that generally worries parents – indeed, when I raise it with them, many wish their offspring would talk *less* rather than more. Young children go through a 'language explosion', which can be quite exhausting. But it's not childish prattle, endless toddlers' questions or pre-teen backchat that teachers are concerned about. It's children's ability to connect and communicate socially, to listen attentively and with comprehension, and to use language for learning – and, according to every primary teacher I've discussed it with over the last fifteen years, these skills began to decline sometime in the 1980s, especially in children from more disadvantaged homes.

Language, literacy and learning

In fact, this is where I came in. My interest in toxic childhood syndrome developed from concern about children's language and literacy skills. At the end of the 1990s, I was an adviser to the British government's National Literacy Strategy, a nationwide drive to raise standards in reading and writing. Within a few years, we realised that the Strategy wasn't working – at least, not as well as it should have, considering the money and effort that were pumped into it.

As government ministers fretted, and literacy experts squabbled over the rival merits of different teaching methods, I became interested in what teachers were telling me on my lecture-tours around the country. Everywhere I went it was the same story: four- and five-year-olds were coming to school with poorer language skills than in the recent past; they didn't arrive with that repertoire of nursery rhymes and songs little ones always used to know; children of all ages found it increasingly difficult to sit down and listen to their teacher or to express complex ideas in speech or writing.

Almost unanimously, teachers put these developments down to the effects of all-day television, which had arrived in the UK in the mid-1980s, and the proliferation of channels that came in the mid-90s with cable and satellite TV. I started researching the subject ... and, as recounted earlier, realised there was a lot more to it than that.

I also discovered that this issue was bothering teachers across the developed world. As long ago as 1990, psychologist Jane Healey noted gathering complaints from American teachers about children's deteriorating language ability. German researchers in the early 2000s found disturbing levels of language difficulty in primary aged children and in a 2003 survey of teachers in Japan, well over half agreed with the statement: 'Academic Japanese-language capability of students is lower than it was in our school years.' One Japanese primary teacher commented: 'Even fifth- and sixth-grade students cannot speak in complete sentences', and a middle school teacher said, 'I feel as if some students do not understand Japanese.'

That term 'academic language capability' is a useful one. It's not that children are unable to understand their mother tongue, or communicate their everyday needs – indeed, in terms of backchat and 'speaking up for their rights', contemporary children are way ahead of previous generations! But academic study requires more sophisticated language to express increasingly complex under-standing and ideas.

Most children develop this sophisticated language through learning to read and write. Reading introduces them to a widening range of vocabulary and language use; writing provides oppor-tunities to use 'literate language' themselves, gaining increasing control over it. These skills are the bedrock of almost all academic learning, and the gradual process of learning to read and write – the 'getting of literacy' – is arguably the most critical stage in children's formal education (see p.215–218).

There's a strong and growing body of evidence that the seeds of success in literacy are sown in the very first year of a baby's existence. Strange as it seems, positive interactions between parent and babes-in-arms can lay the foundations for future success at school. But they can lay many other foundations too. It's not just education that depends upon good communication skills – the development of language is bound up very closely with our sense of identity and self-esteem. Children who can communicate well tend to feel good about themselves, while those who are tongue-tied often feel embarrassed and inferior – the ability to connect with others is a hugely important social skill.

Many psychologists now believe that early parent-child com-munication is one of the most critical elements in nurturing a happy, healthy, resilient child. It's also becoming increasingly apparent that developing all citizens' ability to communicate is a critical element in creating a healthy society.

Here's looking at you, kid

Communication begins when a newborn baby gazes at its mother's face while cradled in her arms. (Of course, it needn't be the mother – a father, grandparent, or any other 'primary care-giver' will do just as well, as long as they really love the child. But as it's usually mum who does the cradling, I'll stick to traditional terminology.) Babies are programmed to gaze at faces, and their mother's face is particularly attractive, being associated with food, warmth and comfort. The mother's smiles, songs, crooning and 'babytalk' as she feeds, carries or comforts her baby are soon rewarded with an adoring gaze and reciprocal smiles, coos and babble from the baby itself.

Professor Colwyn Trevarthen, a child development specialist from New Zealand, calls this mother-baby interaction 'the dance of communication'. Initially based on physical closeness and eye contact, it is critical to mother-baby bonding and the child's developing feelings of security and self-worth – what is known in psychological circles as 'attachment'. The more a child is attached to his early care-givers, the greater his chances of developing as a balanced, secure adult. As child psychiatrist Robert Shaw says, attachment is 'as central to the developing child as eating and breathing'.

Another aspect of attachment (which, in the mother-baby relationship, is wholly the responsibility of the mother) is 'attunement'. To be attuned to a tiny baby's emotional wants and needs, an adult needs to spend a great deal of time in that baby's company, watching, listening, trying to empathise. In 2012, after a ten-year study, researchers at Durham University found that the children of highly-attuned mothers tend to be securely attached, and that the advantages of this secure attachment continue throughout childhood.

To begin with, the dance of communication is mostly to do with body language – in a social species like ours, non-verbal communication (including eye contact, smiles, other facial expressions, pointing and gestures) is as important as talk, and children learn from every interaction. Mothers naturally exaggerate their expressions and gestures – often using rhythmic movements and sounds as part of the communicatory dance – and infants respond by copying. Although children cannot speak themselves at this early stage, they become accustomed to the sounds of the mother's language, and are already tuning their ears and brains to their mother tongue.

The dance soon develops into 'conversations' about what mother and baby see around them. For instance, the mother says '*Look at that doggy!*' and her child looks in the direction she's looking and pointing. Mother says '*He's a lovely doggy, isn't he?*' and – over time, with enough repetition of this sort of scenario – the child connects the furry creature they're both seeing with the repeated word 'doggy'. One day, when he's developed sufficient control of lips, tongue and vocal cords (usually in the months after the first birthday), the child will have a go at saying 'doggy' himself, and mum's excitement and praise will encourage him to try more words. In the meantime, his contribution to the 'conversation' is attention and body language, perhaps along with some excited babble, which makes his appreciation clear.

All this seems so obvious as not to be worth describing, but in fact it's a uniquely human interaction, and one that probably underpins a great deal more than learning what a doggy is. By recognising his mother's intention when she gestures to the dog, the baby is in effect 'reading her mind', something non-human animals simply don't seem to do. The mind-reading potential of human beings is currently an extremely hot topic among neuro-scientists, psychologists and philosophers – indeed, it may be that parent-child interactions of this kind are the key to understanding how human beings think.

The cradle of thought

In 2003 a professor of developmental psychopathology called Peter Hobson published a book about parent-child interaction which, if he's right, puts the dance of communication at the heart of child development. In *The Cradle of Thought* he argues that children's capacity to think, understand and reason arises out of the emotional attachment between parent and child, and their communicative dance.

For Hobson the dance is a triangular arrangement – the parent is at one corner of the triangle, the child at another, and the outside world at the third. Secure in the parent's presence, the child looks out at the world, then back at the parent; the parent looks at the world, then back at the child; their mutual gaze acknowledges a mutual experience – they've both seen the same bit of world. Attachment, attunement, interaction and communication. Hobson argues that, through taking part in this emotionally-embedded triangle of relatedness, children acquire three key insights.

First, there's the dawning realisation that child and parent are separate beings, looking at the same bit of world from different viewpoints – the child is simultaneously attached to and separate from the parent. This is a supremely important insight, because it's the beginning of empathy. If the mind-blowing discovery that other people have their own points of view is rooted in emotional security and pleasurable communication, the chances of the child later extending empathy to a widening range of people are much greater.

The next insight is the infant's recognition of his own personal perspective, different from the parent's ('She's looking at it from there, and I'm looking at it from here – this is *my* point of view'). The child thus becomes conscious of himself as a thinker, an intellectual self-awareness that underpins rational thought and behaviour. It's a charming thought: millions of infant minds throughout the millennia, experiencing their own spontaneous recognition that 'I think, therefore I am'.

Finally, the realisation that it's possible to have more than one perspective points children towards symbolic play ('If I can look at this box in different ways, I can *pretend* it's a car ... brmm, brmm!'). Soon they'll delight in using dolls as symbols for babies, sticks for light-sabres, cardboard boxes for cars. Symbolic play lays the foundation for understanding the many systems of symbols used in our culture, including numbers and letters. Psychologists believe it's also critical for the development of imagination and creative problem-solving abilities.

So the shared gaze of parent and child, along with their shared pleasure of interaction, could be the answer to questions that have vexed philosophers since time immemorial: What does it mean to think? What is it to be human? What is the root of learning? But it also points to other questions: Why do some people think less effectively than others? Why do some seem to have less 'humanity'? Why do others have problems with learning?

Peter Hobson has some suggestions here too. His journey towards *The Cradle of Thought* was via long-term research into autism. He believes an autistic infant's genetic make-up prevents him from acquiring the three insights described above. The autistic child may be able to learn but not to back up that learning with 'human' understanding. What's more, Hobson suggests that if opportunities to participate in emotionally-satisfying interactions are missing in their first eighteen months, even children *without* such a genetic vulnerability may have difficulty in acquiring one or more of the insights. He cites the example of the unfortunate babies raised with little human contact in Rumanian orphanages under the Ceauşescu regime – many more than would be expected in a normal population developed 'autistic-like' behaviour.

There's a growing body of neuroscientific research connecting successful early attachment with the development of neural networks in the prefrontal cortex of the brain – the area associated with rational thought, decision-making, social behaviour and self-control. If Hobson is right, the implications for early childcare are profound. What if a normal child isn't exactly neglected but opportunities for shared gazing and communication are limited? What if parents don't have time, or are too busy, or simply don't know how important it is to interact with their babies? The life we lead today doesn't exactly encourage parents to engage in the communicatory dance – in some ways, it positively discourages it.

How contemporary culture interrupts the dance

In an earlier, less frenetic age, most new mothers had time to devote to the dance of communication – or they delegated someone else to the job: the rich employed nannies; the poor enlisted the services of older siblings or other members of the extended family. Nowadays, it's not so easy. For the many mothers who feel obliged to return to work soon after their babies are born, time for cradling, crooning and pointing at doggies is limited, but – with fewer extended families around and a scarcity of daycare choices – it may be difficult to find someone to whom the child can attach emotionally in its mother's absence. Early communication, with all its attendant developmental implications, may be neglected from the very beginning.

The issue of daycare is discussed in Chapter 6, but even when a mother is at home, there are now many demands on her time to keep her from the 'dance'. Health workers on home visits frequently report seeing mothers with a baby in one hand and a mobile phone in the other, or failing to make eye contact with their suckling infant because they're simultaneously checking the email, catching up on Facebook or watching TV. These mothers are not uncaring or unfeeling – just products of our busy, multi-tasking contemporary culture and utterly unaware of the communicatory needs of their tiny children.*

For well over a decade, organisations such as *Talk to Your Baby*, run by the National Literacy Trust, and the children's communication

---

* The saddest such anecdote I've heard was from a midwife in 2011 who was concerned about the young mothers she works with: 'Many of them are texting their friends and family even as we deliver the baby. They're not even properly present at their baby's birth.'

charity I CAN have been trying to raise awareness of the importance of switching off technological distractions and concentrating – for at least some of the day – on looking at, talking to and singing to babies. Singing seems to be particularly important: the rhythmic movements associated with age-old songs (bouncing a baby on your knee while singing *Bye Baby Bunting*, rocking a cradle to *Rock-a-bye Baby*) seems to affect the patterning of the brain and may have important implications for later social and cognitive development.

The lack of interaction between contemporary mothers and children often continues when they go outdoors. Perhaps because they think children are more interested in watching the world go by, many parents use baby-slings facing outwards, so eye contact is ruled out, and the triangle of relatedness is broken. Then when children graduate to pushchairs the vast majority face away from the pusher: most modern, light-weight, fold-up pushchairs face outwards, because the dynamics of the design require the baby's weight to be behind the front wheels.

Research by Dr Suzanne Zeedyk in 2008 (replicated in New Zealand in 2013) showed that both attachment and communication skills are enhanced if mother and baby are able to make eye contact, and since her study was published there are more parent-facing pushchairs on the market, but take-up is still slow. Even in upmarket middle-class areas, my own informal pushchair counts come out as 75 per cent outward-facing. I suspect that parents believe their children need the 'stimulation' of an outward view: we twenty-first-century adults are addicted to constant rapid visual stimulation, so we assume our tiny offspring are too. And, of course, if we provide it, they soon will be. But in terms of social and emotional development, looking into mum's eyes and face is a far healthier option.

It seems ridiculous that something as simple as pushchair design could affect children's development, but it's one more element in the toxic mix. Before fold-up pushchairs arrived on the scene about thirty years ago (in response to massively growing car ownership) parents ferried their offspring about in old-fashioned prams, which allowed them to look at and talk to the infant as they walked. While I was drafting this chapter, I watched a modern mother pushing her baby son through our local park. She was being a 'good mum' and chatting away to him about the things all around – the squirrels, the trees, my Bedlington terrier ('Look at that doggy!') – and he was totally unaware of her attempts at communication. Facing away from her, he couldn't see where she was looking so the triangle was broken. Her attempts at communication were lost and her words were meaningless, just another noise among many that added nothing to his understanding of the world.

Tuning in or turning off

Even when children and parents can see each other, there's another potential reason for communication failure: constant noise that interferes with children's ability to hear their parents' speech. Outdoors there is traffic noise, increasing every year; indoors, in many homes, there's the day-long noise of television. There is gathering evidence that noise impedes children's educational progress. For instance, schools in airport flight paths tend to have lower than average test scores. This appears to apply indoors as well, as children from homes where the TV is on all day are less likely to read at age six.

For fifteen years at the end of the last century, child language expert Dr Sally Ward investigated babies' listening skills in inner-city Manchester. In 1984, 20 per cent of the nine-month-old infants she tested were unable to listen selectively; by 1999, the proportion had almost doubled. I met her in 1997, when she predicted that 'by the early years of the new millennium, around half the nation's one-year-olds will be unable to listen satisfactorily to the sound of their mothers' voices against the noise of the television' and that this would impact significantly on their language development. Sure enough, in 2006 I CAN collated the findings on children's language skills when they started primary school and found that, in disadvantaged areas of the country, 50 per cent and upwards were arriving in the reception class with significant language delay.

The arrival in the UK of all-day TV in the early 1980s certainly seems to be implicated in this phenomenon. However, as psychologists have probed more deeply into its effects on children's development, it appears that difficulties with focused listening are part of a wider problem with attention skills in general. The issue is discussed in Chapter 9, but in terms of early communication, it requires introduction here. In the UK, for instance, the eminent neuroscientist Susan Greenfield has pointed out that screen-based entertainment offers 'a gratifying, easy-sensation, yuk-and-wow environment. We cannot park our children in front of the TV and expect them to develop a long attention span', and Dr Aric Sigman, who writes widely on the effects of technology on the developing brain, has described young children's state of consciousness when gazing at TV as 'attentional inertia'.

This term was first coined by US media guru Dr Daniel Anderson, a psychologist who advised on many well-known TV series for children, and who also conducts research into television's effects on cognition. In 2008, he pointed out that, since all human beings 'have a natural inclination to look at the shiny, the bright, the mobile', young children playing in a room where TV is on are constantly distracted by it, even if they aren't actually watching a programme: 'being pulled away by the TV all the time, rather than making a behavioural decision to watch'. He found that children focused 25 per cent less on their self-chosen play when the TV was on, and parents interacted 20 per cent less with their children. When they did relate, it tended to be passive: 'Yes, that's nice' or 'In a minute.'

The development of children's listening skills appears to be inextricably intertwined with the development of attentional skills in general, and with the depth of their parents' attention, and thus responsiveness. But as Sally Ward pointed out – in the interview that spawned *Toxic Childhood* – babies who don't learn to listen are likely to have problems acquiring language and, if their awareness of speech sounds is affected, they'll probably also have difficulties with literacy skills.

Sally told me about an experiment she'd conducted with some parents from her study. She simply asked them to turn off the television for half an hour a day, and talk to their children. When they knew why it would be helpful, all the parents were keen to do this ... but they had one, panic-stricken and distinctly chilling question: 'What shall we talk about?'

Dancing to the music of time

Over the second half of the last century, as extended families died away, simple ancient wisdom that had passed through the generations since time immemorial, died away with them. Many of today's parents – and even grandparents – have never themselves witnessed the rearing of children, except perhaps the odd snippet on TV, and the details of their own childhood are now hazy ... so how would they know what to talk about? They haven't watched an aunt, a sister, their own mother with a younger sibling, keeping up a singsong commentary on what she and/or the baby are doing, chanting to accompany a familiar action ('That's one button, two buttons, three buttons...') or rocking an infant to sleep with an ancient rhyme. Indeed, as the child of a nuclear family, the only reason I know such rhymes myself is that we tuned into a radio programme called Listen With Mother which broadcast rhymes and stories every afternoon (sadly, the BBC dropped this in the 1970s because it was 'old-fashioned'). Many of the generation of parents reared since TV became an all-day presence have lost track of this cultural treasure trove.

Old nursery rhymes, songs and jingles may sound nonsensical to contemporary ears, but the reason they've been passed through the ages is that they're ideal for introducing children to the rhythms of language and tuning their ears to language sounds. The rhythmic patterns seem to be particularly important – American researchers have found that a young child's ability to keep a steady beat is one of the best predictors of future success at school. Many of the experts I spoke to, in both linguistics and developmental psychology, commented on the huge importance of music and song in developing children's social and communication skills.

If parents don't know the old nursery songs and rhymes, there are plenty of CDs and many collections on the web. However, in the first couple of years these should be for parental reference only – children need to listen to and learn from a fellow human being, not a machine. Our adult love affair with technology has led many people to believe it can act as a substitute for human interaction. It can't – at least, not with little children. A machine may easily engage a child's attention with lots of bells and whistles and buttons to press, but it isn't genuinely responsive. It has no human warmth, eye contact, facial expression or interest in the child's needs – there is no emotional connection.

The American Academy of Pediatrics (AAP) has long recommended that children under two should not watch television. As a seasoned BBC executive remarked to me, they are almost certainly 'on a hiding to nothing' on this one. TV is such a universal part of our culture that it would be impossible to stop babies and toddlers from seeing it. However, parents should try to limit exposure (see Chapter 9, The electronic babysitter), and they should certainly make time for human connection in a quiet environment.

Connecting with babies and toddlers in the twenty-first century

Once the political and educational establishments woke up to the implications of Sally Ward's research, they began producing initiatives with names like 'Communicating Matters' and 'Every Child a Talker' – in 2011, we even had a Year of Communication (although, ironically, few people outside government circles heard about it). In recent years, therefore, most nursery workers and early years teachers have become reasonably well-informed about the importance of early communication skills, and many of them work valiantly on their charges' language development. But these institutionalised interventions can never be an adequate substitute for attachment and attunement between parent and child. So far there has been little political appetite for increasing new parents' awareness in this respect, which is perhaps why Ofsted repeatedly finds that there has been no real improvement.

Perhaps government's reluctance to address the significance of early attachment and communication is because of political ambivalence about contemporary mothers' problems with work-life balance (see Chapter 6) or perhaps there is a deeper problem buried somewhere in the national psyche. Whatever the reason, apart from a few state-sponsored initiatives like Bookstart, singing sessions in libraries and Scotland's PlayTalkRead (all of which stress their relationship to literacy development), it's been left to charities and commercial organisations to communicate directly with parents about age-old strategies for tuning into and communicating with their offspring.

Organisations such as Talk To Your Baby and I CAN, with its annual 'Chatterbox Challenge', try hard to spread the word to parents across the social classes. Others, like the International Association of Infant Massage (which focuses on the importance of touch and physical connection), Music Bugs and Tiny Talk (baby-signing classes) are obliged to rely on popularity among middle-class parents, who can afford to pay.

Sadly, for new parents who don't know about or can't afford clubs and classes, help in learning how to connect with their little ones is usually available only in extremis. There's an excellent government initiative called the Family Nurse Partnership, in which vulnerable young mums are assigned a health visitor to mentor and 'mother the mother', but lack of funding means this is extremely limited. Many charities, such as Home Start and Gingerbread, also provide personal mentoring services but volunteers tell me that, all too often, their involvement amounts to 'fire-fighting' when an emergency occurs. The government's Sure Start initiative for parents of pre-school children in disadvantaged areas, begun in 1998, should have improved things more widely but made little headway. It was, in fact, roundly criticised in 2005 by one of its original founders because its focus soon changed from child development to childcare and getting mothers back to work.

Only Connect

It's a tragic reflection of our society's value-system that the benefits of attunement and attachment are increasingly available only to well-heeled babies, or the offspring of mums whose lives are so chaotic that the benefits of mentoring are a mere drop in an ocean of poverty and deprivation. It's particularly tragic because classes and courses, meetings and mentors aren't really necessary at all. All a new mother needs to do is turn off the technology, gaze into her baby's eyes, and dance to that long-established music of time. New fathers can do it too. They'll soon discover that, for all small children, jigging on a parent's knee as he or she chants or sings any nonsense they like, is the most enjoyable and rewarding experience in the world. So is bouncing to 'Horsey horsey don't you stop' or collapsing into delighted giggles while playing 'This little piggy went to market' over and over again. And all the time, the constant rhythm, rhyme and repetition is tuning their infant bodies to balance, their ears to sounds and their minds to pattern, opening up the neural networks that lead to fluent speech.

Virginia Beardshaw, CEO of I CAN, a charity that works valiantly to draw attention to this simple fact, recently pointed out to me how easy it is to lose sight of common sense wood among organisational trees: 'The major problem in translating research into policy and practice is that separate streams of research are taken up by different professional groups. Language development is "owned" by speech and language therapists, and kept in their bubble. Attachment theory is the province of psychologists and social workers, and they tend to ignore the key role of communication in it. Health visitors don't tend to "do" communication much, while schools fixate on literacy and overlook the importance of spoken language and, above all, listening skills. In fact, everyone working with children needs to recognise the significance of language as the cement for child development, and use that insight to inform their practice.' Perhaps the words 'Only Connect' should be written above the door of all children's services agencies everywhere.

The language instinct

Human beings are the only animals on earth with the power of speech. It's well over half a century since Noam Chomsky suggested we're genetically programmed to acquire language, just as song-birds are programmed to acquire songs. Neuroscience has since backed up his hypothesis. Unless children are physically or neurologically impaired, or reared in circumstances of extreme deprivation, every one of them learns to speak – usually uttering the first word around the age of one. Language comes as naturally to human beings as smiling, standing or walking.

However, despite being hardwired for language, human babies don't actually learn to speak a particular tongue unless they get plenty of experience of it. (In just the same way, song-birds need to listen to other song-birds in order to sing fluently and freely.) The quality of the engagement and talk surrounding a growing child determines the levels of language, listening and – eventually – literacy that child is personally able to reach. If children are reared in a 'language-rich' environment, they will probably develop good language skills; if their background is 'language-poor', they probably won't.

A major component of a language-rich environment is at least one adult who spends time genuinely interacting with the child, so that the language is meaningful to him and using the exaggerated, simplified language that linguists used to call 'motherese' but now (to emphasise equality of opportunity) is known as 'parentese'. This requires interest and commitment on the adult's part, and many contemporary adults find it difficult (or frankly boring) to 'come down to the child's level'. Perhaps they've been educated out of the ability to communicate naturally to tiny children, but for their children's sake they really need to educate themselves back into it – watching Suzanne Zeedyk's *Connected Baby* DVDs or reading any of the books recommended at the end of this chapter would help.

When children begin to talk themselves, the best way to encourage more talk is to tune in and follow their lead, repeating a child's words, guessing at their meaning and extending the idea. For instance, 'Milk allgone.' 'Has the milk all gone? Oh yes, you've drunk it all up. Do you want some more?' There's no need to get hung up about correctness – children need to experiment with language, which means not worrying about making mistakes. Repetition of the child's words using the correct form shows the adult has understood, and provides a model the child can gradually internalise. By repeating and expanding, parents encourage children to experiment more and more with language, and to grow in confidence in using it.

The power of words

Opportunities for interactive talk with children at all stages in their development abound in daily life. The suggestions in previous chapters – family meals; sharing everyday activities, outings and chores; bedtime routines and stories – are all natural opportunities for shared time and communication. They also provide subject matter for conversations – talking about what you're doing and why you're doing it, pointing out anything interesting, picking up on the child's interests and letting him or her take the conversational lead as often as possible.

Although the minutiae of domestic life may be commonplace for adults, it is still new and original for young children – and seeing it through a child's eyes allows adults to rediscover all the small wonders forgotten in our usual busyness: the sounds, textures, shapes and objects in our homes; how simple gadgets work; the exigencies and effects of the weather; the way a nearby tree changes through the seasons; the buildings, people, pets in the local neighbourhood. As children grow older, they also love talking about themselves and their family – chatting about shared memories, hearing stories about their parents' childhoods and learning snippets of family history. Social psychologist Dr Pat Spungin believes this is an important element in developing a strong sense of identity.

When conversation flags, shared time provides an opportunity for singsongs, reciting rhymes together, number games (starting with counting stairs, cars, cans of beans and graduating to 'Think of a number, double it, etc. etc.') or, whenever time permits, play. Any sort of play is an opportunity for parents to model behaviour and chat about and around the game: 'peek-a-boo' or 'show me the toy' with a baby; painting, playdough-modelling or bouncing a ball with a toddler; playing with soft toys, dressing up and role-play with pre-schoolers; card and board games with school-age children. To return to David Attenborough's quote: for young children, 'play is a very serious business' – symbolic and creative play not only develops physical competence, it underpins their later success at school and general well-being throughout life.

None of the conversational opportunities suggested here are expensive – indeed, with young children, the more sophisticated the purchase, the less time it usually engages them. Most parents have had the experience of watching an expensive present cast aside, because the child was more interested in the wrapping paper or the box it came in. Our consumer society leads us to believe that the more costly and complex an item is, the more its value – this is not the case with children. (Although in a way, it is true: human beings are complex and these days their time is costly ... and time with the human beings who are most special to them is what children most need and crave.)

Interaction versus interactivity

However, there is one form of expensive present that does tend to attract babies' and children's attention, thus releasing parents from the time bind. It's technology, and in recent years manufacturers have devised many ingenious ways for children to develop a technology habit at a very early age: simple computer games that can be operated with a joystick; baby apps to entertain them on the iPad; 'apptivity cases' that allow a tiny baby to grasp said iPad, or an 'apptivity seat' with a clamp to hold the tablet in place so all the baby has to do is swipe its hand around.

For older pre-school children, there are devices such as Ubooly, an educational 'interactive pet' into which parents can insert a smartphone or iPad mini. Using speech recognition technology, it can have a conversation in several languages and immediately recognises the child's name: 'The mobile device operates as a brain of sorts so the Ubooly can tell stories, teach math, demonstrate teeth brushing, suggest healthy eating options, and more.' As one delighted parent explained, it's ideal for keeping her child hooked while she does the dishes. Since 2014 My Friend Cayla, a doll that can be connected to a smart device, has been marketed at seven-year-old girls with homework queries. Similar products are bound to follow.

These developments are so recent that there is, of course, no research to show possible long-term effects. As psychologist and media expert Daniel Anderson has said: 'We are engaged in a vast and uncontrolled experiment with our children, plunging them into home environments that are saturated with electronic media.' However, the findings outlined in the next-but-one section (How technology can dumb children down) suggest that such gadgets are highly unlikely to develop children's all-round communication skills. On the other hand, there's a very good chance they could exacerbate a range of developmental problems that are already on the increase (see Chapters 2, 3, 8 and 9).

Unfortunately, until research can be devised, funded, carried out, peer-reviewed and published, manufacturers will be able to claim, with disingenuous ease, that no research exists. Perhaps one day, a politician will appear who is brave enough to challenge the market on behalf of the next generation. In the meantime, it's up to parents to recognise their babies' essential developmental needs, to remember that mums and dads are perfectly capable of telling stories, informally teaching maths and discussing healthy eating as they and their pre-school children wash the dishes together, and that dolls aren't capable of the social interaction young children need.

Talk so kids will listen, listen so kids will talk

As a child's language skills develop, the best sort of talk encourages creative thinking, and the use of words to communicate those thoughts. In 2004, a UK study described the most valuable educational experience for pre-schoolers (and I'm pretty sure it would apply to school-age children too) as 'sustained shared thinking' – this, of course, is mediated through sustained shared talk. One of the researchers, Iram Siraj-Blatchford, explained to me that in interactions between adults and children the key is 'to open up language, rather than shutting it down'.

Adults who aren't confident about talking with children often ask closed questions, where there's only one right answer ('What colour is that?' 'What was the girl's name?' 'How many blocks do you have?'). Children either get such questions right, and that's that – end of exchange; or they get them wrong, and that's the end of the exchange too – but this time the child also feels bad about it. Much more productive are speculative questions: 'I wonder what would happen if...?' 'What do you think he might do?' 'Wouldn't it be interesting if...?'

Parenting classes and books such as How to Talk So Kids Will Listen, and Listen So Kids Will Talk recommend similar approaches to help children express their feelings. Instead of questioning a child, or providing instant solutions, they suggest acknowledging the way the child is feeling by giving the emotion a name ('Gosh, that must have been *disappointing*' or 'You sound really *frustrated/angry/irritated!*') and offering support with minimal but genuinely interested responses ('Mmmm?' ... 'I see' ... 'Yes') while the child talks through the issue, hopefully arriving at a personal solution.

It is such open-ended approaches to talk – in which the adult respects and pays real attention to the child's contribution – that eventually lead to social awareness, self-esteem and independent thought. On the other hand, a machine, however well-programmed, will never be able to replicate the responses of a warm, caring, empathising human being.

I'm often asked by parents what they can do to help their children do well at school. The simple answer, born out by the research is: talk and listen. Or maybe that should be: listen and talk.

How technology is dumbing children down

In all communication and language, the key is genuine real-time interaction. From the very start, children learn language through human engagement, as illustrated by the story of a little American boy, Vincent, told to me by linguistics professor Jean Aitchison. Vincent's parents were both deaf and communicated in sign language. Their baby, however, was born with normal hearing ability so from the very start his parents made sure he watched TV, expecting him to learn spoken language from the speakers on screen. Vincent didn't learn to speak a single word; but he did become fluent in American Sign Language, his real-life interactive 'mother tongue'. When he was eventually exposed to real-life spoken language at the age of three, his progress in learning to speak was painfully slow.

Language is only meaningful to a small infant if it is part of genuine experience. One of the more alarming developments of contemporary culture has been the increasing use, across the developed world, of technological devices as electronic babysitters, while parents are engaged elsewhere. Vincent's experience shows that very young children don't learn language from a screen – they learn it from people. This has since been confirmed by the work of American neuroscientistist Dimitri Christakis who, as a new parent himself, became interested in whether it was possible to 'inappropriately stimulate the developing brain in ways that are actually not beneficial but harmful.' His subsequent research showed that, in the first sixteen months of life, TV-watching actually depressed language development.

As children grow older, good quality television and computer programs (see Chapter 9) will almost certainly expand their horizons and develop vocabulary – and researchers have found that repeated watching of a favourite DVD by pre-schoolers also means repeated hearing, which can be helpful to language development. But it should still be carefully monitored and limited, because 'receptive listening' is only one side of the language equation – real learning requires children to use the language themselves. Without opportunities to practise any new vocabulary they acquire within a real-life interactive context, children will rapidly lose it.

When first researching this issue, I thought the 'electronic babysitter' syndrome would be a problem mainly in socially-disadvantaged households. A speaking engagement in a very expensive prep school put me right. The staff at this school – which sent many of its pupils on to Eton – recognised the problem immediately. As one teacher put it, 'Here it's not mummy and daddy plonking the child in front of the television – they're both out earning shed-loads of money to pay the fees – it's the Lithuanian au pair!' Teachers in schools serving wealthy families around Europe have given similar reports: where childcare staff don't share a first language with the children, the electronic babysitter comes into its own.

And it's not just child-centred technology that comes between children and parents – technology distracts us in many ways. One constant complaint of children I meet is the extent to which it now interrupts family time. Eight-year-old Lily expressed it very well:

'We'll just be settling down to something – a story or something – and her phone'll go. So then she goes off chatting, and I'm sitting getting jealous, so I just go and put the telly on.' Just as many nursing mothers don't realise that multimedia multi-tasking can deprive their children of essential early communication, parents of older children are often unaware of how much email, phones, Facebook and their own favourite TV programmes come between them and their offspring.

After researching this chapter, I made a conscious effort to treat my family with the same respect I would a business acquaintance – switching to answerphone during 'family time' and leaving the email to stew. It was scary how difficult this proved – we are now so much at the mercy of our machines. No wonder children often give up on us and disappear off to watch TV or surf the Internet on their own.

Stories and screens

Technology has also assisted the decline of another cultural tradition: the bedtime story. There's a huge difference between listening to a story told or read by a loving adult and watching one on a screen, which is how a growing number of children now end their day. Not only does a screen-based story deny parent and child a significant opportunity for emotional connection, it's also less likely to develop children's linguistic and intellectual powers. Stories on screen are mostly visual – viewers *watch* the characters and the setting, following the plot with their eyes. For many contemporary children a story has no verbal narrative thread – just fragmented dialogue, sound effects and background music.

Neuroscientist Susan Greenfield is convinced of the importance of verbal narrative for healthy brain development. Adults throughout history have used stories to introduce their young to important elements of their culture because, as pointed out in the YouTube presentation 'Susan Greenfield on Story-telling', it helps children gradually move from a sensory appreciation of the world to a cognitive one. She explains that, in order to understand any idea, children have to embed it in a wider meaningful context: 'stories give meaning, temporal consequence, ramifications and personal significance – meaning is all-important to human beings ... we need our identity to be acknowledged.'

As well as developing cognitive skills in general, hearing many stories in infancy (particularly favourite stories retold or re-read over and over again) is an important precursor to literacy. If the language of books is unfamiliar to children and their ears untrained to narrative, they may struggle to make sense of it – almost like learning another language. They may also lose out creatively, because if they only ever encounter stories on screen, where ready-made images are provided, children don't learn to make pictures for themselves in their heads – in other words, to use their imagination. Neither do they learn the shape and feel of written sentences – the patterns of literate language that will allow them to express their own thoughts in writing.

Studies have repeatedly shown that children whose parents read to them tend to become good readers themselves, with the many other advantages that literacy conveys. Cuddling up to share a picture book is a source of endless delight to toddlers – and even older children who can read for themselves benefit from hearing good books read aloud. The children's author Robert Louis Stevenson recommended that children at all ages need to *hear* stories, for how else will they learn 'the chime of fair words, and the march of the stately period'?

At this point, I must admit that I have not always practised what I preach. In my capacity as a literacy specialist, I was once on the radio rhapsodising about the importance of reading to children right up to their teens. My daughter, nine at the time and listening at home, turned to her child-minder and said, 'Huh, she hasn't read to me for ages.' It was embarrassingly true: as she'd grown older and her bedtime got later, I was too shattered to sit for twenty minutes reading a story at the end of the day – a classic example of knowing what's right, but not actually doing it. We therefore agreed to import a tape player into my daughter's bedroom and build up a library of good 'talking books'. Sometimes I would still read to her, sometimes she listened to one of her collection instead, and often I enjoyed just sitting, sharing Alan Bennett's rendition of *Winnie the Pooh* as she drifted off to sleep.

This is one sort of technology that may therefore have a place in older children's bedrooms. If you're not able to read to children yourself, letting them listen to a good book, well-read on CD, seems to me a much sounder way of helping them settle down for sleep than the fret and fizz of television. (Talking books are also a boon and a blessing on long car journeys.)

The joy of txt

As children grow older, another factor begins to bother parents: emails and texting. Will children's use of careless, unpunctuated, abbreviated language on chat room messages and mobile phone texts infect their schoolwork? Will using and responding to smiley faces and other icons interfere with their ability to read and write? As a specialist in educational linguistics, I think this is a massive distraction from the real problems, described above. In fact, txt is the least of our worries.

As long as children have well-developed listening and language skills by the time they reach school, and aren't distracted by technological gadgets, there's no reason why they shouldn't learn to read and write (see Chapter 7). And as long as they can read and write according to normal conventions when necessary, there's no reason not to use their own personal style of writing in their spare time. It's normal for human beings to adjust the way they use language depending on whom they're addressing and the message they're conveying. For instance, we speak to children differently from the way we'd speak to the boss, and we express ourselves differently depending on whether our message is serious or flippant, casual or official.

Young people have always had their own specialised slang-languages – largely unintelligible and therefore threatening to adults – which help them proclaim their generation's identity. During the last century most slang was spoken so when, thanks to technology, a written slang appeared it seemed even more threatening to the older generation. However in the past, when letter-writing was fashionable, chatty letter-writers often adopted their own types of speed-writing. I once had the opportunity to look at Queen Victoria's childhood letters (of which she wrote a great many) and was fascinated to find them riddled with strange personal abbreviations and misspellings – it almost looked like 'txt'. Queen Victoria had no difficulty in swapping from that to the language of state when she needed to. And, as cognitive psychologist Steven Pinker once pointed out, 'the telegraph didn't lead people to omit prepositions from their speech or end every sentence with STOP'.

Marketing gurus refer to the language of text as 'TweenSpeak' because it peaks among the ten to fourteen age-group. It's different from previous slangs in being a global phenomenon, uniting young people across geographical boundaries. Like many aspects of technological culture, therefore, it may well prove important in children's development as future inhabitants of the global village.

* * *

There's no doubt that the older children are, the more beneficial technology can be, for widening their horizons and developing knowledge and vocabulary. Nevertheless too much viewing, or too long on the games console, smartphone, tablet or laptop are still not recommended (see also Chapter 9). There's no need to worry that reducing their time online will mean they'll be left behind on the technology front: contemporary children easily learn the 'media literacy' skills required to navigate around computers – these skills are designed to be intuitive, so can be picked up by trial and error. Indeed, as technology develops at an increasingly crazy pace, there's no point familiarising themselves with it from an early age. Any skills learned before the age of seven will be out of date by the time a child is in double figures.

On the other hand, nature has designed children to develop 'old-fashioned' human communication skills during those first seven or so years, including the listening and language skills on which depend the capacity to think, analyse, explore and express ideas, not to mention important aspects of emotional and social development. For the last few millennia, a steadily-increasing number of children have also learned how to use these primary communication skills as the foundation of literacy, thus hugely enhancing their intellectual capacity. If the human race is to continue travelling onward and upward, we can't assume that language and literacy skills will develop 'naturally' unless we adults provide the sort of environment and support they need to flourish.

DETOXING COMMUNICATION

Babies and toddlers

- More than anything else, your child needs the time and interest of a loving adult. Do everything you can to ensure this is available constantly in the first two to three years of life, and frequently and regularly thereafter. Social, emotional and intellectual development are rooted in early attachment and later opportunities for interactive talk.
- Limit electronic noise and visual distraction from TV, CDs, laptop, tablets, etc.
- Talk to your baby as often as possible – when you're playing, when you're out and about, as you do household chores. Make eye contact, smile, and just chat about what you're doing. When you point and talk about something, make sure your child can see where you're pointing.
- Try to ensure that when you're chatting, your baby can see your face, smile and eyes. If possible, find a buggy that allows your baby to face you.
- Listen carefully when your child responds to what you have said, and try always to reply in some way.
- Don't be worried about using 'parentese' in the early stages – the sort of exaggerated, musical pronunciation that most adults find themselves automatically adopting when talking to a very young child. It helps children discriminate the key sounds of the language, which will come in useful when they begin to speak themselves (and later when they learn to read – see Chapter 7).
- Whenever you have time, sing nursery songs and lullabies, recite rhythmic rhymes and chants, use repetitive games like Pat-a-cake, tickling rhymes and number chants – this too lays sound foundations for language and literacy.
- To develop your child's attention skills, play games involving pleasurable anticipation (such as 'This little piggy' and 'Round and round the garden, like a teddy bear') and later play 'Ready Steady Go' games, where they have to wait for a signal.
- Provide opportunities for children to initiate talk, listen carefully and

respond to their verbal and non-verbal communications. As children begin to speak, repeat and expand on their words. If they say something incorrectly, say it back the right way. Praise your child for using new words correctly.

- If possible, don't let under-twos engage in screen-based activity at all – and if it's not possible, keep it to an absolute minimum.

Two-year-olds and upwards

- When sharing precious time with your child, try to minimise inter-ruptions from communication technology. Switch off the mobile, put the phone on answer-machine, resist the temptation to check Facebook or email – you would do this for an important person at work, and who is more important than your child?
- When sharing time with children, try to escape the need to rush and multi-task. Slow down to a more 'human' pace. Do not rush a child who is talking, and don't look away.
- Limit screen-time for older children, keep to programmes and apps designed for your child's age-group and whenever possible watch with them and talk about what you see.
- Encourage your child to speak directly to other adults and children (translate if their language is unclear, but don't 'talk for them').
- Continue to sing with children as they grow older, encourage action songs and dances, and model listening to music. If your child shows an interest in music, encourage it – it is one of the greatest humanising forces there is.
- Ensure that there are regular 'ring-fenced family times' such as mealtimes, shared activities, bedtime routines, when there is plenty of space for talk.
- Use TV as a focus for talk – if you watch together, you can chat about the characters, what they did, why they did it, and so on. (This is particularly useful as children grow older, because the antics of soap stars and celebrities can open up conversations about acceptable and ethical behaviour, including sexual behaviour.)
- Look for ways of 'opening up' your child's language through

speculative language and tentative questions – and thus developing 'sustained shared thinking'. Avoid closing down your child's language with 'closed' questions to which there is only one right answer.

- Encourage children to talk about their own experiences, past, present and future, and model how to listen attentively (see also How to help your child at school, Chapter 7).
- Share family history and lore, tell about what you did 'when you were little' and reminisce about your child's experiences – as well as providing good conversational fodder, this develops a sense of identity and self-esteem.
- Read and/or tell stories every day, whatever the age of your child. With younger children, share a cuddle as you read favourite books repeatedly.
- As children get older, go on reading to them, even when they can read themselves. On long car journeys, listen together to talking books, and when they get too old for a bedtime story, let older children listen to talking books before they go to sleep.

HOW TO TEACH THEM TO TALK IT OVER

Communication is the best way to avoid misunderstandings. Encouraging children to talk things through helps them solve their problems, understand other people's point of view, avoid conflicts and prevent disagreements escalating into fights.

- Acknowledge children's feelings, and give them time to talk through what worries them, rather than immediately offering solutions or opinions (see Faber and Mazlish, below).
- Be a good role model: always try to talk through issues to be sure you understand your child's (and other family members') point of view. This does *not* mean allowing yourself to be drawn into an argument (see Chapter 10: Detoxing behaviour).

- Model how to listen, and to repeat back what someone else has said to be sure you've understood.
- Teach children a four-point 'conflict resolution' technique for resolving their arguments. Model this yourself, and whenever a problem arises help them go through the routine. It does actually work. When someone upsets you so much you want to start a fight, stop and:

  1. state what they've done to make you upset or angry
  2. explain how it's made you feel and why (this will usually be because you are *hurt* or *afraid* of further consequences)
  3. say what you'd like the other person to do to help sort it out
  4. ask for an acknowledgement that the other has understood.

The other party should be helped to listen and show they've understood, then engage in discussion/negotiation about how to solve the problem.

HOW TO GET TECHNOLOGY OUT OF THE BEDROOM

The best way to keep technological items out of bedrooms is never to let them in. If you're not already convinced about the importance of removing screens from bedrooms, read Chapters 8 and 9.

- Make a family rule that no one has any screen in their room. If children already have bedroom screens, plan a campaign to get them out.
- If possible, choose a time when the transition will be easy, e.g. immediately after returning from a holiday when children haven't engaged in much screen-based activity.
- Before removing the screen, plan plenty of activities that your child will enjoy more than sitting alone in the bedroom. See for instance:

  – How to avoid couch potato syndrome, pages 79–80
  – Detoxing family life, pages 172–3
  – How to detox a TV addict, pages 326–7.

- Talk to your child about the fact that the bedroom technology will be removed, and when. Explain clearly why life will be better without it, e.g.:

   – there will be more time for talking, playing, having fun with parents and others
   – the family will be able to share time together (including family viewing)
   – it will help your child sleep better and do better at school.

- Listen to any problems your child voices and respond as positively as possible. But don't get into an argument. If necessary, say you've learned that bedroom technology can be harmful, you love your child and are protecting him/her from harm.
- Keep a 'family' TV and computer in a comfortable family space in the home (see also Introducing children to the Internet, page 323.
- Make sure you have a pleasant bedtime routine in place (see Chapter 3), involving a bedtime story. For older children, you may wish to provide a CD player so they can listen to talking books.
- Place a container at the bottom of the stairs (or similar 'portal' to the sleeping area) and expect *all* family members to deposit *all* handheld devices in it on the way to bed.
- Accept that you and other adults will have to be more selective about screen-based activity when your child is present. Agree strategies for choosing what you'll watch on TV, allow everyone a say and expect everyone to compromise to some extent. As always, adult role models count for a lot.
- When you remove the bedroom screens, ensure you and others are available to talk, play, have fun with your child (for instance, ask friends around to play).
- As time goes on, expect your child to play more independently and need less company – see 'How to encourage creative play' (pages 275–6) and 'How to detox a TV addict' (pages 326–7).

PARENT POWER: GUIDELINES ON TECHNOLOGY AND TALK

Our technological culture has expanded so rapidly that many parents aren't aware of its increasing ill-effects on communication within families. Just as for sleep issues, it would be helpful to have national guidelines delivered through schools and health services, to support parents in promoting children's well-being, for instance:

- the importance of communicating and connecting with children from birth
- how songs, rhymes and moving to music help children's later learning
- why and how to remove TV and other technology from bedrooms
- the importance of developing children's speaking and listening skills in school, as well as literacy skills.

Request such guidelines for your child's school and ask that the Parent Teacher Association lobbies for national guidelines and parent classes about talking and listening to children at all ages.

And when local politicians appear on your doorstep (or inbox) asking for your vote, let them know that it's not just the economy (stupid) that matters, but government support for attachment and attunement between parents and children.

Further reading

Sioban Boyce, *Not Just Talking: Help Your Child Communicate – from Day One* (Not Just Talking, 2014)
Nicola Lathey and Tracey Blake, *Small Talk: Simple Ways to Boost Your Child's Speech and Language* (Pan Macmillan, 2013)
Adele Faber and Elaine Mazlish, *How to Talk So Kids Will Listen and Listen So Kids Will Talk* (Piccadilly Press, 2001)
Sally Ward, *Babytalk* (Century, 2000)

Useful websites

ICAN's 'first stop' website for information on children's
language and communication, aimed at both parents and
professionals: www.talkingpoint.org.uk
Resources from the National Literacy Strategy:
www.talktoyourbaby.org.uk
The ICAN annual campaign: www.chatterboxchallenge.org.uk
Sioban Boyce's website about non-verbal communication: www.
notjusttalking.co.uk
The Scottish Government's website for parents of children ages
zero to three: www.playtalkread.org

Mind the gap

The chorus of concern from teachers in disadvantaged areas about children's level of language competence is now so loud that I could fill this section a hundred times over with their stories. As I was first drafting this chapter, I arrived at a school to address a meeting about 'talking to your child' and I noticed one mother – who didn't attend – sitting in a car outside. She was in the front seat, iPod earphones in place, and her baby was strapped, keening quietly to itself, in the back. But there are also statistics on the subject – some of the most depressing statistics I've ever read.

In the 1990s, two American researchers, Betty Hart and Todd Risley, followed three groups of children through the early years of childhood, from carefully selected 'professional', 'working-class' and 'welfare' families. They regularly tape-recorded hour-long periods of interaction between adults and children in their homes, analysed the findings and extrapolated how many different words the various children had heard, in conversations with adults, by the age of four. On average, it appeared a professional's child has heard around 50 million words, a working-class child 30 million and a welfare child a meagre 12 million. To ram home the alarming difference in language exposure, they found that, by the age of three, the average vocabulary level of professional children was higher than that of the *parents* in the welfare group.

However, Hart and Risley didn't just measure the number of words children heard and spoke. They also recorded differences in the way children were spoken to, and the extent to which parents explained things, gave choices or listened to what they had to say. By the age of three, professional children had heard about 700,000 encouragements and only 80,000 discouragements. In contrast, the welfare child had been encouraged only 60,000 times and discouraged 120,000. Working-class children were somewhere in the middle.

All this backs up teachers' anecdotal evidence about the way parents in poor areas talk to children at the school gate at the end of the day. All too often, instead of a cheerful greeting or enquiry about how the day has gone, the first words these children hear are dismissive and apparently uncaring. When the child presents mum with a picture or something else made in class, it's received not with thanks or praise but with lack of interest or, even worse, a put-down.

Hart and Risley, with their vast experience of parent-child interaction, make it clear the unkindness isn't intentional. These parents love their children just as much as anyone else. They're simply reflecting back their experience of the way people speak to them (disadvantaged parents have seldom received much praise or spoken gratitude themselves, either as children or adults), just as their lack of vocabulary reflects their own impoverished exposure to language.

Right from the earliest stages, attachment is also affected by parents' lack of understanding and personal experience. One mother, asked about how much she talked to her six-month-old child replied she was 'waiting till he talks to me' and another said she *would* like to cuddle her baby but was frightened it would 'spoil' him. It's all too easy to see how children raised in such circumstances become unresponsive themselves, and – if you subscribe to Peter Hobson's theory – fail to acquire the insights that will help them learn once they reach school.

Add to all this the fact that parents at the bottom of the social heap are often so preoccupied with questions of basic survival, it's not surprising that sociable chitchat with a child is an unthinkable waste of time. The constant presence of television and computer games in most homes, as mentioned in Chapter 3's 'Mind the gap', contributes to the problem – why bother talking when technology fills the airways with noise?

Yet poverty does not inevitably lead into a downward cycle of discouragement, impoverished language and failure. Research from thirty years ago suggests that, until social and cultural change began to create barriers between parents and their children, songs, rhymes, cuddles and 'sustained shared thinking' were just as likely to occur in poorer homes as in wealthy ones. (From a personal perspective, I'm sure my own success in the education system was underpinned by the time, love and attention bestowed by my grandmother, who was as poor as a church mouse and barely literate.)

If the technological miracles of the modern world could be rallied to support and inform *all* parents about how real-life interaction enhances children's development (along with the benefits of real food, play and rest), we could break the vicious cycle of social deprivation that undermines our society. But if TV and other technological paraphernalia merely fill homes with noise and distraction, creating an artificial barrier to communication between the generations, the experience of the children at the bottom of the social heap will become ever more toxic.

CHAPTER FIVE

WE ARE FAMILY

The clear message of the previous four chapters is that, for healthy development of body and mind, children need love, stability, attention ... and time. Raising children – even a single child – isn't something you can do in the odd few minutes here and there. Across the animal kingdom, where the young of a species require careful or prolonged rearing, the parents tend to stay together to share the burden – and many species rear their young in packs for extra support. Over the millennia, homo sapiens has developed a similar support system for rearing our young – families, based on parent-child relationships, are supported by their wider community through social, legal and religious frameworks.

The family has had many incarnations over the ages, but the default image for many decades was the nuclear family of the mid-twentieth century (husband, wife, two-point-four children). However, as couples increasingly choose to cohabit rather than marry, and more marriages end in divorce, the stereotypical nuclear family hasn't so much changed as dissolved: the adults who bring up children today may be single or married parents, step-parents, ex-partners, same-sex partners, friends or cohabitees; the children may be siblings, half-siblings or step-siblings; there may also be grandparents, step-grand-parents and a range of other friends and relations that would do justice to Winnie the Pooh's friend Rabbit. This means an infinite number of possible families, each with its own very specific dynamics.

Revolution, relationships and roles

Changes in the way families are structured have necessarily impacted on the way children are reared, and these changes seem at first sight so profound that it's scary. But human beings are flexible creatures who have weathered many revolutions; there's no reason we shouldn't come through this one too. In a 2004 evaluation of the family in Britain for the Gulbenkian Foundation, social scientist Fiona Williams looked on the bright side, towards a future of 'democratic relationships' where partners are bound not by 'obligation and duty' but by independent choice; and in 2011 Dr Katherine Rake, CEO of the Family and Parenting Institute pointed out that 'the modern family is a testament to the rise in tolerance and choice which was not there for generations before.' If these commentators are right, democratic relationships based on tolerance and choice could be just the thing for rearing balanced, civilised children, fit to take their place in a sexually-equal society.

However, as Samantha Callan of the Centre for Social Justice commented in response to Dr Rake's remark, 'The risk of new liberalism is that it may gloss over what some people are experiencing as very real problems' and, according to the research findings in previous chapters, many of these real problems revolve around raising children. At present, millions of disparate contemporary families seem to be trying to sort out the business of twenty-first-century child-rearing from scratch, to fit their own individual circumstances – circumstances which are themselves often subject to sudden change. What's more, they're struggling to do this within the maelstrom of contemporary life, where the rapid pace of change means human beings are constantly running to keep up with machines. Families live – to quote the ancient Chinese curse – in extremely interesting times.

One important driving force of all this social upheaval has been the revolution in the status of women – a revolution that started in the early twentieth century, picked up speed in the 1960s, then accelerated wildly over the last three decades. Aided and abetted by new technology and the media, a majority of women have progressed from helpmates and homemakers to independent earners in not much more than a generation. Sexual equality was inevitable as developed nations embraced a widening ideal of democracy, but it was also inevitable there'd be difficulties of adjustment, especially when it all happened so fast. One of the biggest questions facing all parents today is: how do we define the roles and responsibilities of mothers and fathers within the rapidly-shifting kaleidoscope of the twenty-first-century family?

In the past, for obvious biological reasons, bringing up children was largely 'women's work'. Because they did it at home, unpaid, unsung, along with the cooking and the cleaning, nobody saw child-rearing as particularly important. On the other hand, the father's role was clearly vital. From primitive hunter-gatherer to the archetypal breadwinner of the 1950s, hanging up his hat with a cry of 'Honey, I'm home', he was the protector and provider. His relationship with his children was often distant and centred on the aspect of 'discipline', but his breadwinning work outside the home gave him far greater status in the family than his wife. Whatever you think of the social and economic inequalities in this arrangement, at least roles were relatively clear-cut.

Equality of opportunity and women's increased economic independence blew the traditional roles apart. When there's only one parent in a family, or when both parents are out at work, who is the nurturer and who the provider? As we change the way we view human behaviour and gender differences – men *can* change nappies, women *can* dominate the boardroom – old stereotypes no longer apply. Since the mid-1990s the widespread use of the gender-neutral term 'parenting' has blurred the distinction between motherhood and fatherhood.

As yet, however, there doesn't seem to be a significant move towards genuinely shared parenting – on the whole, twenty-first-century mothers still shoulder the lioness's share of childcare and related domestic responsibilities, often in addition to paid work outside the home. Perhaps a change in terminology isn't enough to wipe out many millennia of cultural evolution, not to mention hormonal differences between the sexes, which have their roots deep in our species' biological inheritance. When couples have a new baby, the vast majority of mothers still feel an extremely powerful urge to care for it, and fathers the need to protect and provide for their families. Interesting times indeed.

The mommy wars

Let's look at mothers first. The opening battles of the mommy wars were fought mainly in the USA during the late twentieth century, but hostilities still linger on across the westernised world and it doesn't seem likely that the guns will fall silent any time soon. Rallying the troops on one side is the women's movement, anxious to consolidate their sex's newfound freedom, especially in term of equal rights in the workplace. Since the 1980s they've gathered increasing support from two unlikely allies – big business and national governments, who quickly worked out that getting women into work meant more consumers, more taxpayers, and a massive boost to corporate profits and national economies.

On the opposite side of the battlefield are champions of the traditional family. They urge a return to 'old-fashioned values' by pleading the case of the child ... and sometimes, as an incidental aside, the return of woman to the home front and the right of man to the role of primary provider. Often the forces of organised religion join in on this side of the debate, making it even more difficult to see the wood for the ideological trees.

In some ways the women's movement has been extremely successful. Most adults reared over the last half-century now take it for granted that the female of the species is just as entitled as the male to participate in the workforce. Women, like men, have therefore come to see their means of earning a living as important to their personal identity and social status, and have used equal access to higher education to make inroads into many previously male-dominated professions. Indeed, by 2011 in the UK, professional women in their twenties were earning slightly more than their male counterparts.

However, this early promise is not maintained. As soon as men and women become mothers and fathers, inequality re-enters the workplace and many new mothers find themselves struggling to adjust not only to the intense demands of childcare, but to the difficulty of fitting these demands into their working lives. The late twentieth-century assumption that working conditions would gradually change to accommodate the domestic needs of sexually-equal adults has turned out to be baseless. On the whole, conditions of paid employment are probably less family-friendly today than they were in the days when Honey stayed at home.

Technological developments, globalisation and the growth of a round-the-clock consumer society have spawned a long-hours culture affecting both men and women. Despite legislation on working hours and lip-service from business-leaders about 'work-life balance', employees often feel obliged to stay at their desks well beyond their official hours of employment ... and, thanks to the wonders of technology, are not even free from work demands at home. What's more, as education systems across the developed world delivered a glut of highly-qualified adults, competition for well-paid high-status jobs has become increasingly fierce – for high-flying women, the prospect of taking time out to raise a family seems extremely hazardous.

In addition, there's now the problem for all parents – well-paid, high-status or not – of ensuring their family has a suitable home to live in: as female earnings helped western economies grow over the last half-century, house prices soared. This causes particular difficulties in the UK where home-ownership is the aspirational norm and obtaining a mortgage for even a modest family home is today predicated on two adult incomes. Women's struggle to maintain their newfound independence in the face of all these developments has also spawned a revolution in childcare practices, now considered by many to be far from optimal for pre-school children (see Chapter 6). It's also an extremely costly business, consuming a great deal of any disposable income families have left after dealing with the rent or mortgage.

Obviously, these developments couldn't have been predicted when the mommy wars first broke out. Nor would 1960s feminists have dreamed that, fifty years on, the cultural and biological factors mentioned at the end of the last section would lead many women to reject the dream of 'having it all'. In fact, research indicates that the majority of mothers are not happy to view motherhood as a brief and insignificant interruption to their working lives. Although fewer than a third of British mothers now stay at home to look after their children, in a 2012 study three-quarters of new mums said they'd do so if they could, and six out of ten explained they'd returned to work only because they had to pay off debt or ease financial pressures. This is almost certainly connected with another survey in 2013, in which 87 per cent of mothers expressed feelings of guilt at having too little time for their children, with a fifth claiming that they felt guilty all or most of the time.

As one mum put it, after giving up her job as a TV features editor to return to the home front: 'I hadn't reckoned with the anxiety, the palpitations, the sheer distress I felt at leaving my year-old baby in the care of someone else.' She was, however, still committed to the ideal of equal opportunities, adding that it would be just as wrong-headed to insist women should stay at home as it is to force them into work: 'Every mother should simply be given the right to choose.'

Mum's the word

This is certainly the opinion of Marie Peacock, chair of the UK pressure group Mothers At Home Matter. She argues that the government's gender-neutral approach to parenting ignores the desire of many mothers to care personally for their children, especially in the pre-school years. Instead, political attention is concentrated on increasing childcare provision so that women can return to the workforce. 'On the one hand policymakers say that the modern choice is "shared parenting" and flexible working for both parents, but on the other hand they claim to champion freedom of choice for families. If they really believe that, they have to accept that choices come in many different guises, often reflecting different circumstances and personal preferences, so they should respect different choices equally, even if they don't agree with them.'

She points out that family taxation, child benefit entitlement and childcare tax allowances are all skewed against the one-wage couple and this, along with media messages suggesting that only working mothers can be 'aspirational' and 'hardworking', influences social norms. The prevailing orthodoxy is that 'the dual-earner model of work and care is preferable to any mother choosing to invest more time in her young children.' Meanwhile, a 2011 research report commissioned by the Labour Party found that 80 per cent of parents questioned would 'in an ideal world' prefer one parent to stay at home with their children. This data was ignored in the party's 2012 policy announcements, which focused – like those of the other main political parties – on affordable childcare. And it's not just in the UK that this is happening: Marie Peacock believes that 'the gender-neutral, women-into-work approach is embedded in international agreements ... worldwide ... UN stuff!' Clearly a significant result for the women's movement.

Psychologist and childhood campaigner, Dr Richard House, agrees with her analysis, describing recent pronouncements from Westminster as 'a toxic Dutch auction between political parties on who can make the best universal childcare offer.' He fears that governmental drives to take parents (generally mothers) out of the home is creating 'a cultural norm which will compromise vital early attachment relationships for young children, and reduce parents' opportunities for learning about the highly complex task of managing family life.'

There's no doubt that, in the first two to three years, secure attachment and interaction with a loving adult is extremely beneficial for children (see Chapter 4). And in recent years attachment theorists have made a powerful case for the knock-on effects of early parent-child relationships as those children grow into adulthood, thus having implications on society as a whole. In her 2010 book *The Selfish Society: How We All Forgot to Love One Another and Made Money Instead*, psychologist Sue Gerhardt explains that: 'the moral and emotional issues we have to deal with as a society are the same as those we begin to grasp in the cradle: how we learn to pay attention to others and their feelings, how we manage conflict and how we balance our own needs with those of others. Morality is about the way we manage the interface between self and society, an interface that starts in babyhood and is learned from the actual practice of early relating. This gives early child-rearing a prime place in our cultural life.'

Since the loving adult who undertakes this early child-rearing is usually the mother, perhaps we should no longer be keeping mum about what this aspect of motherhood involves and its enormous cultural value. Indeed, in the words of psychologist Sammi Timimi, a specialist in children's behavioural disorders, 'the more we've devalued motherhood, the more we need an army of experts to sort out the mess.'

Twenty-first-century mothers

Of course, there's no reason why fathers, or any other loving adults, shouldn't act as primary attachment figures for babies and toddlers. My reason for stressing the significance of motherhood is that a combination of nature and culture still tends to push mothers into the role, and I reckon it's time we all acknowledged the phenomenal contribution to human culture of mothers through the ages. Nor is there any reason why new mums shouldn't hand over the task to a suitable 'mother substitute' if they genuinely believe it would be in the best interest of their babies and themselves.

In his 2010 book *How Not to F*** Them Up*, psychologist Oliver James describes 'Organiser mothers' – often highly-educated women with prestigious careers – who prefer to realise their love for their offspring through organising (and presumably financing) the best possible alternative care. James recommends that the optimal substitute for mum is (a) dad, (b) another family member (very probably grandma), (c) a dedicated nanny or childminder. The point is that, for secure attachment, children need one-on-one, consistent, loving care in the first couple of years. Nursery care is therefore his least preferred option. In twenty-first-century Britain, however, nursery care is increasingly the norm (see Chapter 6).

At the outbreak of the mommy wars, there was little neuro-scientific evidence about the personal and social significance of attachment in young human infants: the cultural spotlight of the time was fixed firmly on women's right to compete with men in the workplace. Our culture has therefore developed in ways that present twenty-first-century women with the mother of all dilemmas. Which should they put first – the biological drive towards motherhood (and the responsibilities this brings in terms of early mothering) or the socio-economic drive towards work and status, in a world where most businesses are un-family-friendly?

There is, of course, no simple answer to the question – it has to be solved by each individual mother, preferably in consultation with her partner (see next section) and in full knowledge of the best childcare options at different stages of development (see Chapter 6). It has, however, become very clear that the twentieth-century feminist dream of 'having it all' is unattainable, except in the case of a few extremely well-heeled and/or fortunate women. The way forward for most twenty-first-century mums must be to find the most personally-satisfying way of 'sharing it all' ... with a partner, other family members, or perhaps other families.

The political journalist (and mother) Gaby Hinsliff makes many useful suggestions for ways of achieving this in her 2012 book, *Half A Wife*. But in the long term, it will require the support of governments, businesses and communities to help the majority of parents find a satisfactory work-family balance. I suspect that support won't be forthcoming without a serious re-evaluation of the significance of motherhood in the early stages of a child's life. Wouldn't it be nice if feminism were to lead the way?

What are fathers for?

Changes for fathers over the last generation have been every bit as profound as those for mothers, and for many men it's been just as confusing. In her 2005 book *The Future of Men*, Marion Salzman recorded that the changes 'appear to be having a negative effect on the male psyche, leaving modern men hesitant, disorientated and, in many cases, more than a little depressed.' Attempts by the media to cheer them up with aspirational images of 'new dads' – generally soft-focused pictures of celebrity fathers, gently cradling their young – haven't met with much success. In the UK, a *New Dad* magazine didn't survive beyond the first edition and similar publications in the USA went belly-up after a couple of issues.

Yet fathers are every bit as essential as mothers in rearing the next generation. There's a growing body of research connecting paternal involvement in child-rearing with educational achievement, social behaviour and long-term mental health. However, in direct contrast to soft-focused media confections, psychologists point out that father-child relationships tend to be rather 'blokeish' – involving lots of joking, teasing, tickling, physical play and shared outdoor interests such as football or camping. Men bounce babies boisterously on their knees, swing toddlers up on to their shoulders, encourage children to ever braver displays on play equipment – often to the horror of their female partners, whose maternal hormones may make them cautious about risk-taking or rough and tumble. By being adventurous in shared play, men encourage their children to be more daring – perhaps fathers' uncertainty about their role helps account for our generally over-protective attitude to children in the early twenty-first century (see Chapter 2)?

Fathers' influence is clearly important for boys – for whom they will always be the most important role model – and many research projects catalogue the problems of boys brought up without the benefit of a father-figure. It's been at various times associated with crime and violence, low income and problems with relationships in adulthood, and the passing on of these problems to the next generation by perpetuating a cycle of fatherlessness. But a man's influence in the home is also important for girls, who – like their brothers – grow in self-esteem by sharing their dad's time and interests (as a daughter who was initiated at the age of eight into the mysteries of cricket, I can personally vouch for the beneficial effect on self-confidence of a father's interest – without it, I doubt I'd have the brass neck to attempt this book).

So, while motherhood usually takes centre stage in the early months and years, a father's natural instinct to protect and provide makes him the best possible secondary attachment figure for a small baby during this time (always remembering that – if it suits mum and dad – the roles can be reversed, or shared equally). The best sort of fathering simply involves ensuring that babies and toddlers get the loving care they need, taking an interest in one's children at all stages of development, spending time in their company, listening, talking and encouraging them to join in with hobbies, interests and everyday domestic chores. In this respect, being a father – like being a mother – is utterly 'natural'. No special skills, qualities or equipment are required, just plenty of time and loving attention.

How technology comes between parents and children

Technology has, however, presented humanity with another hurdle to overcome in the process of rethinking work and family commitments, one that may be more difficult for men than for women. All the prescriptions for successful parenting come back to two key words – time and attention – the two things adults born in the latter part of the twentieth century find it most difficult to spare.

It's not surprising: people reared in an era of labour-saving devices are conditioned to expect simple and instant solutions to domestic issues – food comes pre-packaged, oven-ready and microwavable; machines remove dirt from clothes, carpets and crockery; almost every problem can be solved by turning a dial or flicking a switch. To fill in the time this saves, personalised entertainment is instantly available at all hours of the day and night. For anyone raised in such a quick-fix world, the tiring and often tedious business of looking after small children can seem positively primitive.

At work too, time is of the essence, and the capacity to process information quickly is often highly valued. Working on a computer involves diving in and out of different programs and windows, stopping to deal with phone calls and check emails, juggling a dozen different mental operations a minute. In his book *The New Brain*, neurologist Richard Restak calls attention deficit the 'paradigmatic disorder of our times', as the constant rapid processing of information affects the internal wiring of our brains.

The quick-fire world of modern technology is in direct contrast to the slow process of dealing with biological development. Looking after a small child means putting time on hold to concentrate on his or her human (and, for many adults, often interminable) needs. Playing endless games of peekaboo, telling a favourite bedtime story for the forty-third time, walking slowly through the park with a short-legged infant staggering along beside you, letting your child 'help' wash the car whilst making a sodden mess of the garden borders – all these are in 'slow time'.

If part of one's life demands a degree of attention deficit and the other demands lengthy, time-consuming attention, there is a clear conflict of mental interest. So as well as struggling with new family structures and confusion about their personal role, many contemporary parents find their own attitude to their children deeply perplexing. On the one hand, they love them (nature sees to that – and love for one's children is a particularly deep and powerful love), but on the other, they may find themselves bored and irritated by the business of looking after them.

This phenomenon isn't often mentioned in polite circles, as it seems shameful to dislike spending time with one's children. But if it is a problem, parents must acknowledge, confront and deal with it. Otherwise, another complex emotion enters the familial mix: guilt. And guilt leads to all sorts of strange behaviour (see 'Money can't buy me love', page 199).

For fathers, attention deficit often sets in not long after a baby is born. A harassed new mother may bustle the father away, leaving him feeling sidelined and resentful. Without the benefit of a bodyful of female hormones, he may also be somewhat wary of his muling, puking offspring, and secretly grateful to be let off the hook. Concentrating on breadwinning is a useful displacement activity, and much less messy and confusing than what's going on at home. Unfortunately, once a father has backed off like this, it can be difficult to find a way back into family 'slow time'.

This isn't to say that mothers don't suffer from attention deficit too. As we saw in Chapter 4, even those who've chosen to stay at home are now often distracted from their children by the technological marvels that dominate our lives. And working mothers often find it as difficult as their partners to switch from a work mentality to the tempo of home.

But it's now abundantly clear that if the gap left by preoccupied parents is filled by the fruits of consumer culture, toxic childhood syndrome begins to take hold. Then, as their offspring grow ever more distractible, impulsive, egocentric and difficult to manage, there's an even greater incentive for parents to find alternative, more congenial company. Like sociologist Arlie Russell Hochschild, author of *The Time Bind*, I suspect one explanation for the long hours culture is an unspoken wish on behalf of many parents to escape from bewildering and unfulfilling family life to the 'reliable orderliness, harmony, and managed cheer of work'. Toxic childhood syndrome puts all parents in danger of drifting into the macho workaholism of Japanese salarymen, for whom company culture is often stronger than family ties, and family-friendly legislation has so far made little difference to insane working hours.

Work does indeed provide many obvious and immediate

rewards: social status, mental stimulation, adult company, and of course regular payment, which for most of us is an important measure of our worth. The rewards of raising children are less worldly, there's no salary cheque at the end of the month and you don't know how well you've done until a couple of decades into the job. It's easy to see how contemporary culture lures parents of both sexes into focusing on short-term breadwinning for their children, at the expense of long-term nurturing. But if a family is to flourish, the members of that family have to enjoy each others' company – or the whole thing is likely to fall apart.

Happily ever after?

Sadly, families fall apart rather frequently these days. According to recent research, more than 30 per cent of children in the UK will see their parents separate before they're 14 (the fourth highest number in the Western world). The number of divorces – which rose steadily over the late twentieth century – has more-or-less stabilised, and is falling among younger couples. However, this is probably because, every year, fewer couples get married in the first place. In 2012 the number of adults cohabiting was at its highest since the UK census began, and researchers estimate that by 2016 the majority of children will be born out of wedlock. Worryingly, there is a four times greater chance that these children's parents will split up than there is if mum and dad are married.

Campaigners for 'old-fashioned family values' are anxious to reverse the trends towards both cohabitation and family breakdown. In 2011 Sir Paul Coleridge, a judge in the UK high court's family division, launched The Marriage Foundation to improve public understanding of 'the importance, benefits and nature of marriage, and how healthy married relationships provide the most stable environment in which to raise children.' In an interview with the BBC, he singled out the media as a major factor in the current sorry state of adult relationships: 'What I criticise – what I call the *Hello* magazine, Hollywood approach to the whole business – is that there still is, or maybe more than there once was, a completely unrealistic expectation about long-term relationships and marriage in particular, that if you find the right ideal partner that's all that matters and things will just carry on from there and you will be divinely happy.'

Interestingly, John Baker, another judge in the UK family courts whom I interviewed for the original edition of Toxic Childhood, also suggested that media depictions of family life are causing problems: 'family breakdown – driven by the needs and relationships of the adults involved – has come to be regarded as the norm, to be accepted without criticism by the majority of viewers.' He pointed out that, 'with the honorable exception of Marge and Homer Simpson', we now expect all TV relationships to come under ever more startling pressures until they eventually crumble.

Both these men spend their working lives observing the fall-out from fractured relationships, so their perception that celebrity culture and screen-based entertainment influences young couples' behaviour should be taken seriously. For many decades children have grown up witnessing media coverage of fairy-tale celebrity weddings, and have tuned nightly into soaps, dramas and documentaries focusing on the age-old ingredients of love, desire, jealousy and hate – it's not surprising if these experiences influence their own relationships when they finally reach adulthood. But children in the past were also exposed to fairy-tales and stories of human frailty. There must be some other reason that we no longer expect marriages to end happily ever after...

I must admit to thinking that the main reason for the breakdown of twenty-first-century relationships is that women are no longer economically dependent on the men in their lives. When Father was sole breadwinner and undisputed head of the family, Mother had to bow to his decisions and desires whether she liked it or not; but when both parties in a relationship assume an equal right to self-determination, there are bound to be far more sticking points, and far less compulsion to stay together. As Japanese economist Hiroshi Ono succinctly puts it: 'Lower dependency allows greater voice, and lowers the cost of exiting a marriage'. On the one hand, this means far fewer women are abused, exploited or just taken for granted by high-handed husbands; on the other, both sexes now have to work pretty hard to live happily together in the future.

Breaking up is hard to do

It does, however, seem well worth putting in the effort. The economic cost of leaving a long-term relationship – whether an old-fashioned marriage or a new-fashioned 'cohabitation' – may be affordable for many twenty-first-century women, but the emotional cost to them and their partners is likely to be considerable. And so is the emotional cost to their children, as catalogued in a 2009 report from London University: 'on a range of outcomes, including educational achievement, behaviour, mental health, self-concept, social competence and long-term health there are significant differences between children who experience parental separation compared with children from intact families.'

Parents in the throes of a dying relationship are sometimes so distracted by their own pain that they fail to recognise the extent of their children's suffering. But there's an awful lot for children to cope with. Quite apart from the emotional ordeal of witnessing parental trauma and losing daily contact with one of the defining pillars of their existence, children are often confronted with anxiety-inducing life-changes – maybe a new home, a new school, sharing a house with a parent's new partner ... or even bedrooms with step-siblings or half-siblings. If they end up living with a single parent, it usually means considerably reduced circumstances. For an under-ten, such shifts can be as significant as moving to Mars.

While researching this issue in 2005, I phoned a helpline to ask about advice on minimising the effects of divorce for children. 'Oh, they weather it really well these days,' said the woman brightly. 'It's quite normal really – lots of their friends have gone through it.' When I expressed disbelief, and cited evidence from law journals and transcripts of children's comments, she explained that these were extreme cases: 'Where the divorce is well-managed, children suffer very little. It's just a fact of life for them.'

There is indeed recent research showing that, as family breakdown has become socially acceptable, children seem to suffer less trauma than in the past. However, while it's undoubtedly easier to be one of a crowd than a lone outcast, this doesn't mean the emotional pain of parents' separation is any the less. Apart from anything else, children are powerless in the process – it's mum and dad who are making life-changing decisions and mum and dad are often upset, angry or distracted. Not surprisingly, many children get upset and angry too; others soldier bravely on, to avoid upsetting their parents even more (after all, one of the most important people in the world is leaving home – if they're not careful the other might clear off too).

Primary teachers, being outside the family loop but close to the children, are often more aware of the emotional toll than parents. One told me about a little boy in her class of five-year-olds. 'His dad works nights, so Adam doesn't see him much during the week and he wasn't aware dad had left till a few days after the event. I don't think anyone's really explained. Yesterday I saw him sitting at his desk with two big tears running down his cheeks. He's now absolutely terrified of upsetting me in class – being really good, but in a worrying way – I think he's frightened I'll go too.'

Research also shows that children's insecurity and distress often begins years before the divorce as the parental relationship gradually breaks down. Charlotte, aged 12, gave this interview to a Sunday newspaper: 'Mum and Dad were arguing for ages before they split up: they used to throw things at each other and that made my brother and me frightened and we used to cry ... I think it would have helped if we could have all sat down together and talked about how life was going to be once Dad had moved out, but he and Mum either fought or didn't talk at all ... I really wish we could go back to how it used to be. Everything seemed so easy then, and it all seems so complicated now.'

Children's pain continues if the divorce is acrimonious,

especially if custody becomes an issue: some find themselves being passed back and forth like a parcel, others suffer because of lack of contact with one parent. In the USA, where shared custody is common, air stewardesses are well-used to looking after small passengers winging their lonely way back and forth between parents; in Japan, where shared custody is rare, newspapers are full of lurid tales of abduction. And emotional wounds from childhood often fester for years. Statistics show that children of divorced parents are more likely than others to become depressed, drug or drink-dependent and involved in crime; they're also more likely to have unhappy marriages themselves.

Minimising the trauma

The advice on minimising trauma is fairly obvious (see summary on page 176) and since I originally wrote this chapter a plethora of helpful websites have appeared on the Internet (see page 179). One key aspect is to ensure opportunities for children to talk about what's happening, and listen to their point of view. However, parents aren't always the best listeners – as mentioned earlier, children often fear worrying them further or hurting their feelings. A group of British family law experts observed sadly that 'Some children are only left with "talking to teddy" when things get too much for them.' Children's counsellors may be available – and there are calls around the world for more such services – but formal provision of this kind can look like therapy, shifting the problem away from the parents and on to the children, whose burden becomes even greater. More informal confidants – a trusted school teacher or mentor, non-partisan family friends or relations, or even an anonymous helpline – might be preferable.

Parents are also advised to put their own feelings aside and avoid acrimony for the children's sake. As American psychologist James Kraut puts it: 'It's more important to love your children than it is to hate your ex-spouse.' Sadly, such principles are much easier to list than to follow, especially when the breakdown of the relationship is very painful. It also requires remarkable restraint to ensure that children aren't torn in their allegiances. Not only must both parties resist the temptation to dole out blame, they also have to steer clear of self-justification – one of the hardest things for a bruised human being to achieve. However, if parents can be helped to focus on the present and future needs of their children, it does deflect attention from their own grievances. There is a welcome movement internationally in legal circles to provide conciliation and counselling services rather than the old-fashioned confrontational approach to divorce.

More encouragement in this direction through social pressures could also be helpful to all parties – and the media could play an important part in changing social mores. Their tendency to represent the breakdown of celebrity marriages as a sort of gladiatorial combat takes no account of the significance of the celebrities' roles as parents. If newspapers and broadcasters could report divorces more in sorrow than exhilaration, it would help concentrate everyone's minds on the human costs. Similarly, the producers of soaps, celebrity documentaries and screen drama could more often direct viewers' attention beyond the egos of adult protagonists to the emotional fall-out elsewhere (without, of course, infringing real-life children's privacy or exploiting them in any way). Divorce and separation may be becoming commonplace but breaking up hasn't got any less hard to do.

Once a marriage is over, parents' new relationships often take centre stage. In the throes of a new romantic entanglement, it's again difficult for a parent or a new partner to focus on 'the needs of the children'. But the introduction of another adult into a child's life – let alone a step-parent or ready-made step-family – can be deeply threatening and unsettling. It's an invasion of emotional territory that needs planning with almost military efficiency. Parents who don't think it through, or misjudge children's initial politeness as acceptance, are often amazed at the strength and bitterness of the eventual reaction to their new partner.

There's plenty of detailed advice available to parents on helping children through divorce and remarriage in books and on websites (see page 179), but sadly by the time many people access it, the damage has already begun. When a marriage is crumbling or a new relationship in its infancy, no one can expect to be emotionally balanced. Perhaps the best way to detoxify children's experience would be to ensure parents know how best to mitigate any ill-effects *before* they actually start to happen (see Chapter 10).

Children in the centre

The advice to 'focus on the needs of the children' is not, however, to deny the significance of adult relationships, or indeed the right of every adult to have a life and strive for happiness and self-realisation. Parents shouldn't be focusing on the needs of their children every living minute of the day. Indeed, those who do so run the risk of 'over-parenting'– and flamboyant self-denial can imbue their offspring with a lifetime's guilt or create a self-obsessed little monster. The Swedish psychologist Anna Wahlgren makes a useful distinction when she says children should not be the centre of their parents' world, they should be 'in the centre'.

I love that preposition 'in'. It shows there's room for a number of people and interests in the centre of any adult's life. As long as the focus of attention swivels regularly on to the children and their needs, grown-ups can seek fulfilment for themselves as well as tending to their offspring. The key is finding the right balance – which will change from day to day – and being sensitive to the feelings of children about situations that involve them (not merely assuming they feel what you want them to feel).

These situations usually revolve around family life. If, as seems likely, marriage is of dwindling significance – long-term as an institution or short-term in the case of particular couples – it's the family, in all its contemporary incarnations, that must be preserved and strengthened if children are to thrive. Forging a strong sense of family, with successful child-rearing as its primary purpose, is therefore the major task for twenty-first-century parents.

The key figures in this task, married or not, are biological mothers and fathers. In terms of producing children, this is still the major partnership (and likely to remain so, despite ingenious technological alternatives). But as time goes on, other adults may be pulled into the family circle – most frequently step-parents, but also other family members, friends or employees such as nannies and au pairs (who 'live as family'). There may also be another, over-lapping circle belonging to an ex-partner.

Whatever the mixture, it's critical that all adult members of a family circle (or, after divorce, circles) accept responsibility for children's welfare – putting them in the centre of family life. For a biological parent putting the child's interests in the centre of this circle comes fairly naturally (as it often does for adoptive parents, who have invested a great deal of emotional energy in the quest for a child), but step-parents and other adults can find it more of an effort to focus on children's needs – especially if the children concerned are acting up because they're emotionally disturbed. Anyone taking on the role of 'adult in charge' within a family should think long and hard about it, and prepare themselves well by consulting books, websites or counselling services.

Forging a family

In order to forge a viable family, the 'adults in charge' have to be physically present for a reasonable amount of time every week. This means sorting out their work-life balance (see Chapter 6) so that, even if they work full-time, they still spend plenty of time at home. A snippet of Internet wisdom puts the case rather well: If you died tomorrow, the company that employs you would fill your place within a week or so; your family would miss you forever. (Indeed, in many cases they're missing you already, and toxic childhood is the result.)

All the experts I've met and read on the subject of family welfare and social cohesion condemn the long-hours culture, and commend flexible working practices. Families don't flourish unless their members have time to enjoy each others' company, so it really is time that governments, businesses and individual human beings got their act together on this one – as the political writer Richard Reeves once put it, if our culture is to have a future we need to create 'family-friendly economies, not economy-friendly families'.

When families don't spend enough time in each other's company, special events such as Christmas, one-off celebrations or holidays are often a terrible disappointment. In a 2009 UK survey, 65 per cent of parents said they found family holidays stressful and almost half admitted that they didn't look forward to them, even though these are supposed to be precious opportunities to spend 'quality time' with their children. As social psychologist Pat Spungin says, if parents and children don't spend time together on a regular basis, 'the pressure on everyone to be having a perfect time and the feeling this is a one-off chance can permeate every aspect of the holiday to increase overall stress levels.'

Given that time is available, much of the experts' advice for creating strong families applies to everyone involved, whether they're biologically related or not. For instance, families need to develop their identity as a group, which means shared interests and activities (see the lists on pages 172–3). Adults also need time to bond with children one-on-one – while of course avoiding any suggestion of favouritism between siblings and/or step-siblings.

This one-on-one time doesn't have to be spent doing anything special – indeed, one of the most important parental tasks is to pass on simple life skills to the next generation, just by involving them in day-to-day tasks. The lists on pages 174–5 are a good starting point – let your child watch and chat as you do something; then treat them as a valued apprentice until one day they can do it on their own. There's no rush to achieve, no competition, no prizes – it's just a question of taking your time over the years, gradually initiating your child into adult skills. Involving children in a hobby, sport or other interest can also be fulfilling for both generations. Whether it's sewing or cinema-going, fishing or football, parents who pass on their passions to their children always have a point of communication, even during the difficult years of adolescence.

There's another element of balance here. Spending time with children doesn't mean having to be with them interminably – especially as the children grow older, and their social circle widens. But when adults *are* at home with the family, we should be free to engage with children rather than wishing them out of the way. That means switching off smartphones, ignoring the email, and concentrating on the chosen family activity, or just chatting with and listening to the children. It's shifting from the rapid pace of everyday life to 'slow time', and it's not only good for your family, it's good for your health.

To ensure time spent together is as pleasant an experience as possible, families need carefully formulated policies on issues like discipline, mealtime behaviour, bedtimes, and so on. American researchers Betty Hart and Todd Risley, who analysed forty-two US families over two and a half years concluded that 'what made a family normal was its stable and predictable ways of interacting.' Very young children obviously should have little input into family policies – adults are in charge because they know what's good for them – but as children grow older and wiser, there's room for increased negotiation. At all stages, adults have to agree on a reasonable policy, then keep up a united front (trying never to row in front of the children) and act as role models for the sorts of behaviour they want to see. There's further discussion of 'parenting' in Chapter 10.

For adults who are not biologically related to children in their family, one frequently given piece of advice is to acknowledge the fact that you're not a blood relation. The inevitable step-child's cry of 'You're not my mum/dad!' can be countered immediately with 'You're right. I could never even try to replace your mum/dad. But I'm the adult in charge at the moment, so what I say goes.' Experts generally agree that biological parents should take the lead in discipline, making it clear that other 'adults in charge' are their trusted lieutenants.

Now that many children divide their time between two family homes, it helps if basic rules for behaviour, bedtime and so on are consistent; if they aren't, acceptable boundaries in your own home must be very clearly drawn. Schedules and arrangements for visits are important to children, so it helps if they're easily manageable – if they're not, it behoves adults to put themselves out so children are not let down.

* * *

That is what forging a family is all about: adults putting themselves out so children's developmental needs are met. In the revolutionary whirlwind of the last twenty-five years, the focus has been firmly on the needs of adults – the changes in their roles and the resultant dramas in their relationships. But the quotation from Sue Gerhardt's book on page 155 shows that adults' capacity to form stable relationships depends on what happens to them in childhood, starting with secure attachment.

The family – love it or hate it – is where the grown-up generation forms the generation to come. It's where mothers, fathers and other adults-in-charge develop children's sense of self, security and self-esteem, their ability to get along with other people, their knowledge about life and life skills, and an inner code of conduct to guide and protect them when we're no longer around. So far the human race hasn't come up with any better way of passing on these essential elements of our culture. The family is where, in the words of the old adage, we give our children 'roots to grow and wings to fly'.

DETOXING FAMILY LIFE

- Recognise that, during the pre-school years, child-rearing (and home-making) is not a hobby but a full-time job, and it's at least a half-time job thereafter. If you aren't able to do it, or can only do part of it, you'll need to pay someone else to cover for your absence – see Chapter 6. But the two people most committed to any child's welfare are the parents: take on as much responsibility as possible yourself.
- Break free from the traditional view of low-status nurturing and high-status breadwinning. Rearing children is important, and good childcare will cost you in terms of time and money, however you divide work and care responsibilities with your partner.
- Forging a family is a joint responsibility. Discuss the balance of bread-winning versus child-rearing between yourself and your partner. Keep discussing, and continually adjusting, as circumstances change. Ensure both parents read this list, or compile one of your own.
- Recognise that men and women bring different strengths (and weaknesses) to child-rearing, and children need a balance of both. Learn the art of compromise.
- Recognise the supreme importance of *time* in bringing up children – the younger the child, the more 'slow time' you need. When with your children, find ways of switching from the rapid tempo of daily life into the slower, more natural tempo of child-rearing (e.g. switch off the computer, mobile phone, TV and learn to enjoy their absence).
- Families need to spend time together. Don't let breadwinning activities prevent you from being with your children, for instance:

  – family mealtimes (see Chapter 1)
  – family outings, such as visiting friends and relations, walking the dog, shopping, going to the park, cinema, swimming pool (see Chapter 2)
  – family viewing: sitting down together to watch a favourite TV show or a DVD
  – shared bedtime routines in which mum and dad can take a share (see Chapter 3)

- playing games, such as board or card games, outdoor kick-abouts or digital activities such as Guitar Hero
- family holidays, when you can share new experiences together.

- Try as hard as you can to keep work and family separate, so that work-based stress doesn't overflow into family time.
- Children also sometimes need the exclusive attention of individual parents, for instance:

  - a shared hobby or interest
  - time spent helping with household tasks, car maintenance, gardening, etc. (biting your tongue when the child's 'help' is actually a hindrance)
  - time while travelling (either by foot or in the car) can be a good opportunity to chat – see it as social, not dead time
  - Boys especially need to spend time with their father.

- Time spent with children need not – indeed *should* not – involve spending much money. It should be about:

  - giving children attention and showing an interest in what they say
  - passing on (by example, not in a teacherish way) useful life skills, such as those listed below
  - relaxing and enjoying their company
  - rewarding them with praise for good behaviour
  - modelling the manners and sorts of behaviour you want to see in them

- If you find children's company difficult or personally unrewarding, reading up about child development – and then spotting evidence of your own child's progress – can make it easier to appreciate family time. Parenting courses can also be helpful (see pages 346–7).
- However, ensure there's also time for you and your partner to spend together, for instance:

  - regular evenings out (or in) when the children are looked after by babysitters

– if possible, occasional holidays or weekends away, when the children are catered for elsewhere.

- As well as parents, children benefit hugely from spending time with other family members, such as grandparents, or other adults who know them well.
- In the words of Mary Pipher in *The Shelter of Each Other,* 'love each other while you can'.

TWENTY-FIVE LIFE SKILLS FOR CHILDREN TO LEARN BY THE AGE OF SIX

When you have to do one of the following chores, invite your child to 'help' – let him or her watch as you demonstrate each small stage, then have a go. Give plenty of praise for effort and progress. Next time it crops up, invite your child to help again – and this time do a little more. Give lots more praise. Eventually, you can hand over the task. But don't rush at it – it's not a race, and don't get impatient if your child takes a long time to acquire the skill. Just enjoy the opportunity to spend time together.

Make the bed	Put toys away
Help at the shops	Sort out and put away shopping
Put away own clothes	Set and clear the table
Use a brush and dustpan	Clean a mirror or window
Wash the car (very basically!)	Tidy a room
Use a potato peeler	Chop up vegetables
Sort the recycling	Wash up or fill and empty the
Grow a plant	dishwasher
Send a mobile text	Look after a pet
Help weed a garden	Post a letter
Telephone friends or family	Put flowers in water
Help write a card or simple letter	Answer the phone/take a simple message

Know simple first aid (e.g. cuts, grazes, burns)
Contact the emergency services (don't demonstrate this unless you have to!)

TWENTY MORE LIFE SKILLS FOR CHILDREN TO LEARN BY THE AGE OF TWELVE

Introduce these skills in the same way. Treat teaching the skill as an opportunity to spend pleasant time together, and don't have any expectations about how quickly your child will learn it. Each subsequent time it crops up, be prepared to go back to the beginning if necessary – patience is of the essence. The more lavish you are with praise, the quicker s/he will pick it up. And the more likely you are to have a willing helper in the future.

Make hot drinks

Defrost a fridge

Cook simple meals

Put out the rubbish

Use a vacuum cleaner

Iron a shirt

Clean and dress a wound

Sew on a button

Mow a lawn

Change a fuse

Clean a cooker hob

Take proper phone messages

Handwash clothes

Make conversation with a guest

Unblock a sink

Sort out and put away washing

Use public transport

Go shopping (with a list)

Change the bed

Check a car's oil and water

Tidy up a computer desktop

Get rid of spam

Wire a three-pin plug

Use the local library

Change a plug

Use a washing machine

Use a search engine to find information

Paint a wall, fence or similar

Use hammer, screwdriver, drill, etc. for DIY or home maintenance

Find addresses/phone numbers using phone book, Internet, 118 numbers

Download tunes or programs from the Internet (abiding by safety rules)

Find the way home on foot in the local area (with map or A to Z)

Program the satnav and give directions in the car using a map

Look after a younger child (with adult help available if needed)

HOW TO MAKE BREAK-UPS AS PAINLESS AS POSSIBLE

- The two most important people in a child's life are its parents. If at all possible, it's best that parents stay together – so if your partnership falters, take action to mend it sooner rather than later. That means talking over problems and seeking help – books, websites, counselling services.
- If the partnership can't be mended, do everything you can to protect your children from the adverse effects of family breakdown, for instance:

  – make sure you're fully informed about the pitfalls through books, websites, etc. and try to plan ahead (see lists below)
  – ensure children know that, even if you are quarrelling, you both have their interests at heart, you both love them, and will make sure they're OK
  – keep talking and listening to your children, and help them find other trusted adults in whom they can confide their concerns (e.g. other family members, a favourite teacher or youth worker, a specialist phone helpline)
  – ensure children can feel positive towards both parents, and don't have to take sides.

- Try to ensure custody and visiting arrangements are manageable and take children's wishes into consideration. If possible, arrange to be consistent on issues such as bedtime, diet and behaviour.
- If you're a single parent, seek out trusted friends or relations to help you rear your children, especially male role models for boys. These should be long-term, constant relationships – not threatened by romantic entanglements.
- If you're a single parent embarking on a new relationship, take great care about introducing your new partner to your children. Discuss the issues with your new partner, and consult expert advice through books and websites. Beware! This issue is riven with difficulty.
- If you're about to become a step-parent, seek education! Step-parenting comes even less naturally than twenty-first-century parenting.

BEING AN ADULT-IN-CHARGE: SOME THINGS TO TALK TO A PARTNER ABOUT

Talk to your partner about important issues in your relationship and negotiate solutions that suit you both as far as possible before they become an issue. In terms of children, this could involve:

- how many you both want, and when
- how you feel about childcare (see pages 205–7)
- how *both* parents can make time to give children plenty of attention – around the house, in outdoor activities, at mealtimes, at bedtime
- how work patterns can be changed to ensure more family time
- ways to ensure you don't fall into 'default activities' during family time, e.g. checking email or chatting on the mobile, reading the paper or a magazine, watching TV – the sort of things that 'expand to fill the given space', but also cut you off from contact with others around you
- your expectations of your child's behaviour at each stage in development (this needs constant renegotiation as behaviour changes)
- your beliefs about right and wrong, and how you'll help your children understand these, including what to do when they step out of line (see Chapter 10)
- the sorts of regular routines and procedures you'll adopt (e.g. mealtimes, bedtimes) and how they'll be supervised
- how to distribute the chores of child-rearing on a daily basis, e.g. dealing with crying, nappy-changing, clearing up messes, organising school clothes and equipment, supervising behaviour management, etc.
- how to ensure that each week you get:

  – some individual 'private time' to pursue your own interests or see friends
  – some time together, without the children.

PARENT POWER: THE FAMILY IN THE CENTRE

Just as children must be in the centre of the family, families should be in the centre of public policy. A major function of civilised societies was to protect the interests of law-abiding families, but in recent years politicians have often concentrated on promoting economic growth and individual human rights, leaving families to sort themselves out. It's therefore up to parents to ensure that the needs of the family are returned to the heart of policy by demanding that their elected representatives work for:

- a family-friendly economy, rather than economy-friendly families
- legislation rather than lip service to protect work-life balance
- support for parents and adults-in-charge (see other 'Parent Power' sections throughout this book), rather than disempowering them by over-officious professional intervention
- public policy that supports healthy practices including choice in the early years between home-based and out-of-home childcare.

However, politicians are remarkably good at converting human ideals into mind-numbing bureaucracy, as the next two chapters show. As the social revolutionary dust settles and families become politically sexy again, the real challenge for Parent Power is to keep them on track...

Further reading

Lawrence J Cohen, *Playful Parenting* (Ballantine Books, 2001)

Anna Wahlgren, *For the Love of Children* (Forlag Anna Wahlgren, 2009)

Jane Fearnley-Whittingstall, *The Good Granny Guide* (Short Books, 2005)

Carl Honore, *Under Pressure: Rescuing Our Children from the Culture of Hyperparenting* (Orion, 2008)

Noel Janis-Norton, *Calmer, Easier, Happier Parenting* (Plume Books, 2013)

Gaby Hinsliffe, *Half a Wife: The Working Family's Guide to Getting a Life Back* (Chatto and Windus, 2012)

Paula Hall, *How to Have a Healthy Divorce – A Relate Guide* (Vermilion, 2008)

Karen and Nick Woodall, *Putting Children First – A Handbook for Separated Parents* (Piatkus, 2007)

Useful websites

Family Lives: A national family support charity, supporting all aspects of family life. www.familylives.org

Mumsnet: UK-based information and community network for mothers. www.mumsnet.com

Mothers at Home Matter: www.mothersathomematter.co.uk

The Fatherhood Institute: The UK's 'fatherhood think-and-do tank'. www.fatherhoodinstitute.org

Home Start: a well-established national charity which helps community volunteers to provide support and friendship for families (with the motto 'Reach the family, reach the child'). www.home-start.org.uk

Relate: Family and relationship counselling. www.relate.org.uk

National Family Mediation: Practical non-confrontational advice/ mediation service for all members of families involved in family breakdown. www.nfm.org.uk

Divorce Aid: Independent organisation of professionals giving divorce advice. www.divorceaid.co.uk

Help Guide: US-based non-profit resource, offering wide-ranging advice, including helpful advice on children and divorce. www.helpguide.org

Mind the gap

The influence of family circumstances seems to be paramount in terms of the widening gap between rich and poor. If you're born into a poor family you're far more likely to have lower educational achievement, lower life-long earnings and more relationship problems than folks who live higher up the hill. You're also more likely to have physical and mental health problems, including depression and substance abuse. This means that, when you have children yourself, the cycle of poverty and disadvantage rolls on again ...

It's been clear for many centuries that poverty can have profound effects on physical health, but until very recently there's been doubt as to whether it also causes mental health problems, or whether mental health problems cause poverty. Most social intervention projects have had relatively small effects: for instance, despite throwing large amounts of money at child poverty for fourteen years (Sure Start, various educational changes, parenting programmes and so on) the Labour government of 1997-2011 made very little impact – indeed, the UK poverty gap widened steadily over the period.

The exception to this rule seems to be projects that *empower* disadvantaged parents, rather than deskilling them by handing over the care of their children to professionals. For instance, the long-term success in the USA of Professor David Old's Nurse-Family Partnership (and early indications of improved outcomes since it was imported into the UK, where it's called the Family-Nurse Partnership – see page 125) seems due to the fact that mums choose whether or not to participate and the support provided is intensely personal. The role of Old's nurses is to 'mother the mother', giving practical help when needed and modelling the mothering role. This appears to improve the young mums' self-image and self-belief, helping them hope for a better life for their offspring.

Another example of the effectiveness of parental empowerment was recently spotted in the USA, as the unexpected consequence of a profit-sharing scheme among a community of Cherokee Indians. They shared out the proceeds of a new casino on their land equally among the families who lived there, to spend as they wished. Over time, the number of emotional and behavioural problems among poorer children declined significantly. Indeed, where parents received the cash handouts when their children were very small, they were no more likely to have such problems than the offspring of well-heeled families.

A researcher observed that, when parents were freed from the multiple stresses of poverty, the quality of their interactions with their children improved. In the words of Moises Velasquez Manov, the science writer who reported this story in the *New York Times*, 'Early life poverty may harm, in part, by warping and eroding the bonds between child and care-givers that are important for healthy development.'

If we want to close the poverty gap, sensitive support for the families of young children seems one of the best ways to do it. The best evidence for this comes from the Scandinavian countries, which have a long tradition of enlightened social provision. Finland, for instance, has one of the smallest gaps between rich and poor in in Europe. It also has the highest level of literacy, high levels of childhood well-being and – as those children grow up – the lowest prison population. Interestingly, Finland is also top of the Organisation for Economic Co-operation and Development's (OECD) league for avoiding family breakdown: while only 68.9 per cent of UK families are together by their child's fourteenth birthday, 95.2 per cent of Finnish families have stayed the course. When I interviewed a Finnish politician on the subject, he claimed that concentration of resources at the beginning of children's lives is critical to his country's social success.

For instance, all new Finnish parents are entitled to a large cardboard box containing items such as nappies, babygros, outdoor gear, a sleeping bag and a small mattress (the box is designed to double as a cot for the early months). The only condition is that mum must register for prenatal care by the fourth month of her pregnancy – this way, the health authorities can ensure that all new parents are well-informed about child development, in the same way as the mums in the Family-Nurse Partnership, through personal contact. Then the state pays them a home care allowance until their child is three so that one parent – usually mum – can be a full-time carer. (For those who prefer to work, there's the alternative of a daycare allowance, and well-resourced state daycare facilities.)

All this is expensive in terms of tax, of course, but the Finns are doing very well at reducing the poverty gap, and the social rewards of that are manifold. There's more about Finnish childcare and education systems in the next two chapters, but a critical factor in their success story is clearly the empowerment of families to provide the best possible care for their tiny children.

CHAPTER SIX

WHO'S LOOKING AFTER THE CHILDREN?

However long the mommy wars rumble on, there's little doubt the results of our cultural revolution are here to stay. Family structures have changed, and working mothers are increasingly the norm: in the developed world, around 60 per cent of women over sixteen years of age are now in the workforce. In 2013 figures ranged between 78 per cent (Iceland) and 42 per cent (Greece) – in the USA it was 62 per cent and in the UK 68 per cent.

But just as mothers in their millions started streaming out to work, science began to recognise the huge contribution they'd been making in the home over all those centuries. Neuroscientists tell us that around 75 per cent of children's brain growth happens in the first three years of life, and neural networks continue to develop at an astounding rate throughout childhood, especially in the areas of the prefrontal cortex associated with focused concentration, planning, self-control and empathy. The transformation from helpless babe-in-arms to civilised member of society is clearly influenced by what happens to children in these pre-teenage years. So one of the biggest questions we all have to ask – as parents, and collectively as a society – is: who will do the child-rearing when both parents are out at work?

Childcare and education

Of course, for well over a century parents have enjoyed around six hours of free childcare every weekday, thanks to compulsory education systems which also contribute to the civilization process. Education is not, however, the same as care. School systems are primarily designed to transmit a body of cultural knowledge rather than to nurture children's overall development (in which cognitive development is integrally intertwined with physical, emotional and social factors). While most primary schools also try to provide a warm nurturing environment, especially in the first couple of years, the wider developmental needs of pupils are necessarily accorded less attention than academic progress (see Chapter 7). This chapter is concerned not with education, but with the way we care for children before they start formal schooling, and thereafter at weekends, during school holidays and around the edges of every school day.

There are two ways to approach the question of non-parental childcare. You can concentrate on the children's point of view, considering what they need from adult carers at different ages and stages. Or you can concern yourself with the economic and social requirements of adult society, finding ways of keeping children out of harm's way so their parents can go to work. After many years of monitoring the international literature on the subject, it seems to me the success of any state-based approach to childcare depends upon how far politicians are interested in (and informed about) the first perspective as well as the second.

The countries that seem to make the best fist of it are those with a long tradition of working mothers and a commitment to social provision. Some parts of mainland Europe have well-established, child-friendly systems of childcare, funded by a combination of taxes and parental contributions. For instance, the OECD described Finland's system (see also page 181 and 211) as 'a continuum of support for parents until children are in their teens ... flexible parental leave, high quality childcare and reduced

working hours for parents of young children'. Having shouldered
the burden of childcare for many decades, the Finns recognise 'the
invisible curriculum of child-rearing', and are prepared to invest
money in getting it right.

On the other hand, in countries where, until comparatively
recently, most mothers stayed at home (at least if they could afford
to), there tends to be a hotchpotch of provision, of variable quality.
The UK and USA fit firmly into this category. When British and
American women suddenly moved wholesale into the workforce in
the closing decades of the last century, state and private childcare
facilities began to expand at breakneck speed – sometimes in
breathtakingly inappropriate buildings, staffed by carers with negligible qualifications. In the UK this expansion was swiftly followed
by reams of government regulations to ensure that children weren't
'at risk' in their new out-of-home 'settings'. Since the regulations were also cobbled together rather quickly, they've required
frequent revision; and, since politicians find it very difficult to
discriminate between education and care, they often focus on
children's long-term academic prospects, rather than their social
and emotional development.

For love or money?

This isn't to deny the political and economic significance of
childcare. Most modern women *want* to return to paid employment
– at least when their children reach school age – and the female
half of the workforce has just as significant a contribution to
make as the male half. Childcare is also necessary to help solve
the economic time-bomb of falling birth rates: forced to choose
between career and family, some women – particularly highly
educated ones – choose not to have children at all. In Germany,
where the indigenous birthrate problem is particularly acute and
the hotchpotch of childcare facilities particularly confusing, many
women consider childlessness preferable to the choice between
being a *Rabenmutter* ('raven mother' who pushes her children out

of the nest in order to go to work) and a *Heimchen am Herd* (old-fashioned stay-at-home little woman).

In the UK, childcare has apparently delivered a positive double whammy in the case of thousands of single mothers from disadvantaged homes whom social revolution left cluttering up state benefits systems. Politicians soon worked out that, as well as helping these mums make the wondrous transformation from drain-on-the-public-purse to valued taxpayer, it brought their children under the care of the state during the working day. Just as their nineteenth-century counterparts spotted how universal education could remove poor children from the streets and help a few escape from poverty, early twenty-first-century policy-makers welcomed universal childcare as a way of addressing early deprivation, which science now recognises as a major contributor to the yawning educational gap between the children of the poor and everyone else.

This, however, is where politicians need some understanding of what successful child-rearing actually involves. Just removing children from their homes into childcare settings won't necessarily improve their life chances – the childcare setting has to be well-resourced with trained staff who know what they're doing. In successful countries, qualifications for childcare workers are often of a high level (in Finland, for instance, you need a masters degree to teach nursery children), and long-term investment means buildings and equipment are of a high standard. On the whole, the experience of the Scandinavian countries in general bears out the research that early input pays off – there's less ingrained poverty because, over the years, children from all types of backgrounds have benefited from social and educational provision to close the poverty gap.

Sadly, countries fixated on economic and educational considerations are unlikely duplicate this success. If politicians pay scant attention to children's needs and everyone continues to see child-rearing as something anyone can do (something we expect to 'happen naturally') there's little chance of raising taxes to pay for it. Britain at present leads the world in efforts to provide pre-school education and 'wrap-around' childcare for all ages on the cheap. Promises of free nursery places for the youngest children and 'wrap-around' childcare for older ones are based on the cheapest option available: maximising the use of school buildings, and using low-qualified or even unqualified staff.

Parents deciding how best to provide for their children need to bear these political and economic factors in mind. In market-driven childcare, as in just about everything else these days, you tend to get what you pay for, and the better qualified the people who look after your children, the more likely they'll look after them well.

The hot-housing rat race

On the other hand, there's also a danger of paying through the nose for dubious advantages. One famous neuroscientific experiment of the 1980s showed that rats raised in interesting, stimulating environments grew up smarter than those reared in conditions of abject boredom. Among some highly competitive parents, this fed an already established appetite for 'hot housing' – providing ever greater stimulation for children from as early as possible in an attempt to enhance and accelerate their development.

There are now private nurseries in the United States where two- and three-year-olds are crammed to bursting point with supposedly brain-enriching 'sensory stimulation', and others offering courses for the under-threes in languages, mathematics, logic and music. And around the world there are CDs, videos, clubs and courses offering early enrichment in everything under the sun. Parents who want to rear the next Mozart, Picasso or Andy Murray need only to hand over their hard-earned cash and wait for a decade or so to see if it works.

In fact, it's likely that pressure to achieve too much too soon does more harm than good. There are many tales of hot-housed children who failed to live up to their potential, and others whose eventual success was offset by emotional turmoil or social ineptitude.

Researchers in Montreal in 2005 found 'maternal investment in educational performance' to be 'significantly negatively related to social adjustment' – in other words, the pushier the parents, the more likely their child is to be an unpopular social misfit.

Neither is there any actual scientific evidence that hyper-stimulation creates brighter babies. The environments that bred smart rats in the experiment were, in fact, very like a rat's normal habitat (sewers are actually quite busy and exciting places). What the experiment established was that lack of *normal* stimulation breeds dull, miserable rats. According to US neuroscientist Steve Petersen, the message to parents is simply, 'don't raise your children in a closet, starve them, or hit them over the head with a frying pan'. More temperately, a summary of research by UK psychologists Sarah Blakemore and Uta Frith points out that, while deprivation is definitely bad for the brain, 'hyper-enrichment' doesn't appear to be particularly good for it, and the input children need in the first few years 'is readily available in normal environments'. For young children the most successful normal environment is, of course, a happy family home.

Home sweet home

For the first year or so of a child's life, familiar faces and setting are of paramount importance. This is when attachment (and the loving attunement of a carer) is critical, when calming, sleeping and eating habits are established, and when the process of learning to communicate begins. The opinion of all the developmental and childcare experts I met was that – if at all possible – personal care in the family home is the best option, at least for the first eighteen months, and probably the first two to three years.

As described in Chapter 5, however, for some parents the financial implications of taking time off work may be insuperable. Other parents discover they can't cope with the change in lifestyle – education and work experience has distanced them so far from the domestic sphere that full-time childcare, with no other adults around, plunges them into depression. As one who struggled with this problem myself, I know it's not lack of love that causes it, but the conflict between deep parental love and a desperate need to preserve one's sense of self. A mother tussling with personal mental instability is in no condition to tend to a baby's needs.

After fifteen years of research into childhood and child development, I'm convinced that more information for all adults about attachment and attuned parenting, and its immense social importance, would help solve many of these problems (see Chapter 10). Until this information is widely available, however, all parents can do is work out how best to keep financial or mental meltdown at bay while still spending as much time as possible with their offspring. Part-time work, job-sharing, working from home or arranging flexible hours are much better than disappearing from a child's life almost completely. To fend off depression, the Internet has made it increasingly possible to find sources of adult company and intellectual stimulation through local parents' groups and children's activities (see Chapter 4). An emphasis on home and family in the early years doesn't mean children should be closeted away: babies and toddlers need daily doses of fresh air, as well as opportunities to mingle with other children, which help build immunity to childhood diseases.

From the age of about three, research is clear that children benefit from a widening of horizons, taking them away from home and family for gradually lengthening periods, and leading into increasingly structured sorts of learning. The older the child, the more time they're usually happy to spend away from home – and the more good it can do them. But even then, there's plenty of time at either end of a busy day when home and family remain important to children's development – family meals, bedtime routines, shared talk and activities continue to be important into the teenage years.

Personal versus institutional care

When parents can't be at home, one answer is to employ a sub-stitute carer for all or part of the day. Alternatives range from live-in nannies (very expensive but hopefully well qualified), through registered child-minders (less expensive and usually in their home not yours – but generally good quality care) to unqualified minders or au pairs (you may be lucky, but you never know). A relative is sometimes happy to take on the role and a 2013 survey suggested that three-quarters of UK grandparents now provide cover for their working children for, on average, just over eight hours a week – an increase of around 60 per cent over the previous five years.

One problem with using substitute carers is that parents may find themselves struggling with jealousy if the carer is a hit with their offspring, or panic-stricken with worry if the child seems less than happy. The need to nurture one's own child is a deep one, taking many contemporary parents by surprise and sometimes leading to exaggerated emotional reactions. When grandparents lend a hand, there may also be generational differences relating to aspects of care or expectations about children's behaviour. However, on something as important as looking after a beloved infant, it's essential that everyone involved likes and trusts one another, so if jealousy or anxiety occur, they should be confronted and dealt with as soon as possible, and if a child is genuinely unhappy it's obviously essential to find out why and take immediate action. It's also essential that all carers talk through any problems and agree on domestic routines and behaviour management – otherwise, even very young children will find it easy to play off one half of their caring community against the other.

These problems mean that many parents instead choose insti-tutional childcare – day nurseries for babies and toddlers, 'wrap-around care' for pre-schoolers and primary-age children, and 'kids clubs' to cover during school holidays. These often seem a safer option – the centres are regularly inspected, plenty of staff mean checks and balances, you don't have to share your home with them, and they're not likely to disappear suddenly and let you down. It also works out cheaper than high-quality paid care in the home, and there's no problem about hymn-sheet sharing – here the rules are written for you, and if your own system is slightly different, it doesn't matter so much because a daycare centre is a very different environment.

As institutions are much easier to control and regulate than individual personal care, they are also preferred by politicians so the emphasis in provision of universal childcare (see pages 153–155, 183) has been on increasing the number of places available in formal settings. Indeed, over the last decade institutional childcare has become the norm for working parents – British children now spend more time in formal childcare settings than in other non-parental care. The great question is: how far can an institution duplicate the security and stability of home and the sensitive, personal, human engagement of a single familiar carer?

Birth to three: the great daycare controversy

The younger the child, the more pressing that question is. A good day nursery for very young children tries to duplicate home and family as far as possible, providing a named qualified carer with whom the parents are in regular contact, a low adult-child ratio and a comfortable domestic atmosphere. But parents can't always find (or afford) high-quality provision, and there's a niggling body of research suggesting that institutional care for the under-threes may cause damage in the long-run.

In 2000, two of America's most highly-respected child development experts, Drs Stanley Greenspan and T. Berry Brazelton published a book called *The Irreducible Needs of Young Children*, in which they argued that the most irreducible and important need of all is 'the need for ongoing nurturing relationships'. They also questioned whether 'institutional love' in the early stages can possibly substitute for personal care within the family, and suggested a possible link between early daycare and the explosion in US children's behavioural and mental health problems since institutionalising very young children became widely accepted.

Despite attempts by the pro-day-nursery lobby to counter these arguments, they won't go away. Researchers have found that babies and toddlers in daycare generally have higher levels of the stress hormone cortisol than those cared for at home, which many believe can have a long-term effect on their ability to regulate behaviour. A 2013 study led by Professor Alan Stein of Oxford University's Department of Child and Adolescent Psychology recorded 'children who spent more time in group care, mainly nursery care, were more likely to have behavioural problems, particularly hyperactivity.' An earlier research project found that the risk of problems increases after forty or more institutional hours a week – not unusual if parents are in full-time employment.

On the other hand, there's also clear evidence – much vaunted by government agencies – that children (especially those from disadvantaged backgrounds) benefit educationally from pre-school childcare, at least in the short term. These educational advantages are emphasised by advocates of day nurseries: the Daycare Trust, for example, states on its website that 'early years education benefits children's learning, improves their self-confidence and relationships, and can help break cycles of poverty'. These findings have influenced the drive towards the normalisation of institutional care.

However, most of the research cited in this way relates to pre-school care in general – that is, from birth to the age of six. There's a huge difference between a six-year-old and a three-year-old, and an even greater difference between a three-year-old and a baby. Professor Kathy Sylva, who's been working in this area for several decades and is convinced of the educational value of nursery schooling, has concluded that there's no problem in putting children of three and over into full-time nursery care, but says that between two and three the research is 'mixed' and below the age of two there are 'some serious and valid concerns'.

Over recent years, child development experts around the world have become increasingly vocal about these concerns. The advice of UK psychologist Oliver James has already been outlined on pages 155–6, while the childcare guru Penelope Leach recently said that 'I wouldn't recommend group care in a nursery, certainly for under-twos. I think that there are two-to-threes who are ready, and whose attachment relationships at home are secure enough that they can cope with being away, but again I think it does depend on hours.' Steve Biddulph, Australia's respected childcare expert goes much further: in his book *Raising Babies: Should the Under-threes Go to Nursery?*' he warns that current policies are creating 'a colder, sadder, more stressed and aggressive generation of children' and that 'quality nursery care for young children doesn't exist. It is a fantasy of the glossy magazines.'

My own conclusion after reviewing the huge body of international evidence is that 'East, West, home's best': the sweetest place for a baby or toddler is at home, enjoying the constant, consistent loving attention of a parent or a parent substitute. However, that does assume that the home is a safe and supportive one and that the adult concerned is in a fit state to look after a small child – if not, high-quality 'institutional love' may indeed be preferable. As always in matters of child development, there's no one-size-fits-all solution, the age of the child and the number of hours spent away from home are always significant ... and public policy on 'universal childcare' *should* be taking all these factors into account.

Three to six: the quest for quality pre-school provision

Once children are three, another controversy raises its head: do three- to six-year-olds benefit from a 'child-centred' approach to learning or an early start on more formal education? I've defined the pre-school stage as 'three to six' because around the world three is the age at which nursery education begins (except in France where the Écoles Maternelles start at two) and, internationally, six is by far the most common age for starting formal schooling: almost two-thirds of countries send children to school at that age,

22 per cent at seven, and only 12 per cent (including the UK) at five*.

Early years specialists are universally keen on child-centred methods (where learning arises out of children's play and their natural interests), while non-specialists and politicians often want to crack on with something that looks a lot more like school. Parents tend to be in two minds: on the one hand, they want their children to be happy and small children seem happiest when playing; on the other they're fearful that wasting time on play could mean their offspring is 'left behind' in a competitive educational culture. So what exactly is high-quality pre-school provision?

In countries with a long tradition of pre-school education, such as the Scandinavian countries, Italy, Belgium and Switzerland, a child-centred approach is the norm. Informal play, talk, stories, song, making pictures and models take centre stage (interspersed with *oral* adult-directed activities to develop listening skills, language, understanding of numbers and so on). There's also emphasis on the importance of playing outdoors and learning from nature, and more formal, pencil-and-paper approaches to learning are left until the primary school years. This doesn't mean that children are 'held back' – those who show an interest in reading, writing, numbers and so on are encouraged and supported as they would be in a loving family home; they're just not forced to learn literacy and numeracy skills if they don't show an interest, or taught these subjects formally as a class.

However, in highly competitive countries (such as the USA, UK and Japan), where education systems are driven by tests, targets and concern about literacy standards, children under six are expected to press on as soon as possible with the three Rs of reading,

---

* The UK's early start actually has nothing to do with education. When the English state school system began in 1870, the starting age was set at five for two reasons: first, to get the poorest children out of their homes and off the streets as early as possible; second, because the sooner education started, the sooner it would finish – so the now-educated children of the poor could enter gainful employment. Other UK countries, and a few colonies like New Zealand and Malta, simply followed suit.

writing and reckoning. This is particularly noticeable in the USA and UK. In England, for instance, ever since the 1990s, when it became politically expedient to offer one year's free pre-school education, most four-year-olds have simply been shipped straight into primary school, and their introduction to the three Rs now effectively begins at four. This would be considered unthinkable in many parts of the world: I've heard teachers in several European countries condemn the English system as 'cruel', and a Dutch headmaster simply laughed and said 'Here on the mainland, we educators think you Anglo-Saxons are mad.'

There's particular concern about the long-term effects of this early start on three specific groups of children: those from disadvantaged homes, who often have poor communication skills and need time to develop language and listening skills before pressing on with literacy; boys, who tend to be generally slower in terms of overall development than girls; and summer-born children, who are younger and therefore less mature than their classmates.

The English 'Early Years Foundation Stage' (EYFS) introduced in 2008, expects all children, regardless of social background, gender or birth-date, to master many basic literacy and numeracy skills 'by five'. And the EYFS has the force of law so all paid carers – including childminders – have been subject to this 'schoolifying' influence. (Indeed in the years after its introduction, many talented childminders chose to leave the profession rather than, as one sorrowfully put it, 'acting more like teachers than carers').

In the 2010 book *Too Much Too Soon*, psychologist and childhood campaigner Dr Richard House pulled together evidence from educators, parents, childcare professionals and academics arguing that 'schoolification' is potentially damaging for young children in terms of their overall development, while providing no long-term educational advantages.

Too much too soon?

Wendy Ellyatt, CEO of Save Childhood, which in 2013 launched a 'Too Much Too Soon' campaign, admits that there is much that is admirable about the EYFS in terms of care provision, but expresses deep concern about its emphasis on age-related 'outcomes', especially the goals for literacy and numeracy. She believes they set up expectations in practitioners (nursery workers and teachers) which change their relationship with the children: 'If the adult has an agenda – to achieve the outcome – it becomes not-so-subtle manipulation. There's then a real danger that we pressurize children to achieve goals and outcomes at the expense of their disposition to learn. If you ask children to read, write or count before they're developmentally ready, they may do it, but they probably won't enjoy it – and that can have disastrous results further down the line. We need much more research on the long-term results of early, developmentally-inappropriate practice.'

She points to the very different ethos of Scandinavian and Dutch early years practice, where the emphasis up to the age of six or seven is on social engagement as opposed to cognitive achievement. Children in these countries have far higher levels of overall well-being than in the UK, and also do better in international league tables of achievement in literacy and numeracy. In fact, since the introduction of the EYFS, the UK has slipped steadily down these tables (see also Chapter 7).

Indeed, the overall message of international research and practice seems to be that 'too much too soon' is yet another ingredient in toxic childhood syndrome and in recent years there have been calls to raise the UK school starting age, not least from the largest and widest-ranging educational review for forty years, *The Cambridge Primary Review*. Politicians have, however, preferred to take a directly opposite approach, and in 2014 there were calls from government ministers – supported by the head of Ofsted (the Office for Standards in Education) – to put two-year-olds in school-based nurseries, with an emphasis on structured learning.

Wendy Ellyatt believes that the high level of well-being enjoyed by Dutch and Scandiavian children is every bit as significant as educational achievement: 'Their nurseries concentrate on providing the sort of environment that nurtures the whole child. It's overall development we should be measuring, not just one limited aspect. In the twenty-first century we'll need adults who have a range of skills – not just academic ones – resilient, adaptive, forward-thinking, creative people. It's great to have investment in early years, but the sort of investment we're getting in the UK comes at too high a price.'

This controversy looks set to continue and intensify as time goes on, providing UK parents with further dilemmas in choosing the best type of pre-school care. What's more, however satisfied they are with their choice of provision, children's entitlement to free pre-school places are usually for only a few hours a day and research shows that – for three- and four-year-olds at least – there's no benefit in extending these hours. The rest of the time, working parents still have to make the choice between looking after their own children, finding a parent substitute or relying on institutional care – and the decision doesn't get any easier.

As Mary Bousted of the Association of Teachers and Lecturers pointed out in response to the Ofsted suggestion mentioned above, 'We know that parental attachment is absolutely crucial to children in their early years ... it's where they learn how to speak, they learn their values and they get help with their fine motor skills. All those things also take place in high-quality childcare but nothing can replace the relationship that effective and good parents have with their children. So we need time for both.'

A working mum whose pre-school children are in daycare from 8 a.m. to 6 p.m. told me that 'by the time I've picked them up, I haven't got time to engage with them and they're just too tired and strung out.' While on long-term sick leave she'd discovered the pleasure of looking after them herself, and was now agonising over choosing between her career and her children. The problems of filling the home-and-family gap may be less acute once children are over three, but they can be just as heart-rending for all concerned.

Six to eleven: home from home?

Once children reach school age, childcare problems are less pressing ... but they certainly don't go away. Throughout the Western world, children are required to attend primary school for between five and seven hours a day, which significantly eases parents' childcare burden during term-time. It still doesn't, however, cover full-time work commitments and childcare is also still a problem when schools are closed for holidays, especially the long summer break.

In the UK at the time of writing, politicians are considering extending the school day to nine hours for all five- to eighteen-year-olds, and reducing the length of school holidays. In floating this suggestion, Paul Kirby, a former Downing Street policy adviser, pointed out that a forty-five-hour school week, forty-five weeks a year would 'allow all parents to work full-time, without the need for additional childcare. The average employment leave would cover the school holidays. The average working day would give most parents the time to do a full-time job, in between dropping off and picking up their kids.' He added that a longer school day could also improve educational standards by giving teachers more time for teaching and children more time to learn – the equivalent of an extra seven years' education over their school lives.

The response from educationists was frosty. Christine Blower, General Secretary of the National Teachers Union, replied that 'children and young people deserve a childhood and contrary to the suggestion that this will please parents, the majority will not support this at all. Children are not an inconvenience to fit in around work. Equally, education is not a production line.' And a spokesman for the Association of Teachers and Lecturers said: 'Children need time to learn through play and time with their family and friends. UK parents work some of the longest hours in Europe, putting huge pressure on family life. Parents are often exhausted by these hours and children too are experiencing long hours at school or with childminders. A civilized society would ensure that parents and children spend more time together.'

In fact, because of parents' long working hours, many children already spend nine or more hours a day on school premises. Over the last ten years, schools around the UK often open their doors an hour or so before lessons start, frequently offering breakfast, and stay open for after-school clubs, homework clubs and other activities until around 6 p.m. Parents have to pay for this care and the quality is variable. As always in matters of childcare, successful provision depends on good resources, staffing and organisation.

I've visited a number of primary schools with superb outdoor facilities where, when the bell goes for end of classes, children can engage in free play or involve themselves in gardening, tending livestock (from rabbits and chickens to sheep and goats) or joining in a range of sporting activities. Indoors, there are other free play options, as well as adult-led activities like art and drama clubs. Well-resourced and well-organised 'extended schools' like these can clearly provide valuable social and recreational opportunities that are seldom available on the home front and older primary children often seem to benefit from them (although many only attend on a few days a week). I've also visited primary schools with playgrounds like prison exercise yards, where the extended day is a chaotic, noisy affair, with harassed adult minders trying to contain swarms of children in the school hall while sour-faced school cleaners harrumph around them.

If compulsory schooling were to be extended to nine hours a day, there would undoubtedly be similar differences in the quality of provision – and it's unlikely that extra state funding would be available, so parents would still have to pay for the 'extras'. There's also the question of choice. Many parents (like Marie Peacock, quoted on pages 153–4) prefer to care for their own children, especially younger children, rather than handing them over to the state for most of their waking hours. Other working parents choose a home-and-family substitute, such as grandparents, a child-minder or *au pair* for at least part of the week, rather than institutional care. While extended school days have blurred the distinction between care and education, they still allow an element of parental choice – extending the hours of compulsory schooling would remove that choice.

Whether the idea catches on or not remains to be seen, but it's clear from the variability of extended school provision that expecting school premises to double as childcare facilities isn't the panacea some politicians imagine. In fact, it brings us back to where this chapter started: providing effective childcare costs money – lots of it.

Money can't buy me love

This emphasis on the costs of childcare does not mean, however, that all child-rearing problems can be solved by throwing money at them. Quality childcare outside the home is expensive and, as has been pointed out in previous chapters, quality childcare in the home is costly in terms of time rather than money. But in a competitive consumer culture it's all too easy to equate spending money on children with loving them, and many contemporary children come home not to parental time and attention, but to a relentless schedule of expensive extra-curricular activities.

I witnessed a typical after-school schedule some years ago when visiting a highly-educated couple in a middle-class area of England. On the day I arrived, their eight-year-old son came home to a drink and a sandwich from the *au pair*, then was whisked away to a Kumon maths lesson. On return, he completed his homework before setting off to swimming club; then, after a hasty family supper, he was allowed an hour on the playstation before bed. Other evenings, weekends and holidays were similarly filled to bursting point with extra tuition, clubs, music lessons and special outings – with no time left over for unstructured play or simply 'chilling out'. On one occasion the poor child had a few minutes spare between appointments and his mother seemed to panic: she eventually filled the gap by asking him to entertain me by turning somersaults. He was rather good at this, but then he clearly spent his life turning somersaults to please his parents.

This type of frenzied activity may seem far from the experience of the latch-key child who lets himself in, pops some processed food in the microwave and retires to a bedroom full of electronic equipment, to while away the hours in a 'virtual world'. But both scenarios are caused by the same thing: parents who work long hours and attempt to compensate for their absence (or exhausted presence) by spending money on their children. The educated middle classes justify their extra-curricular payments with the argument that they're providing 'the best possible start in life'; other parents feel their offspring have to keep up with the Jones' children down the road in terms of electronic and designer must-haves.

Their over-spending may be the result of guilt (see Chapter 5), over-protectiveness (see Chapter 2), anxiety for one's child to do well in a competitive world (see Chapter 7), a personal belief that 'stuff = contentment' (see Chapter 8), or a heady cocktail of all four. The world turns so quickly nowadays, and everyone's running so frantically to keep up with it, there's no time to stop and wonder *'Why am I doing this?'* The myth of quality time and the burgeoning market in toys, activities and equipment to fill it have added to the emotionally-charged brew, so that parents feel they have to earn more and more, meaning they spend less and less time at home. But the key to successful child development is presence, not presents; and children suffering from 'too muchness' can be as emotionally impoverished as those who have too little.

Of course, a few extra-curricular activities are valuable – maybe two or three hours a week, depending on children's interests (and assuming they haven't already had it up to the back teeth with organised activities as part of the extended school day). Clubs and sporting activities develop new skills, help children learn to get along with others, and develop their time-management and personal organisation skills. School-age children also benefit from some time relaxing in front of TV – if nothing else, to ensure they can keep their end up in playground conversation – or enjoying other electronic entertainment. But they also need time for the sort of casual family activities described in Chapter 5, for their own unstructured, natural play or for simply daydreaming.

Our adult preoccupations can make us unaware of these developmental needs. As Carl Honore put it in his book *In Praise of Slow*: 'to an adult used to making every second count, unstructured play looks like wasted time.' I suspect the friend who asked her son to turn somersaults was terrified that, left to his own devices, he'd be bored – and she was probably right. Children whose lives are filled every moment of every day with structured activity don't learn to think for themselves or exercise their own imaginations. They become dependent on others to educate, entertain and otherwise occupy them – and, in consequence, are easily bored. They then demand more activities or more stuff to ease their boredom, and parents – under the influence of that potent cocktail of love, guilt and anxiety – fork out more and more cash in a desperate attempt to keep them happy.

* * *

In a world where all adults – women as well as men – expect to have opportunities for self-realisation and economic independence, the issue of childcare raises political, economic, social and emotional problems. To solve them, all adults – men as well as women – have to wise up to what looking after children involves. Effective childcare is not, as many politicians seem to think, the same as baby-sitting. Neither is childhood a race, in which the chances of success are improved by hot-housing, an early start on formal learning or endless 'enrichment'. Caring for young children involves expertise which was, in the past, handed down through the female line, but today has often been forgotten. While genetic inheritance and hormones mean human beings almost inevitably love their children, our species seems increasingly uncertain how best to look after them or to ensure they're well looked after.

This problem is compounded, in the most competitive countries of the developed world, by a confused attitude to love and money. Parents who don't see the point of seeking out and paying for high quality daycare are nevertheless prepared to work day and night to afford expensive extra-curricular activities or gifts of technological paraphernalia. Society has conditioned us all to believe that money, hard work and consumer durables can solve most problems. But the problems of babies with brains bathed in cortisol, pre-schoolers struggling to write before they can talk, and school children coralled for up to ten hours a day in ill-resourced institutions will not be assuaged by purchase of the latest technological gadgets. As the twenty-first century progresses, the problem of who's looking after the children isn't going to go away.

DETOXING CHILDCARE

- Make sure you're clear about the difference between childcare and education. In the early years, learning is largely informal, but once children reach the age of six education becomes increasingly formal. It's useful to think of formal learning as being like children's 'work' (requiring mental effort and discipline), while childcare, with its opportunities for child-centred informal learning, is more like 'family time'.
- Good childcare should, therefore, reproduce as far as possible the conditions we'd expect in a happy family home.
- Plan for childcare well in advance – don't leave it till the last minute and thus end up compromising on quality.

Birth to three-year-olds

- In the early years, children's main requirements are consistent one-to-one personal relationships and familiar surroundings. The possible options are:

    – care by parent(s) or other committed family members (youthful enough to cater for the needs of a baby or toddler)

    – a substitute carer in your own or their home, such as a nanny, child-minder or unqualified minder (the higher the carer's qualifications in child development the more likely they are to be effective)

    – a day nursery which provides one-to-one care with a named carer in a highly domesticated setting.

- Avoid:

    – little contact with parents

    – frequent changes of carer

    – poor quality childcare

    – institutional care for more than a few hours a day.

- Look for: childcare that can provide:

    – the sort of child-rearing practices described in Chapters 1 to 4

    – as seamless as possible a transition between childcare and parents

    – reliability and carer(s) with whom you feel comfortable

    – opportunities for your child to mix with others whilst feeling safe in the care of a beloved adult.

Three- to six-year-olds

- By this stage children need plenty of opportunities to explore and learn, along with the chance to meet and play with other children, so pre-school is important.
- Quality pre-school should provide:

    – child-centred activities arising out of the children's own interests interspersed with adult-directed sessions to lay solid foundations for 'school learning' (the latter increasing in significance as time goes on)

204 **Toxic Childhood**

  - plenty of outdoor play, music, art and 'sustained shared thinking' (see Chapter 4)
  - about three hours a day of this sort of activity for children up to four years old, up to six hours thereafter.

- During the rest of the day, children still need the more familial type of childcare described in 'Birth to three' above. The options are:
  - a day nursery in which pre-school activities are interspersed with 'family-like' mealtimes, rests, quiet time, unstructured play, and so on
  - part-time attendance at a pre-school, with other appropriate childcare around the edges.

- Avoid:
  - little contact with parents
  - frequent changes of care arrangements
  - poor quality pre-school provision or childcare
  - too formal an approach to learning before the age of six.

- Look for: a good balance between exciting pre-school provision and the home comforts listed in the 'Birth to three' 'Look for' bullet points.

Six- to twelve-year-olds

- During this period, children should grow in independence so the need for home and family gradually grows less. However, just like adults, they need respite from 'work' in the hours around the school day (and the younger they are, the more that respite should resemble a happy family home).
- Childcare options around the school day and during school holidays are:
  - family or substitute carers as described above
  - institutionalised care in an 'extended school' or similar provision.

- Good institutionalised care should provide:
  - quality supervision, incorporating the sorts of attitude to eating habits, play, outdoor activity and child-adult interaction described in

Chapters 1 to 4, albeit adapted to fit larger group of children
– organised activities and clubs
– opportunities for unstructured play, reading and quiet relaxation
– the right for children to choose their own balance of organised
and unstructured activities.

- The older the child, the longer and more frequently they are likely to
benefit from being in good institutionalised care. However, all children
still need plenty of time at home with their own family (see Chapter 5).

THE WORK-CHILDCARE BALANCE

- Discuss childcare with your partner – preferably before you have
children – bearing in mind:
    – the available maternal and paternal leave arrangements,
    including benefits
    – your *real* financial needs (i.e. living costs, as opposed to 'lifestyle
    choices')
    – your interest in/ability to look after a baby (you may find this
    changes, for better or worse, when the baby arrives)
    – the effects on your respective careers of taking time off – and
    whether you want a child enough to risk these effects. However,
    bear in mind that the effects of taking time off are not necessarily
    negative. Some people end up with a completely new, more
    interesting career.

There's more discussion of the economic issues behind child-rearing in
Chapter 10 and the Conclusion: Detoxing Childhood.

- Bear in mind that raising a child involves time, effort and attention, and
if you can't or aren't prepared to provide these you have two options:
    – pay someone else to do it as well as possible on your behalf (but
    still making sure you put in enough time to 'forge a family' – see
    Chapter 5)

– don't have children – just get on with enjoying life as a non-parent.

- The options available in terms of parental care are:
  – one parent takes full-time responsibility for childcare, the other for breadwinning
  – one or both parents reduce working hours to allow for childcare
  – parents arrange their full-time working lives so that one is always at home (this is probably the least satisfactory option, as a 'revolving door' situation, where one parent exits as the other enters, is far from ideal for both adults and children).

- Reduced working hours could involve:
  – part-time work (reducing the days worked each week, or hours each day)
  – job-sharing (e.g. do you work with/know other parents who might like to share?)
  – working from home (choosing hours to fit around childcare).

- Childcare options available while you're at work are outlined in Detoxing Childcare above. But remember that these options can themselves be time-consuming and effortful in terms of:
  – arrangements for dropping off and collecting children
  – communicating and liaising with carers to ensure your child is happy
  – providing and keeping special equipment and clothing in good repair
  – any parental 'duties' expected (as one mother put it, 'You're usually required to keep up your end of the grunt work, regardless of whether you work outside the home')
  – dealing with emergencies, e.g. if travel arrangements break down.

- Remember that children thrive on consistency and regularity. The younger the child, the more damaging it is to chop and change arrangements, so:

– put in plenty of groundwork on providing the best possible option from the beginning

– spend time devising efficient emergency systems, including more than one trusty 'safety net' should your arrangements go awry.

- Review your arrangements frequently. Are both partners happy with the way things are? Does your child seem happy?

PARENT POWER: CHANGING THE WORLD

Most parents are so busy coping with their own lives there seems to be no time to exercise parent power to improve work-life balance. But even in the midst of the parental juggling act, there are some simple steps that could improve life for you, and for future generations.

- Talk to other parents (and anyone else who'll listen) about the particular problems you're encountering with work-life balance. As well as helping you develop your own social network, this is a good way of discovering what's available and going on locally. But don't just moan – talk about what can be done to make things better.

- Don't be put off by other parents' apparent competence and organisation. Everyone puts on a front, and every parent I've ever met turned out to be struggling just as hard as me, no matter how swanlike and serene they appeared on the surface. But people always like to be asked for advice, so that's a good way to introduce yourself.

- For further information and advice, consult the web – it's amazing what you can find out with half an hour's Googling – websites such as Mumsnet provide helpful advice and opportunities to chat. But *don't* get stuck on the net when you're supposed to be sharing time with your child (see Chapter 4), and don't use net-based contacts as a substitute for meeting real people.

- Use casual chats and virtual leads to develop real-life contacts with people who share your concerns and interests. Real-life contacts are good for you and your child (see Chapter 10), even if you don't solve the immediate problem.

- Don't be put off going to more formal meetings – PTAs, parent groups, pressure groups for change. You don't have to get involved if you don't want to – but if you don't go you'll never find out what's available. Nobody ever changed anything by sitting around bemoaning the status quo.

- At work, ask about family-friendly alternatives to full-time commitment. Don't enrage the non-parents by expecting special treatment – you chose to be a parent, so can't expect the rest of the world to pay your way. But everyone benefits from flexible work structures that respect employees' right to a life beyond the office.

- When local and national elections come round, make it clear (by emailing, writing to or buttonholing candidates) that your vote will be influenced by policies on:
    - effective childcare provision, *appropriate for each of the three age-ranges in this chapter*
    - work-life balance, including flexible working hours and parental leave
    - genuine choice, including support for home-based as well as institutional care.

- If you're the sort of person who likes to get involved, this really is your chance. As a parent, you have inside, expert knowledge on one of the most significant issues of our generation: use it to help build a better world!

Further reading

Norbert and Elinore Herschkowitz, *A Good Start in Life: Understanding your Child's Brain and Behaviour from Birth to Age 6* (Dana Press, 2002)

Ros Bayley and Lynn Broadbent *Flying Start with Literacy* (Network Educational Press, 2005)

Richard House (ed.), *Too Much Too Soon* (Hawthorn Press, 2010)

Diane Rich and others *First Hand Experience – What Matters to Children* (Rich Learning Opportunities, second edition 2014)

Johann Christoph Arnold, *Their Name is Today: reclaiming childhood in a hostile world* (Plough Book Publishing, 2014 – available free of charge from www.communityplaythings.co.uk)

Tanith Carey, *Taming the Tiger* parent (Robinson, 2014)

Useful websites:

For details on childcare options see national websites, e.g. in UK the Daycare Trust: www.daycaretrust.org.uk

Play Talk Read: Scottish government website for parents of children from birth to three www.playtalkread.org

Zero to Three: independent US website about babies' and toddlers' development http://www.zerotothree.org

What about the Children: UK charity raising awareness about the significance of early attachment www.whataboutthechildren.org.uk

Too Much Too Soon campaign website: www.toomuchtoosoon.org

Mind the gap

In 1999, Hilary Clinton chaired a conference at the White House to discuss the findings of psychological and neuroscientific research about the infant brain. It concluded that 'what happens during the first months and years of life matters a lot, not because this period of development provides an indelible blueprint for adult well-being, but because it sets either a sturdy or fragile stage for what follows.'

Governments around the world suddenly became interested in pre-school children when research quoted at the White House conference showed that for every dollar invested in effective early years provision seven dollars are saved in terms of lower crime, better jobs and improved educational outcomes. It clearly makes sense, for social and economic reasons, to ensure that as many children as possible begin life on a 'sturdy stage'.

However, changing children's life chances requires 'effective' early years provision. As US economist Steven Levitt says, state-providedchildcare won't make much impact if, 'instead of spending the day with his own undereducated, overworked mother, the ... child spends his day with someone else's undereducated, overworked mother. (And a whole roomful of needy children.)' Without considerable investment in early childcare for children from poor families, the poverty gap is unlikely to close and the 'cycle of disadvantage' will continue into further generations.

Birth to three-year-olds

During the first decade of this century, a great deal of UK money was devoted to Sure Start (see page 126) and the building of children's centres, but the economic recession put paid to further investment. Sure Start has now fallen by the wayside, but there are some outstanding examples of children's centres around the country, such as the Pen Green Centre in Northamptonshire and the Thomas Coram Centre in London. However, these successful initiatives rely on highly trained staff, and administrators who can play the system (public and private) to fund their work. The Family Nurse Partnership (see page 180) is proving to be 'effective' too, but is so expensive that the number of parents who benefit from it are a drop in the ocean of poverty.

Three- to six-year-olds

Once children are three, research shows clearly that effective pre-school provision can provide a 'second chance' to escape the heritage of an impoverished family background – but only if their pre-schools are well-run and resourced. The long-term harm caused by over-formal pre-school practice is much greater for children from poorer homes. The High/Scope Foundation in the USA followed the progress of a group of such pre-school pupils from the late 1960s, and found that those who attended a formal pre-school were much more likely to have social problems thirty years down the line. These long-term problems include trouble holding down a job, difficulties with personal relationships, and a significantly greater chance of involvement in crime. In both the UK and USA, recent political emphasis has been on 'schoolification' of nursery education (see Chapter 7), so the prognosis is not good.

Six- to eleven-year-olds

Finally, as children grow older, where do you suppose an 'extended school day' is more likely to be a life-enhancing experience? In a middle-class area, where school grounds are extensive and parental pressure ensures exciting, varied, well-resourced provision? Or in an inner-city school with ancient buildings, limited play areas, little parental involvement and 'someone else's under-educated over-worked mother' keeping an eye on the children?

Inadequate childcare, at any age, has a greater negative impact on children from poor families than on those from more privileged back-grounds. On the other hand, the experience of countries like Finland, Norway and Sweden shows clearly that investment in quality provision (and education) for the first ten years of *all* children's lives benefits everyone. It means less mental instability, less crime, less antisocial behaviour, and less handing on of a disadvantaged, chaotic lifestyle from one generation to the next. If we are to close the widening gap, the best investment we can make is high quality care for all our children, including, particularly in their earliest years, constant, consistent one-on-one care provided by loving members of their own family.

CHAPTER SEVEN

THE BEST DAYS OF THEIR LIVES

Children start learning from the moment they're born. By trial and error they learn to control their limbs, sit up, walk, talk, run and jump. They learn through experience what a vast variety of things look, sound, feel, smell and taste like. They watch adults performing daily tasks, such as buttoning up a coat, and as their own physical dexterity grows they start to copy them, then practise the activity until it becomes second nature. They watch natural events, such as water running down a slope, and make deductions about how the world works – some of which, of course, are wildly wrong ... but surprisingly many turn out to be right. Neuroscientists studying children's brain development in the early years wax lyrical about all the learning they do, which for most of human history we've taken entirely for granted.

And almost all this learning is entirely voluntary, for the sheer pleasure of doing it. There are a few social skills adults insist on – such as toilet training, saying 'please' and 'thank you' and table manners. But children learn these skills quickly too if the adults give lots of praise and compliments on how 'grown up' they're being. On the whole, children want to learn and parents and other primary care-givers are pretty good at gauging what can be expected of them. Even when, at around three years old, children go to pre-school, the routine is hopefully much the same – learning develops out of their interests (loosely known as 'play') and talented pre-school teachers take each child's developmental level into account. Then they start school.

Shades of the prison house ...

When children are around six years old, states across the developed world require them to sign up for formal education. For too many children nowadays – particularly those in countries where formal schooling starts at an ever earlier age – Wordsworth's unenthusiastic description:

> Shades of the prison house begin to close
> Upon the growing boy...

sums up what learning feels like when it ceases to be voluntary and is instead determined by the demands of the curriculum. What's more, in large classes – typically thirty or more in state primary schools – a single teacher isn't usually in a position to take the developmental level of individual children into account.

Nevertheless, society needs schools to help create citizens who'll keep the contemporary cultural show on the road, and primary education has the task of laying the foundations for lifelong learning. This means developing children's motivation to learn, their ability to work, both independently and with others, and – very importantly – their skills in the three Rs. If children are bright-eyed, bushy-tailed and up to speed in reading, writing and basic maths by the end of their primary years, they should be able to take full advantage of secondary education and hopefully go on to be balanced, successful, hard-working adults.

After more than a hundred years of state-aided elementary education, you'd think the nations of the developed world would be able to deliver most children into their teens happy, motivated literate and numerate. However, schools have been battered as much as other institutions by the winds of tumultuous social and technological change. Over the last couple of decades, toxic childhood syndrome has made children harder to teach and more difficult to control. Parents, anxious about their offspring's prospects in an increasingly competitive world and worried by reports of falling standards, bullying and disrupted classes, are less confident about schools' effectiveness. And many national governments, including that of the UK, have assumed increasing control over the way schools are run. Both well-being and education appear to have been affected

One unfortunate result of government involvement in education is mushrooming bureaucracy. Every year has seen new systems, regulations and targets imposed, and more requests for records, statistics and test results. The more teachers are preoccupied with this burden of measurement and accountability, the less time and energy they have for teaching, and the less children's individual needs can be taken into account. There have been repeated attempts to reduce bureaucracy (the latest, scheduled for 2015, involves a change of 'success criteria'), but centralised control inevitably leads schools to over-focus on targets and data at the expense of teaching.

Another problem is politicians' need for quick results to impress the voters and provide statistical evidence of improvement. International league tables for pupil achievement, which began to attract media attention in the early 2000s, have increased this fervour.* In countries such as the USA and UK, which could clearly 'do better', they consolidated a tests-and-targets educational culture with a fierce focus on 'standards'. Elementary schools in the USA, for instance, have been dominated first by George W. Bush's 'No Child Left Behind' legislation, then by Obama's 'Race To The Top', while in the UK millions of pounds were poured into National Strategies for literacy and numeracy, and school inspections results have ever since been highly dependent on test results in these subjects. Parents generally welcome the focus on

---

*	The main international tests affecting primary education are PISA (the Programme for International Student Assessment), PIRLS (Progress in International Reading and Literacy) and TIMMS (Trends in International Mathematics and Science).

the three Rs, since they know how important these basic skills are to their children. But, as the independent *Cambridge Review of Primary Education* found in 2009, this focus has grown increasingly narrow, to the extent that it is now probably damaging children's long-term chances rather than improving them.

Why reading is important in a multimedia age

There's no doubt that the three Rs of reading, writing and reckoning are the bedrock of education, with reading arguably the most important R. Even in a multimedia world, where entertainment and information are increasingly visual, the ability to read is essential in every walk of life. But reading brings with it many extra advantages. The very process of learning to read – 'the getting of literacy' – is a hugely important part of children's intellectual and social development.

For a start, learning to read improves children's thinking skills in general. Written language is more complex and sophisticated than the everyday language of speech, so reading leads to a significant expansion of children's ideas, vocabulary and the capacity to express themselves. The second R – writing – also helps, because learning to write involves slowing down the thought-processes, choosing the best words and expressions to communicate an idea. Since language and thought are closely intertwined, this increased word-power leads to increased brain power – it's long been recognised that, when children become literate, there's a knock-on effect in terms of educational progress in general.

The symbolic system by which we represent language is a human invention – a complex early technology whereby squiggles on a page are converted by the human brain into meaningful words. So learning to read and write doesn't 'come naturally' like learning to walk, talk and so on: each new generation has to acquire the skills by conscious application. This is a long, painstaking process (most adults have forgotten quite how difficult it is), but as children gradually become literate there's steady enrichment of the connections in the prefrontal cortex of their brains, the area associated with focused concentration, planning, self-control and decision-making.

The enriched neural networks in children's brains, created by 'the getting of literacy', may well be significant in the development of civilised behaviour. Apart from anything else, the more fluent readers become, the more they're able to connect through the written word with a vast selection of other human minds, leading to a greater capacity for empathy. I don't think it's any coincidence that written language has proved a key element in all successful civilisations and that universal literacy appears essential to the success of democratic systems. As the American writer Neil Postman put it, 'Print means a slowed down mind ... The written, and then the printed word brought a new kind of social organisation to civilisation. It brought logic, science, education, civilité.' However, Postman also points out that 'electronics speed up the mind', and the long slow process of acquiring literacy is more difficult for children who grow up in a world awash with quick-fix, multimedia gadgets.

True literacy therefore requires motivation and plenty of practice, and this is where a narrow focus on test results can also be damaging. The superficial skills children need to score points on multiple choice tests aren't anywhere near as enriching and civilising as the skills involved in reading for pleasure – they merely skim the surface of literacy. In this respect, J.K. Rowling has probably done more for the children of the developed world than the entire twenty-first-century educational establishment. Nurturing children's motivation to read and their enjoyment of reading is every bit as important as teaching them the under-pinning skills (see also 'Books versus screens', pages 292–5).

Nevertheless, they won't get anywhere without those skills ... and a significant number of children still don't manage to learn them. To some extent this is because the early stages of 'the getting of literacy' involve application and perseverance, so teachers have to convince children to slow down their minds and attend to complex symbolic information on a page. This may be difficult if formal reading instruction begins too early, or at any age if the children concerned are suffering from toxic childhood syndrome. But there are other reasons why children sometimes fail to acquire basic reading skills, associated with the vexed educational question of 'phonics'.

Why Johnny still can't read ... and how he might

Even before politicians became involved, primary schools were regularly bedevilled by the fads and fashions of academic theory. For well over a hundred years, academics have wrangled over the best way to teach reading: phonics (showing children that the sounds /c/ /a/ /t/ go together to make *cat*) or fun (getting children hooked on reading so they want to suss out the phonics for themselves). Schools have been pulled back and forth, and for a prolonged period in the second half of the last century, phonics went completely out of fashion.

Fortunately, there is now general agreement that, in an alphabetic language such as English, phonics teaching is essential. Without some grasp of phonics, most children are unlikely to read at all, let alone get hooked on it. However despite this triumph of common sense, many children are still finding reading difficult: teachers teach phonics, but they don't catch on. Recent research suggests that this – like so many other developmental problems – could be the result of nature or nurture.

For children to take advantage of phonics teaching, they have to be able to distinguish the individual speech sounds (phonemes) of their native language, an ability acquired long before they start school, during the first year or so of life. Newborn babies are equipped to recognise and produce the phonemes of any language, but – as they listen to the adults in their lives – they narrow it down to the speech-sounds of the language they'll need. (This is why Chinese people find it so difficult not only to pronounce but also to hear the sound 'r'. It doesn't exist in Chinese, so in very early childhood they excise it from their phonemic repertoire.) If phonemic awareness isn't acquired naturally at this very early stage, it can be very difficult for children to develop it later.

Scientists have now pinpointed the sections of the brain involved in processing speech sounds, and it's clear that for some children genetic factors make it difficult (in extreme cases perhaps impossible) to discriminate certain phonemes. In such cases, personal biology holds the child back; for other children, hearing problems in early childhood, such as glue ear, may cause difficulties in auditory discrimination.

And there are many children who have poor phonemic awareness because, even though they are physiologically OK, they simply don't get enough exposure to language in the early years. This is one reason why earlier chapters have stressed the significance of a child's constant interaction with a primary caregiver in the first eighteen months and the importance of talking, singing and rhyming with small children. At present, many children's poor phonemic awareness may be due to lack of adult time and attention in their earliest years and/or too much time interacting with screen-based technology.

There's also the possibility that schools are simply homing in on class-based phonics teaching too early, before many pupils are able to make any sense of it (see Chapter 6). For the overwhelming majority of children, the age-old wisdom quoted in Chapter 4 can open up the relevant neural pathways quite naturally, long before anyone even thinks about school. Songs, rhymes, laughter and conversation with a loved one in the earliest years, followed by a play-based pre-school education with plenty of time for music, rhymes, stories and oral language activities, appears to be a more effective way of preparing children to read than too-early drill in the finer points of phonics.

The educational rat race

The 'too much too soon' syndrome described in Chapter 6 is greatly exacerbated by a competitive, tests-and-targets educational culture. It may make sense to adults to think 'there's a lot to learn, so the sooner they get on with it the better' or 'if some children can start reading at the age of four, we can expect them all to manage it … or even to start at three!' but children are all different and develop at different rates, and the younger the child the more significant these differences are. Every developmental psychologist I've met agrees that formal learning is best left till children are at least six years old, when the differences have begun to even out and most are sufficiently mature to cope with abstract ideas. Six or seven are, in fact, the starting age for formal schooling in the European countries that do best on the PISA and PIRLS tests. As pointed out in Chapter 6, they're also the starting age for around 90 per cent of countries worldwide (see pages 192–3).

This doesn't mean that caring adults around the world believe in holding back those children who show an early interest in reading, writing or arithmetic. Holding children back would be as cruel and counter-productive as forcing them to struggle with skills currently beyond them. But rather than attempting to accelerate the progress of intellectually-precocious children, wise kindergarten teachers encourage them to enjoy mastery in their chosen sphere whilst simultaneously developing abilities in other areas. Early readers, for instance, often benefit from attention to social skills, physical coordination and control, music and creative arts, concepts of number or learning how things work. What young children thrive on is personal, individual support, appropriate to their own developmental level (the sort of help they'd get in a loving family home). This is difficult to provide in a busy pre-school – especially if every child is expected to reach the same standard in literacy and numeracy by the time they're five.

Sadly, many parents and teachers in the UK and USA have allowed themselves to be drawn into an educational rat race, modelled on the competitive ethos of big business and focused in the early years on literacy. In a cut-throat world, parents are understandably worried that their child may be 'left behind', but all the research cited in Chapter 6 suggests this is another example of contemporary cultural influences blinding adults to children's biological needs – like letting them feed almost exclusively on junk food or stay inside developing square eyeballs when they'd be better off playing in the fresh air.

We wouldn't dream of suggesting twelve-year-olds should learn to drive (even though technically most of them probably could) because we know that emotionally they're not ready for the responsibility of being in charge of a car. Similarly, we shouldn't force four- and five-year-olds to struggle with skills most would learn easily a couple of years later. Russian researcher Galina Dolya believes this early pressure feeds emotional and behavioural difficulties: 'a child who's accelerated is more likely to experience frustration and burn-out'. Over the last ten years teachers in the pre-school departments of prestigious prep schools have often told me how worried they are about the long-term effects on their pupils of constant pressure to achieve, which may well be connected with a recent warning from the charity Young Minds about a 'mental health time bomb' among British adolescents and soaring rates of anorexia nervosa in high-flying teenage girls.

There's also the problem that it's very difficult to assess the cognitive abilities of little children. In 2014, the English government decided to introduce 'baseline assessment' in the first term of the reception year, when most children are only four years old. According to experts on early development, standardised testing of such young children is notoriously unreliable (one group of four-year-olds, tested on a Monday, appeared to be 'gifted and talented', but by the following Friday the same test registered them as having 'special needs'). There's a real danger of misinterpreting such data and labelling children inappropriately even before they begin their school career.

The self-fulfilling prophecy is a well-known phenomenon in

primary education. A child who – for whatever reason – is labelled an under-achiever is very likely to live up to that reputation. Thomas Jefferson once described childhood as a time when 'the imagination is warm, and impressions are permanent'. Thus the most likely result of early 'failure' is summed up by that other American aphorist, Homer Simpson: 'Kids, you tried your hardest and you failed miserably. The lesson is: don't try.' The US psychologist Carol Dweck calls this a 'closed mindset' and believes it blights the life-chances of innumerable children, many of them high achievers in certain areas of the curriculum but reluctant even to participate in others.

Winners, losers … and cheats

Once children in the Anglo-Saxon countries start formal schooling, testing begins in earnest. In England, the new baseline tests for four-year-olds are followed by national tests of phonics at six, then literacy and numeracy 'SATs' at seven and eleven. Many schools now use standardised tests in every age-group, in order to track pupil progress. 'Aspirational' targets are set for achievement at each stage, so teachers and pupils are under constant pressure to up their game.

Schools must, of course, be accountable and occasional standardised tests help keep tabs on the educational state of the nation*, but when testing assumes too much importance it becomes an end in itself. In both the USA and UK high-stake testing (win or lose, pass or fail) has, in the words of Professor Joe Frost of the University of Texas, turned many schools into 'factories that sort both children and teachers into "winners" and "losers" and grade children like chickens on the assembly line'.

High-stakes tests and test-related targets can also blind teachers, parents and children to the importance of a wide and

---

*   Statistically it isn't actually necessary to test everyone. Carefully-managed sampling, which is all that's required for national and international comparisons, provides reliable data.

national and balanced curriculum. When schools are judged almost exclusively on their test results, and especially when teachers' status and earnings depend on those results, they inevitably begin to focus on the narrow range of skills covered by national standardised assessment. 'Teaching to the test' (training children in tricks and techniques to earn marks rather helping them understand and enjoy the subject) becomes the order of the day, and creativity and the development of enquiring minds fall to the bottom of the educational priority list. All too often in schools today, when a new topic crops up, able children ask 'Is this on the test?' and lose interest if it isn't. This is the sort of mindset that led Einstein to remark: 'It's a miracle that curiosity survives formal education.' A test-based primary school system trains children to think in blinkers.

It also leads to a great many dubious practices. In 2007, the year in which English children were officially recognised as the most tested school pupils in the world, investigative journalist Warwick Mansell published his book *Education by Numbers*, describing the damage wrought by this regime. His revelations about excessive coaching, cramming and – indeed – widespread *cheating* by schools desperate to gain or maintain a high place in the educational league tables caused shockwaves in government circles. As well as trying to close the loopholes by which schools could cheat their way to success, Ofsted issued copious advice on the ill-advisability of teaching to the test.

Seven years on, however, Mansell reckons the situation hasn't improved: 'In fact, I'd say it's getting worse. I'm sceptical about that sort of Ofsted advice – in the end it's still test data that's driving everything – that's the bottom line for schools.' He believes it's more difficult to cheat at primary than secondary level because the assessment system is less complex, 'but some primary schools still use strategies that massage the results, sometimes on the borderline of malpractice, like manipulating their intake to push out children with special needs.'

Yet despite a cacophony of criticism over the last decade, from organizations as diverse as the Qualifications and Curriculum Authority, the National Audit Office and the Organisation for European Cooperation and Development, successive governments have continued to embrace high-stakes testing as the major driver of the English state education system.

What is pupil progress?

Indeed, over the last ten years, improvements in digital technology have allowed the collection of ever greater amounts of data – about specific local education authorities, schools, age-groups and individual children – and ever more specialised crunching of numbers. This proliferation of 'big data' has focused political attention on 'pupil progress' and, since parents and teachers are obviously keen for children to move onward and upward, the phrase is a seductive one. However, politicians are interested in general statistics rather than individual pupils, and the danger is that children become little more than pawns in this political game.

It is, of course, essential that every teacher is well aware of how each child in the class is doing, that school management keeps an eye on individual teachers' performance, that teaching in specific groups of schools is effectively monitored and that there's national measurement of performance around the country. But when 'the bottom line' for all this measurement and accountability is pupils' scores on a limited range of paper-and-pencil tests, the concept of 'education' is easily confused with data analysis.

For instance, in 2014 the Kemnal Academies Trust, which runs forty schools in South-East England, announced that it had sacked twenty-six of its headteachers and many other senior staff. In a submission to the government's Education Select Committee, the Trust's management explained that it sets targets for pupil achievement, linked to data collected on a six-weekly basis and 'if an Academy does not meet these targets, then senior leaders and/ or governance are changed'. At around the same time, the head-teacher of another school in the chain, Simon Wood, abruptly moved to another academy group, to the dismay of pupils, teachers and parents. He'd joined the Kemnal Trust two years earlier when his school was struggling with a very poor reputation and an inspection ranking of 'inadequate'; when he left it was graded 'good' and, according to a parent, 'Simon Wood loved this school, loved the children and had transformed this community over the past two years'. Another remarked that Mr Wood's departure was 'a tragedy for the school'. None of this 'soft' information about the way a school's performance can be transformed by a caring head would, however, register on a spreadsheet.

Anyone who has actually taught young children knows that they don't learn and progress in a neat linear fashion – they make occasional dramatic leaps forward, but (for all sorts of reasons, some of them nothing to do with school) they occasionally also slip back, and all children regularly 'plateau' as they take time to absorb new skills and knowledge. Teachers too have good days and bad days, sometimes even good years and bad years depending on the myriad influences that impact on human beings. I remember a particular year in the classroom when all my pupils glittered like stars, followed by another when – no matter how hard I tried – the class just didn't gel for well over a term. You could call the many factors behind this dramatic difference 'reasons' or 'excuses', but I'm very glad the children and I weren't subjected to a six-weekly analysis of data: it would've been soul-destroying for all of us and would have made things much, much worse.

One step forward, two steps back?

The impact on children of national number crunching is evident in the UK's performance in literacy over the last decade. It seemed to start well, when in 2004 the Westminster government trumpeted that the nation's eleven-year-olds had moved up to third place in PISA's international comparison of reading scores. This was after four years of intensely concentrated effort, with every primary teacher in England retrained in literacy teaching and slavishly following the diktats of the National Literacy Strategy, often to the detriment of other elements of the curriculum. The government was less keen to mention that UK children languished at the bottom of the league for enjoyment of reading – all that over-focusing had created pupils who *could* read, but didn't particularly *want* to.

Indeed, it's doubtful whether many of the children who did so well in those literacy tests in 2004 actually 'could' read, in the fullest sense of the word. Training pupils to tick the right boxes on a standardised reading test is a short-term measure that pushes up test scores – all too often, the skills children demonstrate on the test seem to evaporate a few weeks later. Inspiring them to become genuine, committed, enthusiastic readers takes more time and effort, isn't easy to measure, but bears much more significant fruit in the long run. Not surprisingly, during the decade following that early PISA triumph, UK literacy scores have declined considerably (at the last count we came in 23rd).

There is also disturbing evidence from a long-term study at the University of London that the UK's generally good scores in the international science charts may be built on shaky foundations. Between 1990 and 2004, when English primary school children were doing better on pencil-and-paper tests every year (to the extent that the science SAT was eventually dropped because practically everyone was getting top marks) researchers Philip Adie and Michael Shayer recorded a serious deterioration in the same children's 'conceptual understanding' of basic mathematical and scientific principles – that is, the common-sense understanding of the world that underpins scientific thinking. Indeed, in a large-scale longitudinal study using well-established tests of conceptual understanding, eleven-year-olds in 2004 were shown to be operating at the same level as eight- or nine-year-olds fifteen years earlier. When I met Michael Shayer at a conference, he put this down to a combination of modern children's indoor lifestyles (see Chapter 2) and changes to educational practice in early years: '1990 was the year the National Curriculum moved into schools ... and the sand and water moved out of infant classrooms'.

Triumph and disaster

For the last quarter century, US and UK politicians from the major political parties have ignored inconvenient research findings of this kind, as well as the criticisms of highly-respected academics such as Professor Robin Alexander, whose *Cambridge Primary Review* was the most comprehensive academic analysis of English education for fifty years. The former Minister for Education for England, Michael Gove, referred to teachers and academics who disagreed with his education policy as 'The Blob' and studiously ignored their every pronouncement, and one political adviser I spoke to described all critics as 'bleeding heart sentimentalists'. These are hard-nosed times, he argued, and in a competitive world market we need to rear children who can compete.

There's certainly no doubt that children need to learn about winning and losing. Indeed, schools have traditionally provided opportunities for this in the form of competitive events, from sports days, team games and swimming galas to art competitions, quizzes and spelling bees. The greater the range, the more chance that every child can find an activity in which to excel, and thus experience the delights of success. To be of any value these activities should, of course, be truly competitive, not watered-down events where everyone gets a prize. If the lesson is how to cope with Triumph and Disaster, there must be the possibility of both, and schools where Sports Day means the indiscriminate award of winners' ribbons and certificates clearly miss the point.

However, the difference between competitive events and high-stakes testing is that sports, games, galas and quizzes are 'play'. However much play matters while you're doing it, everyone knows it's play, rather than 'work' – and success or failure isn't going to affect your overall life chances. Learning how to read, write and reckon is seldom a playful enterprise these days: even the youngest child can sense from parents' and teachers' attitudes that acquiring these skills is a matter of serious import. As I tried to explain to that political adviser, the three Rs are not appropriate vehicles for learning about winning and losing. Indeed, this is an area of educational life where all must have prizes – when children leave primary school illiterate or innumerate, society as a whole is the long-term loser.

Over the last few years, the UK political classes and other hard-nosed commentators have expressed warm admiration for the educational methods of Far Eastern countries, such as Hong Kong, Singapore and South Korea, where early hot-housing and a fiercely competitive schooling system have led to top rankings in PISA and PIRLS. But as the race to the top has intensified, the 'tiger parents' of the East have resorted to increasingly harsh learning regimes, including long coaching sessions outside school hours, to ensure their children score well in the tests. There's now growing concern about this, partly because of its effects on creativity ('Korean education cannot produce geniuses,' remarked one local commentator. 'We don't produce any Nobel prize-winners but we can produce lots of Samsung middle-level managers') and partly because of the long-term implications for mental health. Statistics on this aspect of child health aren't collected in Eastern countries as they are in the West, but there's growing concern about escalating suicide rates among children and young people, and the indications are that these are related to early pressure to achieve.

To produce citizens who can think creatively, as well as coping with whatever slings and arrows life throws their way, primary schools must be places where it's OK to 'have a go' – where, like successful scientists and entrepreneurs throughout history, children can discover that 'failure' is a necessary staging point on the route to success. This doesn't mean teachers should let them off with less than their best, praise them indiscriminately or suggest that correctness doesn't matter. But it does mean that the younger the children, the more sensitive adults must be to their different needs, talents and stages of development, and throughout the primary years learning should be as enjoyable and life-affirming as possible, with the emphasis on celebrating strengths and helping overcome weaknesses.

As a society, we also have to recognise that characteristics such as social competence, perseverance and self-control, which can't be measured on pencil-and-paper tests, are in the long run just as important as academic achievement.

The great e-learning revolution

One much vaunted means of engaging children's attention, while at the same time developing twenty-first-century skills, is to make more use of new technology. There's no question that, in a multimedia age, it would be madness to ignore the strengths of e-learning resources – video can transport a class through time and space, information is immediately available on the Internet, and computer graphics can brighten up dull educational chores. But, as usual in education, it's also important not to get carried away. Electronic teaching can enrich real life learning, but it can't be a substitute. Inside as well as outside school, young children need human interaction and hands-on activities more than second-hand experiences on screen. This is acknowledged by e-learning visionaries like Seymour Papert, who have always recommended the use of technology to enhance first-hand experience.

Over the last twenty years, I've seen many exciting projects in upper primary classrooms, where pupils have created their own 'TV programmes', websites, computer games or simple apps, connected with their learning in various areas of the curriculum. However, like many other educationists (including many IT specialists), I remain convinced that mastery of the old technologies – reading, writing and reckoning – must be given pride of place in the early stages of education.

Back in the 1990s, English primary schools introduced calculators, on the principle that contemporary children needed to know how to use them, and within five years they had to be withdrawn, because children around the country were failing to learn how to add and subtract. 'Electronics speed up the mind' and children with easy access to 'the right answer' are unlikely to relish the long slow process of learning to calculate for themselves. Unfortunately, the policy-makers currently flooding pre-schools and early primary classes with hand-held tablets seem unaware of this lesson from the past. Within five years or so we'll know whether, as I suspect, young children's ready access to iPads will make it even more difficult for them to focus attention and acquire the many complex skills underpinning true literacy and numeracy.*

Once children are competent in the three Rs, inspired use of IT can hugely enrich their educational experiences (and for those with special educational needs it can be a godsend, both for helping overcome ingrained literacy and numeracy problems, and for enabling access to the wider curriculum). However, if digital technology is merely employed to support a narrow, standards-driven school curriculum, there's precious little evidence that it makes much difference to educational achievement. Thanks to the blandishments of software manufacturers and the optimism of politicians, practically every classroom in the UK now has an interactive whiteboard ... but standards have not soared. Investment by schools in computers and other electronic paraphernalia continues apace – £550 million pounds in 2013–14, and expected to be £590 million in 2014–15 – and the majority of educational publishing is now directed toward interactive whiteboards and handheld devices. This is despite the conclusion of an international study at Munich University that 'the evidence suggests that computer use in schools does not seem to contribute substantially to pupils' learning of basic skills such as maths or reading' (see also Chapter 9, 'Books versus screens' and 'The medium is the message').

---

* It's interesting that, in California's Silicon Valley, three-quarters of the pupils at the fee-paying Waldorf School of the Peninsula (where technology isn't allowed over the threshold until 8th grade) are the children of high-flying IT specialists. These parents work for companies like Apple, Yahoo and Hewlett Packard, and include the chief technology officer of eBay and the executive communications officer from Google who writes speeches for Eric Schmidt. Such people know a thing or two about technology, and are clearly keen to avoid drowning their offspring in it from an early age (see also page 298).

The Munich researchers pointed out that using home computers for learning improved school performance, but using them for games and gossip had the opposite effect; in school, occasional access to computers led to slight improvement but frequent access was linked to even worse performance than no access at all. All this leads to the common sense conclusion voiced by IT expert Greg Pearson – unless you're using computers knowledgeably for a specific purpose, they can be 'a waste of time and energy much more easily than they can be useful'.

Who's educating the children?

If, according to research and experience, excessive or inappropriate use of IT can be counter-productive in pre-school and early primary school, why is it now so extraordinarily widespread – especially in the USA and UK? I suspect part of the answer is a serious case of technophilia among educational policy-makers: new technology has rapidly transformed so many aspects of our national life that many of the powers-that-be are bedazzled by its potential. There's also the rather disturbing fact that policy-makers in general seldom have much day-to-day experience of dealing with young children themselves (at least beyond their immediate families) and – for the reasons outlined above – they usually ignore the opinions of experts in the field unless these happen to agree with their own.

However, and even more disturbing, there is the increasing influence of global corporations, including IT companies, on educational practice. The educational historian, Professor Diane Ravitch, who was US Assistant Secretary of Education in the 1990's George H.W. Bush administration, has since become profoundly disillusioned with her nation's educational direction of travel. In her 2013 book *Reign of Error*, she catalogues the ways successive US government policies have narrowed the curriculum, favoured testing regimes above mind-broadening educational practice, and widened the achievement gap between rich and poor pupils.

She also describes the steady take-over of US 'charter schools' by commercial organizations, which are essentially siphoning off government funding and redistributing it to their share-holders: the subtitle of her book is *The Hoax of the Privatization Movement and the Danger to American Public Schools*. All these changes have taken place in the name of educational reform, but Ravitch warns that the 'reformers' overall intention is to hand over schools to private managers and 'let the market sort out the winners and the losers'.

American public schools are what's known in the UK as state schools, and US charter schools are similar to England's academies. Many British educators believe that current government policy in Westminster is aimed at the privatization of the school system. The financial recession has caused severe funding problems for public services, so offers of help from commercial organizations are clearly attractive, but anyone concerned about democracy and social justice should heed Ravitch's warning that the reformers 'wish to substitute private choices for the public's responsibility to provide good schools for all children. They lack any understanding of the crucial role of public schools in a democracy.'

Reign of Error also suggests an alternative route for the US educational system, one which would be both democratic and educationally successful. It's extremely similar to that of Pasi Sahlberg in the 2012 book *Finnish Lessons*. Sahlberg, who is Director General of the Ministry for Education in Helsinki, describes his country's system, which results not only in high scores in PISA and PIRLS, but high levels of childhood well-being in the UNICEF survey, as well as the narrowest gap between rich and poor in Europe. Interestingly, as well as starting formal education later than the USA and UK, Finland has no standardised testing until students are in their late teens.

In a presentation at the Scottish Parliament, Sahlberg recommended that any country wishing to emulate Finland's educational record should aim for the following in its school system:

- more collaboration, less competition
- more personalization, less standardisation

- more responsibility and trust, less accountability and control
- more pedagogy, less technology
- more professionalism, less bureaucracy.

The state education system this recipe has produced is valued so highly by the Finnish people that primary teaching is a high-status profession – in 2012 seven out of eight applicants for the primary teaching course at Helsinki University had to be turned away. Teaching young children is, in Sahlberg's words, 'only for the very best'.

Parents and teachers

There are, of course, many excellent primary teachers in the UK (I meet them all the time) but I meet many others who are worn down by measurement and accountability procedures, political micro-management and endless bureaucracy. Unfortunately, as long as government refuses to listen to criticism from the educational world, there's likely to be little change in this 'reign of error'. And yet, I also meet countless parents who are concerned about the educational pressure on their young children, especially the parents of boys, who often find our country's early start on formal education extremely difficult to cope with.

The journalist Warwick Mansell, who's also in frequent contact with parents, believes there is widespread anxiety about the system but that 'the parental voice is not heard because there is no real forum. We need a formal mechanism for government to take it seriously, but the current Ofsted system for reporting parental opinion is laughable.' I'm sure the parents who recently told Mansell that 'My five-year-old son told me he hates learning' and 'Everything [at the primary school] is about data and testing' would welcome an effective mechanism for expressing their concerns. As would the mother who told me at a recent parents' meeting that she dreads the day her four-year-old son starts school and the dad who expressed desperate concern about the pressures on his teenage daughter as she approached her GCSEs.

Margaret Morrissey, former press officer of the national Parent Teacher Association (now PTA-UK), believes that twenty years ago this organisation had some influence on government, but that the influence has been steadily eroded, largely due to parents themselves having less time to spend interacting with their children's schools. 'In the first couple of years they turn up to school events, because it's lovely to see your little one perform in a play or something, but as time goes on they're just so busy with the daily treadmill of getting children to school, going to work, trans-porting the kids to various evening clubs and so on ... the education bit in the middle just turns into "drop me an email".' She believes that electronic communications (schools webmail and texting systems) have eroded genuine parent-teacher interaction: 'Even the PTAs meet on the Internet now.'

Mrs Morrissey, who now runs the website Parents Outloud, battling for 'parental voice' in education, believes changing attitudes to childcare are involved (see also Chapter 6): 'I used to look after my grandchildren while my daughter was at work, and in 2003 I was the only granny at the school gates. Now there are lots – in fact, it's more normal to see grandparents at special school assemblies than parents. One day these children will be parents themselves, and it won't occur to them that mum and dad might be involved with school beyond logging on to the webmail. You wouldn't leave your child all day with a stranger at the supermarket or somewhere – parents need to know their kids' primary teacher.'

The normalisation of parents' withdrawal from their children's educational environment is worrying from an educational per-spective, because studies repeatedly find that parental involvement is a critical factor in children's achievement. But it's also worrying from a sociological one: if it takes a village to raise a child, the villagers should presumably have more personal contact than the odd webmail message that 'Johnny did very well in maths today.'

The most successful schools I visit do still seem able to provide opportunities for comfortable interaction between parents and teachers, in which they focus on common goals, not just educational ones or the running of fundraising activities. There are suggestions throughout this book for ways schools can support parents and parents can support schools, thus creating an 'adult alliance' to detoxify childhood.

Bullying tactics

One worrying example of parents and teachers failing to communicate and thus to see each other's point of view is the vexed question of bullying. Parents often feel schools could be doing more to protect their children from bullying, while teachers reckon some behaviour now labelled as bullying is actually just the cut-and-thrust of playground politics, and that over-zealous interference can do more harm than good.

Bullying was defined on a 2007 UK government website as 'teasing and name-calling, threats and physical violence, damage to property, deliberately leaving children out of social activities, spreading rumours or upsetting mobile phone or email messages'. With boys, it often involves violence; in girls it's more likely to be psychological, which can be just as damaging. A parent whose child comes home complaining of being bullied is understandably anxious, and can reasonably expect the school to take action.

However, small examples of the activities listed above happen every day in every primary school playground in the world – and until children are born fully civilised they'll continue to happen. There's a huge difference between full-blown bullying and playground spats, occasional spiteful behaviour or infant fallings out. Resilient children deal with such episodes themselves and learning to sort them out is an important part of every child's social education. As pointed out in Chapter 2, too much policing of play can create both bullies and victims, rather than helping children develop social skills for themselves. However, all children benefit from talking things over with mum, dad, and/or teacher to work out the best ways of dealing with playground incidents.

Real bullying, on the other hand, is extreme or prolonged damaging behaviour, vindictive enough to deprive victims of the capacity to defend themselves. As one teacher described it to me, 'a spat's like the flicker of a candle, bullying's a continuous burn'. All children need protection from true bullying, and every school needs a clear, no-nonsense anti-bullying policy (with unpleasant consequences for the bullies – see next section) brought rapidly into force when incidents occur. Given that such policies are in place, and their children are well-informed about the best way to deal with bullies (see website addresses on page 244), parents have to trust teachers to decide whether a particular incident is a flicker or part of a first-degree burn.

But the cultural factors described in Chapter 2 have made both parents and children increasingly anxious, and distrustful of others. A competitive consumerist ethos outside school (see next chapter), combined with a competitive academic ethos in the classroom, isn't conducive to an atmosphere of mutuality and trust. One of the most depressing findings in the 2007 UNICEF survey of childhood well-being was that 48 per cent of UK children answered 'No' to the question 'Do you find your classmates kind and helpful?', while in the Scandinavian countries the figure was around 10 per cent. When almost half of a nation's children spend their schooldays watching their backs, it's not surprising if everyday spats are sometimes blown out of proportion.

Media reports of the occasional tragic consequences of bullying, or of faddish policies that let bullies off the hook (such as the 'no blame' strategy that was trialled in some English schools) fan the flames of anxiety. Many parents are less inclined to accept a schools' assessment than in the past. This, in turn, puts schools on the defensive about parental complaints. And this breakdown of trust between partners in the child-rearing enterprise has long-term implications for children and society every bit as worrying as the bullying itself.

Dealing with discipline

No child is born a bully, just as no child is born a nasty little brat. Some poor souls may be genetically pre-destined to lag behind in the development stakes, in which case they need extra help to fit into normal social patterns. But the majority of children brought up in a peaceful, prosperous country should, by the time they're six or so, be able to settle down and take full advantage of school.

So why are so many of them turning brattish? Let me count the ways: diet, lack of sleep or outdoor play, inadequate attachment or opportunities for real-life communication, family problems, early failure at school, lack of motivation, national obsession with 'selfish materialism', a playground culture in which it's cool to be badly behaved (see Chapter 8), exposure to screen-based violence and bullying behaviour (Chapter 9) ... the cocktail will be different in every case, but its origins are in a culture that has forgotten the essential elements of successful child-rearing.

And once bad behaviour at school begins, it adds considerably to the toxic mix. A few misbehaving children in a class means the teacher becomes preoccupied with the business of crowd control. There's less time and energy available for producing motivating lessons, and the education of every child in the class suffers. There are now many schools around the developed world where education is the least of teachers' worries – they spend their days desperately trying to hold back a tide of low-level disruption, refusal to follow instructions and, sadly, physical violence to classmates and teachers.

The issue of discipline is as confusing for teachers these days as it is for parents. During the twentieth century the educational establishment, like the rest of western society, swung from trad-itional authoritarian attitudes to much more liberal views on behaviour, with increasing focus on the rights of the individual. Concern for children's rights, culminating in 1989 in the United Nations Convention on the Rights of the Child, has led some educational policymakers to reject the notion of punishment when children break rules or breach the boundaries of acceptable behaviour, resulting in fads like the 'no blame' policy on bullying mentioned earlier. Teachers, who have to try and maintain order on the ground, are sometimes unconvinced by the 'behaviour modification strategies' foisted on them by national or local advisers.

The problem is compounded by the general erosion of respect for authority over the last few decades. But in order to control a group of thirty or so children, teachers *must* have authority. Research on parenting quoted on pages 96–7 suggests the most effective parental style is 'authoritative', where warmth and respect for a child's point of view are balanced by the need to maintain firm boundaries for behaviour. Teachers too have to strive for an authoritative balance. If they're too indulgent, their class will run rings around them; if they're authoritarian, their pupils are likely to erupt into bad behaviour as soon as they turn their backs.

In a morally relative society, it can be difficult for any adult to feel authoritative. It's particularly hard for a teacher, attempting to balance the interests of thirty or so children in a class. It's therefore important that schools have clearly agreed rules, to which everyone involved – children, teachers, parents, school community – are happy to subscribe. The authoritative teacher then does everything possible to respect individual children's viewpoints, while imposing and maintaining the rules in a firm but friendly fashion.

When children flout the rules, the teacher has to be able to impose some kind of sanction, both to maintain authority and to demonstrate to all pupils that antisocial behaviour has unpleasant consequences. In dealing with children en masse, justice has to be seen to be done – if they get away with bad behaviour, it simply encourages them (and others) to push the boundaries further. Teachers usually have a sliding scale of punishments, culminating in removing the offender from the class. This demonstrates to everyone that breaking the rules, and thus ignoring one's responsibility to the group, can ultimately result in social exclusion.

In the case of the youngest offenders, research suggests it's possible to improve behaviour through kindness. The Nurture Group movement in the UK provides trained staff who work with small groups of emotionally-disturbed young children to teach them social skills in less formal, more domestic settings. The children's reward for learning self-control is to be considered 'grown-up' enough to return to their class.

These nurturing tactics are, however, less likely to make an impact as children grow older. Most teachers I've talked to feel that by the time children are in double figures, it's too late to treat misbehaviour (especially bullying) with overt kindness. The older the child, the tougher the love has to be. What's more, to encourage the others, shame has to be part of the deal. Whatever the sanction is, everyone involved in the social life of the school – teachers, parents and children – has to consider it unpleasant, or it won't have any effect. Whether the miscreant has privileges removed, is sent to a 'sin bin' until prepared to toe the line or, in the worst scenario, excluded from school altogether, there's no getting away from the fact that punishment (even if it's for your child) isn't pleasant.

For well-balanced and happy children, however, tough measures are seldom necessary. So rather than battling with a rising tide of bad behaviour, it makes sense for adults to work together to stop the rot before it begins, which means tackling the causes of toxic childhood syndrome both at home and at school.

* * *

Ensuring that all children win the must-have prizes upon which successful citizenship depends – motivation to learn, the three Rs and the ability to get along with others – has never been easy, but aspects of contemporary culture, and the effects of that culture on children, now make the task more challenging than ever. In the circumstances, teachers and parents – the two groups with the interests of schoolchildren most at heart – would gain immensely from joining forces to tackle toxic childhood syndrome. Yet the social and cultural environment in which the syndrome flourishes has made this 'adult alliance' increasingly difficult.

While the responsibility for reinvigorating the educational aspect of the adult alliance rests with schools, it also relies on parents recognising that 'red carpet treatment' for their own child at the expense of others isn't on the cards. A fiercely competitive culture isn't appropriate for the under-tens – childhood is not a race – but neither should children be coddled, cosseted and shielded from the consequences of their actions. The capacity to co-exist with others (which in the long run is arguably the greatest of the must-have primary prizes) relies on children learning within a safe environment how to deal with success and failure, how to fight their own battles, and how to balance their rights as individuals with their social responsibilities to others.

It's in the interests of parents, teachers and society as a whole to work for a primary education system that prepares all children for successful citizenship ... and to ensure that it isn't derailed by educational fads and fashions, time-wasting bureaucracy or misguided political tinkering.

DETOXING EDUCATION FOR YOUR CHILD

- Recognise from the beginning that primary education is not a race.
- Remember that the children who do well in the long run are those who:
    - enjoy learning for its own sake, not just to get smiley faces, stars or high marks
    - are motivated to learn and don't give up easily
    - get on with other children and with their teacher, and can work well with others.

- Accept that children develop at different rates. A child who's doing wonderfully today may slow off tomorrow; a slow starter may eventually overtake everyone.

- Give heartfelt praise for your child's achievements – especially evidence of hard work and effort. Show your delight when things go well.
- But … don't overdo the praise – if you go into raptures about *everything* your child does, your praise won't carry much weight when it's really justified. And avoid suggesting that your child's successes are due to 'natural talent', which research shows can lead to complacency and/or reluctance to try at subjects in which children don't think they're 'naturally' talented.
- If you think your child isn't achieving as well as he or she could, keep critical comments to a minimum – discuss what's going wrong and look for ways to help.
- But … try not to pile on the pressure. If your expectations are too high, it can damage your child's chances of success.
- The single most important way parents can help children do well is through talking with them, and encouraging them to talk. As well as the suggestions in Chapter 4, ask about your child's day at school with open-ended questions that encourage talk, for instance: 'What was the best thing that happened today, then?' 'How's that story going, the one the teacher's reading you?' 'What's this Roman project all about?' The more interest you show, the more you actively listen to their responses, the more children are likely to open up.
- Make sure your child knows what bullying is (and isn't) and how to deal with it, including reporting straight back to you and/or a teacher. There's good advice on websites such as those listed below.
- Make every attempt to attend school events, no matter how dreary you find them – just by being there you demonstrate your love and support for your child, and you also send a message of support to the school. If you can't make it explain why to your child, and try to send a substitute (for instance a grandparent, childminder or family friend).
- Keep an intelligent eye on the news about education, and make sure you know your school's take on it. But don't be swayed by excessive claims about particular educational strategies – there are no magic

bullets in education, because it depends so much on the personalities of the teachers and children involved. What works for one particular class with one particular teacher may well be a complete fiasco in the classroom down the road.

HOW TO DETOX THE PARENT-SCHOOL RELATIONSHIP

- Choose a school by reading the prospectus, arranging a visit, chatting with other parents in the area – for instance, is this a school that encourages the development of 'the whole child' – not just focusing on tests? (Interestingly, schools that take this approach often do particularly well in the tests too.)
- When your child starts school, make sure you know the organisational ropes, in terms of expectations about homework, arrangements for taking children to school, collecting them, and so on. Integrate these into family routines so they become second nature.
- Keep a folder for the prospectus and any other communications about school procedures and so on, and check it once in a while. It can also be useful for keeping your child's school reports and any special commendations or certificates.
- Always make an effort to turn up to parent-teacher interviews. If you can't make it, write to ask if it's possible to arrange an appointment at an alternative time. Teachers are often rushed off their feet and can't always stop for a chat about a child without notice.
- Try to be positive about school when talking about it to your child – parental attitudes rub off on children, and the more positive their attitude to school the better children will do. So:
    - if you had bad experiences of school yourself, don't let them influence you
    - look for things to praise about the school and your child's teacher, and hold your tongue if possible about anything that annoys you
    - don't gossip carelessly with other parents in front of your children.

- But … this doesn't mean you should lie to your child if anything's amiss. Children know when you're telling the truth. They also need to know that if anything is troubling them, they can speak openly to you about it.

- Take opportunities to get to know other parents, but beware of school gate gossip – it's easy for rumours and misunderstandings to get out of hand. The best policy is probably 'hear no evil, see no evil, speak no evil'.

- If you're able to support the Parent Teacher Association, meetings and functions, do so. Apart from being an opportunity to exercise parent power, it's a chance to meet teachers informally and get to know the parents of your child's classmates.

- On the other hand, no one knows your child, or cares about his or her welfare, as much as you. If, on serious reflection, you believe the school is wrong, you must act.

- On such occasions, don't rush in to complain in an angry or upset state of mind. Try to keep calm and use the correct channels to put your point of view.

- Make sure you are completely sure about school rules and discipline procedures and who to contact in particular circumstances (this is where that folder with the prospectus, etc. comes into its own). Don't be tempted to go 'straight to the top' as this can escalate problems rather than solving them.

DEALING WITH PROBLEMS AT SCHOOL

- If something goes wrong for your child at school, help them talk it through. Try to work out what's actually happened, and see if your child can find a way to deal with it (see Chapter 4).

- If your child's in trouble, try to be dispassionate – don't automatically leap to his or her defence. Try to see both sides of the argument. Loving your child doesn't mean assuming he or she can do no wrong.

- It's a good idea to write a letter about the problem first, keeping it as calm and reasonable as possible. It helps you sort out what's gone on, and you can also be sure the main facts are clearly stated (and that you don't forget any in the heat of the moment).
- Before going to any meetings, think about what outcome you would like to see – do you know what you want the school to do to sort out the issue?
- Putting things in writing from the start is also useful if it's necessary to take the case further – i.e. to school governors, county/city authorities or national organizations or pressure groups.

PARENT POWER: WORKING WITH THE SCHOOL

As one who's been both a parent and a teacher I know that parent-teacher liaison is one of the toughest nuts to crack, but when communication is good everyone benefits – especially the children. Many of the present difficulties in schools are compounded by lack of understanding on both sides. For instance, the parents I speak to think schools cause the educational rat race, while teachers often blame the parents. Since both schools and parents want to raise happy healthy children, it's vital to break through such pointless prejudices.

- Try in any way you can to open up lines of communication through official channels – parents' meetings, PTAs, boards of governors – and raise issues that concern you about children's welfare. When I talk in schools about the ill-effects of testing and targets, I'm amazed by the number of parents who've clearly been worried about this issue, but didn't like to say.
- The thought of school social occasions may be ghastly, but the only way to improve them is to join in. Turn up, smile, socialise, network … and talk about your concerns. Try to avoid outright criticism – you'll get much further by looking for positive ways forward.

- Use 'school gate' conversations and other out-of-school contacts with other parents to develop positive, can-do attitudes to parent-school liaison. If you can find one way of working with the school on a particular issue, opportunities for further collaboration are very likely to arise.
- Do you have a talent (Arts? Sciences? Practical skills?) and some spare time to help make the curriculum (or after-school clubs) come alive? Non-working parents and grandparents can be a huge resource in this respect, and there's great satisfaction to be had in passing one's enthusiasm on to another generation.

Further reading

Bill Lucas and Alastair Smith, Help Your Child to Succeed: The Essential Guide for Parents (Network Educational Press, 2009)

Gary Wilson Help Your Boys Succeed: The Essential Guide for Parents (Network Educational Press, 2010)

Adele Faber and Elaine Mazlich, How to Talk so Kids Will Learn at Home and in School (Scribner, 1995)

Warwick Mansell, Education by Numbers: The Tyranny of Testing (Politico's Publishing, 2009)

Noel Janis-Norton, Calmer, Easier, Happier Homework (Hodder and Stoughton, 2013)

Sue Palmer, Upstart: the case for raising the school starting age (Floris Books, 2016)

Useful websites

The Advisory Centre for Education: independent information and advice: www.ace-ed.org.uk

Coram Children's Legal Centre for advice on education law, admissions, etc. www.childrenslegalcentre.com

Official government websites for information on education: England and Wales: www.gov.uk; Scotland: www.scotland.gov.uk/Topics/Education; N. Ireland: www.deni.gov.uk

Margaret Morrissey's parents' website: www.parentsoutloud.com

Websites for help with bullying: www.beatbullying.org; www.bullying.co.uk; www.kidscape.org.uk

Mind the Gap

One of the aims of a state-sponsored educational system is to provide a 'level playing field' – a certain level of basic education available to all children. Another is to provide an opportunity for children from different backgrounds to mingle, and so promote greater social cohesion. The last primary class I taught back in the early 1980s included children from a wide range of backgrounds – from professional families to those of unskilled workers. They all rubbed along together, and I think both children and their parents benefited from the opportunities this gave to mix with people from different backgrounds.

However, when people lose faith in a system, those who can afford it move out. As childhood became increasingly toxic, and parents became increasingly worried about their own children's success and/or well-being at school, the democratic ethos of state education has been seriously undermined. Despite a world-wide economic recession and rising fees, private education continues to flourish – around 10 per cent of children are now educated privately in the US and 7 per cent in the UK (Indeed, part of the reason many parents have to work so hard is that they're paying school fees). Other families choose to educate their own children at home – in 2012 it was estimated that around 1.5 million children in the USA and 60,000 in the UK were being home-educated. The demand for less highly-regulated education has also led in the UK to a flourishing free-school movement, in which parents have far more say in the sort of schooling their children receive.

Where they stay within the state system, better-off parents have become adept at manoeuvring to get their children into 'good' schools. Their support then makes the good schools better, while the less popular ones sink lower down the heap, leading to a two-tier system where some schools, especially in the inner cities, are now in a desperate plight. This perpetuates and increases the poverty gap, which is worse in the USA and UK than most other western countries.

So far, primary teachers in disadvantaged areas have managed to keep their pupils in school and learning: visiting such schools, I've sometimes been in awe at the talent and dedication of the staff. However, they haven't been helped by politicians insisting that fierce and early concentration on the three Rs is all that's needed to overcome poor children's problems, or that a tests-and-targets culture can encourage everyone to 'aspire'. (In one such school, I spotted a beautifully calligraphed poster in the Ladies loo which read 'The flogging will continue until morale improves!') In fact, the children who suffer most from this winners-and-losers approach are those that governments claim are supposedly trying not to 'leave behind'.

Eight years after *Toxic Childhood* was first published, it's distressing to record that the primary educational rat race has grown steadily more competitive, and the pressures on young children have become ever more intense. How long will it take for politicians to recognise that their educational recipe is counter-productive? How wide must the poverty gap grow before they notice that tests, targets and too-much-too-soon are driving rather than reducing it? And how many mental health problems will this high-pressure regime engender in children across the social classes before they spot its cost to families, communities and the nation?

CHAPTER EIGHT

THE WORD ON THE STREET

I've already quoted the African proverb, 'It takes a village to raise a child'. Children's development is affected not only by their parents, but by other members of the family, friends and figures in the local community. Indeed, the neuroscientist Steven Pinker argues that the influence of this wider community is more important than that of parents themselves.

However, today's children also inhabit the electronic village of mass communications and entertainment. Indeed, many of them spend at least as much of their leisure time in screen-based activities as they do with the real people in their lives. So what children encounter on TV, film, the Internet, social networks and electronic games will clearly affect their overall development. The issues arising from children's movement from real life to screen-time are dealt with in the next chapter. But there's another, highly insidious way in which the mass media affect children's lives, through the influence of marketing on their play, friendships, family relationships and the culture of childhood in general.

Peer pressure has always been an important part of growing up, but in previous generations, children's games and playground interactions were largely their own self-chosen (and self-directed) concern. Fads and crazes would come and go, often related to the adult world, but very much under children's control. However, as their lives have become increasingly dominated by screen-based entertainment, playground culture has moved steadily under the control of the marketing industry. Many parents seem unaware – or are in denial – that behind the TV programmes and computer games that keep their offspring entertained lurks an army of anonymous manipulators – marketing executives and child psychologists employed by big business to capture the hearts and minds of the next generation of consumers. These very powerful 'electronic villagers' now have a huge impact on childhood culture and the ways children relate to both their peers and their families.

From creative play to 'toy consumption'

One obvious illustration of this state of affairs is the changing nature of toys. Psychologists explain that, especially in the case of very young children, the simpler the item, the more likely it is to stimulate the creative play that underpins human learning. A cloth thrown over a table can create a den, an empty box can be transformed through the imagination into a car, a boat, anything in the world ... or, indeed, the universe. Symbolic play of this kind has been significant throughout history in developing children's imagination and problem-solving skills. The inborn drive to explore, experiment and create can be satisfied using the simplest of materials – sand, sticks and stones, water, paper, coloured crayons, a dressing-up box of cast-off clothes, household junk for making models...

The problem is that old clothes and household junk are free, and free stuff has no place in a highly developed consumer culture. Toy companies have therefore devised ever more brightly-coloured sophisticated substitutes (often labelled 'educational') that parents can pay for. And advertisers have devoted much time, money and energy to convincing children that these substitutes will make them happy. Sadly, since manufactured toys often leave little to the imagination, parents around the world have noticed that – once the excitement of acquisition has worn off – children don't seem to play as much as they used to.

In the last couple of decades, there's also been a worrying move towards two-dimensional 'techno-play': a growing number of toys are merely a stepping stone from one screen-based activity to another, part of an all-embracing multimedia experience that starts in the marketing departments of global corporations. Films aimed at children are now designed from the outset to optimise merchandising opportunities, including toys (dolls, models, etc.), paraphernalia (pencil cases, lunch boxes, clothing and so on) and website and console games. Children's TV shows – even those shown on non-commercial stations – also come complete with a range of consumer products which, rather than acting as levers to their own creativity are often merely bridges from one type of passive, sedentary entertainment to another. The proliferation of handheld devices, and a growing range of baby apps, means that techno-play now supplants 'real play' from an increasingly early age.

As pointed out in previous chapters, play is an essential element in children's physical, social, emotional and cognitive development – as important, according to child psychologists, as food and sleep. It seems particularly significant in terms of the factors underlying toxic childhood syndrome: anyone who's watched a small child utterly engrossed in play can appreciate its contribution to the capacity for focused attention and self-regulation. To an adult the play may look like pointless 'messing about' but it clearly involves intense concentration, coming from deep within the child. So the more self-chosen messing about children engage in, the better they'll develop control of both physical and mental faculties – and the greater the range of their play, the wider the range of skills they'll acquire. On the other hand, when children engage with screen-based entertainment, their attention is attracted and directed by its adult creators (children's mental state while watching TV has been described as 'attentional inertia'), so the only faculties they'll develop are those required to interact with the screen.

Of course, in today's world children need to understand screen-based leisure and learning, and it would be ridiculous to deny

them access to technological play. But they also need the skills
and understanding that human beings have always needed: a wide
range of physical skills, including bodily coordination and control;
the social skills that develop through real-life interaction, not only
with adults but with other children; emotional capacities such as
self-confidence, risk-management and resilience; and common-
sense understanding of the real world that can only be acquired
through experience. So it's still important that they're allowed and
encouraged to indulge their inborn drive for 'real play', and the
younger the child, the greater should be the proportion of real to
virtual activity.

In 2013, the American Academy of Pediatrics updated its
guidelines on media use, recommending that children under
two shouldn't engage in any screen-based activity, and that
screen-time for the over-twos should be limited to no more than
two hours a day. In the same year, the United Nations, which
enshrines 'the right to play' as Article 31 of its Convention of the
Rights of the Child, issued a General Comment reminding the
global village that play is 'initiated, controlled and structured
by children themselves' and its key characteristics are 'fun,
uncertainty, challenge, flexibility and non-productivity'. While
some shop-bought items doubtless add to the fun, the current
wholesale switch from real play to toy consumption and techno-
play is clearly a detrimental move.

The strangers behind the screens

A further worrying feature of contemporary play – covered in
Chapter 2 – is that it seldom takes place outside, and one of the
main reasons for the retreat indoors is 'stranger danger'. Yet the
same parents who are desperate to protect children from strangers
outside the home are happy to leave even their youngest offspring
in the care of screen-based strangers for hours on end. And these
strangers, or the commercial forces behind them, inevitably have
something to sell.

We are all, whatever our age, constantly manipulated by the mass media, but most adults are savvy enough to recognise the manipulation, understand the differences between real and make-believe, enjoy our viewing and make rational decisions based on what we see. Children are not. The younger they are, the more the distinction between screen-life and real life is blurred. Responsible programme-makers realise this and take it into account – but marketing agencies are not renowned for responsible behaviour in terms of child development. Their interest in children is to sell more stuff. In a twenty-first-century world, marketeers can influence young consumers through billboard adverts in the local area, marketing strategies in shops, TV ads, product placement in films and TV shows, and a variety of 'viral' techniques, in both the real and the virtual world. Most of these are, to some extent, controlled by regulation. But increasingly the market also reaches out to children via laptops, smartphones and tablets, and the rules for the Internet aren't based on those for TV, press, billboard or other obvious types of advertising.

Children today are growing up in what US psychiatrist Susan Linn has called 'a marketing maelstrom'. Research has shown that up to the age of about eight, they aren't particularly aware of marketeers' intent, seeing adverts merely as an enjoyable form of entertainment and information. Indeed, they have to be around eleven or twelve before they can articulate a critical understanding of marketing messages, and by this age many have been effectively brainwashed, so even if they're perfectly aware of how they're being manipulated they still find it difficult to resist. For this reason, some countries have banned TV marketing to children until twelve, and child development experts around the world are urging other governments and the UN to follow their lead (see 'Turning the tide', pages 269–72).

In the past, advertisements aimed at children related mainly to childish things – toys, chocolate bars, breakfast cereals – and were relatively low-budget affairs. Over the last twenty years there's been a huge change. In his 1992 book *Kids as Customers*, US marketing strategist James McNeal alerted big business to the potential of the children's market: 'Kids are the most unsophisticated of all consumers; they have the least and therefore want the most. Consequently, they are in a perfect position to be taken.'

Most adults are scarcely aware of this bombardment – sophisticated marketing techniques aimed at pre-teens simply don't impinge on adult lives – and their own memories of ads are from another, more innocent age. But as Susan Linn says, 'comparing the advertisements of three decades ago to the commercialism that permeates our children's world is like comparing a BB gun to a smart bomb ... the explosion of marketing aimed at children today is precisely targeted, refined by scientific method and honed by child psychologists – in short, it is more pervasive and intrusive than ever.' In 2000, Dr Linn and a group of US psychologists launched the Campaign for a Commercial-Free Childhood to 'reclaim childhood from commercial marketeers'.

In recent years, CCFC has staged several successful campaigns. In 2008, for instance, they stopped the Disney corporation from claiming that *Baby Einstein* DVDs are 'educational' and persuaded them to offer a refund to any parent who'd bought the product since Disney acquired the franchise. In 2011, they prevented Scholastic from distributing corporately-sponsored teaching materials in US schools. In 2014, the US Federal Trade Commission upheld their complaint against the 'Your Baby Can Read' website (on the very reasonable grounds that babies can't read).

Unfortunately, soon after this triumph, the FTC declined to ban marketing material for a Fisher-Price product that claims to 'teach babies numbers and letters', because the ad doesn't say babies will actually *learn* numbers and letters, merely that the product teaches them. Multinational corporations are quick learners and have legal teams to back up their marketing departments, so I fear CFCC faces an uphill struggle in convincing the parents of America that big business is less concerned about the developmental needs of young children than about the cash they can generate.

Children as customers

There are many reasons that today's multinational corporations show a keen interest in the pre-teen age-group. One is that they recognise the money-making potential of parental love, and the desire of parents to give their children the very best start in life. Another is that contemporary children have increasing amounts of money to spend – or, rather, increasing access to their parents' disposable income. Marketeers now specifically target 'guilt money' – pocket money and presents doled out by parents who are worried that long hours at work keep them away from their children. Conveniently, the absence of parents at home means children spend more time glued to screens, so there's plenty of opportunity to groom young consumers.

In fact, the long-hours culture creates a perfect circle for selling more stuff:

- children are unhappy because of parental absence
- advertisements offer happiness through purchase of products
- children besiege parents with requests for said products and guilt-stricken parents throw money at the problem
- the purchase makes children and parents happy for a nanosecond ...
- ... then unhappiness returns because presents are no substitute for presence, and the cycle goes on – children want ever more stuff, and parents have to earn ever more money to pay for it.

And it's not just infant peer pressure driving this vicious circle: as one parent remarked in a 2011 report, 'The problem is that parents sometimes feel the peer pressure too and often feel almost forced to buy certain products because other parents are. They feel like bad parents if they don't.'

Another factor in the increasing commercialisation of childhood has been the discovery that pester power works not only for children's products but for everything families buy – from cars, holidays and entertainment to food, household items and even cleaning products. As avid TV watchers, children are able to pass on marketing messages to parents, and as avid consumers they're quick to pick up on what's in and what's out. So the marketing industry has recruited children to work on their behalf, and 'nag-factor' now features in all major campaigns for family purchases. US market research has shown that 67 per cent of car purchases are influenced by children while – as indicated in Chapter 1 – the younger generation has considerable input into family food shopping. In one consumer report, 100 per cent of parents of two- to five-year olds agreed that their children have a major influence on their food and snack purchases. Indeed, pester power has become essential to marketing – a US study showed that sales of a product declined by a third if children didn't ask for it, even more in the case of toys and entertainment.

Perhaps the most sinister reason of all for big business's interest in young children is the marketeers' desire to initiate them as early as possible into the cult of the brand. In a cut-throat consumer culture, brand awareness and brand loyalty are priceless assets, so the marketeers' aim is to ensnare consumers while 'the imagination is warm and impressions are permanent'. They devote millions to impressing upon children that a par-ticular brand of fizzy drink, snack food, clothing, transport, entertainment or whatever will make their lives more complete than all the competing brands.

Market research has established that brand loyalty can be encouraged in children as young as two through exposure to brand logos and mascots on screen and on products they enjoy. Three-year-olds can be influenced to ask for brands by name. By three-and-a-half children can be convinced that certain brands transmit certain qualities to the purchaser, so marketing strategies move from awareness-raising to creating dependence on the particular brand they're pushing.

Put bluntly, this means that big business now engages in complex mind games with very small children. Given the tender age of the quarry, this seems an unequal contest – amounting more-

or-less to mass brainwashing. Marketeers argue that children are increasingly consumer-savvy, but they're unlikely to be as savvy as adults armed with multimillion pound budgets and the latest psychological weapons. As Nancy Shalek, president of a major US advertising agency, once explained to colleagues: 'Advertising at its best is making people feel that without their product, you're a loser. Kids are very sensitive to that ... You open up emotional vulner-abilities and it's very easy to do with kids because they're the most emotionally vulnerable.'

Sugar and spice ...

In targeting children, advertisers are acutely aware of gender dif-ferences. While many parents since the late twentieth century have tried earnestly to protect their children from gender bias, the forces of worldwide marketing had other ideas. They quickly embraced the claims of evolutionary biologists that the male and female of the species have different attitudes and interests. And by targeting the differences, they emphasise and exaggerate them, which makes the two markets even easier to analyse for the future.

Whether driven by nature or nurture (or most probably a complex combination of both), girls seem from a very early age to be more socially-inclined than boys. They're more interested in other people and have more well-developed powers of empathy (the downside of which, as many parents know, is a finely-honed capacity for manipulation). Marketing forces long ago chose pink to symbolise these female qualities, and for many decades the psyches of small girls have been addressed through a cloud of pink smog, in which swim a vast array of collectible dolls, small furry animals and grooming products. (Grooming is, of course, of serious evolutionary significance. In the remote past, young human females probably bonded by picking fleas out of each other's fur; their modern counterparts delight in fixing each other's hair, so manufacturers lure them into fixing Barbie's instead.)

Since the early 2000s, pinkness has become closely associated with little girls' desire to dress as princesses, from sparkly shoes to glittering tiaras, which may well be associated with Disney's expansion of its range of princess costumes. Many other companies have jumped on this bandwagon, transforming an age-old aspect of imaginative play into an early introduction to the world of fashion. For many little girls, a preoccupation with apparel and appearance acts as a check on the sort of play by which nature has designed them to learn. Not wishing to dirty or damage their costumes, they begin to see real play as somehow 'childish', and thus undesirable.

This premature self-consciousness blends with a deep human desire to belong to a peer group so, thanks to the commercial hijacking of playground culture, they're ripe for the next marketing bombardment: the cult of the tween. The tween demographic ('too old for toys, too young for boys') has an emphasis on 'cool' behaviour and even more gender-specific consumption. It used to refer to children between the ages of 8 and 12, but over the last few years it's reached down to much younger girls. Websites popular with the under-tens, such as GirlsGoGames, revolve mainly around fashion, makeovers, cooking, shopping and boyz. Collectable dolls like Bratz ('girls with a passion for fashion') and Monster High Dolls provide role models, as do tween celebrities in mainstream media and on YouTube. And social networking sites or smart-phone messaging open up endless opportunities for passing around the current cool girly chitchat – in a 2011 survey, Facebook was the favourite website of girls under ten, despite its official starting age of 13.

As ownership of smartphones and handheld tablets spreads to younger children, this commercial culture of tweeny female 'cool' may soon stretch its tentacles down to the pre-school age range. As well as contributing to the early sexualisation of girls (see next section), it ensures that the next generation is primed for a lifetime of 'super-consumerism' based on a highly materialist value system. Children who learn at an early age to judge themselves and others in terms of what they wear and what they look like will almost certainly be socially and emotionally vulnerable. There's an eleven-year-old girl in the marketing manual BRAND*child* who explains that 'I love brands ... Brands not only tell me who I am, but also protect me from problems with the others in my class'. A child whose self-image and self-opinion is so dependent on superficial appearances is likely to encounter many problems as she goes through life.

... and all things nice

The reason that tweendom starts ever earlier is another marketing strategy: KAGOY, which stands for Kids Are Getting Older Younger. For many decades, advertisers have targeted products on the basis of 'aspiration', and young human beings generally aspire to be like their elders. So when teenagers aspired to adult fashion styles, the market sold them adult fashion styles; then eleven- and twelve-year-olds wanted this new teenage look so they sold it to them; and when under-tens coveted pre-teen fashion it travelled even further down the food chain ... until products that had once been the province of grown women (such as high heels and make-up) were available in the shops for every age-group.

Little girls have always wanted to be grown-up like their mothers – to dress like adults, wear make-up and appear 'sophis-ticated'. But in the past such precocity was frowned upon and the only way to achieve their dream was through play – slathering mum's lipstick across their faces, slopping about in her high heels or swathing themselves in scarves, shawls, baubles and beads. However, as the princess culture developed and the KAGOY approach to marketing normalised the idea of fashion items for all ages, play was side-lined and even tiny children became fashion-victims. Attitudes to precocity changed too. While researching *Toxic Childhood* during the early 2000s, I lost track of the number of parents who resignedly told me that 'Kids grow up so much quicker these days' as if this were due to some inexorable force of nature, rather than a concerted marketing drive.

It was only when worried adults (often from religious backgrounds) drew attention to the fact that mainstream stores were now selling sexy underwear, pole-dancing kits and other clearly dodgy products, that public concern about the sexualisation of girls began to surface. The media made the link between these items and paedophilia, and reputable retail outlets began to review their choice of merchandise. But as long as there's money to be made, an unregulated market will find ways of making it – bras, thongs and other adult female paraphernalia are still widely available in children's sizes from more downmarket retailers, and the KAGOY philosophy is now so 'normal' that you can buy high-heeled shoes and make-up for pre-schoolers in many high street stores. In more upmarket areas, trendy shops are now devoted to fashion items for toddlers, and parents fork out a fortune on designer clothes.

Alongside a preoccupation with fashion goes a preoccupation with body image. Beset on all sides by images of physical perfection (which, in contemporary terms, means stick-thin with improbable Barbie-breasts), girls trying to fit into the mould of 'cool' are subject to horrendous pressure. A 2012 All Party Parliamentary Group found young females' dissatisfaction with their appearance now begins around five years old: by the age of seven, a quarter of the girls surveyed by the group had already tried to lose weight at least once.

In recent years, adult concern about the long-term effects of bombarding young girls with commercially-fuelled gender-stereotypes has inspired a fight-back, led by the feminist movement. Abi Moore, founder of the website PinkStinks, pointed out that 'the princess culture starts the minute a child is born and ends up, for teenage girls, with Paris Hilton'. Natasha Walter, in her 2010 book *Living Dolls: The Return of Sexism* recognised that, while turn-of-the-century feminists assumed society was moving towards 'an honest acceptance of girls' sexuality', the market was stealthily trans-forming 'girl-power' into 'the narrowest kind of consumerism and self-objectification'. In my 2013 book, *21st Century Girls*, I argue that marketeers have cynically exploited the social nature of young human females in ways that not only undermine the drive for sexual equality but also cause long-term damage to girls across the social spectrum.

Snips and snails ...

Marketing to boys exploits the same human vulnerabilities. Since parents decide on purchases in the earliest years, products for babies tend to hark back to their own childhood and the market has found that parents of sons appreciate the muscle-bound masculinity of superheroes, or the reassuring maleness of characters like Thomas the Tank Engine and Bob the Builder. Jocelyn Stevens, the media executive who created Bob's TV series, described his role thus: 'My job is to come up with the gentle, lovely, wonderful pre-school programming so that the company can then go out and do all the marketing and branding, then sell the toys and the DVDs and so on...'

As boys grow old enough to choose products for themselves, they often discover consumerism through quirky (non-pink) collectibles, generally linked to conflict, hierarchies or mechanics. Pokémon, Yu-Gi-Oh!, Dragon Ball Z, Medabots and Cardcaptors have all satisfied the infant yearning for ownership whilst simultaneously appealing to the competitive instinct of the human male. This competitive instinct is known among marketeers as 'mastery' or 'dominion', and involves appealing to little boys' inbuilt desire for 'power, force, mastery, domination, control...'

For some boys the 'dominion instinct' leads to the sports field, and the opportunity to burn off aggression through activity. But why bother with all that effort and team-building when there are now many sedentary ways of achieving the same end? Boys are naturally drawn to technology, and console and website games provide opportunities to score without the effort of physical activity or social interaction. Slogans such as Xbox's 'Life is short, play more' and Nintendo's 'Life's a game' were designed to link the idea of 'play' and 'games' with the products of technology. Most children today associate these words not with outdoor play or sport but with virtual, indoor experiences.

There's no doubt that the best computer games for older children can improve players' IQ, perseverance and concentration, but most games popular with the under-tens involve little more than undemanding choices, coupled with hand-eye coordination. In fact, in the case of many boys, the appeal of the games is not only the challenge but the thrill of forbidden violence. Marketeers know that, although their parents may disapprove, the young male psyche is deeply attracted to violence, aggression and war. In most countries the law stops them from selling these things directly to children but there have always been ways round the law – including some that allow children to demonstrate another sort of 'mastery'.

An astounding number of pre-teens claim in surveys (and in my own experience of interviewing children) to have played violent games such as Mortal Kombat and Grand Theft Auto (GTA). Since these are '18+' products, I'd always taken these claims as bravado – till my daughter came home from babysitting in a respectable British home with the news that her young charges (boys aged six and nine) were playing GTA all evening. When she asked where they got it, they grinned that mum had bought it for them. So I asked my twenty-year-old researcher to give me a demonstration of GTA and was taken aback by the realistic and gratuitous violence. The player is encouraged to steal cars, massacre pedestrians, and engage in other random violent crime, such as beating passers-by into pools of blood with a baseball bat. Since the graphics are extremely realistic, the feeling that you're actually beating someone to a pulp is quite strong. Although my researcher thought this no big deal (he's highly educated with a keen sense of irony), to someone who knows about children's social and emotional development the game definitely merits its 18+ rating.

I was recounting this story to a friend, mother of a ten-year-old, and noticed her become rather agitated. Eventually she admitted she'd got her son a copy too, 'because all his friends have it' – as an Xbox virgin, she had no idea what the game involved. (Although it has to be said that, with promotional material for all X-rated computer games now freely available on Google, ignorance is no longer an excuse.)

... and puppy dogs' tails

The yearning for acceptance by the group is just as strong in boys as in girls, and the reliance on brands to make them acceptable may be even greater – in one survey, 75 per cent of boys said they like to wear clothes with popular labels, as opposed to 67 per cent of girls. However, the definition of 'cool' is different. For marketing aimed at males, cool has 'edge' – it's often humorous, sometimes rather callous, usually anti-authority – and conning a copy of Grand Theft Auto from a mother who'd ban it if she knew the contents is a very good example. Part of the appeal of machismo and violence for many small boys is that it appals the women in their lives, so there's considerable peer pressure for boys to act and talk big, play smart and put one over on the womenfolk.

Successful marketing of 'cool' involves lots of examples of just this sort of behaviour. It's usually funny because ironic humour helps to slip products past the post-modern parent, but by pandering to children's enthusiasm for backchat, sneakiness and challenging authority, it sends a message of endorsement – even encouragement – for breaking parental rules. As contemporary parents often themselves want to appear cool and edgy, they're often happy to be carried along with the joke – until it's too late to reverse their children's anti-authority attitudes. The children's channel Nickelodeon (slogan: 'Kids rule') has a fondness for this type of cool, which it claims is empowering for children.

The potential ill-effects of onscreen violence have been widely discussed (see Chapter 9), but there's been little attention to the long-term effects of encouraging an ironic, adult-mocking, anti-authority attitude in young children. Boys especially are very open to messages that, as US psychologist Juliet Schor puts it, 'adults enforce a repressive and joyless world in contrast to what kids and products do when they're left in peace.' Parental exhortations to eat greens, complete homework, finish chores and get a good night's sleep are much less attractive than assurances that Life's a game. Schor suggests that the long-term effect of drip-feeding children – especially boys – with 'edgy cool' messages is to drive a wedge between them and the adults in their lives. Having watched a lot of commercial kids' TV, I'd go further. The messages that marketing feeds daily to our children now amount to a gradual, oh-so-ironic subversion of civilised values.

Of course, there has always been a subversive, anti-authority children's culture, which in many ways is healthy – indeed a part of the 'real play' I've been recommending throughout this book. Every teacher knows that playgrounds are full of games, stories and rhymes that celebrate the gross, the ghoulish and the scatological – and usually we turn a blind eye to it, because children are like that and, above all, 'boys will be boys'. But a children's culture is not the same as an unholy alliance between children and the forces of international marketing. In the words of Professor Mark Crispin Miller of New York University, 'It's part of the official advertising world view that your parents are creeps, teachers are weirdos and idiots, authority figures are laughable, nobody can really understand kids except the corporate sponsor'. By openly encouraging and validating the subversive side of childhood, marketeers are unleashing forces that are becoming increasingly difficult to control.

For instance, one de-civilising effect of edgy cool is its contribution to the anti-education ethos currently destroying many children's lives – especially boys. When boys fail to prosper in a high-stakes testing regime, many choose to ignore school values and espouse an alternative playground culture. In *The Economics of Acting White*, Harvard economist Roland G. Fryer tells how a high-achieving boy moving into a new area fell foul of this culture: 'I became a target ... I got all As and was hated for it; I spoke correctly and was called a punk. I had to learn a new language simply to deal with the threats.' The nine-year-old boys in this story were black

American, but that same anti-establishment, anti-educational culture can be found in playgrounds in deprived areas around the developed world, whatever the colour of the children concerned. Indeed, it has increasingly found its way into the leafy suburbs. It's difficult for parents or teachers to motivate children to try hard at school if the prevailing pre-teen culture – summed up in everything they wear, eat and do with their spare time – is anti-effort, anti-authority and anti-academic.

It's the economy, stupid

A teacher I interviewed in Spain put it this way: 'Sometimes it seems that what we're trying to teach the children in school is at odds with everything they're learning outside'. It seemed to her that honesty, conscientiousness, hard work, and concern for others were no longer valued in the world beyond school, and children defined their worth not by what teachers thought of them, but by what they owned and their social kudos with their peers. When I argued that most parents, like me, still believed in the virtues she'd listed, she replied: 'Maybe – but they're not passing them on to their children. They're just buying them off.'

Discussing her words with parents over the last ten years, it's been disturbing how many feel powerless to assert these 'old-fashioned values' in the face of cultural influences. Most believe that possessions shouldn't hold such importance in their children's lives, but beset by a combination of pester power and the very reasonable desire to protect their offspring from social exclusion, they see no option but to hand over money to purchase a place in the in-group. Only the most strong-minded can resist the excuse that 'Everyone else does it, so you can't let your child be the odd one out.'

I've also encountered a few parents who don't see it as a problem. They feel that in a consumer culture, love really does equal stuff – indeed, they're keen to push their offspring up the social ladder by investing in even bigger and better brands – thus upping the ante of infant aspiration. They don't disapprove of their daughters' obsession with appearance or their sons' burgeoning insolence, believing these qualities will serve them well in a competitive world.

Perhaps they're right. There's always the possibility that, as human beings evolve, values evolve with them and that, very soon, 'It's the economy, stupid' will prove to be the ultimate truth. Perhaps, as the consumer culture spreads across the globe, what you look like and own will be more important than human qualities such as honesty, trust and kindness. And as mothers and fathers demonstrate their love for children by giving them more and more stuff, money will eventually become the new currency of love...?

In his book BRANDchild, Martin Lindstrom looks forward to this brave new world. He explains that 'as formal religion in the Western world continues to erode, brands move in to fill the vacuum'. Children are apparently to be the main evangelists in this process, since marketeers will increasingly seek to 'make children stakeholders of the company and so part of the company's destiny'. If Lindstrom's right, and marketing continues to follow current trends, coming generations can look forward to a future based on superficial appearances, disrespect, hedonism and instant gratification. Somehow, I don't think that's going to be enough to keep a complex technological culture afloat.

Heroes and villains

Another significant factor in contemporary children's lives that's been increasingly corrupted is the role model. Human beings learn largely by imitation, and in the early years they imitate parents and other family members. As time goes by, teachers or older children can also become important role models – as can admirable personalities from history, fiction and electronic media. These role models from the wider world have always affected children's behaviour and aspirations. Unfortunately, today's wider world is comprehensively infected with the values of 'cool' culture.

When five thousand twenty-first-century parents were asked which fictional character they felt most influenced the way their children behave, top of the list, rather depressingly, was Bart Simpson. Bart's most famous quote, according to *The Simpsons* quotes website, is 'I'm through with working; working is for chumps'. (Response from Homer: 'Son, I'm proud of you. I was twice your age before I figured that one out.') I have to admit to enjoying *The Simpsons* and sniggering along with jokes like that. The trouble is, while adults appreciate ironic humour, children under the age of about eight take such statements literally, and even for many older pre-teens satire remains a mystery. We have no idea how many Bart Simpson act-alikes have actually swallowed his philosophy whole over the years.

Screen-based culture also introduces children to many real-life role models beyond their immediate circle, such as sportsmen and women, TV and film actors (including the child stars alongside whom they grow up), pop singers and other entertainers. Sadly, the human price of fame usually means that even the most squeaky-clean of heroes eventually fall from grace, making them as unsuitable for role models as reality TV 'stars' and other celebrities whose main talent is attention seeking. (I once visited a school in a part of inner-city London that bred one of the early contestants on *Big Brother*, and the teachers told me how difficult it now is to motivate children who expect to become famous overnight without effort or qualifications – 'like Jade did').

Far too many contemporary role models end up modelling a sleazy lifestyle, cheating (on the sports field and in private life) and the ruthless pursuit of money. Child stars are particularly problematic because, as they grow up, the continued pursuit of fame and fortune often leads to extravagantly shocking behaviour. For many years Britney Spears and Paris Hilton led the field in this respect but they were resoundingly eclipsed in 2013 when Miley Cyrus introduced 'twerking' to the general public, including the juvenile fans of Hannah Montana movies. It's increasingly clear that the people who make it big in the hyper-competitive culture of celebrity are seldom the sort of human beings we want our children to emulate.

There is little parents can do to diminish the influence of such role models: they're out there and children are inevitably exposed to them. What's more, even traditional institutions now seem to accept them, warts and all. Susan Linn tells the story of a mother who rang her daughter's school to complain at the use of a scantily-clad image of Britney (whose lifestyle at the time was becoming increasingly seedy) in a healthy food promotion. The school authorities couldn't see the problem, but offered to mitigate her concern by colouring in Britney's midriff with black marker pen. I came across a similar example of cultural drift a couple of years ago when contacted by a mum whose ten-year-old daughter was upset about doing 'nasty dancing' as part of a school performance. This turned out to be a highly suggestive bump-and-grind routine, choreographed by a young female teacher. It wasn't until her mother asked whether the head would be happy for an older, male teacher to insist on this sort of display that the dance was toned down. 'They made me feel like some ghastly old prude,' my informant said.

In a world gone so entirely mad, parents' only immediate line of defence is to establish better role models at home, and to establish them early. This is, however, a very powerful course of action since children are at their most impressionable between birth and about eight. That's why the Jesuits famously claimed 'Give me a child till he is seven years old, and I will show you the man' and it's why advertisers are so anxious to capture this age-group's brand loyalty. Early personal and family loyalties are the strongest, so if parents spend time with their young children, imbuing them with the values they believe will serve them best, and modelling those values themselves, the chances of undesirable role models making an impact are much reduced.

Letting children be children

When I was researching the first edition of *Toxic Childhood*, there was little public awareness of the effects of marketing on children, since there'd been no critical analysis written for a general readership. Books outlining the extent of the problem didn't begin to appear till around 2005, when sociologist Juliet Shor and CFCC's Susan Linn drew attention to it in the US, and consumer expert Ed Mayo and marketing academic Agnes Nairn did the same in the UK. Since then concern has mushroomed.

On this side of the Atlantic there have been many campaigns to ban marketing to children by organisations as diverse as a left-wing think tank and the Mothers' Union, and between 2009 and 2011 successive UK governments published no fewer than three official reports on the subject. The first of these, *The Impact of the Commercial World on Children's Well-being*, edited by David Buckingham (a specialist in media education), concluded that 'the commercial world is here to stay' so parents and schools must educate children to live with it. The second *The Sexualisation of Young People Review* by Linda Papadopoulos, a psychologist who worked as a consultant to *Big Brother*, was shelved due to a change of government, but the third – *Letting Children be Children* by Reg Bailey, CEO of the Mothers' Union, succeeded in making a number of helpful recommendations which were followed through. Unfortunately, it stopped short of recommending any sort of ban on marketing to children, sticking to the usual prescription that the industry should regulate itself.

One outcome of the Bailey Report was ParentPort, a web-based 'one-stop-shop' where adults can register complaints about media and marketing strategies. Launched in 2013, it's also a useful source of information. The downside is that it still throws the burden of dealing with the marketing maelstrom firmly on to the shoulders of parents. Many of the quotes from parent contributors to *Letting Children Be Children* indicate how difficult it is for individuals to confront a market-driven culture:

- 'It's crept up on us gradually and makes it difficult to make a stand'
- 'We have all become so used to the ubiquity of these images and messages that we no longer always register them constantly'
- 'It's the cacophony of advertising messages everywhere that make it hard to escape'
- 'I feel that our society trivialises sex and treats people who complain about inappropriate imagery as foolish. I don't feel that I would be treated seriously.'

Those who had tried to make a difference had often met short shrift:

- 'I have often complained but nothing comes of complaints except polite letters acknowledging them'
- 'Even if the company agrees, they always cite policies, guidelines or rules from above preventing them from doing anything about it'
- 'I felt that I was a small fish in a big ocean swimming against the tide.'

Their comments mirror those heard day after day by Agnes Nairn, professor of marketing and co-author of *Consumer Kids: How Big Business Is Grooming Our Children for Profit*. She believes the main reason parents don't challenge marketeers is that their opinion isn't 'legitimised' by society. 'Every single parent in the country – no, the world! – is frustrated by pester power. But consumerism is the norm – advertising tells us it's good, branding tells us it's good, we're all constantly being socialized into thinking all marketing is fine. So parents don't want to complain because they'll sound like oddballs or killjoys or prudes.' This situation isn't going to change until parental concern is 'normalised', which means national governments would have to do a lot more than commissioning reports.

ParentPort, for instance, won't work unless everyone knows about it. Professor Nairn suggests the UK government should organise a massive publicity campaign, and require the marketing industry to fund it. 'But, even then, why should we have to wait for parents to complain before action is taken? We don't wait for complaints about criminal acts – there are policemen out on the streets making sure they don't happen! As long as the industry is responsible for regulating itself, enormous corporations will go on manipulating children and their parents. And it's simply not fair! It would take the average family about 18,000 years to earn what Apple spends in advertising in one year!'

Turning the tide

The governments of Sweden, Norway, Greece and the Canadian province of Quebec have already begun to normalise (and thus 'legitimise') parental concern about the commercialisation of childhood by banning marketing to the under-twelves. While such a ban is obviously difficult to police, it does give a powerful message to society at large that marketing can be harmful to children. And by defining the age at which children can be expected to articulate their understanding of advertisers' intent, it acts as a partial antidote to the KAGOY strategy.

What's more, the message conveyed by an outright ban isn't just powerful but simple, too. At present, the UK system of market regulation is so complicated that only specialists in the field can find their way around – hence the need for ParentPort. While a blanket ban on marketing to children wouldn't do away with the need for specific regulations (e.g. in areas such as food and alcohol advertising, or violent or sexual imagery), it would make it clear that children's well-being comes first and foremost. It might also mean that fewer new regulations would be required as new products and practices develop. A governmental message that *Marketing to Children is Wrong – Full Stop* could help make marketeers take far greater care about the way they conduct their craft in the first place.

At present, the industry isn't required to act unless scientific evidence proves beyond doubt that particular products are actually harmful, or that marketing claims about them are misleading. As we know from the global experience of tobacco and junk-food marketing, assembling such evidence is an extremely long and difficult process, and – once behaviour has been normalised – changing consumer behaviour takes even longer. In the case of infant consumers, enormous damage may be done in the meantime.

This is why campaigners against the commercialization of childhood are particularly worried about tablet-based techno-play for very young children, including 'apptivity' products for babies under six months old. On the basis of current evidence, and the American Academy of Pediatrics' recommendation of no screen-time for the under-twos, it seems reasonable – at the very least – to put a 'health warning' on the packaging of such items. However, manufacturers and marketeers point out that, as yet, there's no scientific proof that screen-based baby-apps are harmful. (This is, of course, because tablet technology is so new that no one's yet had time to do any research.)

Where there's reasonable cause for concern that children's physical, social or emotional development may be affected by new uses of technology, Agnes Nairn believes it should be up to manufacturers to prove their products *aren't* harmful before putting them on the market. This precautionary principle is already applied to pharmaceutical products and ensures that the industry bears the cost of research. Applying it in this way would be a significant step towards shifting the burden of responsibility for 'letting children be children' in a consumer culture from individual families to the commercial organizations who want those families' money.

At the time of writing, the UK government is resolutely opposed to a ban on marketing to children and Agnes Nairn's suggestion wouldn't even cross their radar. But, less than a decade since information about the commercialisation of childhood began to circulate, public concern has begun to make some impact on policy. As time goes on and vastly different interest groups (including environmentalists, feminists, health authorities, child psychologists, play specialists, consumer associations, teacher organisations and parent groups) coalesce around the issue, the concern is likely to generate a mainstream movement. There is reason to hope that the tide may turn in the not too distant future.

In the meantime, it's up to the loving adults in children's lives to protect them from those who merely want their money. Providing time, loving attention and sound role models for one's own children is an excellent start but we also have to help them deal with marketing pressures (see Detox boxes, below) and the fast-changing world of electronic media (see pages 283–5). And to shame our government into the sort of decisive action already taken by Sweden, Norway, Greece and Quebec, those of us who recognise the danger have to do everything possible to raise public awareness of the exploitation of children by commercial forces for financial gain.

★★★

It's increasingly clear that the twenty-first century will hold many challenges for the upcoming generation. In 2014 Jon Savage, author of *Teenage: The Creation of Youth, 1875-1945*, predicted that 'climate change will begin to test the limits of our civilisation ... and that, at the very minimum, people will not be able to consume in the way they have become accustomed to over the past sixty years.' He believes that today's teenagers are well equipped to deal with these problems because 'they are already familiar with ideas of sustainability at the same time as they swim in a media revolution still ill-understood by adults.'

I hope he's right, and – after a lifetime of working with children – I'm still a great believer in the power of the human spirit to adapt to changing circumstances and overcome the obstacles fate throws in our way. However, as consumerism makes ever earlier inroads into children's consciousness, I fear that many will struggle in teenage and adulthood to turn 'ideas of sustainability' into productive action in the real world. Over the last few decades the commercialisation of childhood has had profound effects on child development in two ways: first, through its influence on the behaviour and values of their families; and second, by changing the nature of play. For a growing number of children real play ('initiated, controlled and structured by children themselves') has now been almost completely supplanted by toy consumption, techno-play and precocious obsession with 'adult' trivia.

A couple of days after reading Jon Savage's words, I interviewed Susan Linn of the Campaign for a Commercial-Free Childhood. She summed up my concerns perfectly: 'Play is the foundation of learning, creativity, problem-solving and the capacity to wrestle with life to make it meaningful but as a society we seem to be doing everything we can to prevent children from playing. And when it comes to children's leisure time the primary deterrent to play is the commercialisation of childhood. When consumerism calls the cultural shots, genuine play disappears because there's no way of making money out of it!'

DETOXING THE CONSUMER CULTURE

- Monitor what children watch on TV, DVD and the Internet – keep screen-based entertainment in a shared area of the house and watch with them as often as possible (see also pages 300–301).
- Limit young children's viewing to non-commercial stations, such as CBeebies, or selected DVDs and videos.
- When they begin to watch commercial stations, play 'Spot the advertisements' to help them learn the difference between entertainment and marketing.
- Don't give your child a smartphone or tablet until you are confident of their Internet safety and savviness (see pages 323–325).
- Keep an eye on ads and marketing, watch out for local trends and sign up for newsletters from CFCC (see page 279) to let you know what's brewing.
- Talk to your child about advertising, products and brands. Watch adverts together and discuss how the marketeers target people's hopes, fears and needs. Discuss:
  - how pictures, music, slogans and so on can affect the way you feel and your attitude to the product being advertised
  - how well products they've tried live up to advertising promises
  - whether the families in the ads correspond to real life (are they like real people?)
  - how far stuff can bring contentment, and what else is important
  - what key advertising words like *freedom, choice, love, natural, exciting* really mean.

- When watching ads with your children, play 'What aren't they telling us?' (what facts about the product might be missed out and why?), e.g. when an ad says a food product is 'low in fat', does it fail to mention other fattening ingredients, such as sugar?
- Video their favourite programmes and teach your child how to fast-forward during ads.
- Do some consumer testing with your child and friends. Try 'blind tests'

of food and drinks (e.g. baked beans, cereals, ketchup, soft drinks, colas) mixing famous brand products and supermarket own labels. Can they tell the difference and how much does advertising influence their guesses?

- Don't give in to pester power. The earlier in a child's life you make a stand on this the better – but whatever the age, once you've decided, be firm. If you stick with it, your child will eventually realise it's not on.
- If your child argues the toss because of market pressure, use it as an opportunity for discussing:
    – the difference between needing something and merely wanting it
    – the reasons you don't want marketing and media to determine their behaviour
    – how you draw behavioural boundaries because you love your child; marketeers just want your family's money.

- Have clear, fair guidelines on money and spending. Decide what you will/won't pay for on a regular basis, then agree on levels of pocket money – if children want something extra to what you provide, teach them to save for it or wait for birthday/Christmas/other regular present-giving time.
- Involve children in making consumer decisions that uses marketing information wisely, along with other considerations:
    – let them help make shopping lists and discuss food choices (see Chapter 1)
    – discuss other family purchases (cars, holidays, etc.), listening respectfully to their contributions and involving them in reasoned choices.

- Limit exposure to consumer culture by doing other things with your children: family outings, activities and hobbies, making things, and so on. See below.

HOW TO ENCOURAGE CREATIVE PLAY

Babies and toddlers

- Very young children don't need encouragement to use their imagination – parents have to be discouraged from stopping them! Create safe environments where they can move and experiment, both inside and out.
- Make a box or basket of interesting but safe items, such as wooden spoons, large pine cones and shells, crackly packaging, discarded lids or boxes, bits of fabric, ribbon or fur. Let your child select items and watch what they do – join in, taking the lead from your child.
- Read and talk about picture books with your child – this will provide lots of ideas for play. Shared TV will give ideas as well.
- Give your toddler cheap items and let them experiment indoors, e.g.:
  - a large empty box can become a car, boat, space rocket …
  - a cloth or sheet can become a den, a bed for dolls or soft toys, a hiding place …
  - pots and pans can be filled and emptied, banged to make music, piled up, knocked down, carried about …

- Choose somewhere you can make a mess (outdoors? a tiled area?) and on different occasions let your child play with sand, water, mud, paint, bubbles, clay, cooking ingredients, snow, any interesting things from the natural and manmade world. Provide lots of sticks and spoons for mixing and containers for filling and emptying, and stay close by on safety watch.
- Let children know that you really value these activities.
- Ensure that other adults who look after your child also know that you really value these activities.

Older children

- Children will play at what they have experienced. The rich experiences offered to them will inform their play and explorations of the world. Going to places, even familiar everyday places very near to them, meeting people, exploring the world around them all offer starting points for play.

- Older children still enjoy messing and discovering with all the equipment listed above. Just leave them to it and see what they do. Continue to let children know that you really value these activities and ensure that other adults who look after your child, also know that you value them.
- Carry on sharing books together and chatting about the ideas they inspire.
- Provide household junk and packaging, along with glue, sticking tape and paint and encourage children to make models and equipment for their play. Don't expect it to be impressive – it's the making that counts, not the product.
- Show how to make a den by throwing a cloth or sheet over a table. Encourage children to look for other ways of making dens, houses, castles, forts, mountains, planets, etc.
- Provide paper, paint, crayons, felt pens, glue, coloured scraps, glitter and suggest making greetings cards, posters for family events, books, albums, or just pictures 'out of your head'.
- Start with music (not just what's in the charts) – listen to it, move to it, try making it with anything around…
- Go out collecting – leaves, stones, shells, cones, insects, worms, tadpoles… (if it's alive, look after it and watch it grow).
- Provide a box of old clothes, shoes, hats, beads, ribbons, fabrics, etc. for dressing up games. Add to this with cheap exotic purchases from second hand shops.
- Buy a cat-litter tray and encourage your child to make 'small worlds' (farms, islands, alien planets, dinosaur world etc.) inspired by your reading or talk. Or help make a doll's house from boxes stuck together, furniture from matchboxes.
- Children love cooking or making mixtures and potions in bottles and jars from household items. Let them become chefs, scientists, inventors, witches or wizards – but keep an eye on safety.
- Don't feel you always have to provide playthings. It's good for older children to think up activities and play for themselves.

DETOXING ROLE MODELS

- Make sure you, your partner and other 'adults-in-charge' are the sort of role models you want your child to copy.
- As children acquire heroes beyond the family, talk to them about the good qualities these heroes show. Discuss any aspects of the character your child may not understand (such as: why is it all right for Spiderman to fight people sometimes?)
- Keep an eye on the TV characters children admire – if they start imitating their speech or behaviour, talk about the character and why they like them. Don't be afraid to discourage your child if they've chosen an inappropriate hero.
- Similarly, when children show an interest in pop stars and other celebrities, talk and listen to your child's opinions. Encourage careful thought about people's worth. What characteristics does your child think are really important – and do these characters live up to their standards?
- If you're a single mother, do everything you can to provide a suitable male role model for your child (such as a family member, a male friend, a youth group leader) – someone who'll spend time with him/her and be there to give advice and support.

PARENT POWER – PUTTING THE MARKETEERS IN THEIR PLACE

Despite warnings that the content of this chapter is 'frightening', I resisted advice to tone it down because I believe the impact of aggressive marketing on children *is* frightening and the only way to stop it is parent power. If you agree, the obvious step is to work with other parents to stem the tide:

- Talk with other adults about commercial pressures on children, and nurture relationships with like-minded families and individuals. They can provide the sort of peer support that's the best defence against unwelcome peer pressure. You may well find that many of the teachers and other parents at your child's school are concerned about this issue.
- Check out the campaign websites below and watch out for new initiatives around consumerism and childhood. Just adding your name to a petition will help, but actually getting together with other people who feel strongly about the issue helps most. Remember the words of the anthropologist Margaret Mead: 'Never doubt that a handful of thoughtful committed citizens can change the world. Indeed, it is the only thing that ever has.'
- Read up on the subject (see the books/video below and keep an eye open for new ones). Share what you learn with friends.
- Make your feelings known to all the politicians who represent you. When they're looking for re-election, ask what they're doing about aggressive marketing to children. In the meantime, you could write and ask them to lend their support to any moves to ban advertising to the under-twelves.
- The main point is to speak up. If parents don't speak up for the welfare of children – all children – who will?

Further reading

Juliet Schor, *Born to Buy* (Scribner, 2004)

Susan Linn, *Consuming Kids: The Hostile Takeover of Childhood* (NY New Press, 2005)

Eric Clark, *The Real Toy Story: Inside the Ruthless Battle for Britain's Youngest Consumers* (Black Swan, 2007)

Mayo, Ed and Nairn, Agnes, *Consumer Kids: How Big Business Is Grooming Our Children for Profit* (Constable, 2009)

Thomas, Susan Gregory, *Buy, Buy, Baby: How Consumer Culture Manipulates Parents* (Mariner Books, 2009)

Reg Bailey, *Letting Children Be Children: Report of an Independent Review of the Commercialisation and Sexualisation of Childhood* (The Stationery Office, 2012)

Diane Rich, Denie Casanova, Annabelle Dixon, Mary Jane Drummond, Andrea Durrant, Cathy Myer, *First-Hand Experience – What Matters to Children* (Rich Learning Opportunities, Second Edition 2014)

Julia Deering, *The Playful Parent: Seven Ways to Happier, Calmer, More Creative Under-Fives* (HarperCollins, 2014)

Useful websites

Campaign for a Commercial-Free Childhood – US-based organisation, providing regular updates on marketing methods: www.commercialfreechildhood.org

Leave Our Kids Alone – UK pressure group, set up in 2013 to campaign for a ban on marketing to pre-teens: www.leaveourkidsalone.org

Save Childhood – coalition of UK childhood campaigners, which includes a call for a ban on marketing to pre-teens in its manifesto: www.savechildhood.net

ParentPort – UK one-stop-shop for reporting inappropriate marketing and media messages, with helpful advice pages for parents: www.parentport.org.uk

Media Education Foundation: *Consuming Kids: The Commercialisation of Childhood*, 2008 Can now be watched free online at: http://topdocumentaryfilms.com/consuming-kids/

Mind the gap

When rioting broke out in Tottenham, North London, in summer 2011, rioters soon forgot their original grievance and began looting local shops. The police failed to contain the trouble and – thanks to smartphones – it spread throughout the capital, then across England. Birmingham, Manchester, Gloucester, Nottingham and Liverpool all experienced serious problems and, nationwide, 2500 shops and businesses were looted before the police regained control. 'It was like Christmas!' said one sixteen-year-old female looter, while a nineteen-year-old man exclaimed, 'Snatch and grab, get anything you want, anything you ever desired.'

A subsequent analysis of the rioters found that around three-quarters were under 25, and the vast majority were from poor backgrounds, with few educational qualifications. They were the products of the most toxic of childhoods – unable, by dint of birth, either to achieve at school or to afford the 'cool' rewards of consumer culture. When an opportunity arose to show how they felt about the society that reared them (and take home a few coveted consumer durables to boot), it's no surprise they took it.

Many police and fire-fighters on the front line feared they would be killed during the riots and senior officers were amazed there was no loss of life – the police were vastly outnumbered and the crowd's frenzy led to unprecedented levels of violence and vandalism. 'They had control and they knew that,' said one policeman. 'It was venomous.' 'It was the best few days of my life,' said a rioter.

Despite several years of recession, Britain is still a rich country, with a welfare state that just about ensures no one yet lives in absolute poverty. In fact, many poor families manage to afford a range of material possessions – TVs, smartphones, various branded goods – beyond the wildest dreams of those in less wealthy countries. But when 'what you are depends on what you own', poverty – however comparative – is personal. Camilla Batmanghelidjh, who's devoted her life to working with poor children in Southwark explains that 'the poverty in Britain is worse than poor countries because it's so isolating. The discrepancy is staring you in the face all the time – on TV, in the shops.'

As the gap between haves and have-nots has widened and the authority of traditional social role models (teachers, religious leaders, law-enforcers) is steadily undermined, the only adult guidance available to many children comes from those glamorous strangers on screen and the anonymous manipulators lurking behind them. So they learn from their earliest years to associate stuff with status, money with respect, and lack of stuff and/or money with lack of dignity. Perhaps this is why, in schools in deprived areas, I regularly hear stories of struggling young mums who prefer to spend what cash they have on keeping their children fashionably dressed, rather than on feeding the family.

The riots of 2011 were, inevitably, hailed as a 'wake-up call'. But the memory swiftly faded: streets were cleaned up; insurance companies settled claims. The police analysed the episode and, if anything similar kicks off in the future, they'll be better prepared and equipped to deal with it. But the social and cultural factors that caused the riots still exist – inequalities of wealth in modern Britain are greater than at any time since the 1920s and on schedule to reach Victorian levels within the next couple of decades – so the problem has simply been brushed under the carpet. Unless we *all* – rich and poor – start learning from an early age that greed is not good, the twentieth-century consumerist dream may turn into the twenty-first century's social nightmare.

CHAPTER NINE

THE ELECTRONIC VILLAGE

It's now well over half a century since families began the move into Marshall McLuhan's electronic, global village. But for most of that time people have had a simple way of returning to real-time reality: it was called the 'off switch'. It's only in the last couple of decades that electric speed has overtaken real time, as technology invaded every aspect of our life and work. PCs, the Internet, the web, smartphones and tablets mean the electronic village is around us 24/7, whether we like it or not. There doesn't seem to be an 'off switch' any more – just a welter of remote controls.

On the whole, most adults seem happy enough in the electronic village – we may have to run twice as fast to stay in the same place, but it's an infinitely more interesting, comfortable and entertaining place than the world our parents and grandparents inhabited. Perhaps it will also become a less divided and prejudiced place? Old geographical and national boundaries certainly seem less significant: social networks unite friends from every corner of the globe, and the world community reacts as one to sporting triumphs and natural disasters. Mass communication has already helped bring about a seismic change in women's status in much of the world: as it continues to challenge ancient prejudices it could also help overcome racism, homophobia and other social evils. Maybe the global village will eventually become a truly democratic community, where everyone has the chance of self-realisation, without interfering with the self-realisation of others?

Clearly, however, this utopian vision depends on everyone sticking to humane, democratic principles. And that depends on each new generation of children being able to think, manage their own behaviour and get along well enough with others to keep the component parts of the village working. For that, as *Toxic Childhood* has shown, they need genuine human nurture, which must proceed at biological, not electric speed. Children need the security of a loving family, opportunities to experience and learn about the world at first hand, real life friends and communities, and human values that will help them resist the siren calls of the market. For that to happen, we have to round up the remote controls, and reinvent the 'off switch'.

Spinning along with Moore's Law

An IT expert I met as a result of *Toxic Childhood* first told me about Moore's Law. It was formulated in the late 1960s by one of the founders of Intel and predicted that the power and potential of digital technology would double roughly every two years. This, of course, meant we were on track for exponential growth in terms of electronic media so it's not surprising that life seems to move faster and faster, especially since IT experts now say the doubling act happens around every eighteen months.

It's a testament to the plasticity of the human brain that we've been able to adapt so readily to each new technological development. Indeed, we've adapted so well that it's almost impossible to imagine life before email and the worldwide web (1993), text messaging on mobile phones (1994), console games (1998), Google (2004), YouTube (2005), Facebook and Twitter (opened to the public in 2006), iPhones (2007), apps (2008) and iPads (2010). By the time this edition of *Toxic Childhood* hits the bookshops (including, of course, Amazon which launched in 1995, introducing the Kindle in 2007) there'll almost certainly be another electronic household name (my bet's on the smartwatch, 2014).

Most parental concern about the effects of this brave new world on their children has so far focused on the content to which the younger generation is now exposed. In the last couple of years, for instance, there has been much publicity around the ready accessibility of pornography and the problems of cyberbullying. These developments are certainly worrying, and will be discussed later in the chapter. But there is another source of concern about the electronic media which has attracted far less attention – the effects on developing bodies and brains of the medium itself.

The UK's major commentator in this area is Dr Aric Sigman, whose personal research interest is the development and control of attention skills. He sums up the problem thus: 'Increasingly the growing preponderance of a child's life is becoming virtual. It's spent looking at a screen and gaining primary information through visual means. But all the evidence points to the need to upload information through real world experience first. The ratio of real to virtual activity for children has shifted and it's up to those who promote this virtual lifestyle to show that it's utterly safe. Until then, we should be careful.' It concerns him that, while there's plenty of public interest in the possible harmful effects of onscreen content, any criticism of this move towards a virtual lifestyle for young children is 'shouted down'.

In fact, Aric Sigman's arguments about children and technology mirror those of Agnes Nairn (see pages 268–270) about the commercialisation of childhood: a screen-based lifestyle has become 'normalised' and adults who question its appropriateness for children are widely labelled uncool and old-fashioned. As one who has raised the question regularly over the last decade, I can confirm this point. I've been called a technophobe more times than I care to remember, which always raises my hackles because I *love* my laptop, my satnav and my smartphone, can't work without access to the web and thoroughly enjoy many types of screen-based entertainment. However, I'm an adult. As Dr Sigman points out, children's bodies and brains are still in transition – what's OK for adults is not necessarily OK for them.

Fortunately, the worldwide medical community is growing increasingly vocal about the issue. Guidelines about screen-time, especially for the very young, have been issued in the United States, Australia and Canada, while France has banned broadcasting to the under-threes. In a 2012 edition of the *Archives of Disease in Childhood*, Aric Sigman called for British medical authorities to follow their lead. He believes there are now excellent grounds for accepting that children's physical and mental health is being compromised by three aspects of the screen-based media:

- the increasingly young age at which children begin to *access* it (tablet-based products are now available for children only a few months old)
- the steadily rising levels of *consumption* (the average screen-time for young British teenagers is currently 6.1 hours per day, while in the US it's 7.5 hours – more than half of their waking lives)
- its ready *availability* (by the age of ten, children in Britain have regular access to an average of five different screens in the home, e.g. TV, handheld games console, smartphone, family computer, laptop, tablet computer).

As Moore's Law rolls on, these three factors are unlikely to change – although, as smartphone technology develops, the availability of electronic media will probably be far greater, but through fewer different screens. If there are reasons for concern about the effects of this technology on children's physical and mental health, parents should be aware of them.

The electronic babysitter

Screen-based entertainment now begins not long after birth. It's been commonplace in Japan since the 1980s, when research found four- and five-month-old babies happily watching more than an hour's TV a day (the set was usually in the room in which they slept, and positioned so they could see it from their cradle). A Japanese educational programme, *With Mother*, became the first broadcasting tailored to the under-twos, and although it was more than a decade before English-speaking programme-makers explored this market, *Teletubbies* eventually opened the floodgates.

At the time of writing, British consumers have access to a twenty-four-hour Baby channel and several commercial channels such as Nick Junior and Tiny Pop, aimed at the very young. Even the BBC's *CBeebies*, originally intended for children of three and over, now has a section on its website for babies, with screen-based activities linked to TV programmes. There are also many DVDs, from pure entertainment like *Peppa Pig* (infant eye-candy, and thus a superb electronic babysitter) to 'educational' fare such as Disney's *Baby Einstein* series, which caters for the 'hot-housing' impulses of aspirational parents (see also Chapter 8, 'The strangers behind the screens').

All this is at odds with medical recommendations that the under-twos should have *no* screen-time at all. This is based on research linking early screen-gazing to later health problems of various types, including obesity and heart disease, but also on evidence linking excessive early screen-time to ADHD, language delay and autism (for further details of the studies concerned, see Notes and References, page 424). On the other hand, there is no evidence at all that very early exposure to TV or video enhances children's learning.

Remember the rats in Chapter 6, who became smarter through living in an interactive 'enriched environment', while rats who sat around with nothing to do became duller by the minute? One of the authors of that study, Dr Marian Cleeves Diamond, once made a guest appearance at a US conference about television and young children to point out that the dull sedentary rats didn't get any cleverer if they were allowed to watch the enriched rats running around having fun. She pointed out that, in order to learn, 'it is important to interact with the objects, to explore, to investigate, both physically and mentally.' Children learn by doing, not watching, just as (as described in Chapter 4) they acquire language skills by interacting with real speakers, not through exposure to screen-based ones. The younger the children, the more vital all these real-life interactions are.

As described in Chapters 4 and 8, we can now add the lure of techno-play to that of TV and video. Children can now 'play' on their baby apps even before they can actually hold the tablet. Again, there's not the slightest evidence that these products are beneficial to babies and toddlers, but there's a real possibility that playing on them will encourage a sedentary, screen-dominated lifestyle. Even though the apps are 'interactive', the swishing of fingers across a screen is a long way from the three-dimensional, multi-sensory, whole-body involvement through which previous generations of children developed their physical, social and cognitive skills.

In 2014, a teacher told me about a three-year-old boy brought to enrol in her nursery. His mother was very proud of her son's prowess on the iPad, and he was indeed extremely adept at working the screen. However, his balance was so poor he could scarcely stand without support, he preferred crawling to walking and his language was, according to the teacher, at around the level of the average 18-month-old. When his mother noticed how much more advanced other children of his age were in these respects, she became rather agitated. 'I think she'd perhaps been isolated,' the teacher said, 'so she'd had nothing to compare him to in terms of overall development. All that little boy wanted to do was play on the iPad.'

Of course, there's no way of knowing whether the child's developmental delay was due to excessive screen-time or some underlying handicap – or, as I suspect, a combination of both. But if any tiny children are constantly distracted from the physical and social activities through which they're naturally adapted to learn, it is bound to have an effect. Every hour of TV-gazing or techno-play displaces time spent on activities known to facilitate healthy development and, since electronic entertainment brings such immediate rewards, it diminishes children's inborn motivation for real-life engagement. Dr David Walsh of the National Institute on Media and the Family puts it very neatly: 'If we orient our kids to screens so early in their lives, we risk making media their automatic default activity.'

From default to dysfunction?

The trouble is that screens are now ubiquitous. TVs and computers are part of the furniture in twenty-first-century homes and the temptation for busy parents to snatch a few minutes peace while the little one gazes happily at a cartoon is enormous. Many families also keep in touch with distant friends and relations via Skype or Facetime, which almost inevitably involves beloved infants communicating via a screen. And most adults now have a smartphone or tablet constantly at hand, in which their infant is deeply interested.

All this means that sticking to the zero option for the under-twos seems so difficult that even those parents who are actually aware of the medical research and recommendations often discount it. They gamble on the probability that most little children won't be adversely affected by occasional screen-time. And indeed I'd have to agree that serious long-term developmental problems are only likely in babies who are frequently left with electronic babysitters for long periods or those who already have an underlying genetic predisposition. (Mind you, except in the case of severe autism, most genetic predispositions of this kind are more-or-less impossible to spot in the first couple of years, so it really is a gamble).

However, as screen-based technology proliferates, another probability has begun to emerge. Parents who don't assume firm control about the use of electronic media right from the start usually find it becomes increasingly difficult as time goes on. The reason that screen-gazing can so easily become children's default activity is that – like junk food – it's highly addictive.

Technology addiction is a new phenomenon, and the first British programme for treating it (aimed at teenagers and adults) was launched by Dr Richard Graham in 2010, coincidentally the same year that the iPad came on the market. By 2013 he was being asked to see children as young as three. 'They see their parents playing on their mobile devices and they want to play too,' he reported. 'It's difficult because having a device can be very useful in terms of having a reward, having a pacifier. But if you don't get the balance right it can be very dangerous. They can't cope and become addicted, reacting with tantrums and uncontrollable behaviour when they are taken away.'

Again, we can't know whether the three-year-olds brought to Dr Graham are somehow genetically-inclined towards technology-addiction. But anyone who's tried to wean a pre-schooler off a much-loved pacifier knows how difficult it is to extinguish behaviour learned in the early months and years. When the pacifier is a dummy, trainer mug or comfort blanket, children soon realise that it doesn't contribute to their street cred at nursery so they're highly motivated to abandon it. But if the pacifier is a technological device, parents can't rely on this positive effect of peer-pressure. The child's dependence is far more likely to grow, and if mum and dad try to enforce time-limits, the possibility of alarming tantrums is considerable. It seems easier to give in.

Behavioural issues around screen-based entertainment are not new: most parents I meet complain that children of all ages become 'wired' or unsettled after too long in front of a screen, resulting in squabbles about when to press the off-switch. The earlier such conflicts begin, the more difficult they are to deal with, so it's best to start as you mean to go on. If children learn from the very beginning of their lives that TVs, laptops, smartphones and tablets are for grown-up use (rather like kettles, cookers and other potentially dangerous household items), they'll be primed to accept parental supervision and boundary-setting when they're finally allowed to use them. And if adults establish their authority from the start they'll feel much more confident about setting boundaries in the long run.

In an increasingly screen-saturated world, the upcoming generation is going to need plenty of self-discipline to 'get the balance right' between real-life and virtual activity. Books such as

Nicholas Carr's *The Shallows: How the Internet Is Rewiring Our Brains*
illustrate how tricky it now is to establish a healthy balance,
even for adults who've been reared in a pre-Internet world. And
the sorts of teenage screen-addiction documented in Beeban
Kidron's 2013 film *InRealLife* – pornography, electronic communication, computer gaming – suggest that these problems
are even greater for the smartphone generation. Until there
is clear evidence that techno-play in the first couple of years
doesn't cause, or at least seriously exacerbate, problems with
attention and self-regulation as children grow older, the precautionary principle should apply.

Technology for tots

Once children are over two (although Aric Sigman would prefer to
say 'over three', since the first three years are the most critical in
terms of brain development), the American Academy of Pediatrics'
recommendation is no more than one or two hours of recreational
screen-time per day. It would make sense to start with short
sessions – perhaps five or ten minutes on an app, or a fifteen-
minute TV programme – to establish the idea of time limits and see
how things go. If a child shows undue distress when it comes to
an end, it'd probably be better to reduce exposure (perhaps letting
him or her go cold turkey for a few days) and concentrate on other
activities, rather than feed a craving.

There is good evidence however that, once children are around
two or three years old, high-quality TV can create talking points
between parent and child, which aids language development and
stimulates ideas for shared activities. Also, as mentioned in Chapter
4, repeated viewing of favourite programmes can extend children's
vocabulary. Research on the advantages of using handheld devices
with the pre-school age-group is still in its infancy and tends to
relate mainly to children's motivation (i.e. they like using them) or
to the development of highly specific skills. For instance, in 2014 a
study by the National Literacy Trust suggested that disadvantaged

children's literacy skills at the age of five were enhanced by the joint use of books and handheld devices, which sounds promising. But the skills concerned were simple phonic decoding and word recognition, and while these are useful short-term achievements, they're not a reliable indication of future reading fluency (see 'Books versus screens', below).

It's also important to remember that all the positive research relates to age-appropriate materials. Clare Elstow, who was head of the BBC's CBeebies pre-school channel when I interviewed her for the first edition of *Toxic Childhood*, explained that for pre-schoolers she avoided fast-moving cartoons and 'montage telly' (cutting rapidly from shot to shot, as on many US children's channels). Instead she aimed for gentle pacing and plenty of real-life presenters, speaking directly to their young viewers, who are more likely to pick up language from TV if they see real lips moving as the words come out.

Aric Sigman also emphasises the importance of slow-paced materials for young children, as well as 'less novelty and more of a single narrative quality'. Adults may therefore find good TV for children rather boring because we've become used to rapid action and editing, but young children need time to process what they see and hear, making links between words and images. If we teach them to speed up their thought processes too soon they may become used to skimming over the surface of ideas, rather than deeper mental processing. For the same reason, they also need the security of familiar content and straight-forward narrative. Research by Professor Angeline Lillard in the USA found that 'nine minutes of viewing a popular fast-paced fantastical television show [*SpongeBob Squarepants*] immediately impaired four-year-olds' EF*, a result about which parents of young children should be aware.'

The best advice in the pre-school years seems to be to choose screen-based media wisely, watch or play with your child

---

* EF = executive function – the control of thought processes such as working memory, reasoning, problem-solving and planning.

whenever possible, and exercise adult authority over the length of time spent in front of the screen, emphasizing that when you say 'Switch off', it means 'Switch off'. As long as the discipline you impose is clearly born of love, the habits of behaviour your child develops during this period are likely to last life-long. With any luck, your cautionary voice will gradually translate into the inner voice of self-discipline so that he or she becomes capable of self-regulation in the future.

One reason parents often give me for allowing their pre-schoolers to engage in techno-play is that 'they're growing up in the modern world, so they need to learn IT skills'. But the electronic media are now developing at such a pace that any IT skills children do learn in the pre-school years will be out of date by the time they reach their teens. It's much more important that children of this age develop imagination, learn essential life skills like problem-solving and getting along with other people, and lay firm foundations for literacy and numeracy through tried-and-trusted human interaction. The age-old human repertoire of cuddling, playing (especially outdoors), singing, reading stories, and just 'hanging out' with babies, toddlers and pre-schoolers will equip them for the future far better than long hours in front of a screen.

Books versus screens

As a literacy specialist, I have a particular interest in the possible impact of techno-play on young children's minds. As described in Chapter 7, the spread of literacy though the centuries has generally had a civilising and democratising effect on societies. I would argue that this is because learning to read and write develops children's capacity for focused attention, self-regulation, rational thought and – in the case of fiction – empathy.

To read a simple story, young children need to rally all their powers of attention because, for novices, reading involves processing written language at three different levels, all at the same time. They have, first, to decode individual words; second, they have to hold these words in their head while making sense of each sentence; and third, they must simultaneously keep tabs on the narrative as a whole. It's a complex and demanding mental task and it can take a lot of practice before children reach what's called 'automaticity' – the point when they're no longer consciously decoding words or struggling to make sense of sentences, but are fluent enough simply to concentrate on the story itself. Some adults remember the moment they achieved automaticity – indeed I vividly remember enjoying a story book (illicitly, when I should have been asleep!) and suddenly realising that, for the first time, I hadn't been conscious of 'reading' it.

Even then, it takes much more practice to develop the mental stamina required to enjoy a full-length novel – following the plot and subplots, envisaging each scene, responding to charac-terisation and becoming personally involved with the fate of the characters. As readers become more fluent, they also have time to respond to the language, to read between and beyond the lines, to 'lock brains with the author' and see the world through someone else's eyes. It takes a lot of time and effort to get to this stage of fluency but, once there, the rewards are considerable – not only at a personal and emotional level, but also in terms of intellectual development.

Language is, by its very nature, linear and sequential, so the complex mental control involved in fluent reading develops readers' capacity for linear, sequential thought – the type of thought that underpins reason and logic. In the words of the Canadian professor of psychology, Merlin Donald, 'literacy skills change the functional organization of the brain', introducing 'the elaborate procedural habits of formal thinking.'

Unfortunately, as any primary teacher will tell you, it's becoming increasingly difficult to persuade children to put in the practice required to become fluent readers. This is partly because they don't need to do so to pass 'short-answer' standardised tests (see Chapter 6) but also because they're simply not motivated to read at any length. Why should they bother when they can watch stories on screen, and engage in a wide range of enjoyable activities without having to make much effort at all?

There's very little deep conscious processing involved in watching a TV programme, playing a digital game or scrolling round the icons on an iPad. All these activities offer opportunities for children to learn, of course, but don't involve the same depth of mental engagement. Instead, children develop their ability to access information from multiple media sources (pictures, sounds, colour, video), using parallel processing and multi-tasking techniques, and applying what Ian Jukes, an expert in digital learning, calls 'continuous partial attention' to make rapid connections between ideas.

I'm not suggesting that this type of thinking skill isn't important. Indeed, it's essential to human survival and children have, in fact, been doing a real-life version of it since they were born because it's the sort of thought that underpins little children's play, especially before they develop language skills. That's why digital learning is, as Ian Jukes puts it, 'relevant, active, instantly useful and fun'. The trouble is that the mental processes involved are at odds with those required for 'the elaborate procedural habits of formal thinking'. Digital learners don't have to focus their attention or exercise self-control in pursuit of a distant reward, and they don't have to process language in increasingly complex ways. It's broad-based 'lateral thinking' as opposed to the deeper 'linear thinking' that literacy develops.

There's no doubt that today's toddlers will one day need to be experts at on-screen multi-tasking and parallel processing – flicking from window to window, making rapid connections between ideas. But, they'll also need to think rationally and sequentially in order to bring these connections together in a logical way. And they'll need to be able to control their thought processes in order to switch back and forth from lateral to linear, rather than continually going off at tangents.

My argument is that encouraging children to develop digital

learning skills too soon might impair their ability to develop fluent reading skills, and could thus deny them access to all the advantages we know that literacy brings. Personally, therefore, I'd prefer to apply the precautionary principle and try to ensure children are relatively fluent readers before encouraging them to develop ever more rapid lateral thought processes. That means prioritising real play over techno-play and books over screens until they're around six or seven, then ensuring plenty of time for practising reading until they're fluent enough to enjoy doing it for pleasure.

As Aric Sigman puts it: 'Ultimately, we have to make a value judgement about the way children are conditioned to learn. Which comes first: breadth and skimming the surface of ideas, or depth and the capacity for deep analytical thought?'

Look up!

The medical advice on recreational screen-time for schoolchildren continues to be a maximum of two hours a day. Since many of them will be spending a fair amount of time looking at screens of various types in school (and will probably have homework to complete onscreen or even online), this seems by no means unreasonable. But now that computer gaming, social networking and YouTube-grazing have been added to TV-watching, it's not easy to maintain sensible limits.

Even the Facebook generation is beginning to worry about the difficulties of tuning out of the virtual world and into the real one. In May 2014 as I was revising this chapter, a YouTube video by a young man called Gary Turk unexpectedly went viral. 'Look Up' began with the words 'I have 244 friends and yet I'm lonely. I speak to all of them every day but none of them really know me' and urged viewers to look up from their smartphones and start interacting with the real people in the real world around them. It must have hit a chord because the last time I checked he'd had nearly 48 million hits.

I was at the time working on a section which, in the 2006

edition of *Toxic Childhood*, was called 'The splintering family'. It was about the alarming number of children with a TV in their bedroom (around 80 per cent) and the growing trend for children to have their own DVD players, MP3 players, laptops and console games. Bedrooms were turning into 'electronic bedsits' where children spent long hours alone away from their families. One little boy I'd interviewed told me proudly about his 'virtual world' adding that his parents had virtual worlds too – mum in her office working on the computer and dad in the living room watching the football. I took the title for the section from a reference in a marketing tract: apparently, the more 'splintered' families are, the easier it is to sell stuff, because advertising can be more efficiently targeted.

Back in 2006, of course, smartphones were in their infancy, Facebook and Twitter were only just getting off the ground and the iPad was a mere twinkle in Steve Jobs' eye. So, thanks to Moore's Law, my research about bedroom TV is now well out of date, because the writing is on the wall for electronic bedsits. Having reached its peak around 2006 the phenomenon has ever since been in decline. By 2013, Ofcom's annual report *Children and Parents: Media Use and Attitudes* recorded that only 52 per cent of British children now had TVs in their bedrooms (still far too many, but significantly reduced), and there was a similar decrease in their ownership of other types of electronic paraphernalia. In fact, 41 per cent of families had actually cut back to just one television, kept in the living room.

Unfortunately, however, this doesn't herald a return to widespread 'family viewing'. Families may be watching screens in the same space but, courtesy of handheld devices, they're often watching different programmes. Or perhaps dad's tuned into sport on the TV while mum logs into Facebook or LinkedIn on her laptop and the children bend over tablets or smartphones, playing games or checking out videos on YouTube. Between 2012 and 2013, the number of families owning a tablet computer more than doubled (from 20 per cent to 51 per cent) and the number of five- to fifteen-year-olds who use them regularly tripled. Since tablets are now, according to Ofcom, the 'must-have device for children', this trend is set to continue.

Just under a fifth of eight- to eleven-year-olds and almost two-thirds of young teenagers also own smartphones, a percentage that's also bound to increase. The World Health Organisation recently stated that research into this area is of 'high priority' – there are possible long-term implications for brain development when young people use mobiles* and very little is known about the effect of smart phones on children's cognitive functions. In autumn 2014 a two-year study was instituted at Imperial College, London, but it's unlikely that many families will resist market pressure to buy technological 'must-haves' before it reports.

Screen-time has become portable, and is likely to become more so as the years go by. Screen use will also become increasingly personalised as major corporations refine their capacity to target each one of us as individuals. All of which means that maintaining a fully-connected family life will become more problematic, as marketeers direct children towards aspects of 'cool' culture appropriate to their personal profiles and adults towards whatever turns them on. If some or all members of a family are locked into personal virtual worlds (or even sporadically distracted into them), it doesn't matter that they're in the same physical space – the connection between them is broken.

This probably means that *everyone* has to accept a degree of discipline regarding the availability of handheld devices. However well-intentioned we are about spending time together, it's astoundingly easy to be distracted by an electronic toy promising constant immediate rewards, so the best way to ensure that we all 'look up' is to remove temptation. I increasingly hear about families who have a 'technology basket' or other container, in which everyone deposits their handheld devices

---

* The current Department of Health advice about mobile phones is that under-sixteens should use them only for essential purposes and, where possible, with hand-free kits.

during mealtimes, other family activities and when going off to bed.

This low-tech parenting approach turns out to be popular with many high-tech parents. Steve Jobs, for instance, wouldn't let his children use iPads at home, imposed limits on their screentime and insisted on a screen-free family meal every evening. Evan Williams, one of the founders of Twitter and Blogger, provides his children with books rather than tablets. Chris Anderson, former editor of Wired and currently CEO of 3D Robotics, limits screentime and has parental controls on all devices in his home: 'My kids accuse me and my wife of being fascists and overly concerned about tech, and they say none of their friends have the same rules. That's because we've seen the dangers of technology firsthand. I've seen it myself and I don't want it to happen to my kids.'

The dark side of the village

Every village has its dark side and, as children's access to the Internet was steadily 'normalised', many sources of danger were found looming in the shadows. At the time of writing, cyber-bullying and Internet pornography top the charts in terms of parental anxiety: in 2013, the NSPCC reported that 38 per cent of young people had experienced cyberbullying and, according to the BBC, by 2014 50 per cent of British teenagers were at least familiar with pornography. But these are just the current horrors. At other times, the focus of concern has been paedophiles grooming children for sex, violent computer games, websites encouraging anorexia or other types of self-destructive behaviour, children racking up huge bills through online gaming sites, cruel crazes such as 'happy slapping' or 'trolling' and many other anxiety-inducing possibilities.

It's important to remember that, as with all media scares, stories about the dark side of the electronic village tend to be pretty hyped-up. As Professor Tanya Byron said in her 2008 review for the UK government (updated in 2010), this sort of reporting 'predominantly focuses on the extreme, often tragic, and thankfully rare cases of harm to children and young people.' Many of the dangers now identified in the virtual world are simply an online version of offline hazards, and children whose real-life experiences have developed their self-confidence, emotional resilience and social skills are unlikely to be at significant risk. General parental guidance about bullying, 'stranger danger', and other aspects of personal safety can easily be adapted to cover the sorts of situations they'll meet online.

However, as usual these days, cometh the problem, cometh the commercial solution, to let parents off the hook. As worries around Internet safety surfaced, a plethora of 'parental controls' appeared on the market, so that mums or (more probably) dads could deny their children access to particular sites. 'Did you know,' asks a brisk female voice on NetNanny's current website, 'that most kids' exposure to porn happens at less than eleven years of age, that one in five children aged ten to seventeen have been approached for sex online, and that 75 per cent of these young people did not tell their parents about it?' She then explains how her product can set parents' minds at rest.

Parental controls are, of course, helpful and it's definitely a good idea to block 'adult content' on any computer children might use (see next section) and to set the inbuilt controls on handheld devices left lying around the home. But outsourcing the problem in this way is unlikely to keep children safe in the long run. That requires continuous hands-on involvement by their parents, who have to do what responsible parents have always done: maintain constant open communication with their children, whilst keeping a keen eye on potential dangerous developments in the outside world.

In fact, if 75 per cent of youngsters don't mention to mum or dad that they've stumbled upon online pornography or been the subject of sexual approaches by strangers, it's evidence of a serious breakdown in intergenerational communication – and buying in an Internet nanny isn't going to solve that problem.

The splintering of family units over the last quarter century has left many children and parents inhabiting vastly different worlds. It's also allowed free access to young minds by anyone with dark intent: the aggressive targeting of children by marketeers, for instance, has been skilfully directed under the parental radar, while most parents had absolutely no idea about the type of hardcore online pornography to which those 2014 teenagers had open access.

It's therefore essential that parents reconnect with their offspring, and take personal responsibility for their safety. In terms of tweaking authoritative parenting to include the electronic media, the lessons of the recent past seem to be:

- keep TV, computers, etc. in family space, where you can monitor and mediate their use
- train young children in Internet behaviour, hygiene and safety by visiting websites with them – 'holding their hand' as you would on a busy street, till you're confident that they're competent enough to go it alone
- check for age recommendations on any site your family visits and any software that enters your home and explain to your child why it's important to abide by them e.g. 18-rated games are rated that way because they can be damaging for still-developing minds; Facebook is for over-thirteens because young people need a certain level of maturity to deal with the content they'll find there*
- stick to the AAP guidelines of no more than two hours a day of recreational screen-time, thus ensuring there's plenty of space in children's lives for family activities, real play, hobbies, sport, music, reading, etc.

---

*   When your child protests that other kids' parents don't abide by these rules, the diplomatic answer is that these families must be unaware of them. But it's worth checking out who the families are and, if your child visits their home, mentioning politely that you don't want him or her viewing age-inappropriate material (and why – see 'A question of rights', below).

- as children grow older, continue to keep a weather eye on their media use and, through regular and frequent family contact, maintain constant communication about where they're going and whom they're meeting online, just as you would in the real world
- don't give them their own mobile devices with Internet connectivity until you're absolutely sure they're mature and informed enough to use them responsibly (personally, I'd recommend no earlier than secondary school age)
- keep abreast of behavioural trends on the Internet via media sources (there's no excuse for ignorance these days – you just Google) and through open communication with your child; talk these through and ensure your child has a healthy value system to help deal with them.

No matter how the digital world develops in the future, I suspect these general guidelines will still apply (for more detailed suggestions see pages 319–29). However, new issues arise with every new development and, after conversations with experts and young people, I reckon that some of the most worrying ones at the moment revolve around questions of identity, privacy and 'sharing'.

Identity, privacy and sharing

Imagine being thirteen (or younger if your parents don't monitor your online activity) and the time has come to begin your personal PR campaign. Henceforth you can choose how you present your image to the world – even airbrushing your photos if you have the right app – and tailor your published comments to project your chosen identity. At thirteen, there is quite a lot of choice involved, because you're still discovering your 'grown-up' identity. This involves learning to live in a confusingly-developing body, adjusting the values you acquired during childhood to fit your new teenage life and finding out where you fit within a peer group that's in a similar state of transition. What's more, the world around you is changing too, so you have to keep up with the trends.

I reckon that, if they've had a good enough shot at childhood, most kids will be resilient and secure enough in themselves to go through the long dark tunnel of adolescence and emerge at the other end relatively unscathed. Indeed, I suspect young teenagers who've benefited from love, play, communication and warm-but-firm parenting will even have enough sense of self to cope with the transition from childhood to adulthood on a social networking site (or to dump social networking if they're not enjoying the experience). But what if they've not had a good enough childhood? What if they've spent much of the preceding thirteen years in the company of marketeers, gazing at two-dimensional screens?

The neuroscientist Susan Greenfield points out that, since 'the physical brain adapts exquisitely to the environment, and the 21st century environment is changing in unprecedented ways' we may be undergoing a significant change in the nature of identity. In their 2013 book *The App Generation*, psychologists Howard Gardner and Katie Davies suggest that young people who've led a largely two-dimensional existence may not develop a deep sense of their own inner selves, but instead begin to define identity in terms of an online persona. They seek confirmation of their personal significance in the number of hits for their photos, videos, bon mots and anecdotes, rather like small children clamouring for attention ('Look at me, mummy! Because if you don't look at me maybe I don't exist...').

This isn't a criticism of social networking (indeed, I believe that, used positively, it's a remarkable resource – see 'And now the good news', below). Instead, it's yet another argument for limiting children's media use and instead making sure they have a flourishing real life of their own. And it's also another reason for preparing them throughout childhood to use technology wisely – in the age of social media, they need to be clear about the differences between authentic and commodified identities. They also need to think about the manifold implications of 'sharing'.

In 2010, Facebook founder Mark Zuckerberg announced that privacy is 'no longer a social norm' because 'people have really gotten comfortable not only sharing more information of different kinds, but more openly and with more people.' In the same year I interviewed a group of fifteen-year-old girls who'd been on Facebook since its public launch, when they were eleven or twelve. I asked what they thought should be the lower age limit, and was initially surprised when they decided on eighteen. Apparently, they'd been dead keen on having a profile 'when we were young' but now concluded 'the grief wasn't worth the hassle'. Although they claimed to be as relaxed as Mark Zuckerberg about the idea of 'sharing', much of the grief they described resulted from posts being misinterpreted or falling into the wrong hands. They'd also had problems deciding who to accept as 'friends' and with people making comments online that they wouldn't dream of in real life, because 'it's different when you can't see them.'

Over the last few years, attitudes to privacy have certainly changed – bloggers share their lives (and often the lives of their small children) with the world, Tweeters keep followers up-to-date with their every passing thought, Facebook, Instagram and Flickr are awash with photographs. But I suspect that, as people become more familiar with the implications of sharing, the pendulum will swing back. It's now clear that the 'digital footprints' we leave every time we go on the net are of interest to all sorts of people for whom they weren't intended.

Apparently, by 2010 half of employers had rejected a potential employee after checking out his or her Facebook pages, so photos of drunken high jinks can blow their protagonists' chances of a job. It seems that burglars refer to social networks as 'Internet shopping', because it's a great way to find out homeowners' personal details and holiday plans. Internet phishers have worked out that email-users are more likely to open spam if it features a Facebook friend's name and the odd buzz word when they send it (often, these days, with a view to identity theft). And if, for any reason, a social networker acquires a public profile, journalists are likely to trawl through their archives in search of a story. In 2013, seventeen-year-old Paris Brown was obliged to stand down from her new job as local youth crime commissioner because of a racist tweet a couple of years earlier.

Perhaps the most distressing possibility is that confidential information – particularly photos – may be misused by people whom sharers do know, but for some reason have antagonised. No matter how close young adults may be (and in the case of romantic relationships, that may be very close indeed), the course of true love doesn't always run smooth, and neither does the course of every friendship. Children therefore need to know well before such incidents can arise that it's unwise to trust anyone with access to photos you wouldn't want made public and 'sexting' is *never* a good idea.* (Proud parents might also bear in mind that secondary schools are now reporting incidents of cyberbullying based on photos shared on family Facebook pages, sometimes from many years earlier.)

Google's Eric Schmidt is less convinced about the death of privacy than his counterpart at Facebook. In 2013 he told an audience in Cambridge: 'I'm absolutely sure that parents will have to have the "online privacy talk" before the "sex talk". It might be when they're eight years old you're saying "Don't put that online – it'll come back and bite you" and then you'll have to explain why.' One way of ensuring plenty of 'online privacy talks' is to set up a family Facebook page, which your child can help you compile and edit. This provides opportunities to talk naturally about all the major issues, including how to set privacy settings, the hazards of sharing, and the fact that Mark Zuckerberg may be so keen on it because the more information Facebookers share about

---

* Sexting = sending sexually explicit pictures via smartphones. A couple of years ago an app called Snapchat became a popular sexting device, since the images it sent self-destructed after a specified length of time (up to 10 seconds). However, recipients soon worked out how to snap the Snapchat picture on another mobile device.

themselves, the more money his organization earns from market developers and targeted advertising.

All these lessons are, with hindsight, simple common sense. But in the excitement of a new social phenomenon it's easy to lose sight of common sense – and, anyway, teenagers haven't had time to acquire much of it. It's up to older, wiser members of the real-life community to help them strike a balance between the thrill of a rapidly-changing present and the hard-won lessons of the past.

O tempora, o mores

In fact, parents have always had to be aware of dangers in the environment, to second-guess their children's needs in the future, and to prepare them to survive and thrive in adolescence and adulthood. In that respect there's no difference between twenty-first-century parenting and parenting through the ages. But as illustrated in Chapter 8 (pages 247–81), modern parents have the added problem of swimming against a cultural tide that's turned out to be damaging for children. If the electronic village isn't to become an ever-darker and more anxiety-inducing place, it seems to me the time has come to challenge some recent cultural assumptions.

The Papdopoulos and Bailey Reviews into the sexualisation and commercialisation of childhood (see Chapter 8) clearly showed that one significant side effect of hyper-competitive consumer culture has been the steady sexualisation of society. Sex sells, so commercial companies naturally exploit it whenever possible. Shock also sells, so film- and programme-makers, pop singers, celebrity-endorsers, and creatives in every area of the visual media have to find ever more shocking and titillating ways of attracting an audience. Thus, as well as sexual content becoming sexier, violent films have become more violent, horror movies more horrific, and cutting-edge comedy has grown coarser and crueller.

Such media fare is, of course, originally aimed at adults and it's now widely agreed that adults should be entitled to view anything they like, subject to minimal censorship based on public safety and criminal law. The arrival of the Internet, with its policy of completely open access, was in keeping with this view of human rights, and so incidentally fuelled a cultural climate of 'anything goes'. Few people questioned what was happening at the time, for fear of being thought prudish or out of touch – indeed, after the vitriol and ridicule heaped on Mrs Mary Whitehouse during the late twentieth century, it would be a brave individual who dared poke a head above the parapet.

But alongside the steady degradation of adult culture, commercial forces were also normalising the notion that twenty-first-century children 'grow older younger'. As a result, many parents grew careless about age-restrictions on movies, websites and computer games. Official regulators, also influenced by cultural trends, gradually eased age restrictions, and films which would once have definitely been X-rated became 15s … then 12s … then PGs (I'm still reeling at the PG rating for *Batman: the Dark Knight* in 2008). TV programmers grew steadily more daring about the sorts of content shown before the 9 p.m. watershed, including levels of violence in footage shown on the daytime news broadcasts.

A question of rights

The UK forensic psychologist Professor Kevin Browne once commented that adults should exercise 'the same care with adult media as they do with medication or chemicals around the home', since unrestricted viewing could be regarded as 'a form of emotional maltreatment of the child'. In a cultural free-for-all, however, how are parents to tell what is 'adult' and what isn't? We've arrived at a point where many children under ten are regularly exposed to visual media that leaves them confused, frightened and emotionally destabilised. The long-term emotional toll is yet to be discovered, but among the obvious short-term results are problems with sleep (see Chapter 3) and reluctance to play outdoors (see Chapter 2), both of which impact on overall development and well-being.

I believe the worst of the media has now become a child protection issue and, just as real life villages protect law-abiding families from damaging assault, we need a more serious approach to policing the electronic village. Over the last couple of decades, many organisations have called for greater government restrictions on what children see and hear on-screen but now that the subject is entangled with the much wider debate about censorship, the question of children's right to a healthy environment is often lost in controversy about the rights of adults to read, view and listen to whatever they like.

Take violence, for example. In the year 2000 a number of highly influential institutions including the American Medical Association, American Psychological Association and American Academy of Pediatrics issued a joint statement 'At this time well over 1000 studies ... point overwhelmingly to a causal connection between media violence and aggressive behaviour in children'. This concerted stand immediately drew counter-fire from anti-censorship experts around the world, rubbishing the studies cited and pointing to others proving the opposite. A decade and a half later, the situation hasn't changed. Parents are understandably confused by these conflicting messages – and, of course, anxious not to be fuddy-duddy old killjoys if the anti-censorship lobby proves correct.

Nevertheless, if we rise above the bickering, most parents would agree that in real life they want to protect their children from witnessing extreme violence. As screen images become ever more realistic, research repeatedly shows that they stimulate the same emotional centres in the brain as genuine violent experiences. What's more, video can be rewound, slowed down or freeze-framed and computer games are played repeatedly. We aren't talking about Tom and Jerry here, or the Roadrunner being beaten over the head with a frying pan, but about highly realistic – and, indeed, in news broadcasts completely realistic – bloody murder, sadism and mayhem.

Psychologists point out that when children watch such violent material the possibility of increased aggressive behaviour is only one of a range of effects. Others are desensitisation to pain and suffering (which could contribute to the bullying explosion) or increased fear of the world around them (which makes children afraid to venture beyond the safety of their own homes). The American writer Neil Postman maintains that the most significant effect is the undermining of children's confidence in adults' ability to protect them in a violent world.

Another flashpoint is the sexual content of many TV programmes. The effects on children of casually witnessing graphic sex scenes or tuning into salacious discussion (as seen on daytime shows like *Jeremy Kyle*) are also lost in the debate about what's acceptable for adults. No one has yet proved that exposure to salacious chit-chat or televised sexual dramas at an early age is associated with a rise in underage sex, teenage porn addiction, or the sexualisation of young girls ... but we've already seen the effects that unmediated consumer pressure has on children. The same media that sell little girls an interest in clothes, dieting, make-up and 'boyz' also introduce them, through regular programme content, to the fascination of sexual intrigue. Again, parents have to wonder whether they'd be happy for their children to witness these scenes in real life.

It seems we've reached a point when adults' right to media freedom is in direct conflict with children's right to grow up in a non-toxic environment. There's an urgent need for more effective application of the 9 p.m. TV watershed and a tightening up of film categorisation and regulations surrounding pop music videos. It would also be helpful to have a public information campaign to raise awareness about the reasons for age-related guidance in these areas, as well as those on electronic games and social networking sites.

Inching in the right direction?

There are, however, some areas where policy and policing do take parental anxiety about the Internet seriously, two of which are paedophilia and pornography. Thanks to the sensational nature of these topics, there's been no shortage of outraged media coverage, so law-makers and law-enforcers have had to make efforts to keep up with developments.

Internet freedom must have seemed like a blessing to paedophiles. In the past, child sex abusers were sad isolated individuals for whom feeding the habit was wracked with personal danger, but the world wide web provided ready access to thousands of fellow-deviants and a global library of images, often available for purchase from commercial organisations that quickly recognised a money-spinner. Not surprisingly, the perversion flourished, with media publicity attracting other sad individuals who probably wouldn't even have contemplated it in pre-web times.

Eventually, however, there were corresponding changes in policing. For instance, in 2002 sexual grooming on the Internet became a criminal offence in the UK; in 2004 the British police joined a Virtual Global Task Force to collaborate in breaking up international paedophile rings, and in 2006 the Home Office established CEOP (the Child Exploitation and Online Protection Centre). They're kept pretty busy: in 2013 a journalist, under police guidance, logged on to a chatroom posing as a fourteen-old girl – within ten seconds she was contacted by two men who were very keen to make her acquaintance and after three minutes the list of interested punters was so long it went off the screen.

High levels of public concern and legislative response can make a difference. The CEOP 'thinkuknow' website is extremely useful for parents and teachers, with well-made videos about Internet safety for different age-groups of children. The publicity surrounding online grooming and high-profile arrests brought discussion of child sexual abuse firmly into the mainstream, and has ensured that other crimes achieved wide coverage (the earlier reluctance of the Catholic Church, the BBC and other arms of the Establishment to acknowledge abuse going on under their noses shows this is a significant move forward). It illustrates how powerful media coverage can be in highlighting and combating issues affecting children's safety and well-being, as long as the media can be persuaded to take an interest in the first place.

Developments during the last couple of years regarding online pornography have been just as dramatic. Since the 1960s, few people apart from faith groups openly questioned the increasing sexualisation of society – a more open attitude to sex was generally considered healthy. Feminism had embraced the idea that open displays of female sexuality were empowering, which made it difficult to criticise some of the sleazier manifestations of 'openness' in the media. As explicit sexual content became commonplace, purveyors of pornography had to up the ante in terms of the shock value of their products. They were fortunate that the Internet provided a new and financially-rewarding platform and, since their materials could be viewed in the privacy of consumers' own homes (thus avoiding the embarrassment of going into a shop and buying them), the porn industry flourished as never before.

Teenagers are, of course, deeply interested in sex so they soon logged on in their millions. Secondary teachers rapidly noticed the damaging effects on young people's relationships but it took a while before the general public caught up and, by this time, the type of pornography freely available online was shocking even to twenty-first-century sensibilities (even the former editor of the 'lads mag' *Loaded* was horrified when he checked it out). An unlikely alliance sprang up between the faith groups who'd long waged war on the sex industry and feminists who were appalled at Internet porn's misogynistic overtones. They were joined by worried parents in lobbying the government to introduce an 'opt-in' clause on Internet-enabled devices, so that consumers had to prove they were eighteen and actually wanted this stuff delivered to their machines before it cascaded into their lives.

The media were also naturally interested: they brought some

of the more jaw-dropping facts about what kids were watching to the nation's attention and the Daily Mail gave its backing to the campaign. Even then, to interested observers like myself, it seemed probable that the government would take a less controversial route and go for 'opt-out' rather than 'opt-in'. But in late 2013, the opt-in option was adopted and Britain's four major Internet providers signed up to deliver it by the end of 2014.

There has been the predictable outcry from the anti-censorship lobby (even though it's not censorship – anyone's welcome to opt in once they're eighteen) and there are bound to be problems with implementation. But it's a significant change in public policy, very welcome to childhood campaigners, and perhaps heralding a turn of the tide in national attitudes to child protection.

And now the good news …

Children's descent into the dark side of the electronic village is certainly not inevitable. The developments listed in the previous section show that legislation and regulation can be positively helpful to parents. And as we learn how to adapt to constant change, parents can also take control of the electronic media in their own homes, so there's no reason why technology shouldn't enrich children's lives as much as it has enriched the lives of most adults over the last thirty years.

When television is reinstated in a family space, family viewing once again becomes an opportunity to share time and con-versation, with negotiated periods for children to watch their own special programmes. If family computers and console games also inhabit shared space, everyone knows what's happening on them, and children can be reared to use them responsibly. As long as parents take note of medical advice, raise their offspring to respect themselves and others, and ensure they understand the rules of Internet safety, the next generation can grow up to be confident, competent electronic villagers.

So while it's important to recognise the problems for child-raising that come with modern technology, it would be downright reprehensible to ignore the benefits. Good children's television can be a magnificent resource, touching parts of the infant consciousness that other media cannot reach. It can transport children to any part of the globe, any period of history, any realm of the imagination. TV can also help children see how other people live and understand their point of view. American psychologist Paul Bloom argues that children grow as moral beings through stories that help them take the perspective of distant others – TV can provide these stories, and the opportunity to empathise with people across the global village.

What's more, it can provide these experiences in an informal, non-didactic way and, with an ever-expanding capacity for interactive involvement via related websites, the potential to build on TV-inspired interest is now phenomenal. Increasingly, public service broadcasters are working alongside other agencies to develop new approaches to education – in the coming years, we may well see wonders.

This isn't to say that all encounters with TV should be educational. Today's children, like their parents, lead exhausting lives – they too have to sit in the traffic queues on the way to and from school, and deal with a world of rapid responses and constant change. A bit of mindless visual chewing gum is a great way to relax, and one could scarcely begrudge them an hour or so chilling out in front of children's programmes at the end of a hard day.

It would also be madness to deny the potential of computer technology to enrich children's experience. Today's youngsters have access to limitless information and technological tools for exploring and expressing their ideas in ways unimaginable even a decade ago. Building websites, creating apps or making multimedia presentations all involve higher-order thought processes and command of language and literacy skills, not to mention the development of self-control and perseverance. Many computer games also involve considerable mental effort and self-control, and interaction with fellow-players develops virtual social skills. There are now even ways that web-based developments encourage new forms of outdoor activity, such as geocaching.

Once they're equipped with the skills to negotiate it wisely and safely, the Internet offers young people innumerable ways to develop current interests and discover new ones. If they've something to communicate they can set up their own blogs on sites like Wordpress and Tumblr or post videos on YouTube; if they want to make art or music they've only to click on apps such as ArtStudio or Soundbrush; for those who just want to listen there are iTunes and Spotify; and anyone who's still at a loose end will find countless productive ways to use their energy on sites like Pinterest. Meanwhile, half an hour a day on Facebook keeps them in touch with friends and up to date with topics of interest (while those who are addicted to gossip can sign up to Twitter). If they've learned how to keep a sensible balance between virtual and real life – and can concentrate on chosen experiences long enough to enjoy them – the world really does seem to be the next generation's oyster.

Village wisdom

There's plenty more good news in the global village in terms of help for parents. As social problems – including those associated with toxic childhood syndrome – become apparent, technology provides new ways of helping to solve them. There are now vast numbers of websites offering information, advice and support for parents – it's never been easier to call on help from experts or from other parents who've been there before. For factual help, it's safest to avoid commercial sites and stick with those created by well-established charities or respected institutions, such as the ones listed at the end of each Chapter in *Toxic Childhood*. For peer support, there are networks like Mumsnet and the websites of local groups, offering opportunities to meet up with other local parents.

The web also provides ways of bringing people together to protect children's right to a healthy childhood, such as the

Campaign for a Commercial-Free Childhood in the United States. Over the last ten years, I've been involved in a number of UK childhood campaigns, each of which has rallied support via the Internet. Gradually, the different organisations involved in specific areas of child development have begun to forge alliances, and in 2013 Wendy Ellyatt (interviewed on pages 195–6) launched the Save Childhood movement, with a formidable list of expert advisers and organisational support. She hopes to collate all future developments on the website and, once I've finished revising this book, I hope to be helping.

Television programme-makers have also devised many ingenious methods of spreading good ideas and useful knowledge. From chat shows to reality TV, they've looked for ways of providing modern substitutes for the trusted authority figures to whom families turned in old-fashioned villages – the family doctor, the kindly schoolteacher, the moral or spiritual leader. In terms of childcare, there are dispensers of wisdom on daytime chat show sofas, regularly throwing hints and advice in parents' direction. (In France, a daily hour-long programme about raising children, *Les Maternelles*, provides a wide range of information in typically urbane French style that could act as an object lesson to programme-makers in other countries.) There are also documentary-style programmes, such as the BBC's remarkable *Child of Our Time*, following the lives of various children born in the year 2000, and linked to a course in child development through the Open University's Open Learn website. The opportunity to tap into advice and video footage of parenting skills could be the twenty-first-century equivalent of learning through growing up in an extended family.

I've come to the conclusion, however, that edu-tainment programmes such as *Supernanny*, demonstrating how desperate parents can tame their out-of-control children, aren't the best way forward. They may give useful messages about behaviour management but, in order to retain an entertaining edge, the behaviour of onscreen children in successive series has to get worse and worse, which doesn't give a particularly hopeful message and may even help normalise 'naughtiness'. There's also usually an expert imported to solve the problem – a supernanny figure or a child psychologist – giving the impression that parents aren't capable of raising their children unaided. And there's the problem of electric speed. On TV, transformations have to happen in the half an hour or so that the programme lasts. We see only edited highlights – the reality of raising children in 'slow time' can't possibly be addressed.

The medium is the message

A week or so after the 'Look up' video mentioned earlier, a couple of responses appeared on YouTube, predictably entitled 'Look Down!' and making an impassioned case for virtual communication. They were just as enjoyable to watch but their antagonistic edge (and the sort of feedback they inspired) illustrated how discussion of emotive subject matter can so easily become polarised.

It's an age-old problem because, no matter how civilised human beings are on the surface, the minute we become emotionally involved it's very difficult to maintain a reasonable tone and demeanour. I struggled with the problem constantly while writing this book, and even more so during the updating process. Over the last eight years, I've had opportunities to learn much more about child development, so I've grown ever more worried about the ways modern culture can inhibit children's ability to self-regulate, control the focus of their attention and empathise with others. If these qualities are generally eroded, it won't do much for their capacity for reasoned argument.

So, while technophobia is clearly ridiculous, so is unbridled technophilia, and the excitement of living in an age of marvels mustn't blind us to its potential dangers. In arguing for a more balanced approach to raising children in a screen-based culture, therefore, I've found myself continually pondering on Marshall McLuhan's most famous aphorism: 'the medium is the message'.

The message (or content) of any communication is hugely

affected by the medium through which it's conveyed, so humanity's sudden shift into an electronic village, where messages are conveyed through fast-moving multimedia channels, is a highly significant one. It's particularly significant from the point of view of child-rearing because, as Susan Greenfield has said, 'the physical brain adapts exquisitely to the environment' and childhood is obviously the most important period for brain development – it's when we learn to talk, to think, to operate socially, and to read and write.

The natural medium for human communication, integrated into our DNA, is face-to-face interaction. This is critical to human development from the very beginning (see Chapter 4) and it continues to be essential to our well-being throughout life. If we value our humanity, we must continue to cherish real-life, real-time interaction as the first and fundamental medium for passing on all the most vital messages about what it is to be human. It's not only how our species has learned language and basic attention skills for several million years; it's also where we've acquired the capacity for empathy that allows social groups to work together.

Around six millennia ago, humanity made a massive step forward. We built on our facility for language to develop ways of communicating via the written word. As writing systems developed, this new medium became steadily more widely available and – especially after the invention of the printing press – literacy hugely increased humankind's capacity for rational thought (see 'Books versus screens', above). So this second-level medium is also well worth cherishing – it doesn't come naturally, but it's been an essential element in the growth of civilisations and the spread of education and democracy.

It's an enormous privilege to live at a time when the human race is taking its third great communicatory step forward. The electronic media offer new ways of building on language and literacy, so that everyone can now benefit from quick-fire, easily-accessed, multimedia message-bearing systems to extend our knowledge, understanding and potential for further progress.

The trouble is that, whenever anything new and exciting comes along, it's easy to take what's gone before for granted. Adults who can already talk and listen tend to assume that these skills developed 'naturally', unaware of how much human input was involved. They also tend to forget the amount of time and effort involved in learning to read and write and – unless they're psychologists or neuroscientists – are probably unaware of the effect that process had on their capacity for 'the elaborate procedural habits of formal thinking.'

If we're to raise bright, balanced children, fit to meet the challenges of the twenty-first-century, we have to stop taking these essential stepping-stones for granted. Children need to be fully equipped to function at all three levels of human thought and communication. In the words of IT writer Edward Tenner, 'It would be a shame if brilliant technology were to end up threatening the kind of intellect that created it.'

* * *

In 2001 Marc Prensky, an American educationist, came up with the rather strange idea that the younger generation were 'digital natives' who, having been born into a world of electronic media, were somehow more competent at finding their way around it than old-fashioned 'digital immigrants', born on that other planet known as the past. From the moment I heard this conceit being bandied about I was filled with dread. It seemed to me a gift to unscrupulous marketeers, who could use it to divide and conquer both groups of consumers.

It's clear from the evidence described throughout Toxic Childhood that de-skilling adults by suggesting they're less competent than the younger generation hasn't contributed to the mental and physical health of children, or of society in general. Nor has 'empowering' children by suggesting that they're somehow imbued with esoteric wisdom denied to their elders. No matter how rapidly the world changes, children will always need adult care and guidance as they grow and mature – indeed, in a culture moving at such hectic speed, authoritative parenting (see page 334) is more important than ever. Fortunately, we've now reached the stage when most parents are 'digital natives' themselves so, until someone comes up with another clever slogan, they should feel empowered to assume full responsibility for their offspring.

Evolution has not furnished us with a technology gene, and young children are no more naturally equipped to wander freely round virtual worlds than they are around the real one. Twenty-first-century parents must ensure their children are fully prepared to deal with the real environment and real interactions, and to benefit from old-fashioned literacy as well as the digital variety.

And from the moment they introduce modern technology into their offsprings' lives, they also have to teach safety rules for the Internet super-highway, just as they teach those for the busy highways outside their homes.

DETOXING THE ELECTRONIC VILLAGE

The aim of the suggestions in this and the following boxes is that, by their mid-teens, young people will be confident, competent, and *independent* electronic villagers. By taking authoritative control in the early stages, parents should themselves feel confident to give their children increasing freedom to navigate their way around the virtual world, just as they need increasing freedom to explore the real world (see Chapter 2).

The first two to three years
- As with all aspects of child-rearing, start as you mean to go on, if possible before you even have a family. Discuss your attitudes to electronic entertainment with your partner and devise policies that will work for you.

- Until there is firm evidence to the contrary, in the early years remember the precautionary principle. You can't, as they say, put the toothpaste back in the tube, so try to stick to the medical recommendation of zero screen-time till children are at least two.

- There may sometimes be pressing reasons to make an exception to the zero screen-time rule (e.g. a weekly chat to grandma via Skype), but always ask yourself whether any projected deviation is mainly for your own convenience. If so, make every possible effort to find an alternative way forward.

- Make it clear to your child that screen-based technology is for grown-ups. Like the car and the cooker, it's off-limits until (and unless) you say so.

- Your attitude is of paramount importance here. If you genuinely believe that these things must be off-limits, that belief will communicate itself to your child, making it much easier to establish the rule.

- Don't have TV on in the background as, even if a child isn't watching it, it can disrupt their attention during play and distract you from genuine interaction.

- Spend plenty of time chatting, singing and reading to your child – this is by far the best way to prepare him or her for literacy. Don't be fooled by products that offer a short cut – at this stage short cuts are almost inevitably counter-productive.

Three- to seven-year-olds

- Keep all screen-based media, including handheld devices and console games, in family space, and introduce children to them gradually, monitoring and mediating their use. Gradually work up to, then stick to the medical recommendation of no more than one to two hours of screen-time a day.

- Remember that the benefits of multimedia relate only to *appropriate* material – that is programmes, games, apps and software specifically designed for your child's age-group.

- Keep the rest of your family time screen-free, e.g. TV off, handheld devices placed in a 'technology basket' or other container *outside* the living room. While this may involve a degree of sacrifice on everyone's part, bear in mind that there are hugely important benefits:

  – time (without distraction) for communication, forging a family and passing on life skills (see Chapters 4, 5 and 6)
  – showing your children that they come first in your life, and modelling the self-discipline they'll need in the future.

- Don't let electronic entertainment ever become a 'default activity' – for instance, make it a rule that no family members automatically switch on the TV or log on to a computer when they enter the family space. Ensure that engagement with electronic media is always purposeful, intentional and finite (see 'How to detox a TV addict', below – all these suggestions can be adopted to apply to other electronic entertainment).
- Talk to your child about the electronic media and the reasons for your decisions and rules. Ensure they know that your key concern is their welfare and well-being.
- Before bringing any electronic game into the house, make sure it's suitable for your child's age-group and play it with him/her so you're fully aware of what it's all about.
- Talk also about what you see on screen – TV especially provides openings for conversations about life in general, including love, sex and relationships (the sooner conversations about these issues begin, the easier it is to maintain open communication throughout your child's life).
- If your child is frightened by something seen on TV (e.g. the news) or film, give them a cuddle and warm reassurance that you're always there to keep them safe. Simple explanations like 'That's just a story – it's not real' or 'That sort of thing doesn't happen round here' are generally effective.
- Continue to read to your child and gradually encourage him or her (in his/her own time) to develop reading skills and reading stamina.

As long as you provide an environment in which literacy is seen to be valued and fun, most children should be well on the way to being readers by the time they're seven.

- See also 'Detoxing the Internet' below and the detoxing boxes for Chapter 8.

Seven- to twelve-year-olds

- Stick with the 'maximum two hours of recreational screen-time a day' rule, thus ensuring your child still has plenty of time for other activities. As time goes on, s/he may also have screen-based homework – ensure this doesn't go on too long (contact the school if it does), and insist on regular breaks every half hour.
- Maintain the rules about keeping electronic media in family space, screen-free family time, and no 'default screen use' (see above).
- Continue to take great care over the electronic resources brought into your home, and explain to your child why it's important to abide by age restrictions.
- Chat with your child about the electronic media with which they come into contact at friends' homes and, if you're worried about any of it, contact the parents concerned and talk it through. It may mean you have to adjust your child's social calendar in future … but, on the other hand, it may mean you convince another family to be more authoritative about their children's electronic entertainment.
- Gradually give your child greater choice and control over the use of screen-time, but maintain open communication and encourage them to talk about what they've watched or played, and also the websites they've visited.
- If your child is frightened or disturbed by anything they've seen, talk it through. Children over seven still need reassurance that their parents will protect them from violence or disaster but also benefit from logical explanations, e.g.:

  – 'it can't happen because it's fantasy'

– 'it couldn't happen here/to you because ...'
– 'if it ever did happen, this is what we'd do ...' (making plans to deal with vaguely possible scenarios is a good way to defuse their scare potential).

- See also 'Detoxing use of the Internet' below and the detoxing boxes for Chapter 8.

Twelve-year-olds and older

- If parents maintain authoritative control over media use during the first twelve years, children should by this stage be capable of exercising self-discipline. They should also have enough other interests to ensure they need plenty of screen-free time.
- However, teenagers are inclined to go over the top with new freedoms, so keep lines of communication open and make it clear that:

    – adult privileges come with corresponding responsibilities
    – age-restrictions on any TV programmes, DVDs, computer games and websites continue to apply, no matter what other families do (see page 322)
    – you're still responsible for their welfare, so what you say still goes (and if you say 'Switch off', it's because you love them).

- Maintain the rules about keeping electronic media in family space, screen-free family time, and no 'default screen-use', as above.
- See also 'Detoxing use of the Internet' below.

DETOXING USE OF THE INTERNET

The web is a fantastic resource for parents and children. Check out the websites below to find ways of using it positively.

Three- to seven-year-olds

- Gradually introduce your child to the Internet on the family laptop or your own handheld device, but make sure they understand that it's a 'grown-up' world and not to be visited without supervision until they're older.
- Visit only age-appropriate websites or those, such as a family Facebook page, over which you maintain control. Explain about the importance of privacy settings.
- Gradually teach your child how to behave on the net and ensure s/he knows the difference between real-life friends/relations and people that you've never actually met. Again, check out detailed suggestions on the websites listed below.
- Watch and talk about the age-appropriate video on the CEOP thinkuknow website, below.
- Make sure your child knows how to recognise suspicious emails and hyperlinks. Give dire warnings about viruses that knock out the system, how you could be spammed to death, etc.
- Make sure they also know never to give out an address, phone number or any information that could identify them (e.g. photos in school uniform) to anyone they meet in the electronic village.
- See also the general points in 'Detoxing the electronic village', above.

Seven- to twelve-year-olds

- Continue to spend time on the web with your child but, once you feel confident that they're reasonably Internet-savvy, allow them to visit trusted websites without supervision.
- Don't rely on parental controls to protect children from inappropriate materials. They aren't completely reliable and, like computer firewalls,

are rapidly outdated. Use them to help by all means – especially in blocking adult content – but assume major responsibility for your child's safety yourself.

- Talk about the dangers of sharing information and the ways posts 'can come back to bite you' (see 'Identity, privacy and sharing', above). Encourage your child to be particularly circumspect about sharing photographs. Unless they'd be happy to have the photo displayed on a billboard in the middle of town, it's not a good idea to send it spinning into cyberspace.
- Watch and talk about the age-appropriate video on the CEOP thinkuknow website below.
- When you feel your child is sufficiently Internet-savvy, gradually relax the rules about which websites s/he may visit on the family computer. Keep up regular communication about web-based activities just as you would about his/her activities in the real world. Continue to emphasise the importance of abiding by age-restrictions.
- Ensure your child knows that if s/he encounters anything in the electronic village that makes her/him feel uncomfortable, embarrassed or worried, s/he should let you know. See the websites below for details of what to do in specific cases, e.g. cyberbullying, stranger danger.
- Remember that all villages have their dark sides, even if their PR personnel prefer to gloss over them. Since PR people for the electronic village now control most of the information that circulates in our world, be wary. Don't trust them to make decisions for your family – make them yourself.
- One of the most important decisions is when to allow children to have their own smartphones or tablets. Since handheld devices allow them to wander freely in the virtual world, be sure you feel as confident as possible about their competence to do so. And make it clear that, if you find the device being misused, it'll be immediately confiscated. Your trust depends on their trustworthiness.
- See also 'Detoxing the electronic village', above.

Twelve-year-olds and above

- By the teenage years, children need increasing opportunities to spread their wings and increasing privacy in the virtual world, just as they need it in the real world. If they've been well-prepared, they should be fine. However, make sure they understand that you are still responsible for them so expect them to abide by the established rules:

  – stick to age-restrictions in terms of the sites they visit
  – no more than a couple of hours' recreational screen-time per day
  – family-time is screen-free (e.g. all handhelds in the technology box).

- Ask them to watch the CEOP videos for teenagers on the thinkuknow website listed below. Keep an eye open for other useful material, e.g. at time of writing, there's an excellent short video called 'Tagged' on the Australian Cybersmart site (see also below).

- Maintain communication about screen use, e.g. talk about and share any new apps, discuss new developments in the news. Ensure your child feels confident to talk to you about anything that concerns or upsets him/her on screen and online.

HOW TO DETOX A TV ADDICT

Some parents assure me the best system is to go cold turkey. Just remove the TV from the house and start life without it. If you can live without TV yourself, that would probably work a treat, but personally I enjoy watching occasionally and love films on DVD. And there's always the problem of 'forbidden fruit' – the point of the exercise is to help children acquire a balanced attitude to screen-based entertainment.

- Look at the viewing habits of the family as a whole – it may be you all need detoxing.
- Discuss with your child why he or she is a TV addict. Is it because there's nothing else to do? Is it a default activity and they've never thought about alternatives?
- Make sure the TV is in a shared space (see 'How to get technology out of the bedroom', page 142–3).
- Find ways of rationing 'electronic time' that suit your family, e.g.:

  – buy a TV guide every week, and let everyone circle the programmes they want to see (up to an agreed level) in advance, so you can just switch on when required and tape any overlaps
  – have agreed time limits for viewing each day and stick to them (like anything else involved in child-rearing, if you are *utterly* consistent and determined for a few weeks, the arrangement will become habitual).

- Perhaps you could have a regular 'family TV evening' when everyone settles down together with popcorn and drinks for some shared viewing of DVDs or digitally-recorded programmes you all want to share.
- Make sure there are lots of real activities on offer to compete with electronic entertainment and, especially in the early stages, make time to share these. They don't have to be complicated or expensive. For instance, with your child:

– make a pile of family photographs and sort them into albums / scrapbooks / biographies / make a collage for your child's wall (whilst sorting, take the opportunity to reminisce and talk)
– get out recipe books, and go through them together choosing meals you fancy cooking. Make menus for the week, take your child shopping for ingredients and do some shared cooking.
– investigate your local area. Get a map, and go on expeditions to find out about all the places you don't know (however unpromising they sound). Make sure you're properly equipped – camera or smartphone for taking photos, notebook, food supplies – and collect information, pictures, souvenirs to make a scrapbook of your travels.
– throw a party. With your child, decide on a theme (e.g. pirates, storyland, robots) and a budget (keep it low). Then enjoy planning and making costumes, decorations, food, invitations, activities – the lower your budget, the more ingenious you'll have to be. Invite a few of your child's friends and their parents, and enjoy yourselves.
– see also 'How to avoid couch potato syndrome'; '50 things to do before you're 11¾'; 'Detoxing communication'; 'Twenty-five life skills for children to learn by the age of six', 'Twenty more life skills for children to learn by the age of twelve'; 'How to encourage creative play'.

- Or perhaps you could just go for a walk, a bike ride, a swim ... it doesn't have to be anything spectacular.
- Demonstrate to your child that, while it's fine occasionally to slump in front of a screen and be entertained, it's much more fun to entertain yourself and others. But if you don't switch off the magic box and make the effort to do something, you'll never discover the joys of living in the real world.

PARENT POWER: POLICING THE VILLAGE

When I started researching this subject, I soon learned that Googling for information on children and the media could fill several lifetimes. I also discovered that, while there are plenty of helpful websites about Internet safety, one could search forever for a truly balanced approach to safe TV and DVD viewing. The ferocity of opinion on either side of this issue is testament to its importance – but it also deters decent non-extremist parents from speaking up, and that's bad. So here are a few modest proposals by which parents could help the move towards reasonable policing of the electronic village:

- Talk to other parents about what worries you. The more discussion there is on this subject the better, not only for the good of your family and community but of society in general.
- Register your concern when anything on the electronic media disturbs you on www.parentport.org.uk
- Give your backing to calls for media education in school. While it's infinitely better for parents to assume this responsibility themselves, many will not so it's the only way to help develop all children's awareness of the advantages and dangers of life in the electronic village.
- Lend your voice to future campaigns for broadcasting authorities, film regulators and Internet providers to exercise tighter control over the content they make universally available. This doesn't have to be a question of censorship or denying adults' right to view and say what they like, simply that extremely violent or sexually explicit material should be available only to adults on demand, rather than automatically accessible by everyone.
- When your MP is up for re-election, ask what he or she thinks about giving specialists in child development greater influence in decisions on film, video and computer game certification, tightening up controls on the sale or rental of adult-rated materials to children, and policing of the Internet.

- If any of these subjects crops up in the press, find the article on your
newspaper's website and register your point of view in the comments
section at the end. Media opinion is influenced by the number of reader
responses, so your voice could help direct future editorial policy.

Further reading

Aric Sigman, *Remotely Controlled: How Television Is Damaging Our Lives and
What We Can Do About It* (Vermilion, 2005)

Gary Small and Gigi Vorgon, *iBrain: Surviving the Technological Alteration
of the Modern Mind* (Harper, 2008)

Maryann Wolf, *Proust and the Squid: The Story of Science and the Reading
Brain* (Icon Books, 2008)

Howard Gardner and Katie Davis, *The App Generation: How Today's Youth
Navigate Identity, Intimacy and Imagination in a Digital World* (Yale
University Press, 2013)

Paul Levy, *The Digital Inferno* (Clairview Books, 2014)

Susan Greenfield, *Mindchange: How Digital Technologies are Leaving their
Mark on our Brains* (Rider, 2014)

Useful websites

The CEOP website on Internet safety mentioned in the detox sections,
with videos for children of different age-groups: www.thinkuknow.
co.uk

UK-based not-for-profit website aimed at 'making the Internet a great
and safe place for children': www.childnet.com (Childnet also runs
www.kidsmart.org.uk)

The UK government's 'preferred online security advice channel',
covering all aspects of Internet safety, with a useful section on safe-
guarding children: www.getsafeonline.org

Webwise is the BBC's Internet advice and information service, with
plenty of material for parents and children: www.bbc.co.uk/webwise

Australia: www.cybersmart.gov.au

USA: www.safekids.net 'digital citizenship, online safety and civility'

Cyberbullying sites: see recommended websites for Chapter 7

Mind the Gap

The positive side of life in the electronic village as described on pages 311–13 applies mainly to wealthier families with up-to-date electronic media, where parents' educational background allows them to keep up with research findings and hopefully adjust family life to ensure their children are enabled by new technology rather than becoming dependent on it.

However, over on the other side of the tracks, where parents are not so fortunate either in terms of income or education, children's experience of the digital world tends to be very different. Children from poor backgrounds are usually disadvantaged on several fronts:

- lack of access to worthwhile technology in the home, so their media literacy skills are less well-honed than those of children from more advantaged backgrounds
- too wide an access to junk TV and low-grade technoplay, which shut down minds rather than opening them up
- less parental supervision and mediation of their on-screen and on-line activity.

The 'digital divide' is now helping to drive all the other aspects of toxic childhood syndrome and, over time, is helping the poverty gap grow ever wider.

Society can try to even out these disadvantages through education and access to appropriate and useful technology in after-school clubs. But initiatives of this kind have so far made little difference. If children suffer from too early an introduction to TV and handheld computer games, too much time spent on daily screen-gazing, and a media diet of lowest-common-denominator content, it's unlikely that they'll be able to adjust their habits as time goes on.

This is why governments must make a concerted drive to inform *all* parents about medical advice on screen-time and screen-use, starting before their babies are born. It's also why we need adequate policing of the electronic village, since the children of the poor are, as usual, the most vulnerable to corruption and abuse. While parents should take responsibility for monitoring what their children see and do online, there will always be some (and unfortunately it's currently very many) who either can't or won't take this responsibility.

CHAPTER TEN

MANNERS MAKETH MAN

The electronic village may exert an increasing influence on children's lives, but they still have to live in the real world. Getting along in a community of real-life neighbours, shopkeepers and other random adults requires social skills that can't be learned in a virtual environment. For their first eight or so years, children are usually accompanied when out and about by parents, teachers or others in loco parentis but, as they grow older, they increasingly wander abroad without supervision.

The adult alliance

Civilised societies have in the past relied on an unwritten code of behaviour between children and the adults they meet outside their home. Children were expected to behave with respect towards their elders – for instance, giving up a seat on public transport, speaking when spoken to and trying, as far as possible, not to disturb adults with their play. Since this sort of 'well-mannered' behaviour, drummed in by parents, reflected well on their family, 'well-brought-up' children were motivated to abide by the unwritten rules and avoid overtly antisocial activities (or at least to make sure they didn't get caught).

In return, most adults would keep a weather eye open for children's welfare, and even complete strangers would sometimes act *in loco parentis* – warning errant infants about unsafe behaviour, protecting them from obvious harm, and generally keeping them on the straight and narrow. A tacitly agreed 'adult alliance' kept this cycle of trust and respect going: if children were accused of misbehaving by a neighbour, teacher or other respectable adult, most parents would take the adult's part and the children would be given short shrift.

Over the last quarter of a century, and especially in crowded inner-city areas, this behavioural code seems to have evaporated. Children in general are no longer as respectful or well-mannered as they were in the past. Similarly, the neighbourliness and fellow-feeling that fuelled the adult alliance has waned. Indeed, in most of Britain it's almost disappeared – a phenomenon that's run alongside the changes in childhood culture recorded in Chapter 2, from active outdoor play to indoor screen-based entertainment. Which caused which? Did the breakdown in neighbourliness fuel the withdrawal of children from the streets, or vice versa? Certainly the two seem interconnected, since initiatives to get children playing out around their homes are often associated with the revival of community spirit.

So far, sadly, such initiatives are few and far between. In most urban British communities (and a disturbing number of rural ones), free-range children are now regarded by older citizens as a threat. Adult witnesses of juvenile misbehaviour tend to look away; and if they do intervene, they may find it is they who get the short shrift. Today's children often stand and fight their corner – perhaps with colourful verbal displays – and if affronted adults take the case to a higher authority, today's parents frequently take their children's part.

This change has largely been blamed on poor parenting but, as I hope this book has shown, it's not that simple. Most parents are frantically doing their best in a world where the goal posts are not just moving – they've actually disappeared.

The parental balancing act

Ironically, there's now little doubt what good parenting involves. Over the last twenty-odd years, psychologists have identified the features of a variety of parenting styles, and long-term research has indicated clearly what works best for families in today's global village. The key – as usual in human behaviour – is balance.

There are four broad styles of parenting, based on the balance mothers and fathers strike between two elements: warmth and firmness. Warmth is the measure of how much love and support they give their children; firmness relates to the level of control they exercise over their children's lives.

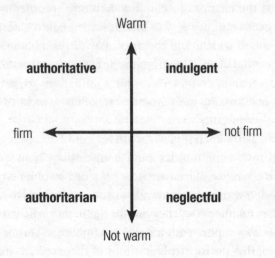

I've already mentioned that, according to research, the most effective parenting style is *authoritative*. Authoritative parents treat their children warmly, which in practical terms translates into giving them plenty of time and loving attention, listening to them, responding to their concerns, and allowing some (safe) choices. But they're also firm, ensuring rules and routines to provide stability, security and safety – for instance, regular family meals, bedtime schedules and rituals, a sensible media diet and plenty of technology-free family time. The advice of every expert I spoke to whilst writing and revising *Toxic Childhood* pointed towards an authoritative parenting approach. According to psychologists, a successful balance between warmth and firmness should produce 'self-regulating' children, well-balanced, resilient, with plenty of initiative, optimism and genuine self-esteem. Such children are likely to do well at school, make (and keep) plenty of friends, and go on to lead happy, successful lives.

Parents who are firm with their children but lacking in warmth are labelled *authoritarian*. They tend to lay down the law, without listening to children's point of view or offering opportunities for discussion, choice or negotiation. Maybe they believe this law has been handed down to them from on high; maybe they're replicating the parenting style they experienced themselves; or maybe they're just too unsure of themselves to brook any argument. Their regime means plenty of stability and security, but little consideration for the child's feelings or point of view. The outcome is often a well-behaved, obedient child but with a poor self-image – and in a generally liberal society poor self-image can lead to problems (in terms of self-destructive or antisocial behaviour) once the child is out of the parents' immediate control.

On the other hand, parents with high warmth but low firmness rating are labelled *indulgent*: they're the ones who make a habit of loving 'not wisely but too well' – giving into requests, letting children make more choices than is good for them, putting their offspring' interests above other people's and automatically springing to their defence if they get into trouble. Some of these parents may be over-reacting to their own authoritarian upbringing; some may like the idea of being their children's 'friend' rather than parents; others may have let the child lead from the start – for instance, by using a tablet computer as a pacifier – then found themselves unable to recoup and establish parental control. The children of indulgent parents usually feel loved and are generally self-confident, but they often have problems conforming at school and getting along with other children or adults (as one teacher described it to me, 'Their sense of entitlement is breathtaking.') They may also go off the rails later – studies have found that as adolescents they're more likely to be involved in drug or alcohol abuse – or find it difficult to accept that the world doesn't owe them a living.

The final parenting style – neither warm nor firm – is labelled *neglectful*, and involves giving one's children neither loving attention nor behavioural boundaries. Many 'Mind the gap' parents may be the result of a neglectful upbringing themselves and too pre-occupied with the dramas of their own lives to expend much effort on their children. As Philip Larkin said: 'Man hands on misery to man – it deepens like a coastal shelf'. But it can also happen in more economically successful families when parents are simply too wrapped up in their work to spare the time for child-rearing. Children brought up in neglectful homes grow up with low self-esteem, poor powers of self-regulation and a far higher than average chance of behaviour problems – leading later to self-destructive and antisocial behaviour.

Most parents can probably recognise elements of their own parenting style in more than one category – these things are never clear cut. What's more, mothers and fathers sometimes have different styles and, unless they can find a happy medium, the resultant conflict is bad for their relationship as well as their children. But, whatever one's own shortcomings, it's obvious that authoritative parenting will lessen the effect of toxic childhood syndrome while the other styles will magnify it. So if we know the problem and we know the answer, why can't more parents move towards an authoritative style?

The case of the missing goalposts

Unfortunately, as pointed out in Chapter 3, to be authoritative you need to feel confident about what you're doing. In a world of tumultuous change, confidence is thin on the ground. The moral and social certainties that once produced the adult alliance have disintegrated, and there seems to be nothing to put in their place.

If we think of society as acting like a parent to its citizens, the parenting style has moved – over the course of a couple of generations – from authoritarian to downright indulgent.

In the not very remote past, you couldn't move for rules about behaviour – many of them highly restrictive. Religious conventions, rigid class structures and long-established social norms all provided clear guidance for citizens, laying down the law in no uncertain terms. Not much more than half a century ago, for instance, English church-goers were still belting out the words:

> The rich man in his castle,
> The poor man at the gate:
> God made them high and lowly
> And ordered their estate.

There was certainly order, but – unless you were one of the lucky ones with a castle – it came at a cost.

Then suddenly the process of democratisation, which had been creeping slowly and steadily through western civilisation for several centuries, shifted up several gears. Within a couple of generations much of the old guidance was swept away. Respect for traditional authority figures declined, as the mystique on which they relied dissolved in the glare of the TV lights. Social attitudes relaxed and interactions became increasingly informal – even between people who'd always been considered of different status, such as boss and employee, teacher and pupil, or different generations. Religious traditions, deeply ingrained in the authoritarian culture of yesteryear, seemed increasingly irrelevant. Across much of the developed world, the old authoritarian social norms disappeared and no other value system – apart from a vague moral relativism – has emerged to replace them. For many people, self-realisation is now the only guiding star in a darkling sky.

Parenting styles have simply followed the same social and cultural trends. Parents know an authoritarian approach is 'old-fashioned', but without some sort of moral compass, they lack the confidence to be authoritative. So they're blown by the prevailing wind towards more indulgent behaviour. After all, in an egalitarian society, everyone has the same human rights as everyone else, so why shouldn't that apply to children too? If everyone's entitled to self-realisation, why should children be expected to defer to others just because of their age? Why should they give up their seat, hold their tongue, restrain their play so as not to offend some adult stranger?

In the case of 'warm' parents, this attitude blends neatly with their fear – born of Freudian psychology and nurtured by the advertising industry – that repressing children's natural inclinations will somehow damage their development. In the case of neglectful parents, it's a good excuse for letting children run wild. And the models of children's behaviour parents seen on TV shows and advertisements back up the impression that 'normal' children are sassy, quick-witted little characters who operate close to the edge of acceptable behaviour. These models are, of course, also available to children and – as we saw in Chapter 8 – there's considerable pressure from marketeers for children to exercise pester power and to take authority figures with a pinch of salt.

The late twentieth century also saw great deal of talk about children's rights. The 1989 UN International Convention on the Rights of the Child ushered in even more uncertainty about how far children should be constrained by adults. The actual convention is extremely reasonable and fair, but people who've never read it often assume it's a charter for indulgent parenting.

Research now shows that several decades of a generally indulgent ethos has taken its toll. The American professor of psychology, Jean Twenge, has recorded the growth of narcissism and related traits (such as materialism, unrealistic expectations and low empathy) in young people, together with increasing individualism and waning collectivism. Carol Dweck, another US psychology professor, has shown that indiscriminate parental praise can lead to children developing a 'fixed mindset', preventing them – no matter how bright they are – from reaching their full potential as individuals and citizens. Her research builds on the work of Professor Martin Seligman about 'learned helplessness', a conditioned response based on repeated experiences and related to a wide range of mental health problems, of the type recorded increasingly among US and UK teenagers.

For loving parents, determined to do their best for their offspring – but bombarded with commercial messages, short on time to spend with the family and uncomfortably aware of judgemental attitudes on all sides – child-rearing is probably more confusing and demanding than at any time in human history. It's not surprising that many lack the moral confidence to be authoritative, but for the sake of their children's mental health and happiness they have to find it from somewhere.

The pursuit of happiness

Most parents would say that, above all, they want their children to be happy. However, the World Database of Happiness, available on the web, shows that despite vast increases in wealth the people of the USA, Britain and Japan are no happier than they were fifty years ago. Our quest for consumer-based self-realisation – along with the ability to pay through the nose for it – has not increased the sum of human happiness by one iota. The influential British economist Richard Layard has put this down to a combination of consumerism and constant economic growth luring people in highly successful nations into over-competitiveness: 'Our fundamental problem today is a lack of common feeling between people – the notion that life is essentially a competitive struggle. With such a philosophy the losers become alienated and a threat to the rest of us, and even the winners can't relax in peace.'

In 2010, Professor Layard – concerned at the long-term implications of these changes on mental health – helped found an international movement called Action for Happiness, which defines ten research-based keys to happier living:

- Do things for others
- Connect with other people
- Take a positive approach
- Take care of your body
- Notice the world around you
- Kccp learning new things
- Find ways to bounce back from adversity
- Have goals to look forward to
- Be comfortable with who you are
- Be part of something bigger.

The first two of these keys (and possibly the last) relate to the importance of social interaction for human well-being, and Layard argues that it's also important for societies, which depend for their success as much on 'social capital' as on the monetary capital that drives economic growth.

The term 'social capital' was popularised by Harvard professor Robert Puttnam, who explains that it flows from 'the trust, reciprocity, information and cooperation associated with social networks' when people come together with a shared purpose. In his book *Bowling Alone*, Puttnam defined these real-life social networks as religious congregations, political and pressure groups, sports or social clubs – anything from a bowling league to a book group. But as westernised society stayed home nursing its 'affluenza' and connecting remotely on the web, membership of such groups declined considerably – society splintered in the same way that family members were splintering into their own individual virtual worlds.

Being part of a real-life social network – like being part of a successful family – involves time and commitment. But it's worth the effort. As Puttnam explains: 'people in relationships can reach goals that would have been far beyond the grasp of individuals in isolation' while at the same time enjoying 'the intrinsic satisfaction of association, of being part of a community'. Perhaps the best way for parents to gain moral confidence in our changing world is to accept that self-realisation isn't just about making oneself (or one's offspring) happy but about working together with others for a common purpose. This isn't exactly a new idea – in fact it underpins every major religion and ethical system that's ever existed. Not surprisingly, now that science is the nearest thing we have to a religion in the secular west, it's currently being promoted through neuroscientific evidence about the role of empathy in human development and culture. In his 2014 book, *Empathy: A Handbook for Revolution*, political philosopher Roman Krznaric defines it as '*the art of stepping imaginatively into the shoes of another person, understanding their feelings and perspectives, and using that understanding to guide your actions.*' Authoritative parents have a natural opportunity to develop this art as they tune into the feelings and perspectives of their child at each stage in development. They also have many good practical reasons to cooperate with other parents and adults in their local community; if they do so empathically, they can reinstitute the 'common feeling' described by Richard Layard.

Throughout this book there have been many detox recommendations that could lead to the creation of real-life social networks – for instance, parents making contact with neighbours to provide eyes on the street (Chapter 2), or collaborating with other members of their local child-rearing 'village' to ensure children's well-being outside the home (Chapters 6 and 7). Many detox sections advise talking with other parents to establish general social norms (such as suitable bedtimes and rules about media use) and coming together to improve the local environment or stem the assault on children's minds by marketeers and other dark forces in the electronic village. All of these provide reasons for adults to work together for the common good – indeed, there can be no more important shared purpose than raising the next generation. Parents interested in detoxing childhood have strong motivation to re-establish the social capital that once underpinned the adult alliance.

Getting along in the real world

Working together with others depends on mutual trust and respect, and a common purpose can generate these qualities, even among people from vastly different backgrounds. If a cause is important enough, other differences must be put on one side, new relationships forged, and reciprocity established. Unfortunately, as social change has made us all more preoccupied and suspicious, people have increasingly withdrawn from face-to-face contacts outside their own immediate circle, and relied instead on virtual friendships online and watching other people's social lives on screen. But real-life hands-on help with the day-to-day socialisation of children requires real interaction within a real community. If we rely too heavily on virtual interactions and technological solutions, we hazard our children's chances of successfully growing into fully functioning human beings.

Perhaps, to re-fashion a splintered world, the present generation of parents needs help in greasing the wheels of everyday transactions with people whose previous life experiences have been very different from their own. This skill – taken for granted in most communities in the past – isn't acquired through virtual relationships, where individuals assume complete control of their interactions with others (choosing the 'where', 'when' and 'how much' of all engagements, with the capacity to melt into cyberspace if anything goes wrong). Netiquette is different – and much easier – than getting along with real people in real time and space, especially if you seem to have little in common. And that's especially the case now that our international cultural revolution has swept away the hugely important social toolkit known as 'good manners'.

For many people today, manners are tarred with the same brush as deference and snobbery – the poor man at the gate doffing his cap to the rich man in his castle. The screen-dominated world in which recent generations have grown up compounds this mindset, because high viewing figures rely on frequent emotional outbursts, conflict, intrigue and abrasiveness. So these behaviours have been normalised, while well-mannered characters in TV dramas often generate suspicion (and frequently turn out to deserve it).

But 'good manners' have always been part of the currency of social capital. In real life, the more each individual can put others at their ease, deal with misunderstandings and demonstrate respect, the more easily the world turns on its axis. It's the first step that parents have to take if they're going to 'build their own village'.

By making an effort to be socially active, even on a very small scale (such as chatting briefly with neighbours), and ensuring that our exchanges are pleasant and respectful, we facilitate the growth of trust and reciprocity in the community. It takes courage to initiate new social contacts, especially in modern cities and housing estates, and may be bruising if others are ungracious. On the other hand, it's worth pressing on because of the immense gratification when they're responsive. And if you press on sufficiently to create a small 'village' with a shared child-rearing purpose, there may be untold benefits.

Indeed, reforging the adult alliance to help all local children have 'a good childhood' could turn out to be the holy grail of social capital. It ticks at least six of the boxes in the Action for Happiness list on page 339, while apparently passing on the potential for happiness to the next generation. A 2014 research study by Richard Layard and colleagues at the London School of Economics found that emotional health in childhood is 'the key to future happiness': 'By far the most important predictor of adult life-satisfaction is emotional health, both in childhood and subsequently,' his team reports.

Social capital begins at home

Since manners are habits of behaviour, they also matter at home. From their earliest days on earth children can develop good habits or bad ones. In order to establish respectful behaviour parents have to accept responsibility, set up routines and rules for the family, and train infants to abide by them. This, of course, involves constantly demonstrating the same good manners yourself – children will copy what you do (and also what you say, so mind your language!).

The firmness involved in establishing family rules should, of course, always be balanced by warmth. Children deserve warm praise for good behaviour and, if they question the rules, it behoves adults to listen and respond respectfully. Opportunities for children to make reasonable choices within agreed limits will also help the growth towards self-regulation. As children grow older and more able to think for themselves, the responsibility for defining appropriate behaviour is increasingly shared with them. The whole process of authoritative parenting involves mutual respect between parents and their offspring, based on mutual trust.

The family rules to be observed usually cover a number of areas:

- aspects of safety, health and hygiene (including aspects of media use)
- social conventions such as table manners
- moral precepts (Thou shalt take turns; Thou shalt not hit thy sister, etc.)
- simple practices to ease the running of the household, such as taking off muddy boots at the back door and closing doors to keep the heat in.

In a time of social upheaval and chaos, it may take a leap of faith to believe such rules can be agreed and kept by all. But if adults accept the responsibility for enforcing behavioural boundaries with reason and consistency (trying valiantly never to lose their temper), all the studies show that children soon learn to do-as-they-would–be-done-by and family life becomes much more enjoyable.

The extension of respectful behaviour to others outside the home shows children how the policy of doing-as-you-would-be-done-by reaches beyond the family circle, and makes sure they know how to behave respectfully to other adults. At the same time, parents and children begin to roll the snowball of trust and respect that builds communities.

In 2003, the Commission for Children at Risk, a panel of leading children's doctors, research scientists, and youth service professionals in the USA, recommended that the best way to address social concerns about children's deteriorating mental health was through 'authoritative communities'. By this they meant a culture of authoritativeness within all civic, educational, recreational, community service, business, cultural and religious groups that serve or include young people under the age of eighteen. Authoritative communities would be warm, nurturing, respectful to children's and teenagers' point of view, but would also set clear boundaries, encourage moral development and equal respect for all. If this could be brought about, I suspect we'd have achieved the ultimate detoxification of childhood.

Of course, it would help a lot if the visual media – the window through which we now all see the world – could reflect the advantages of healthy social interaction, rather than concentrating so much attention on dysfunctional relationships and social breakdown. Positive depictions of trust and cooperation seldom seem to occur on screen outside the confines of *Sesame Street*. As Richard Layard said, when I asked how we could achieve authoritative communities: 'We have to change the relative prestige accorded to smart-arsed behaviour and that accorded to kindness'.

Knowledge is power

While the simple ethical guiding star of do-as-you-would-be-done-by could do a lot to help parents feel more authoritative, there's another important route to confidence: knowledge. The more parents know about child development the better equipped they are to aim for a productive balance between warmth and firmness. But researching this book has taught me how little most adults know about children. As a teacher, working with them every day, one soon learns a few essential truths, otherwise, one doesn't last long in a classroom. One important truth is that children – even very small children – are naturally manipulative. They have to be to ensure their survival – as the smallest and weakest of humans, they instinctively rely on basic rules of human psychology to make sure their needs are noticed. So they learn very early how to reward adults with smiles and punish them with loud noises, and as time goes on many become extremely adept at getting their own way.

Teachers and others in children's services learn about childish wiles through wide experience, but most parents' experience of children is limited. With the death of the extended family, contemporary adults' knowledge about child-rearing is often limited to vague memories of their own childhood, in a world vastly different from the world today, assisted perhaps by a few impressions from TV and the Internet. As more families now stop at one child (meaning no points of comparison, and no need to share), parents are often at the mercy of their children – held to ransom by the power of love.

Parental love takes most people completely unawares. Take Julia Roberts' letter about her newborn twins, read out on The Oprah Winfrey Show at the beginning of 2005: 'The babies are amazing. The way they stare into your eyes, their exuberant smiles, how they begin each day all warm and sleepy, smelling of promise. I suppose I never realised it before – babies aren't really born of their parents, they're born of every kind word, loving gesture, hope and dream their parents ever had. Bliss.'

If you've gone through the experience of motherhood (or the more hands-on type of fatherhood), Ms Roberts' outpourings may bring a tear to your eye. If you haven't, it'll probably make you reach for the sick bag. The trouble is, there's a very fine line between the deep parental urge to care for a child and crippling sentimentality. If you land on the wrong side of it, even the youngest child – indeed, especially the youngest, with its charming gurgles and terrifying screams – could soon have you performing somersaults at its behest.

It seems only fair, therefore, to prepare parents for this experience. The media are already lending a hand (see Chapter 9), but TV crazes come and go, depending on the ratings. There are also many excellent books and courses available, such as the Australian *Triple P* (Positive Parenting Programme) and the American *Incredible Years*, both of which have a well-established evidence base showing how they can reduce disruptive behaviour and parental stress. The Internet now provides easy access to these and many other resources – and, as mentioned in Chapter 9, there is now immense potential for spreading information about child development and helpful parenting strategies via the electronic media.

However, it's still up to parents to seek out support. On the whole, most only do so when a problem arises, by which time the habits of behaviour underpinning the problem are well-established. If child-rearing is to take its rightful place in the centre of our culture, we need to ensure every parent knows the nuts and bolts of child development *before* things go awry – and this probably means governments have to get involved. But here we run into the problem that's raised its head repeatedly throughout *Toxic Childhood*: how much should the state interfere in the way families function and children are brought up?

Can Nanny know best?

The question of state intervention into the way we rear our young always raises fierce opinions. There was, for instance, an extreme reaction in Germany in 2004 when a government minister, reporting that childhood obesity had reached near epidemic proportions, called for an initiative to change children's eating and exercise habits. Critics condemned her suggestion as 'reminiscent of regimented youth programmes under the Nazis and Communists' and a political opponent reflected that 'the whole thing raises an eery spectre, especially talk about mandatory PE and intimidating manufacturers into "doing the right thing".'

This particularly deep-rooted resistance to any sort of intervention in child-rearing seems to stem from a feeling that raising children is a 'natural' human process, not requiring guidance or regulation by the state. Yet one of the key factors behind toxic childhood syndrome is that profound social and cultural changes have cut parents off from the child-rearing lore that was once passed down through the female line. We no longer have any 'natural' access to knowledge about children and how they develop because we no longer live in extended families within tight communities, with grandmothers and other 'wise women' on hand to proffer help and advice. And unless we start acquiring this knowledge from somewhere else, the damage to children – especially in Mind the gap families – seems likely to increase.

States around the world have often intervened to protect children's interests in the past. The banning of child labour and the introduction of compulsory schooling, two instances of 'Nanny statism' now normalised by custom, both arose in response to significant social and cultural change, and were both at the time considered a gross infringement of parental rights. The state intervention I'm suggesting here is not government diktats about child-rearing, but simply sharing the key messages now learned from science about how children develop and what they need at different stages with every citizen.

In the first instance, this could be done via the education system. At the moment, most countries provide sex education lessons, but nothing about the needs and nurture of the living products of sexual relationships – a strange and worrying omission. The best way to ensure a minimum baseline of knowledge for all adults would be to include the study of child development within the secondary school curriculum, when students are in their mid-teens. A short course on human development based on developmental psychology and neuroscience could be both interesting and informative for teenagers, as well as arming them in advance for parenthood.

A second blast of information could be delivered through the health service as an integral part of antenatal and post-natal care – when prospective parents really have a reason to listen. And perhaps further instalments could be provided when parents take their children to nursery, when they enrol them for full-time education, and every few years thereafter. Short presentations at antenatal clinics and school parents' meetings could convey the key facts about child development, relevant to each age-group and using up-to-date technology to provide information as memorably as possible. Access to further detail and advice could then be available on demand via the web. As recommended elsewhere in this book, schools could also be valuable distributors of research-based advice for rearing healthy children – such as recommended bedtimes, information on healthy eating and guidance about electronic entertainment.

A friend once sent me a cartoon from the *New Yorker* showing a pair of exhausted parents, surrounded by the products of global technology and telling their children: 'Your mother and I are feeling overwhelmed, so you'll have to bring yourselves up.' In the maelstrom of social change and moral disorientation, a few simple shared facts about children's developmental needs could help all parents feel less overwhelmed. If nothing else, many would find it helpful to have the state's muscle behind them when explaining to their children why early bedtime is important, electronic entertainment must be limited, and many of the things they see advertised on TV aren't good for them.

Undermining parent power

At present, however, most governments dare not risk opening this particular can of worms. Perhaps this is because it involves the implicit suggestion that parents need to spend lots of time with their children, especially when they're very small. And this, of course, is at odds with current political orthodoxies about economic growth and gender equality. For politicians, the main function of all adults in today's 'hard-working families' is to con-tribute to continued economic growth (see Chapter 6, 'Mum's the word').

So instead of empowering and trusting parents to be authoritative carers in the home, government policies have resulted in a steady expansion of 'support services' – medical, social and educational – which take ever greater responsibility for children away from home, leaving mums and dads free to work longer and longer hours. The cumulative effect of this has been to deskill and disempower parents by:

- suggesting, through this 'professionalisation' of childcare, that raising twenty-first-century children requires specialist knowledge, premises and equipment
- separating parents from their children for most of the day so that, during what little family time remains, everyone is tired and in no condition to enjoy it.

As described in Chapter 6, for instance, the English government suggested in 2014 that schools should take children from the age of two and that school opening times for children over five should be extended to forty-five hours a week. In the same year, they also toughened up the regulations preventing parents from taking children out of school for family events and holidays, meaning that many families now lose important opportunities for valuable shared experiences and time in each other's company.

Both of these suggestions seem to me prime examples of 'nanny statism' – drawing children under increasing control by the state while distancing them from their parents. The obvious alternative – improvements to working hours and practices so that parents can spend time actually caring for their children – simply isn't on the agenda of the mainstream political parties. Yet there are many ways in which enlightened politicians could help develop a family-friendly economy, rather than continuing the drive towards increasingly atomised, economy-friendly families. The political journalist Gaby Hinsliff provides a raft of practical suggestions in Half A Wife: The Working Family's Guide to Getting a Life Back, all of which could benefit businesses as well as families.

Meanwhile, lack of political attention to the effects of marketing and media on children simply compounds the problems for parents. So do the increasingly critical and judgemental attitudes of non-parents towards children and young people's behaviour, and the media-borne anxiety of countless worried child development experts like myself...

* * *

Different cultures have always taken different attitudes to the moral and ethical education of their young, depending on religious, philosophical or political traditions. In terms of the relationship between individual and state, the Japanese for instance broadly recognise social conformity as the route to personal fulfilment, while the American dream is one of individual success eventually benefiting the whole of society. In a global village driven by the ideal of economic growth, the loss of traditional cultural reference points adds to parental uncertainty. But whether you take the American view that 'it's the squeaky wheel that gets the grease' or believe with the Japanese that 'the nail that stands up must be hammered down', it's the balance of individual rights with social responsibilities that underpins life in a democratic society.

At present, that balance is threatened by a terrible brew of market-driven self-indulgence, lack of moral direction and political attempts to paper over the cracks with short-term, economy-driven solutions. It's not surprising that many young people seem to be unimpressed by the concept of social responsibility. Someone has to challenge the destructive elements of the status quo, and it probably has to be parents, since it's their children who'll have to live in the world we're creating today. As Julia Neuberger says in *The Moral State We're In*: 'Unless we rethink our social obligations and reassess the value of trust, we will become even more cynical, even more atomistic, ever more individualistic – and there really will be no such thing as society.'

DETOXING BEHAVIOUR

- Aim for an authoritative style in all dealings with your child. Try to be constantly aware of the need for *warmth* balanced by *firmness*.
- Parents' job is to give children what they need – this is not always the same as what they want. If your child wants something you know isn't good for him, it's your responsibility to stand firm.
- Authoritative parenting is much easier when all adults-in-charge agree (see 'Being an adult-in-charge: some things to talk to a partner about' page 177). If you can't agree, find ways to differ amicably – but keep a united front for the children.
- The younger the child, the more adults have to decide on the behaviour required and gently train the infant into that behaviour. The aim is to show children how to control their emotions so they can eventually become *self-regulating*. See for instance the advice on helping small children become self-soothers (page 106) and preventing screen-time becoming a child's default activity (pages 289 and 320).
- The more you can ensure that the behaviour you want becomes ingrained as habit, the easier your child will find it to follow the rules – regularity, routine and consistency are critical, e.g. bedtime and ready-for-school routines, regular mealtimes and so on.
- Routine and regularity are also helpful to you. When particular aspects of the day-to-day grind are relegated to habit, you don't have to think about them. Then you can enjoy the chance to chat, think or perhaps listen to music as you get on with it.
- Decide with your partner on appropriate family rules and manners:

    - safety, health, hygiene rules (including media use)
    - social conventions, such as table manners (see page 43)
    - moral rules to help children do-as-they-would-be-done-by
    - family rules to make everyone's life easier and more pleasant.

- Express rules positively as often as possible – what children should do, rather than what they shouldn't.
- Recognise that some of these rules (and the routines you embed

them in) will change over time, as children get older, e.g. bedtimes. The older the child, the more important it is to involve him or her in discussion and negotiation of family rules. Gradually, over the course of a child's first ten to twelve years, the aim is to move from parental regulation to self-regulation.

- Avoid falling into authoritarianism by remembering that chidren have to learn how to manage their *own* behaviour and emotions. The rules and routines parents establish are to help them towards this goal – they aren't holy writ. Don't let yourself get bogged down in petty issues of discipline.

- The language you use about behaviour should also be warm but firm:

  – praise good behaviour (don't take it for granted) but don't overdo the praise – if a child is praised to the skies for everything, it devalues real achievements

  – when giving praise avoid suggesting that your child's achievements are due to inborn natural ability (which can lead to a 'fixed mindset' – see pages 338–9 and associated Notes and References), as opposed to effort and perseverance (which develop a 'growth mindset')

  – describe what your child's done that's made you pleased ('I love the way you're putting the bricks away!')

  – if your child behaves badly explain what you don't like and why, but don't criticise more than is absolutely necessary (and never nag!)

  – to elicit the behaviour you want, ask politely: if they don't respond, state firmly once more what you want the child to do – and expect it to happen. (see also How to Detox a Little Monster)

- If your child puts a point of view, listen respectfully and respond to it honestly. This shows you think the child competent and value his or her opinion. But it doesn't mean you have to agree – in the end, the responsibility for decisions rests with the parent.

- Be a good role model. Remember that your child will copy:

  – what you do, how you do it
  – what you say and how you say it.

RE-ESTABLISHING THE ADULT ALLIANCE

- Teach your child from the beginning to think about other people's feelings and needs, and to treat *everyone* with respect.
- Start when your child's a baby by acting in this way yourself. In public places (e.g. restaurants, church services, shops, museums, any sort of performance) try to position yourself where you can make a quick getaway if your child cries or misbehaves. Removing a distressed or disturbed infant means:

    – you don't disturb other members of the public
    – you can calm the child without risking escalation of the problem.

- On the other hand, don't panic if your baby cries, your toddler throws a tantrum or your young child acts up in circumstances where you can't remove them (e.g. on public transport). Deal with the problem as calmly as you can and don't worry about being judged – there are almost certainly other parents in the vicinity thinking 'There but for the grace of God go I'.
- As well as trying to be considerate and trustworthy to others, it helps to assume that they'll reciprocate. While there are a few people around who can't be trusted, the vast majority are good-hearted. Start by hoping you can trust everyone, while keeping a wary eye open for any evidence to the contrary. Gradually teach your child to aim for the same balance.
- Explain that older people are less fit than younger ones, and age earns concessions (such as a seat on the bus or extra tolerance of irritating behaviour).
- This does not mean children should suffer behaviour which makes them uncomfortable or frightened – make sure they tell you about anything that worries them.
- Model respectful behaviour to other adults in the community yourself at all times. Don't be put off when other people don't keep up the same standards – someone has to start this ball rolling, and it's your child

who should ultimately benefit from an increase in social capital.

- Make social contacts with other adults in your community, and – when an opportunity arises – talk about how important the adult alliance is. Listen to their opinions and concerns and try to draw them into re-establishing the alliance.

- If your child is disrespectful to an adult, apologise and show your disappointment to your child. Explain later to your child what was wrong with the behaviour and why.

- Bear in mind that no child is perfect. Even a little angel may misbehave sometimes (I have watched delightful children lie in their teeth). If other people question your child's behaviour, listen respectfully to their point of view. Try to imagine how you'd feel if someone else's child had behaved in that way to you.

- If your child complains that an adult is behaving unpleasantly, talk it over and think about why they might be acting that way. (Once when my daughter's teacher was being strangely snappy, we wondered if perhaps something was upsetting her outside school. My daughter decided to make her a 'My favourite teacher' card, and we were amazed at how much it cheered her up.)

- If all else fails, and an adult seems to have it in for your child, teach them how to keep out of their way. And if that's impossible, help them learn the art of keeping a low profile to avoid incurring displeasure.

HOW TO DETOX A LITTLE MONSTER

- See 'Detoxing behaviour' above. If your little monster's bad behaviour is deeply embedded, consult one of the books/websites below. This short section cannot give more than a few starting points.

- Make sure you never inadvertently reward misbehaviour, e.g.:

    – by giving attention to a child who's misbehaving
    – by giving a treat to stop a child doing something
    – by laughing at bad behaviour

All these will encourage the child to do it again.

- Choose your battles. You can't make a child perfect all at once. Decide which aspect of behaviour you're going to tackle first and ignore other aspects till you've made some headway with that. Then you'll have something positive to praise.
- With younger children, keep an eye open for behavioural flashpoints and distract your child before trouble can start, e.g.:

  – have a 'distraction bag', where you can stockpile interesting but safe items for ready access (see Chapter 8 – 'How to encourage creative play')

  – songs, games, rhymes, etc. make good distractions (see page 129)

- With all ages, be prepared. The more you think through possibilities, the easier it is to deal with problems if they arise. If you know the sort of mischief your child's likely to get into, you can try to stop it happening, e.g.:

  – tell your child exactly what you want, discussing any difficulties he or she has with it

  – keep children occupied, e.g. colouring books, songs and story tapes in the car

  – offer a reward for the behaviour you want (but only give it if you're satisfied)

  – use a system of incentives, e.g. a wall chart with stickers for good behaviour (but think this through carefully beforehand: if you start it, you have to stick with it, and reward systems can get very complicated)

  – a simple reward system is the Marble Jar: put 20 marbles in a jar (well out of reach of your little monster) and take one away for every misdemeanour while adding one for every good deed – if by the end of a decreed period there are more than 20 marbles in the jar, convert them into previously agreed rewards

- If possible, ignore silly, attention-seeking behaviour. The more fuss you make, the more likely your child is to repeat it.
- If you can't ignore it, nip it in the bud – don't let it escalate:

    - explain immediately and calmly what you don't like, what behaviour you want, and what will happen if you don't get it – then expect your child to respond positively
    - don't get into an argument – wait for them to comply and if they don't, follow through calmly with the punishment.

- Don't ever let bad behaviour escalate to the point where you lose your temper, i.e. don't join in! Just look disappointed, act grown-up and continue to request the behaviour you're after. Don't give in, and don't keep telling the child off. Just wait, if necessary restraining the child gently and guiding them into the behaviour you want. It can help to have a little mantra you recite to yourself on these occasions ('warm but firm, warm but firm'…).
- Establish some sort of punishment for bad behaviour, e.g. time out on a naughty chair or docking of pocket money, so you have something to use as a threat if your child misbehaves. (Plucking threats out of the blue is not a good idea because you can't always follow them through.)
- The younger the child, the more immediate any punishment should be.
- If you threaten your child with anything, *always* follow through. If you don't, they'll just learn you didn't mean it.
- However, don't let yourself become focused on punishment. Find ways of being positive, such as praising good behaviour, and as soon as possible move into the general behavioural policies in Detoxing behavior above.
- There's much more specific advice in the books and websites listed throughout these detox pages.

PARENT POWER: FROM AUTHORITATIVE PARENTING TO AUTHORITATIVE COMMUNITIES

The suggestions throughout this book provide many vehicles for linking child-rearing to the re-establishment of social capital:

- work with grandparents, extended family, neighbours and other parents to make communities safe for children
- collaborate with school and childcare agencies to look after all children's interests, not just your own
- develop real-life social networks to help not only with raising your children, but also to establish a better work-life balance, find effective ways of policing the electronic village, and so on
- lobby for education about child development so the next generation don't have to try and find out about it haphazardly – a three-pronged approach would reach everyone:

    – a child development module in secondary citizenship classes
    – 'developmental needs birth to five' as part of ante- and post-natal care
    – child development meetings for parents when children start nursery and primary school, and every couple of years thereafter.

Parenting is not just about looking inward, at the children in the centre of the family; it's about looking outward at the world where those children, and successive generations of children, will grow and live. It's only through families pooling their expertise and parents exercising their power as citizens that authoritative communities will come into existence.

Further reading

Richard Layard, *Happiness: Lessons from a New Science* (Allen Lane, 2005)
Sue Palmer, *Detoxing Childhood: How to Raise Bright Balanced Children*
(Orion, 2007)
How To Traumatise Your Children: Seven Proven Methods to Help You Screw Up Your Kids Deliberately and with Skill (Knock Knock Books, 2011) – This book, which I picked up in a card shop, describes itself as a 'parody of parenting and psychology books'. However, the psychological evidence on which it's based is spot on and it's the only book on parenting I've ever read straight through in a sitting (whilst laughing immoderately).

See also 'Further reading' in Chapters 6, 7 and 8

Useful websites

Action for Happiness – evidence-based information about happiness and well-being, with many links and resources: www.actionforhappiness.org
Centre for a New American Dream – a helpful organisation with sections on 'Beyond consumerism' and 'Collaborating communities': www.newdream.org
Save Childhood – UK charity campaigning on a wide variety of childhood and parenting issues: www.savechildhood.net

Mind the gap

I'm sure it's no coincidence that happiness reached its peak in the UK (see page 339) at the point when our society was at its most equal. In 1910, Britain was a very unequal nation, with the richest 10 per cent of the population accounting for a fifth of total income. By the mid-twentieth century their share had dropped by half as income became more widely distributed, but the process then went into reverse and by 2013 the rich were back with a fifth again.

The Labour government of 1997–2010 was determined to reduce inequality and, since politicians were now aware of the relationship between early childhood experience and adult success, declared war on child poverty. Their two key strategies in England were support for parents of pre-school children through the Sure Start initiative (see pages 126 and 128) and fierce attention to standards of literacy and numeracy for primary pupils. However, to keep middle-class voters on board, these strategies were extended nationwide, which (along with other developments related to child protection) led to extraordinary levels of spending on local government reorganisation, new buildings and the employment and training of a rapidly expanding workforce.

The money for all this investment, of course, came from the free market economy – i.e. increasingly hyper-competitive consumerism – so parents constantly had to work harder and for longer hours to keep up their levels of consumption and pay for somewhere to live. Parents of young children in disadvantaged areas (often single mums) were urged, like other 'hard-working families', into the workforce, meaning that the Sure Start support for families rapidly gave way to institutionalised childcare (see Chapter 6). And the competitive consumerist ethic also infected the national literacy and numeracy strategies, intensifying the 'winners and losers culture' described in Chapter 7.

As a consultant to the English Department of Education during the first few years of these changes, I went from enthusiastic support for their original principles to horrified disgust at the resultant practice, eventually leaving to write *Toxic Childhood*. It seemed to me that, instead

of empowering and supporting disadvantaged families in giving babies
and toddlers the love, time, song, talk and play they needed for healthy
development, the government was separating mothers from their children.
And instead of trusting nursery and primary school teachers with time
and professional freedom to help disadvantaged children learn, they
were swamping them in measurement and accountability procedures,
micromanaged from Whitehall. Meanwhile, the twin forces of media and
marketing were intensifying a national culture of selfish individualism in
which the rich were getting richer and the poor poorer.

However, government policy has to be seen to succeed so statistics
were assembled showing over half a million children technically transferring from one side of a poverty balance sheet to the other. Evidence
of this transformation was sadly unavailable in the real world, and by
summer 2008 even the *Guardian* was expressing horror at the government's faith in centralised, systemised reform: 'Evidence, reality,
consequences, the classroom failures of struggling pupils – none of these
matter. The statistics, however flawed and unreliable, are all that count.'
Later that year, the global economic crisis put an end to massive social
investment, so these particular flawed statistics ceased to flow.

However, we can't let one government's failure to close the gap
prevent us from trying to replicate – and improve on – the positive social
changes of the mid-twentieth century. As Richard Wilkinson and Kate
Pickett showed in their 2009 book *The Spirit Level: Why Equal Societies
Almost Always Do Better*, equality is good for the mental and physical
health of everyone – rich and poor alike. What's more, the most basic
ingredients of a good childhood – love, talk, song, play, warm-but-firm
parenting – are all free, so should be within the grasp of all parents,
whatever their economic background. We just, somehow, have to rally
the power of social capital, reinstate essential knowledge about child-
rearing and help everyone understand that the raising of healthy balanced
children is the key to national well-being.

CONCLUSION

DETOXING CHILDHOOD

The Conclusion of the 2006 edition of *Toxic Childhood* began with these words:

> It is the best of times; it is the worst of times. We live in a world of comfort, convenience and promise, a wonderful world for grown-up human beings to work and relax. But it's not the best of all possible worlds for children. Deep in our hearts we all know it, but we're frightened to admit it: the world we've created is damaging our children's brains.

How times have changed. In 2008, the world we'd created came to the brink of economic collapse, and for most citizens of the wealthy west, life after the crash has been rather less comfortable, convenient and promising than it once was. (I've often wondered whether those reckless young 'Masters of the Universe' on Wall Street might have foreseen the consequences of constantly slicing up subprime mortgages if they'd played outdoors more, rather than honing their intellectual powers on two-dimensional computer games – see the Adie and Shayer research quoted on page 225.)

The rebalancing act

Before 2008, however, the only voices regularly questioning the widespread political faith in free-market capitalism were those of environmentalists and spiritual leaders, two groups who could easily be dismissed by dedicated secular consumers as 'flaky'. In recent years, there's been a growing cacophony of dissent, widespread recognition that the poverty gap is expanding daily (to the detriment of society as a whole, including the 'squeezed middle') and increasing appearances in the media of words like 'ethical' and 'values'. When French economist Thomas Piketty, author of the 2014 bestseller *Capitalism in the 21st Century*, pointed out that 'there is a limit to what the market can do' I suspect most grown-up human beings were inclined to agree.

Attitudes to the digital revolution are currently undergoing a similar process of reassessment. In 2006, my suggestion that new technology might not be an entirely benevolent force was received with considerable scorn but by 2010 Nicholas Carr's book, *The Shallows: How the Internet Is Rewiring Our Brains*, was well-received by the reading public. It was suddenly permissible to think out loud about the subject. Recent contributions to the debate, such as the film *InRealLife* (2013) by the distinguished film maker Beeban Kidron, and *The App Generation* (2014) by highly-respected American psychologist Howard Gardner et al., have looked critically at the effect of screen-based technology on teenagers. We seem to have reached a stage when many grown-ups also suspect that there's a limit to the beneficial effects of technology on young minds.

This process of rebalancing is still in its early stages and there's clearly a long way to go before global corporations realise that targeting small children is unethical or politicians clock that dishing out handheld devices to pre-readers might affect the development of their higher thinking skills. But it's a start.

The perfect storm

There is, however, another key element in toxic childhood syndrome of which I was only vaguely aware when writing the 2006 Conclusion, which focused mainly on (1) rapidly accelerating technological change and (2) increasingly competitive consumer capitalism. It wasn't until the next year, when I immersed myself in research on gender differences for *21st Century Boys* and *21st Century Girls* that I recognised the significance of element (3): the steady movement of mothers out of the home and into the workforce. Just like the digital revolution and consumerist fervour, this movement began to gather speed in the mid-1980s, and has made an increasing impact on the quality of children's lives. These three socio-cultural phenomena swirl together, creating a perfect storm for childhood.

As a woman born in the mid-twentieth century, I have always been totally committed to sexual equality so it wasn't easy to confront this aspect of change. Like most of my contemporaries, I'd hitherto believed that, as equal rights for men and women became normalised, child-rearing would become a genuinely shared activity, summed up by the gender-neutral term 'parenting'. It was startlingly apparent, however, that parent audiences for *Toxic Childhood* talks were overwhelmingly female, and as I ploughed through the latest research on gender, I began to understand why. Whether by nature or nurture, there are clearly significant differences in the interests and value-systems of male and female adults which thirty years of equality haven't changed, and I suspect that females will always remain more predisposed than males towards personally *caring* for their children in the early months and years. This is, of course, in direct conflict with mainstream feminist philosophy, in which motherhood is seen as little more than an inconvenient interruption in a woman's working life.

Of course, feminism has developed alongside the other two elements of the perfect storm – both of which are based on exclusively materialist values – so it's not surprising that it ascribed little significance to the human values underpinning 'women's work' through the millennia. The consequent devaluing of motherhood is a highly significant factor in toxic childhood syndrome (not least because much child-rearing wisdom, once passed around the females of the village, is no longer transmitted through the generations) and if women themselves don't value the traditional maternal role, I can't imagine many men will step up to the plate begging to share it. Yet women's contribution to human culture – unpaid, unsung and therefore largely unnoticed – has been every bit as important as that of men, and if we're to achieve genuine sexual equality we must, as a society, embrace that fact and find sexually-equal ways of recalibrating the balance between work and family life.

This subject is touched on briefly in Chapter 5 but I set out the arguments and evidence in *21st Century Girls*. It was predictably dismissed – I maintain, misunderstood – by mainstream feminists, so it's been cheering to discover through research for this edition of *Toxic Childhood* that many other women have come to similar conclusions, including the original leader and founder of third-wave feminism, Rebecca Walker, whose 2014 lecture on the subject to a Swedish audience can be found on YouTube.

Weathering the storm

For some years now, I've been talking about this perfect storm in presentations for parents about *Toxic Childhood*, and it's interesting that the first mention of each of the elements tends to arouse emotional responses in some members of the audience. When I talk about children and technology, for instance, one or two people usually look twitchily irritated, perhaps because they assume I'm a rabid technophobe, but more likely because their child is at home, tucked up in a technology-rich bedroom. Once I get onto the damaging effects of consumer capitalism, a cloud of unease often descends on the whole room – I'm never sure whether it's due to fear that I'm some sort of left-wing activist or discomfort about their own guilty shopping habits. And, almost always, as soon as I suggest that part of the problem may be due to working mums, you can cut the tension with a knife. For many audiences, the first emotional reaction to this suggestion is probably embarrassment – such a politically incorrect statement is clearly a massive social gaffe on my part. But I reckon guilt is a significant factor here too (the marketing industry definitely think so, as evidenced in the term 'guilt money' – see page 253).

After a little explanation (including a personal admission of considerable guilt), these heightened emotions generally die down and we can return to discussion of childhood. But the phenomenon has helped me understand why toxic childhood syndrome has flourished, despite the fact that twenty-first-century parents love their children as passionately as any previous generation. Three of my expert interviewees for this revision – Marie Peacock (Chapter 5), Agnes Nairn (Chapter 8) and Aric Sigman (Chapter 9) – stressed the significance of 'normalisation' in creating childhood toxicity. The perfect storm, each element of which is driven by adult needs, has normalised adult behaviour that may well be fine for childless adults, but is seriously damaging for children and their families.

It's emotionally difficult to challenge 'normal' behaviour. People may think that you're a technophobe, a political misfit, old-fashioned, fuddy-duddy or 'flaky'*, so most people choose to go along with the flow. Unfortunately, in the case of loving parents, this has further emotional repercussions, because 'deep in our hearts we all know it, but we're frightened to admit it: the world we have created is damaging our children's brains'.

However, as outlined above, there are signs that the prevailing orthodoxy is beginning to crumble. There's also a huge mass of scientific evidence showing the ways in which that orthodoxy is damaging children's brains. So I reckon it's now time to feel the fear, and detox childhood anyway.

---

* My fellow childhood campaigners and I have had many such epithets thrown at us. For a couple of years, representatives of the former Secretary of State for Education dismissed us a parts of 'The Blob', but that was recently changed to 'middle-class do-gooders who don't understand the problems of disadvantaged children'. Ho hum.

I ♥ my attitude problem ... and my mum and dad ♥ me

Do you remember the child on the steps of the Uffizi? Ten years old at the most and the unhappiest of bunnies. How did she get like that? Perhaps she spent ten years feeding on burgers, pizzas and ice cream, washed down with sugary cola. Maybe she's whiled away long hours in a virtual world of her own, absorbing the messages of marketing men, playing computer games rather than real ones, staring at TV rather than going out to play in the sunshine. Does she lie awake till the early hours, checking the status of Facebook friends and messaging her chums on the iPad? Has a sedentary, screen-based lifestyle led to problems at school in concentrating, controlling her temper or relating to other people? Or maybe – like many girls – she has managed to do well enough in a test-and-target regime, but is starting to wilt under the constant pressure to do even better?

Of course, her mother and father are products of twenty-first-century culture too. Throughout their lives, they've absorbed the message that it's good for both men and women to work hard, aim high, drive themselves to ever-crazier deadlines. So they may have taken the same approach to child-rearing, wanting their little princess to be the best, the first, the winner. Perhaps they felt obliged to enrol her in a day nursery when she was very young, so their dual income would provide her with the best possible lifestyle. By the time she was three, they probably wanted her to be doing a bit of 'proper' schoolwork to ensure she was always one step ahead of the herd, and I bet that ever since she's had a busy schedule of clubs and classes to keep her productively busy. They've probably pushed her to achieve at school and supplied state-of-the-art technological gadgetry to help with the homework. They've certainly let her 'grow up' very fast, dressing like someone twice her age – although the ironic comment on her chest suggests that, actually, she sometimes behaves like an angry, bewildered toddler.

I also bet that, to keep their daughter in consumer goods, both parents work long hours and bring projects home with them, ready to respond to emails and phone calls twenty-four hours a day. Parents who work so intensely often find it difficult to break away and slow down to the ancient, human rhythms of family life. What's more, their twenty-first-century minds are programmed to seek constant change and stimulation – not the same rites and rituals every day. So there's probably not been much domestic stability in their daughter's life – the security of knowing that mum and/or dad are home, ready to share an evening meal, a family evening and her bedtime routine.

I shouldn't think they worry about how much time she spends in front of screens. They'll be lifelong TV-watchers themselves, and early up-takers of each new screen-based gadget, so they probably trust technology more than they trust the natural world, with its unpredictable weather, unexpected physical hazards and unknown passers-by (possibly lurking with criminal intent). They feel better knowing their daughter's safe in her electronic bedsit, rather than interacting with all that terrifying reality. It's never occurred to them that letting her wander alone in the electronic village now exposes her to far greater dangers than playing out with friends in the local park.

Above all, it's easy to imagine their parenting style – warm, but far from firm. When their little one was born they probably hadn't the foggiest idea what was involved in bringing up a child and thought that love would conquer all. I suppose she led them a merry dance from the beginning. Once the marketing men inveigled their way into her life, her poor parents didn't stand a chance – the need to supply more and more consumer goods ensured they were trapped forever on their career paths, earning money to feed their little princess's attitude problem.

My heart goes out to those parents. Nobody told them about cultural side effects – indeed, until about a decade ago, nobody really knew. Having fallen into so many of the same traps myself (albeit – thank God – in an earlier age, when the consequences were nowhere near as dire) I have nothing but sympathy for their predicament. They loved their princess not at all wisely, and far, far too well.

Detoxing childhood

However, now we *do* know. Knowledge is power, so the evidence below empowers parents to detoxify their children's lives. We know that the following factors can affect healthy physical, social, emotional and cognitive development:

- the food they eat, and the circumstances in which they eat it
- the amount of exercise, activity and unstructured play they engage in
- the amount of time spent outdoors, especially in natural surroundings
- the length and regularity of sleep
- the potential for attachment in the first eighteen months to three years
- the amount adults talk and sing to them, and the way they communicate
- the amount they're read to and encouraged to enjoy books
- the level of first-hand experiences they have throughout childhood
- the age-appropriateness and consistency of childcare arrangements
- the extent to which adults limit, monitor and mediate screen-time
- the extent to which adults resist marketing messages on their behalf and help them become market-savvy
- the degree to which they're helped to be self-regulating
- the role models available to them
- the level of emotional security and stability throughout childhood
- the time available for social interactions within the family
- the ethos of the pre-school and schools they attend, including

the age at which they begin formal schooling
- the confidence of their parents in all aspects of child rearing
- the 'adult alliance' of neighbourhood support.

Detoxification simply requires parents to make a few lifestyle adjustments which, once they've got over the emotional shock, aren't particularly taxing. Cheeringly, in an uncertain economic climate, most of them also have the advantage of being completely free of charge. In fact, that's probably why so many parents have lost track of them as the perfect storm raged: in a consumer culture, no one values the free stuff.

If you're a parent wondering where to start, don't panic – it's not a race. Neither do you have to be a perfect parent: just, in the words of psychologist Donald Winnicott, 'good enough'. Take a long look at your child's lifestyle, and talk with your partner, other family members and – if he or she's old enough – your child, to plan a strategy. Then remember the mantra 'warm but firm, warm but firm', as you start putting it in place.

Once you get going, you'll probably find the detoxification process leads to some changes in your own life:

- You'll have to slow down, smell the roses, and notice the real life going on around you
- You'll have to spend time talking, doing, sharing, connecting with those close to you
- To establish routines and habits for your child, you'll need to find ways of organising your life to give more time to home
- This may mean re-examining your values and establishing what's really important to you and your family
- With luck, you'll also become more involved with your real-life community – meeting other adults with interests that overlap with your own

Interestingly, these are the same changes you'd pay a fortune to hear from a lifestyle guru, life coach or psychotherapist.

A helping hand for parents

There are, however, an increasing number of Mind the gap parents who, through no fault of their own, aren't likely to take action. We can't rely on a 'trickle down' effect to help them out, so society as a whole has to get involved. Successive UK and USA governments have focused on reducing inequality by raising educational standards, so current childcare policies concentrate on research linked to children's cognitive development, without taking into account its intricate inter-relationship with physical, social and emotional development, particularly in the first seven years.

Throughout *Toxic Childhood*, I've identified a number of policies which evidence suggests can help to detox these children's lives, while lending a helping hand to all parents and – coincidentally – helping to reduce inequality. For instance, in various parts of the world, you'll find:

* healthy, compulsory, attractive school meals in pleasant surroundings
* initiatives to promote healthy eating, such as the Edible Schoolyard Project where children grow and prepare foods for school meals
* 'walking buses' taking children to and from school, thus doing away with the school run
* child-friendly city planning, such as home zones and shared space, making safer streets for children to play out
* movements for the greening of cities and the creation of natural playgrounds
* information on child development disseminated at ante- and post-natal classes and through the education system
* children's centres offering a range of parenting support
* homecare allowances enabling parents to stay at home during the first three years of their children's lives
* well-funded play-based nursery schools for children between

the ages of three and (at least) six, with highly trained early
years staff
- a school starting age of six, or preferably seven, and no standardised testing during the primary years
- an exciting primary school curriculum, with a balanced
  approach to literacy
- flexible, affordable, high quality childcare, appropriate to
  various ages
- the banning of marketing to pre-teen children
- authoritative advice to parents, from governments and/or
  medical authorities, on screen-time and media use
- television programmes and websites to help parents
- successful, widely-used parenting programmes.

Some of these ideas have already been adopted in the UK, but others
seem almost impossible to achieve in the current climate. However,
with enough pressure from the electorate (parent power), there's no
reason why a future government shouldn't recognise the long-term
importance of taking a holistic approach to childhood. In this case,
a good first step would be to set up a National Institute of Child
Development and Well-being, consisting of respected academics
and other experts in the field, to provide genuine evidence-based
advice to government on matters relating to families, childcare
and education. Like the National Institute for Health and Clinical
Excellence, it must be politically-neutral and all governments
would have to be answerable to it, rather than pursuing their own
short-term agendas.

The setting up of such an Institute would, of course, involve a
serious political paradigm shift because scientific, evidence-based
advice about child development and well-being doesn't accord
with the current orthodoxy that parents should work all hours God
sends, feeding the global economy to the serious detriment of their
families and communities. Perhaps the evidence from the London
School of Economics outlined on pages 343–4 will help to start that
change.

How detoxing childhood makes everyone happier

The beginning of the twenty-first century saw a glut of books about human happiness. They include lifestyle books, psychotherapy books, scientific tomes and, increasingly, books on politics and economics, such as Richard Layard's *Happiness* and Wilkinson and Pickett's *The Spirit Level*. All of them tell us what science has shown: given a certain level of economic well-being, happiness in a social animal such as *homo sapiens* comes not from more money but from successful personal relationships with family and friends, and in the local community.

This finding is, of course, at odds with the interests of global corporations. To increase their wealth and power, they need us to believe that the true route to happiness is through shopping. Hence the concerted drive of marketeers, aided by images of the 'perfect' lifestyle beamed through those ubiquitous screens, to make us judge each other's worth in terms of appearance, possessions, and other indicators of material wealth. By splintering us off from our communities and families, luring every man, woman and child into personalised virtual worlds where advertisers can exploit their particular psychological vulnerabilities, the market creates the conditions in which to sell more stuff.

Limiting the time children spend in front of screens and concentrating instead on real-life human interaction isn't just the first step in detoxing childhood, it's also the first step to becoming happier ourselves. When parents join together to organise 'eyes on the street' or lobby for better child protection in the global village, they not only help the detoxification process for their own and their neighbours' children, they start reactivating the social capital communities need to thrive.

This doesn't mean turning our backs on the wonders of technology, foreswearing all luxury good, sending 'Honey' back into the kitchen, or failing to embrace exciting developments in the future. It simply means finding a sensible balance between quick-fix twenty-first-century culture and the 'slow time' nurture all children require. That means being warm but firm with ourselves about the extent to which we allow the market to determine our lifestyle, and recognising that the loving care traditionally provided by women is as essential to child-rearing as the wage packet traditionally provided by men. However we choose to share these two responsibilities within our own families we should value them equally.

It seems to me that, if we get the balance right for the children, we'll get it right for the whole electronic village. And if we start today, we might even be in time to save the world.

NOTES AND REFERENCES

INTRODUCTION: TOXIC CHILDHOOD SYNDROME

What's happening to children?
- 2014 figures for UK from the Mental Health Foundation: http://www.mentalhealth.org.uk/help-information/mental-health-statistics/children-young-people/. For US, from the Centre for Disease Control and Prevention:http://www.cdc.gov/features/ childrensmentalhealth/
- UNICEF report: UNICEF Innocenti Research Centre: *An Overview of Child Well-being in Rich Countries: A Comprehensive Assessment of the Lives and Well-being of Children and Adolescents in the Economically Advanced Nations* (UNICEF 2007) http://www.unicef.org/media/files/ChildPovertyReport.pdf

Revision of 'special educational needs' guidelines in England
- Between 2003 and 2010 the number of children assessed as having 'mild' SEN problems increased from 14% to 18% of the school population. Ofsted suggested (in its 'SEN and Disability Review' of September 2010) that these probems did not require special help, just better teaching and pastoral care. This was accepted by government and ever since SEN figures have fallen (neither Ofsted nor the DFE ever mentioned that the cost of SEN provision was becoming unsustainable). See 'Half of some special needs children misdiagnosed' by Jeevan Vasager, the *Guardian*, 14/9/10.

The special needs explosion

- 2014 ADHD statistics for the US: http://www.cdc.gov/nchs/fastats/ adhd.htm. For UK: http://www.nhs.uk/conditions/attention-deficit-hyperactivity-disorder/Pages/Introduction.aspx
- Since 2013 there has been concern at the year-on-year increases in prescriptions for medication such as Ritalin on the principle that, in many cases, simple lifestyle adjustments are more effective than medical interventions: see NHS news 11/11/13 www.nhs.uk/news/2013/11November/Pages/Experts-argue-that-ADHD-is-overdiagnosed.aspx
- Dyslexia statistics from the Dyslexia Research Trust (www.dyslexic. org.uk), run by John Stein, a professor of neuroscience at Oxford University.
- 'Dyslexia May Not Exist, Warn Academics' Sarah Knapton, *Daily Telegraph*, 26/2/14
- Dyspraxia: www.nhs.uk/conditions/Dyspraxia-(childhood)/Pages/ Introduction.aspx and www.dyspraxiafoundation.org.uk/about-dyspraxia/
- ASD: Frith, Uta, *Autism and Asperger Syndrome*, (Cambridge University Press, 1991)
- ASD statistics: American Academy of Pediatrics website, 2005, Centre for Disease Control and Prevention, 2014: www.cdc.gov/ ncbddd/autism/data. UK autism figures: *Survey of the Mental Health of Children and Young People in Great Britain*, 2004 commissioned by the Department of Health and the Scottish Executive, carried out by the Office for National Statistics. See also the UK National Autistic Society website: www.autism.org.uk/about-autism/myths-facts-and-statistics.aspx

Nature, nurture and behaviour

- Nature and nurture are vibrantly interactive: see for instance Rose, 2005, Greenfield, 2003, Ridley, 2003. For a more recent survey of the debate, see the book review 'Untangling the Morass' by Professor Daniel McShea in *American Scientist*, Vol. 99:2 2011: www. americanscientist.org/bookshelf/pub/untangling-the-morass
- Monkey research quoted in National Research Council, Institute of Medicine, et al. 2000.

Learning to behave

- I am indebted for neuroscientific advice on the three 'key' areas of development ('executive functions', relying on neural networks that develop during childhood in the prefrontal cortex of the brain) to Professor Norbert Herschkowtiz, during a series of personal interviews in 2005. In the succeeding decade, most of the scientists I've read and interviewed have pointed me in the same direction.
- Experiment on deferred gratification: see Goleman, 1997, replicated by BBC *Child of our Time* programmes, see Livingstone, 2005
- Redefinition of Special Educational Needs – see above in 'The Special Needs Explosion'

A twenty-first-century report card

- Primary teachers' concern: as a literacy specialist, I've spent much of my professional life over the last two decades travelling around the UK (and occasionally to the other countries mentioned here) talking to many hundreds of teachers every year. It was their widespread concern that led me to do the initial research for this book. Further details on my experiences are recounted in Palmer, 2013. See also www.suepalmer.co.uk
- The process of learning to read actually develops children's powers of thought and understanding – see Chapter 7, and Donaldson, 1978 and 1989.
- Street-Porter, Janet, 'I've Changed My Mind Over Smacking', *The Independent*, 4/11/2004
- Increases in bullying are reported across the developed world, e.g.: Ernest Gill 'Bullying Takes on Epidemic Proportions in German Schools' *Deutsche Presse-Agentur*, 7/7/05; Amelia Hill 'Children's Czar Warns of Huge Increase in Bullying' *Observer*, 13/11/05

The blind men and the elephant

- Commentators have been complaining about reduced attention span ever since television became widespread in the 1950s and over the last 20 years children's viewing has escalated wildly. e.g. Winn, 2002.
- The poem by John Godfrey Saxe, *The Blind Man and the Elephant*:

It was six men of Indostan
To learning much inclined,
Who went to see the Elephant ⁓ (Though all of them were blind),
That each by observation ⁓ Might satisfy his mind.

The First approached the Elephant,
And happening to fall
Against his broad and sturdy side, ⁓ At once began to bawl:
'God bless me! but the Elephant ⁓ Is very like a wall!'

The Second, feeling of the tusk,
Cried, 'Ho! what have we here?
So very round and smooth and sharp? ⁓ To me 'tis mighty clear
This wonder of an Elephant ⁓ Is very like a spear!'

The Third approached the animal,
And happening to take
The squirming trunk within his hands, ⁓ Thus boldly up and spake:
'I see,' quoth he, 'the Elephant ⁓ Is very like a snake!'

The Fourth reached out an eager hand,
And felt about the knee.
'What most this wondrous beast is like ⁓ Is mighty plain,' quoth her;
''Tis clear enough the Elephant ⁓ Is very like a tree!'

The Fifth who chanced to touch the ear,
Said: 'E'en the blindest man
Can tell what this resembles most; ⁓ Deny the fact who can,
This marvel of an Elephant ⁓ Is very like a fan!'

The Sixth no sooner had begun
About the beast to grope,
Than, seizing on the swinging tail ⁓ That fell within his scope,
'I see,' quoth he, 'the Elephant ⁓ Is very like a rope!'

And so these men of Indostan
Disputed loud and long,
Each in his own opinion ⁓ Exceeding stiff and strong,
Though each was partly in the right ⁓ And all were in the wrong!

The past is another planet

- 'The past is a foreign country' L.P. Hartley, *The Go Between* (Penguin, UK, 1953)
- Canadian media visionary Marshal McLuhan: see McLuhan and Quentin, 2001

Detoxing childhood

- We could dole out drugs: Wong I., Murray M., et al., 'Increased Prescribing Trends of Paediatric Psychotropic Medications', *Archives of Disease in Childhood*, 89:1131-1132, 2004
- Recent increase in British prescriptions for Ritalin: 'Ritalin Use for ADHD Children Soars Fourfold' by Jamie Doward and Emma Craig, *Observer*, 6/5/12 www.theguardian.com/society/2012/may/06/ritalin-adhd-shocks-child-psychologists
- Courtney Love quote: see Eberstadt, 2004

Mind the Gap

- For more background on the connection between poverty and poor educational attainment, see Palmer 2009, Chapter 10
- Wilkinson and Pickett quote from 'The Spirit Level authors: Why Society Is More Unequal than Ever' in *The Observer*, 9/3/14 www.theguardian.com/commentisfree/2014/mar/09/society-unequal-the-spirit-level
- *The Spirit Level*: see Wilkinson and Pickett, 2009
- Nelson Mandela quote from his speech at the launch of the Nelson Mandela Children's Fund, 1995

CHAPTER ONE FOOD FOR THOUGHT

- Dangers of unhealthy eating are widely reported, e.g. Olshansky S., Passaro D., et al. 'A Potential Decline in Life Expectancy in the United States in the Twenty-first Century' *New England Journal of Medicine* 253;11, 17/3/05.
- Quote about brain degeneration: report of plenary address by Anthony E. Kelly, George Mason University, USA, to the OECD Brain Research and Learning Science Symposium, Germany, 2003
- International seminars in London: *Omega-3 DHA and Children's Behavior and Learning*, the Royal College of Surgeons, London,

4/9/13; *Feeding Healthy Minds: maternal and infant nutrition and children's brain development*, Royal College of Surgeons, 29/10/13
- The Institute for Food, Brain and Behaviour: www.ifbb.org.uk
- International food guidelines: Knight, Jonathan: 'Around the World in Three Square Meals', *Nature*, 24/2/05; US 2005 food pyramid: www.mypyramid.gov
- US 2005 nutrition guidelines update: www.healthierus.gov/dietary-guidelines
- Quote about guidelines by Michael Jacobson, head of the Center for Science in the Public Interest, a nutrition advocacy group in Washington DC, quoted in Butler, Declan and Pearson, Helen: 'Flash in the Pan', *Nature*, 24/2/05
- US MyPlate: see www.choosemyplate.gov/dietary-guidelines.html
- UK MyPlate: see www.food.gov.uk/multimedia/flash/Alisha_and_Ronnie_e.swf

Junk-food junkies
- I'm indebted throughout this section to Dr Susan Jebb, Head of Nutrition and Health Research at the Medical Research Council (HNR) Centre, Cambridge: personal interview, 2004.
- Sugar content of canned drinks: Warren S. Jafferian, Vice President, Worldwide Education Market, Sodhexo USA: personal interview, 2004
- Addiction quote: Deanne Jade, psychologist and founder of the UK Centre for Eating Disorders, reported by Rachel Newcombe, 'Is Junk Food Addictive?', BUPA *Investigative News*, 19/07/03

Marketing messages
- Research on Coca-Cola's effect on the brain: Dr P. Read Montague of the Brown Human Neuro-imaging Laboratory at Baylor College in Houston, Texas. Reported in the *Independent*, 17/10/04.
- Children and brands: from the Ofcom report: *Childhood Obesity – Food Advertising in Context: Children's Food Choices, Parents' Understanding and Influence and the Role of Food Promotions*, UK, July 2004
- Fruity snack advertising campaign: Felicity Lawrence, consumer affairs correspondent, 'Revealed: How Food Firms Target Children', the *Guardian*, 27/5/04. The campaign was for Kellogg's Real Fruit Winders, a snack which is one third sugar, and Lawrence's article was based on the submission from an

advertising agency to the Institute of Practitioners of Advertising for an 'effectiveness award' in 2002.

It's just a bit of fun

- Information about junk food advertising in children's programmes: details from Malcolm Clark of *Sustain*: personal interview, October, 2013
- Advergames, apps, etc: *Through the Looking Glass: A Review of the Topsy-turvey World of Regulations That Are Supposed to (but Don't) Protect Children from Online Marketing of Junk Food* by Malcolm Clark and Charlie Powell, April 2013 (Children's Food Campaign, London)

Trapped in the junk-food jungle

- Schools promoting unhealthy food: For details of Jamie Oliver's magnificent campaign – www.feedmebetter.com
- Nestle Healthy Kids Initiative: http://www.iaso.org/site_media/uploads/A_Junk-free_Childhood_2012.pdf
- Lack of parental control over diet: Ofcom report, 2004 (see above)
- 'Not wisely but too well': Othello, Act 5, Scene 6

Sugar rush

- See also: 'Sugar Rush' Karen Schmidt in *New Scientist*, October 2002, Ursell, 2005 and Robert Lustig's YouTube lecture: *Sugar: The Bitter Truth*, 2009
- Quote from Robert Lustig MD, Professor of Paediatrics, Department of Endocrinology, University of California at San Francisco: from 'Sugar Is Toxic and Should Be Regulated' by Tiffany O'Callaghan, *New Scientist*, September 2011
- Review of studies about vitamin and mineral deficiencies: *Nutrition, Health and Schoolchildren*, British Nutrition Foundation, 2003
- Bernard Gesch, Senior Research Scientist, Oxford Department of Physiology, in *Food on the Brain*, Independent TV, UK, 29/4/05
- Study at University of Southern California: Jianghong Liu, Ph.D., Adrian Raine, D.Phil., Peter H. Venables, Ph.D., D.Sc., and Sarnoff A. Mednick, Ph.D., D.Med. 'Malnutrition at Age 3 Years and Externalizing Behaviour Problems at Ages 8, 11 and 16 Years', *American Journal of Psychiatry* 161:2005–2013, November 2004

The additive cocktail

- See Ursell, 2005
- Dr Vyvyan Howard, toxico-pathologist, Liverpool University, quoted by Tim Utton, 'Children's Drinks Are a Chemical Cocktail', *Daily Mail*, 11/5/04
- 2011 US study: see Food And Behaviour Research website, http://www.fabresearch.org/view_item.aspx?item_id=1846&list_id=search1-search_page&list_index=4&is_search_result=true 'Food Navigator: no link between ADHD and Food Colouring But More Science Needed, Says Expert', 15/6/2011
- Alex Richardson quote: personal interview, October 2013

Fats and fish oil

- I am indebted for information in this section (and general background information throughout this chapter) to Dr Alex Richardson, Senior Research Fellow, Mansfield College and the University Laboratory of Physiology, Oxford
- Among the 'other contemporary ills' that may be linked to an Omega 3/6 imbalance are inflammatory diseases (including heart disease, high blood pressure and strokes) and depression.
- Recent research into fish oil supplements: Richardson A.J., Burton J.R., Sewell R.P., Spreckelsen T.F. and Montgomery P.: *Docosahexaenoic Acid for Reading, Cognition and Behaviour in Children Aged 7-9 Years (the DOLAB study)*, Centre for Evidence-Based Intervention, University of Oxford, published online September 2012 http://www.ncbi.nlm.nih.gov/pubmed/22970149

The wrong sort of fats

- WHO and NICE comments on trans-fats: 'Dying for a Burger: Why Are Transfats Still Legal in the UK?' by Clare Dwyer Hogg, *Independent*, 10/9/11
- Alex Richardson quote – further information on this and other nutrition research on the Food and Behaviour Research website: www.fabresearch.org

The decline of the family meal

- Sheila Pell's article: 'Family Dinner Minus Family' *Washington Post*, 11/1/05
- Rutgers University report: *The Real Value Meal: Eating Together*, 2006

http://njaes.rutgers.edu/spotlight/eating-together.asp; see also *Family Dinners: Much More Than a Meal*, CBS News, 11/2/09 http://www.cbsnews.com/2100-3480_162-1482571.html
- UK survey of toddlers' eating habits: research conducted by GrowingUpMilkInfo.com reported in 'Toddlers Glued to Screens at Mealtimes' *The Times*, 10/12/13

Meals, manners and marijuana
- Richard Woolfson quote: see *Times* article, above
- Table manners survey, by Brewsters Restaurant chain, quoted by Adam Powell, 'Pupils Get Lessons in How to Use Knife and Fork', *Daily Mail*, 7/4/05. He also provided the following quote from a headteacher, which is typical of what teachers tell me everywhere I go in the UK (although, interestingly, less so in mainland Europe): 'There has been a trend in the last five years for children to come to school unable to hold a knife and fork or sit at the table properly because of the decline in family meals and the availability of convenience foods. I think you would find that the majority of family homes do not have a table any more, and the only time the family is together is in the car. It's amazing how many children go home in the evening just as their father is coming home and their mother is going out to do an evening shift.'
- Decline of family meals in Japan: Yukio Hattori interviewed by Masami Ito, staff writer, 'Food for Thought', *Japan Times*, 02/11/05
- Quote from Dr Pat Spungin (www.raisingkids.com) in same article (also personal interview, 2005)
- Richard Harman quote: 'Children's Social Skills "Eroded by Decline of Family Meals"' by Graeme Paton, *Daily Telegraph*, 30/4/12
- Social significance of family meals: Eisenberg, Marla E. et al., *Correlations Between Family Life and Psychological Well-Being Among Adolescents*, Archives of Pediatrics and Adolescent Medicine Aug 2004, Vol. 158
- Survey of twenty years' worth of National Merit Scholars in the USA showing they all ate family meals by the National Merit Scholarship Corporation, reported in 'The Family that Eats Together...' by Mimi Knight in *Christian Parenting Today*, January/February, 2002

Feeding a family

- The chopstickless tribe quote: Asako Aranaki in 'Pick Up Those Sticks: Chopstick Use Seen as a Sign of Healthy Diet', *Trends In Japan*, edited by Japan Echo Inc, 8/7/05 www.web-japan.org/trends00/honbun/tj990708.html
- Long-established Italian feeding routine for babies – I was told about this by several Italian mothers who swear by it, but couldn't find any official references – I suspect it dates back to before the Second World War!
- Two-year-old fussiness: Cooke, L., Wardle, J., Gibson, E.L., 'Relationship Between Parental Report of Food Neophobia and Everyday Food Consumption in 2-6 Year-old Children', *Appetite* 41, 2003, 205–206 **or** Wardle, J., Cooke, L. et al., 'Increasing Children's Acceptance of Vegetables; A Randomized Trial of Parent-led Exposure', *Appetite Journal* 40, 2003, 155–162
- What, when, where; how much and whether: Satter, 2000
- Susan Jebb quote: personal interview, 2004

Cutting back on snack attack

- Healthy snacks list: Better Health Channel, Victoria Australia, 2005 www.betterhealth.vic.gov.au
- 80–20 nutritionist quote: personal interview recounted in my later book *21st Century Girls*, 2013: I'd love to give my 80–20 nutritionist credit for her idea. She's anonymous only because she asked to be: 'Please don't quote me on that. That's me being a mother, not an academic. The official line is zero tolerance!'

CHAPTER TWO: OUT TO PLAY

- Stevenson, Robert Louis, *Good and Bad Children*, Child's Garden of Verse
- The term 'eyes on the street' comes from Mary Eberstadt: Eberstadt, 2004

The fear of fear itself

- Research on effects of World Trade Centre attack: see Restak, 2003
- Negative content of TV news: Szabo, Dr Attila, study by Nottingham Trent University's School of Biomedical and Natural Sciences, UK, Press Release – 'TV News Can Make Us Miserable' 22/3/05

- The chances of children being killed: according to a 2012 NSPCC document 'Child Killings in England and Wales: Explaining the Statistics', on average 55 children in England are killed each year. Of these, eight out of nine victims are under 1 year old, two out of three are under 5 years old and the vast majority are killed by a parent or step-parent – mostly in the family home.
- Quote about Beslan siege: Melanie McDonagh 'How Close to Home These Terrified Children Seemed' *Sunday Times*, 5/9/04

Cottonwool kids

- Children's fears: see Cantor, 2001, Bourke, 2005
- Quote from Kansas professor: Eric M. Vernberg, 'Psychological Science and Terrorism: Making Psychological Issues Part of Our Planning and Technology' in http://merrill.ku.edu/publications/2002whitepaper/vernberg.html
- Hugh Cunningham references: personal conversation, 2007 and Cunningham, 2006
- Debate about safety surfacing in playgrounds: see Gill, 2007
- Debate about cycle helmets: see Cairns, 2008
- Tim Gill quote is from the film *Project Wild Thing*, Green Lions films, 2013
- Asthma boom research: see 'Factors Associated with Different Hygiene Practices in the Homes of 15 Month Old Infants' and 'Hygiene Levels in a Contemporary Population Cohort Are Associated with Wheezing and Atopic Eczema in Pre-school Infants' both by A. Sherriff, J. Golding and The Alspac Study Team in *Archives of Disease in Childhood*, 2002; 87; 26–29

Getting children off the couch

- I am indebted for much of the information in this section to Dr Amanda Kirby, Director of the Dyscovery Centre for Learning Difficulties, Cardiff UK: personal interview, 2004
- Dr Christine Mcintyre has also provided me with information on early physical development: we met at an Early Years Education Conference, Harrogate, 23/9/05, and had several helpful conversations between then and 2012: see also Macintyre and McVitty, 2004.
- Sunshine avoidance: for information about Vitamin D see Gillie, 2004 and www.healthresearchforum.org.uk

- Early levels of activity: see 'Active Parents Raise Active Children' in www.sciencedaily.com/releases/2007/11/071126105434.htm
- Activity and obesity links: see 'Early Life Risk Factors for Obesity in Childhood: Cohort Study' by Reilly J.J., Armstrong J., et al., *British Medical Journal*, 11/6/05 and many subsequent studies by the NHS.

Family time ... and having fun

- UNICEF survey on childhood well-being (2007): UNICEF Innocenti Research Centre: *An Overview of Child Well-being in Rich Countries: A Comprehensive Assessment of the Lives and Well-being of Children and Adolescents in the Economically Advanced Nations* (www.unicef.org/media/files/ChildPovertyReport.pdf)
- Dr Amanda Kirkby quote: personal interview, 2004
- Dr Agnes Nairn's findings in Ipsos MORI Social Research Institute report: *Children's Well-being in the UK, Sweden and Spain: The Role of Inequality and Materialism*, June 2011. See also an excellent 2013 TEDx talk by Agnes Nairn on www.youtube.com/watch?v=fXTaRN DwigA&list=PLsRNoUx8w3rOrE_cFJh3y-3ppiFiySDyf&index=3

PE, playtime and paranoia

- Japanese children's physical fitness: Ihara, Atsushi, 'Japan Perspective; Kids, Society Becoming Weak', *The Daily Yomiuri*, 9/8/2002
- Children's running speed: Study led by Dr Grant Tomkinson at the University of South Australia, findings presented at a Scientific Session of the American Heart Association in Dallas, Texas. See 'Children Take One and a Half Minutes Longer To Run a Mile Than Their Parents at Their Age' by Richard Gray, *Daily Telegraph*, 19/11/13
- Decline of *raijo taiso*: Alice Gordenker, 'Better Off Sleeping Than Working Out', *Japan Times*, 16/8/02
- *Managing Risk in Play Provision: Implementation Guide* by David Ball, Tim Gill and Bernard Spiegal, published by Play England on behalf of the Play Safety Forum, 2013
- *The Good School Playground Guide: Developing School Playgrounds to Support The Curriculum and Nurture Happy, Healthy Children*, Learning Through Landscapes, 2013 (funded by the Scottish Government).

The decline of the free-range child
- I'm indebted for many of the ideas in this and the following two sections to Tim Gill, Director of Rethinking Childhood: personal interviews, from 2004–present day. See also *The Power of Play: An Evidence Base* by Issy Coles-Hamilton (Play Scotland, 2012)
- Natural Childhood Report by Stephen Moss (National Trust, 2012)
- The Good Childhood Enquiry (2009): see Layard and Dunn, 2009, also an update at www.childrenssociety.org.uk/sites/default/files/tcs/good_childhood_report_2012_final_0.pdf
- Stephen Moss quote from a video to launch the Natural Childhood Report in August 2012 www.youtube.com/watch?v=rBwKrbfhgDU

Back to Nature
- David Attenborough quote from an address to the Communicate Conference: *Connecting With Nature*, November 2010, University of Bristol
- Information on Forest Schools and Beach Schools from Sarah Blackwell of Archimedes Forest Schools: personal interview, summer 2013
- Outdoor nurseries, e.g. The Secret Garden in Fife, Scotland, where children play outdoors all day in all weathers; the Red Hen Nursery in Lincolnshire, based on a working farm; and Farley Outdoor Nursery in Wiltshire whose founder and headteacher is, coincidentally, called Sue Palmer
- National Play Day is organised by the four National play associations, see www.playengland.org.uk , www.playscotland.org, www.playwales.org.uk, www.playboard.org (Northern Ireland)
- My favourite books on getting children of all ages outdoors are Fiona Danks and Jo Schofield: see their website: www.goingwild.net.
- The guerrilla geographers' organisation (The Geography Collective: www.thegeographycollective.wordpress.com) launched Mission Explore in 2008 www.missionexplore.net
- *Cotton Wool Kids* documentary, Channel 4, 10/4/08
- *Natural Childhood Report* by Stephen Moss for the National Trust, 2012
- *Project Wild Thing* by Green Lions films, released October 2013 www.projectwildthing.com. The project was sponsored by the National Trust, the Royal Society for the Protection of Birds, the National

Health Service and the four national Play Associations (see above)
- List of advantages of children reconnecting with nature: see *Natural Childhood Report* and *Project Wild Thing*, above

It takes a village
- Playing Out movement: www.playingout.net
- Streets Alive: www.streetsalive.org.uk

Safer streets
- David Bann quote: personal correspondence, 2014
- Ben Hamilton-Baillie, urban designer, address to Royal Society of Arts, Bristol, and personal interview, 2005
- Home zones: see www.homezonenews.org.uk
- Yellow school buses: successful pilot schemes in Wrexham and Hebden Bridge by the Sutton Trust were reported in 'It's Time for the Yellow Solution' by Hilary Wilce, *The Independent*, 16/6/05
- Walking buses in Japan: see Ashby 1994. British example: http://www.worcestershire.gov.uk/home/large_text/cs-sus-transport-ooschool-plan-walking_buses
- Scottish National Play Strategy, 2013: see http://www.scotland.gov.uk/Publications/2013/06/5675. At the parliamentary launch of this document on 31/10/13, many MSPs vowed to challenge the 'no ball games' culture, currently endemic across Scottish cities. Whether this will translate into action remains to be seen.

Places to play ...
- Quotes from Don Early of Fields in Trust: personal interview, 2013
- The Canadian Evergreen movement: www.evergreen.ca
- Parks in Freiburg: Tim Gill – 'In Need of an Unlevel Playing Field', *Guardian*, 3/8/05
- *Learning Through Landscapes*: www.ltl.org.uk

... people to play with
- Issy Coles-Hamilton quote: *Best* magazine, May 2003
- Playwork – my original information on playwork and playworkers came from yet another Sue Palmer, Head of School of Film, Television and the Performing Arts, Leeds Met University: personal interview, 2005. However, since researching *Toxic Childhood*, I've

become personally involved with the UK play movement, and
have been lucky enough to learn from playworkers in all four UK
countries, as well as serving on the Board of Play Scotland.

CHAPTER 3: TIME FOR BED

- General background on sleep – Martin, 2003
- US National Commission on Sleep Disorders Research, *Wake Up America: A National Sleep Alert*, Washington DC, Dept. of Health and Human Services, 1993.

Tired families
- Recommended sleeping hours and 2004 sleep poll: the US National Sleep Foundation www.sleepfoundation.org
- UK figures from UK Sleep Council Report, see 'Two Thirds of Children Not Getting Enough Sleep' by Nigel Bunyan, reported in *Daily Telegraph*, 23/4/12
- International research: 'Never Enough Sleep' Mattricianni et al., *Pediatrics*, February 2012

A good night's sleep
- For advice on this and the next two sections, I'm indebted to sleep researcher Professor Jan Born, Director of Neuroendocrinology at Luebeck University, Germany: personal interviews, 2005 and 2014.

Learn while you sleep
- Yvonne Kelly quote from 'Children With Regular Bedtimes Less Likely to Misbehave, Research Shows' by Alexandra Topping, *Guardian*, 14/10/13
- Professor Kelly's research project: 'Changes in Bedtime Schedules and Behavioural Difficulties in 7-year-olds' Kelly et al., *Paediatrics*, 2013. There have been many earlier reports on this subject, such as the The National Sleep Foundation's assertion that 'children who get enough sleep are more likely to function better and are less prone to behavioural problems and moodiness', backed up by studies, e.g. Fallone, G., Acebo, C., Seifer, R. & Carskadon, M.A., 'How Well Do Children Comply with Imposed Sleep Schedules at Home?', *Sleep Medicine Review*, 25, 739-745, USA, 2002.

- Sleep provides opportunity for brain to reorganise and prune: Terry Sejnowski, Director of Computational Neurobiology Laboratory, Salk Institute, USA, quoted in *Time Magazine*, 2005

Why it's important to sleep on it

- REM sleep and learning: Maquet P., Laureys S., et al., 'Experience-dependent changes in cerebral activation during human REM sleep, *Nature Neuroscience* pp. 831–836, August 2000
- Slow wave sleep and learning: Huber R., Ghilardi M., et al., 'Local sleep and learning', *Nature*, Vol. 430, 1/7/04
- Born J., Gais S., 'Low acetylcholine during slow-wave sleep is critical for declarative memory consolidation' PNAS, Vol. 101, No. 7, pp. 2140-2144, February 2004
- Born's creative thinking experiment and work relating to children's learning: personal interviews, 2005 and 2014. See also 'System consolidation of memory during sleep' Born J. and Wilhelm I., *Psychological Research*, March 2012

Hush, little baby ... stopping sleep problems before they begin

- My overview of recommendations was taken from the American Academy of Pediatrics, the National Sleep Foundation and, in the UK, Livingstone, 2005
- Professor Helen Ball quote: 'Supporting parents who are worried about their newborn's sleep' editorial in British Medical Journal, 15/4/13. Also personal interview, December 2013
- ISIS website (www.isisonline.org.uk)

The babies who haven't read the book

- One of the most popular books of recent years has been *The Contented Little Baby Book* (Ford, 1999) – parents of babies who respond well to its strict sleep regime tend to love it; those whose babies respond badly seem to hate it.
- 'Fussy' babies: see Shimada, M. and Takahashi, K., 'Emerging and Entraining Patterns of the Sleep-Wake Rhythm in Preterm and Term Infants' in *Brain Development* 21, 1999 and National Research Council Institute of Medicine, 2000
- For more information on ways of soothing children, see Woodhouse, 2003
- If you've tried all the recommended techniques, and your child still

has problems going to sleep and/or staying asleep beyond the age of nine months, check with a doctor or paediatrician, and perhaps ask for referral to one of the new 'sleep clinics' springing up all over the developed world.

Time for a nap
- 'Napping Helps Preschoolers Learn' – commentary piece by Sara C. Mednick in *Proceedings of the National Academy of Sciences of the USA*, October 2013
- 'When Children Do Not Nap Well, They Pay a Price': Weissbluth, 2003
- TV and naps: Winn, 2002

Sleepy schoolchildren
- Research on children's lack of sleep: Silentnight Beds poll, reported in the *Guardian*, 1/5/03; Chervin, R.D., Archbold K.H., Dillon J.E. et al., 'Inattention, Hyperactivity and Symptoms of Sleep-Disordered Breathing', *Pediatrics*, 2002; 109: pp. 449-456; Yoshimatsu, Shingo and Hayashi, Mitsu, 'Bedtime and Lifestyle in Primary School Children' *Sleep and Biological Rhythms*, Vol. 2, Issue 2, p. 153, June 2004
- Brillat-Savarin, Jean-Anthelme, *The Physiology of Taste*, France, 1825
- Studies linking sleep with obesity: this link is now well-established. For a summary of current knowledge see: science.howstuffworks.com/life/sleep-obesity.htm

Snoring and other worries
- Sleep and ADHD: see 'Sleep and alertness in ADHD children' Cortese et al., *Sleep*, Vol. 4, No. 29, 2006
- Snoring research: Gozal, David et al., 'Sleep Disordered Breathing and School Performance in Children' *Pediatrics*, Vol. 102, No. 3, pp. 616-620, September 1998; Chervin, R.D., Archbold K.H., Dillon J.E. et al., 'Inattention, Hyperactivity and Symptoms of Sleep-Disordered Breathing', *Pediatrics*, 2002; 109: pp. 449-456; see also Weissbluth, 1998
- Quote about tonsillectomy by Professor Jim Horne: 'In the US experts have found that 20 per cent of children with mild to moderate forms of ADHD seem to have a disturbance of their sleep due to chronic colds, enlarged tonsils and breathing problems. The

implication is that these sleep disturbances are the cause of mild
to moderate ADHD behaviour but parents should make sure their
children are not experiencing a sleep disorder before checking for
ADHD. Sometimes, just removing a child's tonsils, for example,
can solve the problem.' in Niki Chesworth's 'How Lack of Sleep
Can Turn Little Angels into Nightmares' in Sunday Express, 4/8/04
- 'Media Screens in Bedroom Tied to Less Sleep for Boys with
  Autism' by Traci Pedersen on Psychcentral.com, 3/1/14
- For information on the significance of children's sleep on their
  and their family's mental health, see the American Psychological
  Association website: http://www.apa.org/pi/families/resources/
  primary-care/sleep.aspx

A regular bedtime
- Changes in children's behaviour due to sleep improvements: Dahl,
  R.E., Pelham, W.E., Wierson, M., 'The Role of Sleep Disturbances
  in ADD Symptoms' Journal of Pediatric Psychology, 16, 1991 and Gozal,
  Dr David, et al., 'Sleep and Neurobehavioural Characteristics of
  5- to 7-Year-Old Children With Parentally Reported Symptoms of
  ADHD', Pediatrics, Vol. 111, No. 3, March 2003

The real monsters in the bedroom
- American Medical Association warning re media use in the
  bedroom: see Report 4 of the Council for Science and Public
  Health, June 2012 at http://www.ama-assn.org//resources/doc/
  csaph/a12-csaph4-lightpollution-summary.pdf
- TV and sleep problems: Owens J., Maxim R., McGuinn, M. et
  al. 'Television Viewing Habits and Sleep Disturbance in School
  Children' Pediatrics Vol. 104, No. 3, September 1999; The Brown
  University Child and Adolescent Behaviour Letter, January 2000.
  Resetting circadian rhythms: John Herman, Associate Professor
  of Psychiatry, in press release from the University of Texas
  Southwestern Medical Center, Dallas, USA, 30/9/02. Effects of
  TV lights: Salti, R. and Galluzzi, G., et al., 'Nocturnal Melatonin
  Patterns in Children', Journal of Clinical Endocrinology and Metabolism,
  Vol. 85, No. 6, pp. 2137–2144, University of Florence, Italy, 2000
- Figures for TVs in bedrooms: under-fours – US Kaiser Family
  Foundation survey 2003; over-fives – ChildWise Monitor Trends
  Report 2005, www.childwise.co.uk/trends.htm

Monsters on the move

- Ofcom statistics: *Children and Parents: Media Use and Attitudes Report*, Ofcom Research Document, 3/10/13
- Reduction of TVs in middle-class bedrooms in Mayo and Nairn, 2009
- Short wavelength blue light, including quote from Dr Steven Lockley: 'Light from Electronic Screens at Night Linked to Sleep Loss' by Monica Eng, *Chicago Tribune*, 8/7/12. 'Experts Say Exposure to Artificial Light from Tablets Causing Sleep Disorders' by Deborah Rice, ABC Australia News, 1/7/13
- Long term sleep problems: Johnson, J.G. et al., 'Association Between Television Viewing and Sleep Problems During Adolescence and Early Adulthood', *Archives of Pediatrics and Adolescent Medicine*, 158, 2004, pp. 562-568
- Mobile phones disturbing sleep: Van den Bulck, Jan, Senior Lecturer in Psychology, Catholic University of Leuven, Belgium, Letter to the journal of sleep research, 2003: 12: p. 263
- Ofcom figures re smartphone ownership: see Research Document 3/10/13, above
- Franklin, Benjamin, *Poor Richard's Almanack for the Year 1735*

CHAPTER 4: IT'S GOOD TO TALK

- Communication by thumb. In Japan texters are known as 'the thumb tribe' (*'oyaj ubi zoku'*) – this used to refer to people who spent their time playing a card game. Now it means those who prefer texting to speaking face to face.

Language, literacy and learning

- American teachers' concerns: Healy, 1990
- German research: Herschkowitz, 2004
- Japanese teachers' concerns: '80 per cent of Teachers Say Language Skills Declining', *The Daily Yomiuri*, 8/8/02 quotation from Hidefumi Arimoto, Senior Researcher for National Institute For Educational Policy Research
- The psychological implications of early communication: see Gerhardt, 2004 and 2011
- The social and health implications of early communications: see ICAN briefing paper: *Children's Poor Speech, Language and Communication as a Public Health Issue*, 2013

Here's looking at you, kid

- 'The dance of communication': Dr Colwyn Trevarthan, personal
  interview, 2005. Over the years since publication of *Toxic Childhood*,
  I have become increasingly convinced that this early cross-gen-
  erational gazing is of immense importance, both for individual
  human beings and for our species as a whole. It is therefore central
  to my book *21st Century Girls* (2013), which looks at the scientific
  evidence in much greater detail. I'm also deeply grateful to Colwyn
  Trevarthan and other Scotland-based attachment theorists, notably
  Dr Suzanne Zeedyk and Dr Jonathan Delafield-Butts, with whom
  I've been privileged to have many conversations over the last five
  years.
- *The Epidemic*: Shaw, 2003
- Attunement: I was alerted to the significance of mothers'
  empathetic input into the attachment process by a paper by E.
  Meins, C. Fernyhough, R. Wainwright, D. Clark-Carter, M.D.
  Gupta, E. Fradley, and M. Tuckey. 'Pathways to Understanding
  Mind: Construct Validity and Predictive Validity of Maternal Mind-
  Mindedness' in *Child Development*, Vol. 74, Issue 4, 2003. As I
  completed *21st Century Girls*, I was able to quote Dr Elizabeth Meins'
  latest findings (see below). See also Dr Stacey Annand's website:
  http://theattunedparent.com and Zeedyk, 2012
- Non-verbal communication: see Boyce, 2009, 2012 and her website
  www.notjusttalking.co.uk
- Early parent-child communication/ 'mind-reading' see e.g. Bloom,
  2004, Baron-Cohen, 2004, Zeedyk, 2012
- For more on the significance of infant 'mind-reading' see Bloom,
  2004

The cradle of thought

- *The Cradle of Thought*, Hobson, 2002, and personal interview, 2005
- The second 'insight' gained in the triangle of relatedness is known
  as 'theory of mind' and is very popular at present among psychologists and philosophers, e.g. see Bloom, 2004.
- The importance of children's symbolic play was clarified by the
  Russian psychologist Lev Vygotsky. He believed it was humans'
  ability to use symbols that set us apart – symbols are 'mental tools'
  which help us extend our control over our mental world in the
  same way that physical tools such as hammers and levers help us

extend our control over the physical world. See also the article 'Lev Vygotsky' by Galina Dolya and Sue Palmer, on my website: www. suepalmer.co.uk (first published in the *Times Educational Supplement*, July 2004)

- Early years practitioners recognise symbolic play as critical to children's cognitive development, e.g. Bergen, Doris, 'The Role of Pretend Play in Children's Cognitive Development', *Early Childhood Research and Practice*, Vol. 4, No. 1, Spring 2002

- 'A Growing Body of Neuroscientific Research Suggesting Hobson Is Right' – this case is powerfully argued in Gerhardt, 2004 and 2011

How contemporary culture disrupts the dance

- The descriptions of parents failing to communicate with children are anecdotal evidence, gathered from health visitors, speech and language therapists, and nursery practitioners on home visits – the same story is told all over the UK

- The Talk To Your Baby website (www.talktoyourbaby.org) is run by the National Literacy Trust

- I CAN runs an annual Chatterbox Challenge. See www.ican.org.uk

- The importance of singing to babies and small children – see later section: 'Tuning in and turning off' and 'Dancing to the music of time'

- Forward-facing pushchairs: I was first alerted to this in the conversation with Sally Ward described later in the chapter, and as a result persuaded the National Literacy Trust to set up *Talk To Your Baby*. Liz Attenborough, who chaired TTYB, checked out with manufacturers to find out why the pushchairs face the wrong way. After many unsuccessful attempts to turn them round, in 2008 TTYB commissioned research from Suzanne Zeedyk, then at Dundee University. The study is available on the TTYB website: www.literacytrust.org.u/talk_to_your_baby/resources/1555_whats_life_in_a_baby_buggy_like

- The pushchair study was replicated in 2013 by Dr Ken Blaiklock of Unitech Institute of Technology, New Zealand ('Talking with Children when Using Prams While Shopping' in *New Zealand Research in Early Education Journal*, 16). Our lack of success in alerting parents to this small but significant factor in child development sums up for me the frustrations of being a 'childhood campaigner'

in a hyper-consumerist culture. I therefore tend to go on about
it a bit and, when *Who's Who* invited me into its pages in 2014,
listed 'ranting against forward-facing pushchairs' as one of my
recreations.

Tuning in or turning off

- Noise affecting children's school achievement: e.g. Hygge, S.,
  Evans, G.W., and Bullinger, M., 'The Munich Airport Noise Study
  – Effects of Chronic Aircraft Noise on Children's Cognition and
  Health', *7th International Congress on Noise as a Public Health Problem*,
  Sydney, Australia, November 1998, pp. 268–274
- TV noise affecting children's reading at six: research reported in
  review by the Kaiser Foundation: *Zero to Six: Electronic Media in the
  Lives of Infants, Toddlers and Preschoolers*, 28/10/03 see www.kff.org
- Sally Ward's research: personal interview, written up in several
  articles, e.g. 'Time For Teletubbies?', the *Independent*, 30/10/97. See
  also Ward, 2000
- I CAN research into children's language development on arrival at
  school: *The Cost to the Nation of Children's Poor Communication*, ICAN,
  2006
- Susan Greenfield quote from *The Scotsman*, 2006 http://www.
  scotsman.com/news/health/the-trouble-with-childhood-1-1139872
- Aric Sigman quote from an address at *The Child: The True Foundation*
  conference, London, 12/6/10
- Interview with Daniel Anderson in Jackson, 2008
- Sally Ward writes about her work with parents in Ward, 2000

Dancing to the music of time

- Steady beat research: see Kuhlman, K. and Schweinhart, L.J., *Basic
  Timing and Child Development* (High/Scope Educational Research
  Foundation, Ypsilanti, Michigan, USA, 2000) and Palmer and
  Bayley, 2004
- Songs and rhymes on the web e.g.: http://www.bbc.co.uk/cbeebies
- American Academy of Pediatrics recommendations on TV: *Television
  and the Family* – http://www.healthychildren.org/English/family-
  life/Media/Pages/The-Benefits-of-Limiting-TV.aspx

Connecting with babies and toddlers in the twenty-first century

- Government initiatives: Hall, N., *Communicating Matters*, DfES

2006; *Every Child A Talker*, DFES 2008; the national Year of
Communication, also known as HELLO 2011

- Ofsted's 2012 Annual Report found that 34 per cent of children are
not working securely in language, communication and literacy by
the end of the Foundation Stage. This increases to 50 per cent in
disadvantaged areas.

- Bookstart is run for the government by Book Trust www.bookstart.
org.uk; singing sessions in libraries come under various guises,
e.g. 'Bounce and Rhyme'; PlayTalkRead is a Scottish government
initiative www.playtalkread.org

- I CAN Chatterbox Challenge: see above.

- International Association of Infant Massage: www.iaim-
babymassage.co.uk. Being typically English, I was very doubtful
about this organisation when I first heard about it, but on investigation I decided it would be my number one recommendation to
any new mum who isn't sure how to tune into her baby.

- Music Bugs is a nationally-franchised commercial organisation,
offering 'sensory music classes' for babies and toddlers. The
classes are usually led by enthusiasts and are an excellent way for
mothers to meet up with fellow-mums.

- Tiny Talk is a franchised operation for baby-signing, often popular
with middle-class mothers who (perhaps due to high educational
achievement) find it difficult to interact naturally with their infants.
While singing and talking seem to me a far more effective introduction to normal human communication, I've always reckoned
that baby-signing is at least a way of promoting parent-child
interaction. Recently, however, doubt has been cast on its effectiveness in improving language skills: 'Baby Signing Classes "Fail to
Boost Toddlers' Language Skills"' by Graeme Paton, *Daily Telegraph*,
3/11/12. Perhaps parents would just be better reclaiming their own
ancient expertise.

- Family Nurse Partnership: see http://fnp.nhs.uk. This programme
was imported into the UK from the US, where it was developed
by Professor David Olds of the University of Colorado and is,
rather confusingly, known as the Nurse Family Partnership. I've
been asked to point out by a number of people that Olds based his
'mothering the mother' model on the role of health visitors in the
UK, so the project appears to have come full circle.

- Home Start (http://www.home-start.org.uk) and Gingerbread

(http://www.gingerbread.org.uk) are two charities with whom I've been privileged to work over the last few years, and find totally awe-inspiring.
- Sure Start was criticised by Norman Glass in a *Guardian* article 'Surely Some Mistake?' 5/1/05. His point about the shift from family/community support to institutionalised child care is only one of his criticisms about the way the project developed (with all of which, as a dedicated Sure Start watcher, I heartily agree) and the piece is still well worth reading for anyone with an interest in this area: www.theguardian.com/society/2005/jan/05/guardiansociety-supplement.childrensservices

Only connect
- Virginia Beardshaw quote: personal conversation, January 2014

The language instinct
- The title of this section was taken from Steven Pinker's 1995 book, which summarises the Chomskian arguments, but doesn't acknowledge the importance of exposure to a particular language in order to internalise it – see Tomasello, 2003, Palmer and Bayley, 2004
- *Connected Baby* DVD: see Zeedyk, 2010 and http://www.suzannezeedyk.com
- Early language development: Herschkowitz, 2004; Law 2004; Woolfson, 2002

The power of words
- Dr Pat Spungin quote: personal interview, 2005

Interaction versus interactivity
- Wide range of Fisher-Price 'apptivity' products to help babies access their baby apps. See 'Where Apps Become Child's Play' by Nicole La Porte, *New York Times*, 17/7/12 on http://www.fisher-price.com/en_US/brands/babygear/products/78030 and http://www.fisher-price.com/en_US/brands/babygear/products/78030
- I'm indebted to Lynn Oldfield for letting me know about the Ubooly – see Venturbeat.com: 'Meet Ubooly, the Smart Toy that Can Teach Your Child Math' by Christina Farr, 19/10/13
- My Friend Cayla: www.myfriendcayla.co.uk

- Daniel Anderson quote in Strasburger V: 'First Do No Harm: Why Have Parents and Paediatricians Missed the Boat on Children and the Media?' *Journal of Paediatrics*, 151 (54)
- Government advice on parental media use: at time of writing I'm still working with other childhood campaigners to persuade the Scottish government that this is a good idea, so perhaps least said soonest mended.

Talk so kids will listen, listen so kids will talk

- UK study recommending 'sustained shared thinking': Siraj-Blatchford, I., Sylva, K., Muttock, S., Gilden, R., Bell, D., '*Researching Effective Pedagogy In The Early Years*', Institute of Education, University of London, Department for Educational Studies/University of Oxford, UK, updated November 2004
- Quote from Iram Siraj Batchford: personal interview, 2004
- Faber and Mazlich, *How to Talk so Kids Will Listen, and Listen so Kids Will Talk*, 2001

How technology is dumbing children down

- Vincent's story told by Jean Aitchison, Professor of Language and Communication, Oxford: personal interview, 2005
- Dimitri Christakis: see TEDxRainier, Dimitri Christakis, Media and Children. Research reference: Zimmerman, F.J., Christakis, D., Meltzoff, A.D., 'Language Development in Children under Age 2 Years'
- In the original edition of *Toxic Childhood*, I based my review of research into effects of TV and video on 'Television and Language Development in the Early Years' by Close, Dr R., on behalf of the *National Literacy Trust*, March 2004. Since then there has been a plethora of reports on the subject, and a reasonably recent comprehensive survey by the University of Michigan can be found on http://www.med.umich.edu/yourchild/topics/tv.htm, last updated 2010.

Stories and screens

- Decline of the bedtime story: 'Decline of "Once upon a Time" as One Third of Parents No Longer Read a Bedtime Story to Their Children, *Daily Mail*, 11/9/13 http://www.dailymail.co.uk/news/article-2418076/Third-parents-longer-read-bedtime-story-children.html

- Susan Greenfield YouTube talk 'Susan Greenfield on Story-telling', posted by School of Life, 13/1/13
- Importance of bedtime stories: see e.g. www.literacytrust.org. uk/news/5578_report_shows_just_ten_minutes_reading_a_day_boosts_school_achievement, National Literacy Trust, 17/9/13. For further arguments as to why reading to children is helpful, see Palmer and Bayley, 2014 and Bayley and Broadbent, 2005
- The lovely quote from RLS is in Essays of Travel, ii.

The joy of txt
- Queen Victoria's letters: display at Buckingham Palace, World Writer's Day, 2003
- Steven Pinker's quote about the telegram and definition of TweenSpeak: Lindstrom, 2004
- The intuitive nature of computer literacy: see Johnson, 2005

Mind the gap
- Hart and Risley, 1995
- Research from thirty years ago: Young Children Learning Tizzard B. and Hughes M., Blackwell 1984

CHAPTER 5: WE ARE FAMILY

Revolution, relationships and roles
- 2004 evaluation of the family: Williams, 2004
- Quotes from Drs Rake and Callan from Family: Helping to Understand the Modern British Family from the Centre for the Modern Family, October 2011 www.centreformodernfamily.com
- See October 2011 report, above
- No significant move towards genuinely shared parenting: see Banyard, K. (2010) and Asher, R. (2011)

The mommy wars
- The expression 'mommy wars' was used in the press during the mid-nineties to describe contemporary women's dilemma.
- Over the last seven years I've published two books about child development and gender, so have become very aware of the deep antagonism between the more extreme arm of the women's

movement and organisations devoted to 'family values', e.g. the books by Banyard and Asher (see above) put the feminist case; the Family Institute (familymen@eir.com) makes the case for the opposite side.

- Young professional women's earnings (women between twenty-two and twenty-nine earned just over £10 an hour, as opposed to less than £10 for men in the same age-group): see 'David Willetts Warns about Striking University Gender Gap' by Graeme Paton, *Daily Telegraph*, 6/11/12
- Conditions of paid employment: e.g. see Report on British Social Attitudes, *Horizons* magazine, UK National Statistics Office, March 2005
- Fewer than a third of British mothers stay at home to look after children: OECD, 2013 http://www.oecd-ilibrary.org/employment/employment-rate-of-women_20752342-table5
- 2012 study showing mothers' wish to stay at home by uSwitch: see '75 per cent of New Mothers Would Stay at Home to Look After Their Children if They Could' by Steve Doughty, *Daily Mail*, 6/9/12
- Guilty mothers survey by a babycare company, NUK: see 'Guilt of Modern Mothers at Having Too Little Time for Their Children' *Daily Telegraph*, 21/1/13
- Mum who returned to work: quote in 'Why Is the State Obsessed with Subsidising Childcare when Most Mothers of Young Children Want to Stay at Home' by Kathy Gyngell, *Daily Mail*, 5/11/12

Mum's the word

- Quotes from Marie Peacock: personal interview, 2014
- 2011 Labour think tank report by Britain Thinks: *The Modern British Family* http://britainthinks.com/sites/default/files/TheModernBritishFamily-print.pdf
- Quote from Dr Richard House: personal correspondence, 2014
- Attachment, neuroscientific evidence and current theory: during 2013, I was fortunate enough to attend a series of seminars organised by the Scottish Universities Insight Institute, entitled 'The Well-Connected Child', featuring many international authorities. Its Final Report is a useful summary of major findings in this field up to the end of 2013: http://www.scottishinsight.ac.uk/Portals/50/ias%20documents/Reports/Well%20Connected%20SUII%20Narrative%20Report%20091213.pdf

- Quote from Sue Gerhardt, see Gerhardt, 2010
- Quote from Sammi Timimi: personal interview, 2009

Twenty-first-century mothers
- Phenomenal contribution of mothers through the ages: many of the issues discussed in this and the two preceding sections are covered at much greater length in my 2013 book *21st Century Girls*. Shortly after the interview quoted above, Marie Peacock sent me the following link and personal comment: http://www.opendemocracy.net/5050/jennifer-allsopp/state-feminism-co-opting-women%E2%80%99s-voices 'But what a shame there's no fundamental understanding that care work is in itself important, equal, dignified, a gift, honourable, and to be lifted up in recognition of its fundamental importance to the human condition. Women, in solidarity with their sisters, should be standing up to save all women's different choices and roles in life, not just the choice to be economically productive without a break!'
- Oliver James reference: see James, 2010
- 'Having it all': I suspect the final nail in the coffin for this myth was Allison Pearson's novel, *I Don't Know How She Does It*, 2002
- Gaby Hinsliff's suggestions: see Hinsliff, 2012

What are fathers for?
- Marion Salzman quote: Salzman, 2005
- Paternal involvement: e.g. see www.fatherhoodinstitute.org ('If you have a positive relationship with your dad, you're likely to do better at school, be happier, have high self-esteem, and even form better relationships when you're an adult', on front page of website, January 2014) and www.modernfatherhood.org, which began a long-term research programme in 2013
- New Dads: 'Baby Sling? All that Says Is "Eunuch on Board". . .', by Toby Young, *Night and Day*, 3/10/04
- Disadvantages of fatherlessness for boys: see for instance *Experiments in Living: The Fatherless Family* by Rebecca O'Neill for the think tank, Civitas, September 2002 http://www.civitas.org.uk/pubs/experiments.php

How technology comes between parents and children
- Restak quote: see Restak, 2004

- Arlie Hochschild quote: Martin Carnoy, *Sustaining the New Economy: Work, Family and Community in the Information Age* (Harvard University Press, 2002)
- The problems of Japanese salarymen: 'Family Support Policies in Japan' by Pat Boling www.yale.edu/leitner/pdf/Boling.doc

Happily ever after

- High level of family breakdown: research by the Organisation for Economic Cooperation and Development found the UK came fourth in the family breakdown league, after Belgium, Latvia and Estonia. 'UK high in OECD's family breakdown table' *BBC News*, 29/12/12 http://www.bbc.co.uk/news/uk-20863917 http://www.ons.gov.uk/ons/rel/vsob1/divorces-in-england-and-wales/2011/sty-what-percentage-of-marriages-end-in-divorce.html
- Couples choose to cohabit rather than marry: figures from the Office for National Statistics: see 'Most Children Will Be Born out of Wedlock by 2016' by Steven Swinford, *Daily Telegraph*, 10/7/13 (Incidentally, the census began in 1801)
- Marriage Foundation: see 'Marriage Breakdown a Scourge, Says High Court Judge' *BBC News*, 3/5/12 http://www.bbc.co.uk/news/education-17906017
- John Baker quote: personal interview, 2005
- Ono, Hiroshi, economist, 'Divorce in Japan: Why It Happens, Why It Doesn't', *EIJS Working Paper Series* 201, The European Institute of Japanese Studies, 2004

Breaking up is hard to do

- Emotional repercussions of divorce on children: Mooney, A., *Impact of Family Breakdown on Children's well-being*, (Institute of Education, London University), 2009
- Is divorce becoming less traumatic for children?: Neale, Bren and Flowerdew, Jennifer, *Parent Problems: Looking Back at Our Parents' Divorce: No.2*, (Young Voice, 2004)
- Charlotte's quote: Dodd, Celia and Guest, Katy, 'How To Survive Divorce Without Damaging Our Children', the *Independent on Sunday*, 10/10/04
- Long term results of divorce: Sun, Y., 'Family Environment and Adolescents' Well-being Before and After Parents' Marital Disruption: A Longitudinal Analysis', *Journal of Marriage and Family*, 63, pp. 697–713, 2001

Minimising the trauma

- Talking to teddy quote: Professors Douglas, Butler, Murch and Fincham, family law specialists, Cardiff and Keele Universities, UK, *Family Law Journal*, May 2001
- Dr James Kraut quote in 'Children Centered Divorce': www.divorcesource.com/FL/ARTICLES/kraut1.html

Children in the centre

- For advice on this and the following section I am indebted to family experts Pat Spungin and Jill Curtis: personal interviews 2005
- Information on Anna Wahlgren's work: Cecilia Weiler, personal interview, 2005. Since *Toxic Childhood* was first published, one of Wahlgren's books has been translated into English and is highly recommended (Wahlgren, 2009)

Forging a family

- I found the expression 'economy-friendly families' in the chapter by Richard Reeves in Diamond et al., 2004
- Family holidays: 'Parents Find Family Holidays More Stressful Than Work' by Sarah Gordon, *Daily Mail*, 15/5/09
- 'What makes a normal family' quote: see Hart and Risley, 1995

Mind the gap

- Family Nurse Project: www.fnp.nhs.uk
- 'When the Poor Get Cash' by Moises Velasquez-Manoff in *New York Times*, 19/1/14
- 'toxic time bomb' quote: see 'Mental Health Risk to Children Trapped in a Toxic Climate of Dieting, Pornography, School Stress' by Ian Johnson, *Independent*, 20/1/14
- For information on Finnish family policy see: 'Policy: The Case for Finland': www.york.ac.uk/inst/spru/research/nordic/finlandpoli.pdf
- Baby box: http://www.bbc.co.uk/news/magazine-22751415

CHAPTER 6: WHO'S LOOKING AFTER THE CHILDREN?

- Figures on women in the workforce from OECD, 2013: http://www.oecd-ilibrary.org/employment/employment-rate-of-women_20752342-table5

- Neuroscientific research on the developing brain: the most comprehensive survey to date was commissioned by the US government in the late 1990s and published in 2000: *From Neurons to Neighbourhoods*, see National Research Council, Institute of Medicine, 2000. For a clear summary of key issues in brain development for parents, see Herschkowitz and Herschkowitz, 2002

For love or money

- Information on childcare provision – see *Doing Better For Families:* http://www.oecd.org/social/soc/doingbetterforfamilies.htm. The 2011 update on *Babies and Bosses – Reconciling Work and Family Life* (OECD Publishing) Vol. 1: Australia, Denmark, The Netherlands, 12/11/02; Vol. 2: Austria, Ireland and Japan, 13/11/03; Vol. 3: New Zealand, Portugal, Switzerland, 05/11/04; Vol. 4: Canada, Finland, Sweden and the United Kingdom, 27/05/05
- Quote about Finland from Vol. 4 of *Babies and Bosses*, see above
- UK provision since 2005 has changed considerably since the OECD survey but, as in the USA, drives to improve educational attainment have significantly influenced the type of care provided (see 'Birth to three: the great daycare controversy' and succeeding sections, and Chapter 7)
- 'invisible curriculum of childcare' quote: Todd and Risley, 1995

Childcare on the cheap

- Falling birth rates: Lutz, W., Scherbor, S., Sanderson, W., 'The End of World Population Growth' *Nature* 412, 2001; Foreign Press Centre Japan Brief 10/6/05: *Concern Deepens over Continuing Slide of Birth Rate in Japan, No Stop in Sight:* www.fpcj.jp/e/ and *Doing Better for Families*, 2011
- German low birth rate reference: *Germany's New Children:* BBC Radio 4, 24/1/14
- Different sorts of mothers – see 'Fighting Over the Kinder', *Economist*, 13/6/13 http://www.economist.com/news/europe/21583676-cr-ches-trump-euro-and-much-else-german-election-campaign-fighting-over-kinder
- Early input pays off in closing the poverty gap: see Wilson and Picket, 2009

The hot-housing boom

- 1960s smart rats experiment at Berkeley by Mark Rosenzweig,

Edward Bennet and Marion Cleeves Diamond. See also Diamond, M.C., 'Response of the Brain to Enrichment,' in *New Horizons for Learning*, 2001: newhorizons.com
- Information on early hot-housing, Blakemore, Dr Sarah-Jayne, 'Life Before Three: Play or Hot-housing?' *RSA Journal*, February 2005
- Steve Petersen quote: see Bruer, 1999
- Canadian research into pushy mothers: Joussemet, M., Koestner, R., Lekes, N., Landry, R., 'A Longitudinal Study of the Relationship of Maternal Autonomy Support to Children's Adjustment and Achievement in School', *Journal of Personality*, Vol. 73, Issue 5, pp. 1215-1236, Oct 2005
- Recent UK summary quote: Blakemore and Frith, 2005

Home sweet home
- There is now an immense amount of literature on the significance of early attachment. My most recent updates have been through personal correspondence with Dr Suzanne Zeedyk and attendance at a series of seminars organised by the Scottish Universities Insight Institute on *The Well-Connected Child*: http://www.scottishinsight.ac.uk/Portals/50/ias%20documents/Reports/Well%20Connected%20SUII%20Narrative%20Report%2020091213.pdf

Personal versus institutional care
- Increase in grandparents providing care: survey by RIAS insurance group in 2013, 'Britain's Grandparent Army Swells by 60%': http://www.rias.co.uk/about-us/news-and-press-releases/britains-grand-parents-army-grows/ See also *The Role of Informal Childcare*, Nuffield Foundation, 2012

Birth to three: the great daycare controversy
- 'institutional love': see Greenspan and Brazelton, 2000
- Cortisol studies: see Ahnert, L., Gunnar, M.R., Lamb, M.E., Barthel, M., 'Transition to Child Care: Associations with Infant-Mother Attachment, Infant Negative Emotion, and Cortisol Elevation' *Child Development*, 2004 75(3) and 'Children's Elevated Levels of Cortisol at Daycare: A Review and Meta-Analysis' Vermer, H., van IJzendoom, M.H., *Early Childhood Research Quarterly*, Vol. 21, Issue 3, 2006 http://www.sciencedirect.com/science/article/pii/S0885200606000421

- Professor Alan Stein's research: 'The Influence of Different Forms of Childcare on Children's Emotional and Behaviour at School Entry', *Childcare: Heath and Development*, September 2013: http://onlinelibrary.wiley.com/doi/10.1111/j.1365-2214.2012.01421.x/abstract
- An earlier study: see Professor Ted Melhuish, quoted in 'The Effective Provision of Pre-School Education (EPPE) Project: Final Report', Institute of Education, University of London, November 2004
- Daycare Trust benefits of childcare: http://www.daycaretrust.org.uk/pages/benefits-of-childcare-and-early-learning.html. Note, however, the comment of a spokeswoman for the charity Working Families in the UK magazine *Children Now* 31/8 (6/9/05), 'What isn't measured in the research is the emotional health of the child'.
- Summary of research on favourable effects of pre-school education from three: Goodman, Alissa and Sianesi, Barbara, *Early Education and Children's Outcomes: How Long Does the Impact Last?*, (Institute for Fiscal Studies, July 2005)
- Dr Kathy Sylva was lead researcher in 'The Effective Provision of Pre-School Education (EPPE) Project' which reported in 2004. The quotes given here are from 'The Great Nursery Debate' by Amelia Gentleman, the *Guardian*, 2/10/10
- Oliver James advice: see James, 2010
- Penelope Leach: *Woman's Hour* interview, BBC Radio 4, 16/12/13.
- Steve Biddulph quote: see Biddulph, 2010

Three to six: the quest for quality pre-school provision

- Comparative school starting ages: 'What Age Should Children Start School' by Richard House in *The Mother* magazine, Sept/Oct 2013 (statistics taken from World Bank data, calculated from: http://data.worldbank.org/indicator/SE.PRM.AGES)
- The Dutch headteacher is right that it's the Anglo-Saxons. In 2008, the Welsh amended their curriculum for the under-sevens to a more European model, Northern Ireland has an 'enriched curriculum' for early years, and Scotland has a long tradition of child-centred early years provision. However, all these countries are inevitably influenced by policy decisions emanating from Westminster (for instance, the child-centred ethos of the Welsh Foundation Phase is now threatened by changes to the testing regime in early primary

schools). In the USA a previously child-centred approach to kindergarten teaching has become increasingly formalised.
- Concern re three groups of children: see research summaries
  and discussion on the website run by the Too Much Too Soon
  campaign: www.toomuchtoosoon.org.
- Early Years Foundation Stage in England: see https://www.gov.uk/
  early-years-foundation-stage
- Evidence on the 'schoolifying' effects of the EYFS: see House, 2010

Too Much Too Soon

- Wendy Ellyatt quotes: personal interview, 2014
- International league tables of achievement: Since the start of the
  twenty-first century, these regular league tables have had profound
  influence on educational policy. They are PISA (the Programme
  for International Student Assessment), PIRLS (the Progress in
  International Reading and Literacy), and TIMMS (Trends in
  International Mathematics and Science). In recent years the UK
  has consistently fallen in the PISA tables (latest report 2013),
  PIRLS results have been inconsistent between 2001 and 2011, and
  on TIMMs over the same period the UK has fallen in Science and
  plateaued in Maths.
- Overall message of international research and practice: see www.
  toomuchtoosoon.org and House, 2010. The latest summary I've
  read is 'Hard Evidence: At What Age Should Children Start School?'
  by Dr David Whitebread, Senior Lecturer in Psychology and
  Education at the University of Cambridge, 11/7/14: http://thecon-
  versation.com/hard-evidence-at-what-age-are-children-ready-for-
  school-29005
- 'Start School at Six, Key School Report Recommends' by Polly
  Curtis, the *Guardian*, 16/10/09
- The Cambridge Primary Review (sometimes known as the
  Alexander Report) was compiled between 2006 and 2009. See www.
  primaryreview.org.uk/
- No benefit in extending pre-school hours: Sylva, Kathy, Melhuish,
  Edward, Sammons, Pam, et al., 'The Effective Provision of
  Pre-School Education (EPPE) Project: Findings from the Pre-School
  Period', Institute of Education, University of London, March 2003
- Mary Bousted quote: 'Infants "Institutionalised" by too Early
  Childcare' by Graeme Paton, *Daily Telegraph*, 7/4/14:

www.telegraph.co.uk/education/educationnews/10749840/Infants-institutionalised-by-overexposure-to-childcare

Six to eleven: home from home?

- I'm indebted to the playwork specialist Sue Palmer, Head of School of Film, Television and the Performing Arts, Leeds Met University, for many of the ideas in this section: personal interview, 2005
- Paul Kirby's quotes: 'Lengthen School Days and Cut Holidays Says Former Tory Adviser' by Richard Adams in the *Guardian*, 30/1/14
- Christine Blower quote: 'Longer School Days, Shorter Holidays and 45 Hour Weeks "Could Be the Perfect Manifesto to Win the Tories the Next Election"' by Felicity Morse in the *Independent*, 30/1/14
- ATL quote: Dr Philip Dixon, Director of ATL Cymru, in 'Parents' Long Hours Mean Children Are Losing Out on Growing Up, Say Teachers' by Gareth Evans, *Wales Online*, 15/4/14: http://www.walesonline.co.uk/news/wales-news/parents-long-hours-means-children-6988197

Money won't buy me love

- Carl Honore quote: Honore, 2004

Mind the gap

- Findings of the White House conference: see Shonkoff and Phillips (eds.), 2000
- Savings made by early years help: see Diamond et al., 2004
- Quote re Headstart: Levitt and Dubner, 2005
- Study on long term effects of too formal an early start: Schweinhart, L. J., & Weikart, D.P., 'Lasting Differences: The High/Scope Preschool Curriculum Comparison study through age 23', *Monographs of the High/Scope Educational Research Foundation*, Ypsilanti, MI: High/Scope Press, 1997

CHAPTER 7: BEST DAYS OF THEIR LIVES

- Lyrical neuroscientists: e.g. Gopik et al. 1999; www.zerotothree.org

Shades of the prison house

- Wordsworth quote: *Intimations of Immortality from Recollections of Early Childhood*, 1803-1806
- Boys more likely to be affected by less-than-perfect early educational experiences than girls: there's evidence (e.g. Baron-Cohen, 2004, Palmer, 2008, 2013) that boys are generally slower in terms of social and language development, which are critical for success at school. In 2012–13, 60 per cent of girls in English schools achieved an overall 'good' level of achievement at the end of the Early Years Foundation Stage, compared with 44 per cent of boys: www.gov.uk/government/publications/early-years-foundation-stage-profile-results-2012-to-2013
- Cambridge Primary Review: www.primaryreview.org.uk/

Why reading is important in a multimedia age

- Reading's effect on the brain: Wolf, 2006, Blakemore and Frith, 2005; see also Donaldson, 1990.
- Neil Postman quotes: Postman, 1994
- JK Rowling's *Harry Potter* books have inspired millions of children to read.

Why Johnny still can't read … and how he might

- Phonological basis of reading problems: Snowling, 2000
- Up-to-date information on dyslexia is available from the Oxford University-based charity, The Dyslexia Research Trust, run by Professor John Stein: www.dyslexic.org.uk
- The major researcher into the effects of screen-based technology on attention skills is Dimitri Christakis, Professor of Pediatrics and Director of the Centre for Child Health, Behaviour and Development in Seattle. In 2011 he gave a TEDx talk on the subject: www.youtube.com/watch?v=BoT7qH_uVNo

Educational rat race

- In 2012, the three European countries that did best in the PISA tests (www.oecd.org/pisa) were Switzerland and Finland, both of which have a school starting age of seven, and the Netherlands where children start formal lessons at six.
- Six or seven is the starting age for almost 90 per cent of countries in the world: see 'What Age Should Children Start School' by Dr

Richard House in *The Mother* magazine, Sept/Oct 2012. The data for this article was from the World Bank: www.data.worldbank.org/indicator/SE.PRM.AGES

- Amplification as opposed to acceleration: I'm indebted for ideas in this section to Galina Dolya, researcher at the Russian Academy of Education and co-author (with Professor Nickolai Veraksa) of the *Key to Learning* developmental cognitive curriculum for early years: personal interviews, 2004-present

- Young Minds' warning about 'a mental health time bomb', January 2014: www.youngminds.org.uk/news/blog/1830

- Anorexia nervosa: 'The Silent Epidemic Hitting Top Girls' Schools' by Katie Gibbons in *The Times*, 22/2/14

- Early Years experts pronouncements about the unreliability of early standardised testing: e.g. Jan Dubeil of Early Excellence at the Westminster Education Forum, January 2014, pointed out that 'If it is very young children [you are testing], you are not going to get meaningful data'. The anecdote about four-year-olds was recounted at the same conference, referenced in 'Chalk Talk' by Richard Garner, the *Independent*, 5/2/14

- Thomas Jefferson quote: quoted from a letter to J. Bannister, Paris, 15 Oct 1785, contained in *Memoirs, Correspondence, and Private Papers of Thomas Jefferson*, Vol. 1, Thomas Jefferson Randolph, ed., 1829, pp. 345–347.

- Homer Simpson quote from *I Love Lisa*

Winners, losers ... and cheats

- Professor Joe Frost quote from 'Bridging the Gaps: Children in a Changing Society', University of Texas, 2003

- Warwick Mansell's work: personal interview, February 2014 and Mansell, 2007; see also www.educationbynumbers.org.uk/

- Criticism from QCA ('the assessment load is ... far greater than other countries, and it is not necessary for purpose': see Claxton, 2008), National Audit Office (*The Use of Sanctions and Rewards in the Public Sector*, September 2008), OECD ('high stakes tests can have negative consequences for educational outcomes': 'Reforming Education in England' OECD Economic Surveys, United Kingdom, 2011)

What is pupil progress?

- Kemnal Academies: thanks to Warwick Mansell for alerting me to this story; see 'More Headteachers Vanish from Large Academy Chain' by Warwick Mansell, the *Guardian*, 28/1/14 and www.getsurrey.co.uk/news/local-news/weyfield-primary-academy-parents-shocked-6495000
- Simon Woods' abrupt departure is catalogued by a Weyfield School parent in her blog: http://pinchypants.com/2014/01/08/the-mysterious-case-of-the-disappearing-head-teacher/

One step forward, two steps back

- Long-term London University Study: see 'Have the Norms for Volume and Heaviness for Year 7 Changed Since the mid-70s?' Report to the ESRC by Michael Shayer and Philip Adie, January 2006. Explanation and quote: personal conversation with Michael Shayer, 2007

Triumph and disaster

Since 2009, South Korea, Singapore, Hong Kong and other Far Eastern countries have dominated the PIRLS and PISA leagues, but according to local commentators this test success comes at a price. See for example: 'The Singapore Rat Race Starts at Age Seven' by Singapore journalist Elaine Ee on CNN travel, 2011: www.travel.cnn.com/singapore/life/tell-me-about-it/elaine-ee-ridiculous-rat-race-singapore-starts-7-years-old-132289; 'OECD Report: Korea's School System a Pressure Cooker for Children' by Andrew Salmon, *Daily Telegraph*, 2/12/13: www.telegraph.co.uk/education/10491289/OECD-education-report-Koreas-school-system-a-pressure-cooker-for-children.html; 'Hong Kong's Deadly Exam Culture' by Alastair Sharp, *South China Morning Post*, 21/3/13: www.scmp.com/comment/insight-opinion/article/1195545/hong-kongs-deadly-exam-culture: 'Asia's Parents Suffering "Education Fever"' by Yojana Sharma, BBC *News*, 22/10/13: http://www.bbc.co.uk/news/business-24537487

The great e-learning revolution

- For more about Seymour Papert's work: http://www.papert.org/ and http://www.mamamedia.com
- Silicon Valley school 'A Silicon Valley School that Doesn't Compute' by Matt Richtel, *New York Times*, 23/10/11

- Info on technology spending: 'Schools Say Yes to Tablet Computers as ICT Spending Soars' by Richard Vaughan, *Times Educational Supplement*, 20/9/13: http://www.tes.co.uk/article. aspx?storycode=6358755
- Munich Research: Fuchs, T., Woessmann, L., 'Computers and Student Learning: Bivariate and Multivariate Evidence on the Availability and Use of Computers at Home and at School' October 2004, presented at the Royal Economic Society's 2005 Annual Conference at the University of Nottingham, 23/3/05
- The great calculator scandal: see Ben Preston, 'Inquiry into Pupils' Use of Calculators' *The Times*, 23/5/95
- Greg Pearson quote: Alliance for Childhood, 2004

Who's educating the children?
- Diane Ravitch arguments and quotes: see Ravitch, 2013
- Many British educators are concerned about privatisation: everyone I've met recently in English educational circles is convinced that this is the long-term policy of at least one major political party, and at the time of writing the UK press is beginning to mention it too, e.g. 'Secret Memo Shows Michael Gove's Plan for Privatization of Academies' by Jane Merrick, *Independent on Sunday*, 10/2/14: http://www.independent.co.uk/news/education/education-news/secret-memo-shows-michael-goves-plan-for-privatisation-of-academies-8488552.html
- Pasi Sahlberg: see Sahlberg, 2012
- Presentation at the Scottish Parliament: Finnish Lessons, 2/5/12

Parents and teachers
- Warwick Mansell quote: personal interview, February 2014
- Margaret Morrissey quote: personal interview, February 2014; see also www.parentsoutloud.com
- I am indebted for ideas about this section to Hilary Wilce, author of *Help your Child Succeed at School*: personal interview, 2005

Bullying tactics
- Bullying definition: www.direct.gov.org.uk, 2008
- The 'no blame' approach to bullying, trialled (often unsuccessfully) around the UK, was supposedly based on the principles of restorative justice. Problems appear to have arisen because its pro-

ponents often confused restorative justice with 'mediation', see the paper 'Mediation versus Restorative Justice Practices' Brookes, D. and McDonagh, I., on www.restorativejusticescotland.org.uk/html/mediation.html. Where restorative justice techniques are appropriately used in schools – alongside sanctions for bad behaviour – they can be highly effective.

Dealing with discipline
- United Nations Convention on the Rights of the Child, 1989: see www.unicef.org/crc
- Nurture groups: see Bennathan and Boxall, 2002, Boxall 2002
- 'red carpet treatment': in Wilce 2004, the educational journalist Hilary Wilce argues that 'teachers and parents come from different corners, and have different goals. Parents want red carpet treatment for their children; teachers want to keep their classroom show on the road. Parents get frustrated when schools don't take them seriously; schools get hostile and defensive when parents make demands they think unreasonable.' The only way to avoid this situation is better real-life relationships between parents and their children's teachers.

Mind the gap
- 2014: 10 per cent of children are now educated privately in the US: see www.statisticbrain.com/private-school-statistics; and 7 per cent in the UK: see www.isc.co.uk/research. There has also been an increase in parents removing children from school and teaching them at home: see http://www.home-education.org.uk/ and http://www.nheri.org/
- Figures for home schooling in the USA: www.a2zhomeschooling.com and in the UK www.home-education.org.uk

CHAPTER 8: WORD ON THE STREET

- Influence of wider community: Pinker, 2003

From creative play to toy consumption
- The case for 'real play': see Rich, D., Drummond, M.J. and Myer, C., 2014 and Gray, 2014

- Move to techno-play: see also Palmer, 2009, 2013
- 'attentional inertia': Dr Aric Sigman, speech at *The Child: The True Foundation* conference, London, 12/6/10
- American Academy of Pediatrics recommendations: see *Media and Children* pages on the AAP website at http://www.aap.org/en-us/advocacy-and-policy/aap-health-initiatives/pages/media-and-children.aspx
- UN Convention on the Rights of the Child can be found on the UNICEF website: http://www.unicef.org/crc/
- Quotes from UN General comment No. 17 (2013) on the right of the child to rest, leisure, play, recreational activities, cultural life and the arts (article. 31) are taken from this passage: 'Children's play is any behaviour, activity or process initiated, controlled and structured by children themselves; it takes place whenever and wherever opportunities arise. Caregivers may contribute to the creation of environments in which play takes place, but play itself is non-compulsory, driven by intrinsic motivation and undertaken for its own sake, rather than as a means to an end. Play involves the exercise of autonomy, physical, mental or emotional activity, and has the potential to take infinite forms, either in groups or alone. These forms will change and be adapted throughout the course of childhood. The key characteristics of play are fun, uncertainty, challenge, flexibility and non-productivity. Together, these factors contribute to the enjoyment it produces and the consequent incentive to continue to play. While play is often considered non-essential, the Committee reaffirms that it is a fundamental and vital dimension of the pleasure of childhood, as well as an essential component of physical, social, cognitive, emotional and spiritual development.'

The strangers on the screen

- Background on marketing to children in this and subsequent chapters: see Schor, 2004, Linn, 2005, Gregory, 2009, Mayo and Nairn, 2009
- James McNeal quote: see McNeal, 1992
- Information on the Campaign for a Commercial-Free Childhood: personal interview with Susan Linn, 2014. See also www.commercialfreechildhood.org

Children as customers

- For further information on guilt money, pester power and 'winning for brands': see Schor, 2004, Lindstrom, 2003
- Parent quote re peer pressure: from Bailey, 2011
- Children's influence on car choice: research by ad agency Millward Brown, cited on BRANDchild website: www.dualbook.com
- 100 per cent children affecting food purchases: Griffin Bacal ad agency survey cited in 'Preschoolers: an Emerging Consumer Set' *Kidscreen: Reaching Children Through Entertainment*, 1999: www. kidscreen.com
- Sales decline by a third if children don't ask: Idell, C., 'The Nag Factor', Western Media Initiative, 1998
- Brand awareness at different ages: Lindstrom, 2003
- Nancy Shalek quote: quoted in 'Why They Whine: How Corporations Prey on Our Children' in *Mothering*, November-December 1999

Sugar and spice...

- Marketeers' appreciation of evolutionary gender differences: see Del Vecchio, 1997
- Barbie website: www.everythinggirl.com
- Little Kitty website: www.hellokitty.com
- Disney princesses: the earliest commentary I've found is 'What's Wrong with Cinderella?' by Peggy Orenstein, *New York Times*, 24/12/06 and the phenomenon is explored in detail in Thomas, 2007
- Tween culture: see 'Marketing and Tweens: BFF', Alycia de Mesa, *brandchannel*, 10/10/05, Palmer, 2013
- Girlsgogames: www.girlsgogames.co.uk
- Bratz dolls: www.bratz.com
- Monster High dolls: www.monsterhigh.com
- Most popular websites among the under-tens: Childwise research pocket fact sheet, 2011–42012. See also: http://www.huffingtonpost.com/michael-gregg/8-scary-social-network-sites-every-parents-should-know_b_4178055.html?

... And all things nice

- Further background on KAGOY: Lindstrom, 2003, Schor, 2004
- How the sexualisation of children became normalised: The

Sexualisation of Young People Review, Linda Papadopoulos (see below in 'Letting children be children') and Walter, 2010

- Children's attitudes to their bodies: *Reflections on Dissatisfaction with Body Image*, published by the All Party Parliamentary Group on Body Image and Central YMCA, May 2012: www.ncb.org.uk/media/861233/appg_body_image_final
- Abi Moore quote: 'Role Models: Someone to Look up to' by Kira Cochrane, the *Guardian*, 31/10/10

Snips and Snails . . .

- Background on marketing to the parents of boys, and Bob the Builder quote: Gregory, 2009
- The case for computer games: see Johnson, 2005
- Background on dominion and computer games: see Linn, 2005
- Promotional material on X-rated computer games: mothers who would like to find out more about Grand Theft Auto can Google GTA and spend time on the latest 'walkthrough guide', bearing in mind that the content is toned down for general viewing and that (at least when I last checked it on 17/4/14) all anyone needs do to sample the fun is enter a date of birth that makes them over 18.

. . . and puppy dogs tails

- Boys who want to wear popular labels: see Mayo, 2005
- Background on Nickelodeon: see www.nick.com
- The Nickelodeon 'empowerment' agenda is explained Kevin Sandler's 'A Kid's Gotta Do what a Kid's Gotta Do' in *Nickelodeon Nation*, reviewed in *Academia*, February 2005: www.ybp.com/acad/reviews
- Juliet Shor quote: Shor, 2005
- Mark Crispin Miller quote: from *The Merchants Of Cool* broadcast on PBS, 27/2/01 (full transcript on www.pbs.org/wgbh/pages/frontline/shows/cool/etc/script.html)
- Austen-Smith, David and Fryer Jr., Roland G., *The Economics of Acting White*, National Bureau of Economic Research working paper, USA 2003

Heroes and villains

- Fictional character survey by Tomy Toys, reported on *CBBC News* 24/4/03

- Bart Simpson quote: www.thesimpsonsquotes.com
- Children and irony: see McGhee, Paul, *Humor: Its Origins and Development*, WH Freeman, 1979
- Britney Spears story: see Linn, 2005

Letting children be children

- Books outlining the extent of the problem: Shor, 2004, Linn, 2005, Mayo, 2005, Mayo and Nairn, 2009
- UK anti-commercialisation of childhood campaigns by the left-wing think tank Compass 2007, the National Union of Teachers 2008, the Mothers Union 2010. The most recent, *Leave Our Kids Alone*, was launched in 2013 on Facebook (LeaveRkidsalone)
- Government reports: Buckingham, 2009: http://webarchive.nation-alarchives.gov.uk/20130401151715/https://www.education.gov.uk/publications/standard/publicationdetail/Page1/DCSF-00669-2009 ; Papadopoulos, 2010: http://webarchive.nationalarchives.gov.uk/+/http:/www.homeoffice.gov.uk/documents/Sexualisation-of-young-people2835.pdf?view=Binary Bailey, 2011: www.gov.uk/government/uploads/system/uploads/attachment_data/file/175418/Bailey_Review.pdf
- ParentPort: www.parentport.org.uk
- Agnes Nairn quotes: personal interview, 2014

Turning the tide

- Countries which have already banned marketing to children: see Bailey, 2011 and www.leaveourkidsalone.org
- American Academy of Pediatrics recommendations: see above in 'The death of creativity'
- Agnes Nairn and 'the precautionary principle': personal interview 2014
- John Savage quote: from 'Time Up For Teenagers', *RSA Journal*, Spring 2014 and on http://www.thersa.org/fellowship/journal/features/features/time-up-for-the-teenager

Mind the gap

- Details on and quotes from the 2011 riots: 'Reading the Riots' analysis by *Guardian* journalists in partnership with the London School of Economics, 2011–2012: www.theguardian.com/uk/series/reading-the-riots

- Camilla Batmanghelidjh quote: Mayo, 2005
- Inequalities of wealth: 'Pay Gap Widening to Victorian Levels' by Graham Snowden, the *Guardian*, 15/8/11 and 'Why Inequality Leads to Collapse' by Stewart Lansley, *Observer*, 5/2/12

CHAPTER 9: THE ELECTRONIC VILLAGE

Spinning along with Moore's Law

- Aric Sigman quote: personal interview, 2014. For more information see: www.aricsigman.com
- Information in 2012 BMJ document: 'Time for a View on Screen Time' by Aric Sigman, *Archives of Disease in Childhood*, 2012

The electronic babysitter

- Tots' TV in Japan: 1986 survey by Kodaira, S.I., 'Television's Role in Early Childhood Education in Japan' Tokyo Broadcasting Culture Research Institute, 1987
- American Academy of Pediatrics recommendations re screen time were reviewed in 2013: www.aap.org/en-us/advocacy-and-policy/aap-health-initiatives/pages/media-and children.aspx
- Some of the studies behind the medical advice on zero-screen time:
- the most prominent US researcher in this field is Dimitri Christakis (Associate Professor of Pediatrics at University of Washington and Children's Hospital in Seattle). Two studies are particularly relevant: (1) 'Early Television Exposure and Subsequent Attentional Problems in Children' by Christakis, D.A., Zimmerman F.J., DiGuiseppe, D.L., McCarthy, C.A., *Pediatrics*, 2004 (2) 'Associations Between Media Viewing and Language Development in Children under Age Two' by Zimmerman, F.J., Christakis, D.A. and Meltzoff, A.N., *Journal of Pediatrics*, 2007
- links with ASD are difficult to establish, largely because of the chicken and egg problem, and the only data-driven evidence so far has been 'Does Television Cause Autism?' by Michael Waldman, Sean Nicholson and Nodir Adilov, published by the National Bureau for Economic Research (Working Paper 12632), 2006 (since this is such an emotive subject, it predictably caused a media firestorm)
- general review: Anderson, D.R. and Pempek, T.A., 'Television

and Very Young Children', *American Behavioural Scientist*, 2005:
summary and a list of other studies can be found on http://abs.
sagepub.com/content/48/5/505.short
- See also many more recent studies sited in Sigman article, above.
- Smart rats researcher: Dr Marian Cleeves Diamond, Professor
of Neuroanatomy at the University of California, addressing
the Department for Health and Human Services Conference,
'Television and the Preparation of the Mind for Learning', 1992:
Quoted in Winn, 2000
- Default activity quote: Dr David Walsh, President of the National
Institute on Media and the Family, 2002: www.MediaFamily.org

From default to dysfunction
- Dr Richard Graham quote: see 'Toddlers Becoming so Addicted to
iPads They Require Therapy' by Victoria Ward, *Telegraph*, 21/4/13
www.telegraph.co.uk/technology/10008707/Toddlers-becoming-
so-addicted-to-iPads-they-require-therapy.html
- *The Shallows* (see Carr, 2010)
- *InRealLife* (see Kidron, 2013)

Technology for tots
- Positive effects of good educational TV: e.g. Huston, A.C., Wright,
J.C. et al. 'Development of TV Viewing Patterns in Early Childhood:
A Longitudinal Investigation' in *Developmental Psychology*, 26 1990;
Watching Children Watch Television and the Creation of Blues Clues, Daniel
R. Andersen in Hendershot 2004; *Deferred Imitation from Television
during Infancy*, Rachel Barr, Georgetown Early Learning Project,
Georgetown University, 28/10/05
- National Literacy Trust study (interestingly, in partnership with
Pearson, an international publisher of screen-based learning
materials) by Suzie Formby 'Children's Use of Technology in the
Early Years': there are two papers (1) 'Parents' perspectives' and (2)
'Practitioners' Perspectives', March 2014: www.literacytrust.org.uk
- Clare Elstow, Director of Pre-School, BBC: personal interview, 2005
- Aric Sigman quote: personal interview, 2014
- *SpongeBob Squarepants* research: Lillard, A.S. and Peterson, J., 'The
Immediate Impact of Different Types of Television on Young
Children's Executive Function', *Pediatrics*, 2011

Books versus screens

- For general background on the neuroscience of reading, see Wolf, 2008
- Merlin Donald quote: see Donald, 2001
- Ian Jukes quotes: transcribed at the 'Bridging the Gap conference', International School of Yokohama, Japan, 29/10/07
- Aric Sigman quote: personal interview 2014

Look up!

- The splintering family (and the rise of the electronic bedsit): see Chapter 9 and associated notes in first edition of *Toxic Childhood*, 2006. This chapter also contains information on the Japanese phenomenon *hikikomori*, which is still of great concern but had to be omitted in this edition due to lack of space.
- Ofcom Report: *Children's and Parents' Media Use*, 3/10/13. These are now published annually and are a stunning illustration of the effects of Moore's Law
- 'container in the hall' for handheld devices: I'm indebted to Professor Andy Phippen of the University of Plymouth for first pointing this idea out to me (and for other background information about children's media use): personal interview, 2014
- High-tech parents: 'Steve Jobs was a Low-tech Parent' by Nick Bilton, *New York Times*, 10/9/14

The dark side of the village

- NSPCC report on cyberbullying, 2013: www.nspcc.org.uk/Inform/ resourcesforprofessionals/bullying/bullying_statistics_wda85732. html. See also information on www.beatbullying.org
- 50 per cent of British teenagers and porn, 2014: 'Mobile Porn Access "Damaging" Children and Teenagers' by Jonathan Blake, *BBC Newsbeat*, 11/2/14: www.bbc.co.uk/newsbeat/26122390
- Tanya Byron quote: from 'Safer Children in a Digital World' review for the UK government, 2008, revised 2010: www.dera.ioe. ac.uk/7332/1/Final%20Report%20Bookmarked.pdf
- Netnanny: www.netnanny.com

Identity, privacy and sharing

- Susan Greenfield, Professor of Pharmacology at Oxford University, has written and spoken widely on the question of identity in a digital world (e.g. Greenfield, 2009)

- For more on the question of identity and social media: see Gardner and Davis, 2013
- 'See me mummy…' quote: from a YouTube video 'Susan Greenfield on Storytelling', 23/1/13
- Mark Zuckerberg quote: from 'Privacy No Longer a Social Norm, says Facebook's Founder' by Bobbie Johnson, the *Guardian*, 11/1/10: www.theguardian.com/technology/2010/jan/11/facebook-privacy
- Half of employers: 'Half of Employers Reject Potential Worker after Looking at Facebook Pages' in *Daily Telegraph*, 11/1/10
- Burglars: 'Facebook and Twitter Users Could Be Targeted by Burglars' by Chris Irvine, *Daily Telegraph*, 27/8/09
- Phishers: 'Phishing Attacks Target Users of Facebook, Other Social Networks' by Robert Westerfelt in *SearchSecurity*, 8/9/10: www. searchsecurity.techtarget.com/news/1519804/Phishing-attacks-target-users-of-Facebook-other-social-networks
- Paris Brown story: 'No Further Action to Be Taken over Paris Brown Twitter Comments', Press Association, the *Guardian*, 21/4/13:www. theguardian.com/uk/2013/apr/21/paris-brown-no-action-twitter-comments
- Eric Schmidt quote from 'Google's Eric Schmidt: Drone Wars, Virtual Kidnap and Privacy for Kids' by Charles Arthur, the *Guardian*, 29/1/13: www.theguardian.com/technology/2013/jan/29/google-eric-schmidt-drone-wars-privacy

O tempora, o mores
- See also Palmer, 2013, Chapter 10
- Batman reference: See also, Palmer, 2009, Chapter 10

A question of rights
- Quote from Professor Kevin Browne (Forensic and Family Psychology Unit) and Catherine Hamilton-Giachritsis, Birmingham University: 'The Influence of Violent Media on Children and Adolescents – a Public Health Approach', *The Lancet*, 19/02/05
- 2000 institutions calling for restriction on violence: American Academy of Pediatrics, *Joint Statement on the Impact of Entertainment Violence on Children*, presented at the Congressional Public Health Summit, Washington DC, 26/7/00 www.aap.org/advocacy/releases/jstmtevc.htm. For further details on desensitisation research see 'Effects of Televised Violence on Aggression' in *The Handbook of*

Children and Media, Dorothy G. Singer and Jerome L. Singer (eds.), Thousand Oaks, CA: Sage, 2001

- Arguments against screen violence/aggression link: e.g. see 'Playing with Fire?' Tony Reichardt, *Nature*, 24/7/03
- The three effects of screen violence are listed in the AAP et al. statement above
- Postman reference: see Postman, 1994

Inching in the right direction?

- The journalist logging on to a chatroom was Louise Tickell, see 'How Police Investigators Are Catching Paedophiles Online', *Guardian Professional*, 22/8/11: www.theguardian.com/social-care-network/2012/aug/22/police-investigators-catching-paedophiles-online
- CEOP website: www.thinkuknow.co.uk
- Former editor of *Loaded*: Marin Daubney in *Porn on the Brain*, a Channel 4 documentary, 13/10/13: www.youtube.com/watch?v=3prZNYccxek
- Online porn block: 'Online Pornography to Be Blocked by Default, PM Announces', *BBC News*, 22/7/13

And now the good news…

- I am indebted to Dr Jackie Marsh, Sheffield University, Professor Andy Phippen, Plymouth University, and Jon Audain, University of Winchester, for their help in reviewing the overall positive effects of technology on children's development: personal interviews, 2005 and 2014
- American psychologist Paul Bloom, see Bloom, 2004

Village wisdom

- Family help websites: these are referenced throughout *Toxic Childhood*
- *Les maternelles*: see www.lesmaternelles.com
- BBC *Child of Our Time*: www.bbc.co.uk/childofourtime and Open University Open Learn site: www.open.edu/openlearn/

The medium is the message

- The discussion about the circularity of culture's influence on brain development, and the influence of the human mind on culture is a long-standing one. A recent, extremely helpful contribution comes from Professor Iain McGilchrist, in *The Master and his Emissary*, McGilchrist, 2009. I've been fascinated by the subject since reading Marshall McLuhan in my late teens and Neil Postman (especially *The Disappearance of Childhood*) during my years as a literacy specialist. The argument here is my best shot at explaining why a too-early introduction to screen-based technology isn't a good idea.

- Edward Tenner quote: 'Searching for Dummies' Edward Tenner, *New York Times*, 26/3/06. It's also quoted in the article 'Our "Deep Reading" Brain: Its Digital Evolution Poses Questions' by literacy specialist Maryann Wolf, *The Neiman Reports*, Harvard, Summer 2010, which opens with the ominous words: 'Will we lose the "deep reading" brain in a digital culture? No one knows – yet': www.nieman.harvard.edu/reports/article/102396/Our-Deep-Reading-Brain-Its-Digital-Evolution--Poses-Questions.aspx. See also Wolf, 2008

CHAPTER 10: MANNERS MAKETH MAN

The parental balancing act

- Authoritative parenting: for summary of research see Martin, 2005, Lee and Lee, 2009, Larzelere, Morris and Harrist, 2013 and Dr Gwen Dewar's 2010 article, 'The Authoritative Parenting Style: Warmth, Rationality and High Standards: a Guide for the Science-Minded Parent': www.parentingscience.com/authoritative-parenting-style.html. Although most researchers use the term 'authoritative', the terminology for other parenting styles varies from study to study. I've chosen what seemed to me the simplest, clearest vocabulary for the concepts involved. The conclusion that an authoritative parenting style is most successful applies to child-rearing in westernised democratic societies – in different cultural circumstances other styles may be more appropriate.
- 'Man hands on misery to man': Philip Larkin from 'This be the verse' in *High Windows*, 1974

The case of the missing goal posts

- 'The rich man in his castle' is a verse from the hymn 'All Things Bright and Beautiful' by Cecil Alexander's *Hymns for Little Children*, 1848

- The Freudian theory that frustration of childhood desires leads to neurosis has been hotly contested by many psychotherapists, including his daughter Anna. In lectures at Harvard, Anna Freud claimed her father actually said that 'the incapability to overcome frustration can lead to neurosis', i.e. that children need to learn the self-regulatory skills that allow them to deal with frustrated wishes. Thanks to Professor Norbert Herschkowitz for this reference.
- United Nations Convention on the Rights of the Child, 1989: see www.unicef.org/crc
- Jean Twenge's work: see Twenge and Campbell, 2009, and a 2013 summary at http://www.psychologytoday.com/blog/the-narcissism-epidemic
- For a summary of Carol Dweck's work on fixed and growth mindsets see https://alumni.stanford.edu/get/page/magazine/article/?article_id=32124
- For a summary of Martin Seligman's work on learned helplessness see http://www.education.com/reference/article/learned-helplessness/

The pursuit of happiness
- Veenhoven, R., World Database of Happiness, *Distributional Findings in Nations*, Erasmus University Rotterdam, 2005: www.worlddata-baseofhappiness.eur.nl
- Richard Layard quote: from Layard, 2005
- The Action for Happiness website was set up in 2010 by Lord Richard Layard (Professor of Economics at the London School of Economics), Antony Seldon (political biographer and Master of Wellington College) and Geoff Mulgan (CEO of NESTA, political strategist and founder of the Demos think tank). It provides research-based evidence about the science of well-being and a variety of resources: www.actionforhappiness.org
- Robert Puttnam and social capital: see Puttnam 2000
- Quote re social networks: from Puttnam and Feldstein, 2003; see also www.bowlingalone.com and www.bettertogether.org

Getting along in the real world
- Research at London School of Economics: 'What predicts a successful life? A life-course model of well-being' by Layard R, Clark AE, Cornaglia F, Powdthavee N, Vernoit J., *Economic Journal*, November 2014

Social capital begins at home
- Commission for Children at Risk reference: from Herschkowitz and Herschkowitz, 2002
- Richard Layard quote: personal interview, 2005

Knowledge is power
- Julia Roberts quote: *Oprah Winfrey Show*, USA 10/02/05
- Triple P parenting programme: www.triplep.net; Incredible Years parenting programme: www.incredibleyears.com

Can Nanny know best?
- German dismay at suggestions of Minister Renate Künäst: *Deutsche Welle*, 17/6/04: www.smh.com.au
- Julia Neuberger quote: Neuberger, 2005

Mind the gap
- Information on income distribution: 'From Rich to Richer: the Rise of the Top 1%', Philip Inman, the *Guardian*, 2/5/14 http://www.theguardian.com/business/economics-blog/2014/may/02/from-rich-to-richer-rise-of-the-top-1-per-cent
- Quote re flawed statistics from 'Balls Test Answer? More of the Futile Top-Down Plans that Labour Loves', Jenni Russell, the *Guardian* 28/7/08

CONCLUSION: DETOXING CHILDHOOD

- Masters of the Universe: see 'Greenwich Time', Tom Wolfe, *New York Times*, 27/9/08: www.nytimes.com/2008/09/28/opinion/28wolfe.html?_r=0

The rebalancing act
- Thomas Piketty quote from 'Thomas Piketty's Capital' by Paul Maso, the *Guardian*, 28/4/14: www.theguardian.com/books/2014/may/02/thomas-piketty-capital-in-the-twenty-first-century-french-economist

The perfect storm
- Rebecca Walker film: www.youtube.com/watch?v=-i8cYU9Yh7A

Detoxing childhood

- Winnicott's 'good enough' parenting – see 'In Search of the
  Good-Enough Mother', Jennifer Kunst, *Psychology Today*, 9/5/12:
  www.psychologytoday.com/blog/headshrinkers-guide-the-
  galaxy/201205/in-search-the-good-enough-mother

BiBLiOGRAPHY

Abbott, John and Ryan, Terry, *The Unfinished Revolution: Learning, Human Behaviour, Community and Political Paradox* (Network Educational Press, 2000)

Adams, Sian and Moyles, Janet, *Images of Violence – Responding to Children's Representations of the Violence They See* (Featherstone Education Ltd, 2005)

Aitchison, Jean, *The Seeds of Speech – Language Origin and Evolution* (Cambridge University Press, 2000)

Alliance for Childhood, *Tech Tonic* (Alliance for Childhood, 2004)

Asher, Rebecca, *Shattered: Modern Motherhood and the Illusion of Equality* (Harvill Secker, 2011)

Bainbridge, David, *Teenagers, A Natural History* (Portobello Books, 2009)

Banyard, Kate, *The Equality Illusion: The Truth about Women and Men Today* (Faber and Faber, 2010)

Baron-Cohen, Simon, *The Essential Difference: Men, Women and the Extreme Male Brain* (Allen Lane, 2003)

Bayley, Ros and Broadbent, Lynn, *Flying Start with Literacy* (Network Educational Press, 2005)

Bennathan, Marion and Boxall, Marjorie, *Effective Intervention in Primary Schools: Nurture Groups*, Second edition (London: David Fulton Publishers, 2002)

Biddulph, Steve, *Raising Babies: Why Your Love Is Best* (Harper Thorsons, 2006)

Biddulph, Steve, *Raising Boys: Why Boys are Different, and How to Help Them Become Happy and Well-balanced Men* (HarperCollins, 1998)

Biddulph, Steve, *Steve Biddulph's Raising Girls* (Harper, 2014)

Blakemore, Sarah-Jane and Frith, Uta, *The Learning Brain – Lessons for Education* (Blackwell Publishing, 2005)

Bloom, Paul, *Descartes' Baby: How Child Development Explains What Makes Us Human* (William Heinemann, 2004)

Bloom, Paul, *How Children Learn the Meanings of Words* (A Bradford Book, The MIT Press, 2000)

Blythman, Joanna, *The Food Our Children Eat: How to Get Children to Like Good Food*

(Fourth Estate, 2011)

Bourke, Joanna, *Fear – A Cultural History* (Virago Press, 2005)

Boxall Marjorie, *Nurture Groups in Schools: Principles and Practice* (London: Paul Chapman, 2002)

Boyce, Sioban, *Not Just Talking: Helping Your Baby Communicate from Day One* (Not Just Talking, 2009)

Boyce, Sioban, *Not Just Talking: Identifying Non-verbal Communication Difficulties – A Life Changing Approach* (Speechmark, 2012)

Bradley, Alan and Beveridge, Jody, *How to Help the Children Survive the Divorce* (Foulsham, 2004)

Brazelton, T.B. and Greenspan, S., *The Irreducible Needs of Young Children* (De Capo Press, 2000)

Bruer, John, *The Myth of the First Three Years*, (Free Press 1999)

Byron, Dr Tanya and Baveystock, Sacha, *Little Angels: The Essential Guide to Transforming Your Family Life and Having More Fun with Your Children* (BBC Books, 2003)

Cairns, Warwick, *How to Live Dangerously: Why We Should All Stop Worrying and Start Living* (Macmillan, 2008)

Cantor, Joanne, *Mommy, I'm Scared: How TV and Movies Frighten Children and What We Can Do To Protect Them* (Harvest Books, 2001)

Carey, Tanith, *Taming the Tiger Parent: How To Put Your Child's Well-being First in a Competitive World* (Robinson, 2014)

Carr, Nicholas, *The Shallows: How the Internet Is Changing the Way We Think, Read and Remember* (Atlantic Books, 2010)

Cohen, Laurence J., *Playful Parenting* (Ballantyne Books, 2001)

Clark, Eric, *The Real Toy Story* (Black Swan, 2007)

Claxton, Guy, *What's The Point Of School? Rediscovering the Heart of Education* (One World, 2008)

Cunningham, Hugh, *The Invention of Childhood* (BBC Books, 2006)

Curtis, Adam, *The Century of the Self* (BBC, 2002; available on Google Video)

Curtis, Adam, *The Trap: What's Happened to Our Dream of Freedom?* (BBC, 2007; available on Google Video)

Curtis, Jill, *Find Your Way Through Divorce* (Hodder and Stoughton, 2001)

Damasio, Antonio, *Descartes' Error: Emotion, Reason and the Human Brain* (Vintage, 2006)

Danks, Fiona and Schofield Jo, *The Wild City Book: Fun Things to Do Outdoors in Towns and Cities* (Frances Lincoln, 2014)

Deering, Julia, *The Playful Parent: Seven Ways to Happier, Calmer, More Creative Under-fives* (HarperCollins, 2014)

Dolya, Galina, *Key to Learning: The Technology of Child Development* (G.D.H. Publishing, 2008)

Donald, Merlin, *A Mind So Rare: The Evolution of Human Consciousness* (W.W. Norton, 2001)

Donaldson, Margaret, *Children's Minds* (Fontana Press, 1978)

Donaldson, Margaret, *Human Minds: An Exploration* (Allen Lane, 1992)

Donaldson, Margaret, *Sense and Sensibility: Some Thoughts on the Teaching of Literacy*

(Reading and Language Information Centre, 1989)

Editors of Scientific American, *The Scientific American Book of The Brain* (Introduction of Antonio R Damasio) (The Lyons Press, an imprint of The Globe Pequot Press, 1999)

Eberstadt, Mary, *Home Alone America: The Hidden Toll of Daycare, Behavioural Drugs and Other Parent Substitutes* (Sentinel; Penguin Group USA, 2004)

Elkind, Ph.D, David, *The Hurried Child: Growing Up Too Fast Too Soon* (Da Capo Press; Perseus Books Group, 2001)

Erikson, Martha Farrell and Aird, Enola G., *The Motherhood Study: Fresh Insights on Mother's Attitudes and Concerns* (Institute for American Values, 2005)

Faber, Adele and Mazlish, Elaine *How to Talk So Kids Will Listen and Listen So Kids Will Talk* (Piccadilly Press, 2001)

Faber, Adele and Mazlish, Elaine, *How to Talk So Kids Will Learn at Home and in School* (Scribner, 1995)

Fearnley-Whittingstall, Jane, *The Good Granny Guide* (Short Books, 2005)

Frith, Uta, *Autism and Asperger Syndrome* (Cambridge University Press, 1991)

Frost, Jo, *Supernanny* (Hodder & Stoughton, 2005)

Garbarino, James, *Raising Children in a Socially Toxic Environment* (Jossey-Bass, 1995)

Gardner, Howard and Davis, Katie, *The App Generation: How Today's Youth Navigate Identity, Intimacy and Imagination in a Digital World* (Yale University Press, 2013)

Gerhardt, Sue, *The Selfish Society: How We All Forgot to Love One Another and Made Money Instead* (Simon and Schuster, 2010)

Gerhardt, Sue, *Why Love Matters: How Affection Shapes a Baby's Brain* (Brunner-Routledge, 2004)

Gilbert, Daniel *Stumbling on Happiness* (Harper Perennial, 2007)

Gill Tim, *No Fear: Growing Up in a Risk Averse Society* (Calouste Gulbenkian Foundation, 2007)

Gillie, O., *Sunlight Robbery* (Health Research Council, 2004)

Goddard Blyth, Sally, *The Genius of Natural Childhood* (Hawthorn Press, 2011)

Goleman, Daniel, *Emotional Intelligence* (Bantam Books 1997)

Gopnik, Alison, Meltzoff, Andrew N., Kuhl, Patricia K *The Scientist in the Crib: What Early Learning Tells Us About The Mind* (HarperCollins, 1999)

Gray, Peter, *Free To Learn: How Unleashing the Instinct to Play Will Make Our Children Happier, More Self-reliant and Better Students for Life* (Basic Books, 2013)

Greenfield, Susan, *The Human Brain: A Guided Tour* (London: Phoenix, 1997)

Greenfield, Susan, *ID: The Quest for Identity in the 21st Century* (Allen Lane, 2009)

Greenfield, Susan, *Mind Change: How Digital Technologies are Leaving their Mark on Our Brains* (Rider Books, 2014)

Hall, Paula, *How to have a Healthy Divorce – A Relate Guide* (Vermilion, 2008)

Hart, Betty and Risley, Todd R., *Meaningful Differences in the Everyday Experience of Young American Children* (Baltimore: Brookes Publishing Co, 1995)

Healy, Jane M., *Endangered Minds – Why Children Don't Think – and What We Can Do About It* (Simon and Schuster, 1990)

Herschkowitz MD, Norbert and Chapman Herschkowitz, Elinore, *A Good Start* in Life: Understanding your Child's Brain and Behaviour from Birth to Age 6 (Dana Press, 2002)

Heymann MD, Jody, The Widening Gap: Why America's Working Families are in Jeopardy – and What Can Be Done about It (Basic Books; Perseus Books Group, 2000)

Hinsliffe, Gaby, Half A Wife: The Working Family's Guide to Getting a Life Back (Chatto and Windus, 2012)

Hobson, Peter, The Cradle of Thought: Exploring the Origins of Thinking (Macmillan, 2002)

Holloway, Susan D., Contested Childhood: Diversity and Change in Japanese Preschools (Routledge, 2000)

Holmes, Jeremy, John Bowlby and Attachment Theory (Brunner-Routledge, 1993)

Honore, Carl, In Praise of Slow: How a Worldwide Movement Is Challenging the Cult of Speed (Orion, 2004)

Honore, Carl, Under Pressure: Rescuing Our Children from the Culture of Hyper-parenting (Orion 2008)

House, Richard (ed.), Too Much Too Soon: Early Learning and the Erosion of Childhood (Hawthorn Press, 2010)

Jackson, Maggie, Distracted: The Erosion of Attention and the Coming Dark Age (Prometheus, 2008)

James, Oliver, They F*** You Up: How to Survive Family Life (Bloomsbury, 2007)

James, Oliver, Affluenza (Vermilion 2007)

James, Oliver, How Not To F*** Them Up: The First Three Years (Vermilion, 2010)

Janis-Norton, Noel, Calmer, Easier, Happier Parenting (Plume Books, 2008)

Janis-Norton, Noel, Calmer, Easier, Happier Homework (Hodder and Stoughton, 2013)

Johnson, Steven, Everything Bad is Good for You (Allen Lane, 2005)

Kerr, Alex, Dogs and Demons: The Fall of Modern Japan (Penguin Books, 2001)

Kidron, Beebron, InRealLife (dogwood DVD, 2013)

Kirby, Jill, Choosing to Be Different: Women, Work and the Family (Centre for Policy Studies, 2003)

Knock Knock Books How to Traumatise Your Children: Seven Proven Methods to Help You Screw Up Your Kids Deliberately and With Skill (Knock Knock Books, 2011)

Krznaric, Roman Empathy: A Handbook for Revolution (Random House, 2014)

Lamb, Michael (ed.), The Role of the Father in Child Development, Fourth Edition (John Wiley and Sons, 2004)

Lanier, Jaron, You Are Not A Gadget (Penguin, 2010)

Lawson, Neal, All Consuming: How Shopping Got Us into this Mess and How We Can Find Our Way Out (Penguin, 2009)

Layard, Richard, Happiness – Lessons from a New Science (Allen Lane, 2005)

Layard, Richard and Dunn, Judy, A Good Childhood: Searching for Values in a Competitive Age (Penguin, 2009)

Lathey, Nicola and Blake, Tracy, Small Talk: Simple Ways to Boost Your Child's Speech and Language (Pan MacMillan, 2013)

Levitt, Steven D. & Dubner, Stephen J., Freakonomics: A Rogue Economist Explores the Hidden Side of Everything (Allen Lane; an imprint of Penguin Books, 2005)

Levy, Paul, *The Digital Inferno* (Clairview Books, 2014)

Lewis, Bex, *Raising Children in a Digital Age: Enjoying the Best, Avoiding the Worst* (Lion, 2014)

Lindstrom, Martin (with Seybold, Patricia B.) *Brand Child*, Revised Edition, (Kogan Page, 2003)

Linn Susan, *Consuming Kids: The Hostile Takeover of Childhood* (NY New Press, 2005)

Livingstone, Tessa, *Child of our Time: How to Achieve the Best for Your Child From Conception to 5 Years* (Bantam Press, 2005)

Louv, Richard, *Last Child in the Woods: Saving Our Kids from Nature-Deficit Disorder* (Algonquin Books, 2005)

Lucas, Bill and Smith, Alastair, *Help your Child to Succeed: The Essential Guide for Parents*, Second Edition (Network Educational Press, 2009)

Macintyre, Christine and McVitty, Kim, *Movement and Learning in the Early Years – Supporting Dyspraxia (DCD) and Other Difficulties* (Paul Chapman, 2004)

Mansell, Warwick, *Education by Numbers: The Tyranny of Testing* (Politico's Publishing, 2009)

Martin, Paul, *Counting Sheep – The Science and Pleasures of Sleep and Dreams* (Flamingo, an imprint of HarperCollins, 2003)

Martin, Paul, *Making Happy People: The Nature of Happiness and Its Origins in Childhood* (Fourth Estate, 2005)

Matsumoto, David, *The New Japan: Debunking Seven Cultural Stereotypes* (Intercultural Press, 2002)

Mayo, Ed, *Shopping Generation* (National Consumer Council, 2005)

Mayo, Ed and Nairn, Agnes, *Consumer Kids: How Big Business Is Grooming Our Children for Profit* (Constable, 2009)

McEvedy, Flora, *The Step-Parents' Parachute: The Four Cornerstones to Good Step-Parenting* (Time Warner, 2005)

McGilchrist, Iain, *The Master and His Emissary: The Divided Brain and the Making of the Western World* (Yale University Press, 2009)

McLuhan, Marshal and Fiore, Quentin, *The Medium is the Massage*, (Gingko Press, 2001)

McNeal, James U., *Kids as Customers: A Handbook of Marketing to Children* (NY: Lexington Books, 1992)

Medhus MD, Elisa, *Hearing is Believing: How Words Can Make or Break Our Kids* (New World Library, California 2004)

Melville, Sandra, *Places for Play* (London: Playlink, 2005)

Motherhood Project, The *Watch Out for Children: A Mothers' Statement to Advertisers* (Institute for American Values, 2001)

National Association of Elementary School Principals *Standards for What Principals Should Know and Be Able to Do* (National Association of Elementary School Principals, 2004)

National Research Council, Institute of Medicine *From Neurons to Neighborhoods – The Science of Early Childhood Development* (National Academy Press, 2000)

Neuberger, Julia, *The Moral State We're In: A Manifesto for a 21st Century Society* (HarperCollins, 2005)

Noel, Brook, *Back to Basics: 101 Ideas for Strengthening Our Children and Our Families* (Champion Press Ltd, 1999)

Nutbrown, Cathy, *Threads of Thinking – Young Children Learning and the Role of Early Education* Second Edition (Paul Chapman Publishing Ltd, 1999)

Orange, Teresa and O'Flynn, Louise, *The Media Diet for Kids* (Hay House, 2005)

Paley, Vivian Gussey, *The Kindness of Children* (Cambridge Mass/London, 1999)

Palmer, Sue, *21st Century Boys* (Orion, 2009)

Palmer, Sue, *21st century Girls* (Orion, 2013)

Pearson, Allison, *I Don't Know How She Does It* (Chatto and Windus, 2002)

Phillips, Melanie, *All Must Have Prizes* (Time Warner Paperback, 1998)

Pinker, Steven, *The Language Instinct* (Penguin, 1995)

Pinker, Steven, *The Blank Slate* (Penguin, 2003)

Pipher PhD, Mary, *The Shelter of Each Other – Rebuilding our Families* (Ballantine Books, New York, 1997)

Postman, Neil, *Amusing Ourselves to Death* (Random House, 1985)

Postman, Neil, *The Disappearance of Childhood* (Vintage Books; Random House, 1994)

Putnam Robert D., *Bowling Alone: The Collapse and Revival of American Community* (Simon and Schuster, 2000)

Putnam, R.P. and Feldstein, L., *Better Together* (Simon and Schuster, 2003)

Ramachandran, Vilayanur, *The Emerging Mind* (Profile Books, 2003)

Restak, Dr Richard, *The New Brain: How the Modern Age Is Rewiring Your Mind* (Rodale Ltd, London 2004)

Rich, Diane, Myer, Cathy, Durrant, Andrea, Drummond, Mary Jane, Dixon, Annabelle, Casanova, Denise, *First Hand Experience – What Matters to Children* Second Edition (Rich Learning Opportunities, 2014)

Richardson, Alex, *They Are What You Feed Them* (HarperCollins, 2006)

Robertson, Juliet, *Dirty Teaching: A Beginner's Guide to Learning Outdoors* (Independent Thinking Press, 2014)

Rose, Steven, *The Making of Memory – From Molecules to Mind* (Vintage, 2003)

Rose, Steven, *The 21st Century Brain: Explaining, Mending and Manipulating the Mind* (Jonathan Cape, 2005)

Salzman, Marian, *The Future of Men* (Palgrave MacMillan, 2005)

Satter, Ellyn, *How to Get Your Kid to Eat ... But Not Too Much* (Bull Publishing, 1987)

Satter, Ellyn, *Secrets of Feeding a Happy Family: How to Eat, How to Raise Good Eaters, How to Cook* (Kelsy Press, 2008)

Sax, Leonard, *Why Gender Matters – What Parents and Teachers Need to Know about the Emerging Science of Sex Differences* (Doubleday, 2005)

Schor, Juliet B., *Born To Buy* (Scribner, 2004)

Shaw MD, Robert, *The Epidemic: The Rot of American Culture, Absentee and Permissive Parenting, and the Resultant Plague of Joyless, Selfish Children* (ReganBooks, an imprint of HarperCollins Publishers, 2003)

Sheppard, Philip, *Music Makes Your Child Smarter: How Music Helps Every Child's Development* (Artemis Editions, 2005)

Sigman, Aric, *Remotely Controlled; How Television Is Damaging Our Lives and What We Can Do about It* (Vermilion, 2005)

Sigman, Aric, The Spoilt Generation: Why Restoring Authority Will Make Our Children Happier (Piaktus, 2009)

Snowling, Margaret J., Dyslexia, Second Edition (Blackwell, 2000)

Small, Gary and Vorgon, Gigi, iBrain: Surviving the Digital Alteration of the Modern Mind (Harper, 2008)

Smith, Tracy and Dewar, Tammy, Raising the Village: How Individuals and Communities Can Work Together to Give Our Children a Stronger Start in Life (BPS Books, 2009)

Stevens MS, Laura J., 12 Effective Ways to Help your ADD/ADHD Child – Drug Free Alternatives for Attention-Deficit Disorders – A Guide to Controlling Attention and Hyperactivity Using Nutrition and Other Safe, Natural Methods (Avery, a member of Penguin Putnam Inc. New York, 2000)

Storr, Anthony, Music and the Mind (HarperCollins, 1992)

Thomas, Susan Gregory, Buy, Buy, Baby: How Consumer Culture Manipulates Parents (Mariner Books, 2009)

Twenge, J.M. and Campbell W.K., The Narcissism Epidemic: Living in the Age of Entitlement (Free Press, 2009)

Ursell, Amanda, What Are You Really Eating?: How to Become Label Savvy (Hay House Publishing, 2005)

Wahlgren, Anna, For the Love of Children (Forlag Anna Wahlgren, 2009)

Ward, Dr Sally, Babytalk (Century, 2000)

Weissbluth MD, Marc, Healthy Sleep Habits, Happy Child (Random House, 1998)

Wender MD, Paul H., ADHD Attention-Deficit Hyperactivity Disorder in Children, Adolescents and Adults (Oxford University Press, 2000)

Whalley, Margy and the Pen Green Centre Team, Involving Parents in their Children's Learning (Paul Chapman Publishing Ltd, 2001)

Wilce, Hilary, Help Your Child Succeed at School (Piatkus, 2004)

Williams, Fiona, Rethinking Families (Calouste Gulbenkian Foundation, London 2004)

Wilson, R. and Picket, K., The Spirit Level (Penguin, 2009)

Wilson, Gary, Help Your Boys Succeed: The Essential Guide for Parents (Network Educational Press, 2010)

Winn, Marie, The Plug-in Drug: Television, Computers, and Family Life (Penguin, 2002)

Wolf, Maryann, Proust and the Squid: The Story and Science of the Reading Brain (Icon Books, 2008)

Woodall, Kate and Nick, Putting Children First – A Handbook for Separated Parents (Vermilion, 2008)

Woodhouse, Sarah, Sound Sleep: Calming and Helping Your Baby or Child to Sleep (Hawthorn Press, 2003)

Woolfson, Dr Richard C., Small Talk: From First Gestures to Simple Sentences (Hamlyn, 2002)

Zeedyk, Suzanne, The Connected Baby DVD (2012)

INDEX

streets, increasing the safety of, 71–3
Streets Alive, 71
substance abuse, 2
Sudden Infant Death Syndrome (SIDS; cot
   death), 57, 95
sugar, 30–1
'sugar high', 30
suicide, 2, 227
Sun newspaper, 64, 111
sunshine, 58–9
Supernanny, 315
Supersize Me, 47
support services, 350
Sure Start, 126, 210, 360
'sustained shared thinking', 131, 141
Sweden, 34, 211, 269, 271
Switzerland, 34, 193
Sylva, Professor Kathy, 191
symbolic play, 118, 248

table manners, 37–8, 43
tablets, 104, 229, 257, 273, 288, 289, 297,
   325 *see also* iPads
talking books, 136, 141
Talk To Your Baby, 119–20, 125
targets (in education), 214, 219, 221, 223
teachers
   and behaviour, 9, 10, 236–8
   and bullying, 234, 235
   and communication issues, 112–13,
      124–5, 133
   and education, 214, 219–20, 223, 224,
      232, 236–8, 238–9
   and family breakdown, 164
   and food, 38
   and outdoor activity, 63, 68
   and parents, 234, 235, 238–9, 241,
      243–4
   risk assessment, 63
   and sleep issues, 87
   and technology, 112, 133, 287
   wide experience of children, 345–6
   see also schools
team games, 64
technology/electronic devices
   addiction to, 288–9
   attitudes to, 315–16, 363, 365
   and the bedroom, 103–5, 107, 109, 136,
      142–3, 296
   and behaviour, 11

benefits of, 282–3, 312–15
books versus screens, 292–5
and commercial forces, 247–8, 260–1,
   270–1, 305–6
and communication, 112, 124, 130–1,
   132–4, 136, 137, 140, 142–3, 144, 147,
   316–18
concerns about impact on physical and
   mental health, 284–5
dangers, 298–301
and data collection, 223
detoxing, 319–28
'digital natives', 318
during first two or three years of life,
   285–8, 319–20
during pre-school years / three-to-seven-
   year-olds, 290–2, 320–1, 323–4
and dysfunction, 288–90
and education, 228–30
'electronic babysitter', 132, 133, 285–8
electronic village, 282–337
further reading, 329
issues of identity, privacy and sharing,
   302–5
and need for connection to the real
   world, 295–8
pace of change, 13, 149, 283, 363–4
and paedophilia, 309–10
parent power, 328–9
parents' spending on, 200, 202
and play activities, 52, 58
and pornography, 284, 298, 299, 300,
   309, 310–11
recommended websites, 329
and relationships, 158–61, 295–8
and rights concerning violence and
   sexual content, 307–9
seven-to-twelve-year-olds, 321–2, 324–5
and sleep issues, 103–5, 107, 109, 111
twelve-year-olds and older, 322–3, 325
'techno-play', 249, 270, 287, 290, 292
teenagers, 2, 38, 105, 257, 272, 285, 302,
   310, 322–3, 325, 348, 363
Teletubbies, 286
television
   in the bedroom, 103–4, 296
   and behaviour, 11
   benefits, 312–13, 314–15
   and commercialisation of childhood,
      249, 251, 254, 259, 262